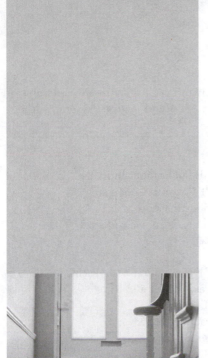

ISSUES FOR DEBATE
IN FAMILY VIOLENCE

SELECTIONS FROM CQ RESEARCHER

SAGE

Los Angeles | London | New Delhi
Singapore | Washington DC

For information:

SAGE Publications, Inc.
2455 Teller Road
Thousand Oaks, California 91320
E-mail: order@sagepub.com

SAGE Publications India Pvt. Ltd.
B 1/I 1 Mohan Cooperative
   Industrial Area
Mathura Road, New Delhi 110 044
India

SAGE Publications Ltd.
1 Oliver's Yard
55 City Road
London EC1Y 1SP
United Kingdom

SAGE Publications Asia-Pacific Pte. Ltd.
33 Pekin Street #02-01
Far East Square
Singapore 048763

Printed in the United States of America

Library of Congress Cataloging-in-Publication Data

Issues for debate in family violence : selections from CQ researcher.
    p. cm.
ISBN 978-1-4129-9032-5 (pbk.)
   1. Family violence. 2. Women—Violence against. 3. Abused women. 4. Child welfare. 5. Family violence—United States. 6. Women—Violence against—United States. I. CQ researcher.

HV6626.I87 2011
362.82'920973—dc22   2010018623

This book is printed on acid-free paper.

10   11   12   13   14   10   9   8   7   6   5   4   3   2   1

Acquisitions Editor:	Kassie Graves
Editorial Assistant:	Veronica Novak
Production Editor:	Laureen Gleason
Typesetter:	C&M Digitals (P) Ltd.
Cover Designer:	Candice Harman
Marketing Manager:	Stephanie Adams

Contents

Annotated Contents

Women's Rights: Are Violence and Discrimination Against Women Declining?

Women around the world have made significant gains in the past decade, but tens of millions still face significant and often appalling hardship. Most governments now have gender-equality commissions, electoral gender quotas and laws to protect women against violence. But progress has been mixed. A record number of women now serve in parliaments, but only 14 of the world's 193 countries currently have elected female leaders. Globalization has produced more jobs for women, but they still constitute 70 percent of the world's poorest inhabitants and 64 percent of the illiterate. Spousal abuse, female infanticide, genital mutilation, forced abortions, bride-burnings, acid attacks and sexual slavery remain pervasive in some countries, and rape and sexual mutilation have reached epic proportions in the war-torn Democratic Republic of the Congo. Experts say without greater economic, political and educational equality, the plight of women will not improve, and society will continue suffering the consequences.

Domestic Violence: Do Teenagers Need More Protection?

On a typical day in the United States, three women are murdered by their spouses or partners, and thousands more are injured. While men are also victims of domestic violence, women are at least five times more likely to suffer at the hands of a loved one. Young people between the ages of 16 and 24 are most at risk. The victims include teens who are abused by their parents as well as young parents who assault each other or their children. Moreover, teen-dating violence touches more than 30 percent of young men and women. The good news is that domestic violence against women has dropped dramatically in recent years. Now Congress has just approved a measure that advocates say will provide much-needed funding to try to stop domestic violence before it starts. Meanwhile, some fathers'-rights and conservative groups say too many domestic-violence programs demonize men, promote a feminist agenda and do not try hard enough to keep families together.

Sex Offenders: Will Tough, New Laws Do More Harm Than Good?

In response to horrific sex crimes against children, Congress and the states have passed hundreds of new laws in recent years to crack down on offenders. In addition to much longer sentences and more rigorous tracking of sex criminals upon release, some of the new laws place limits on where offenders can live, banning them from neighborhoods surrounding schools, parks and playgrounds. But critics warn the laws may prove counterproductive, driving sex offenders further underground. They also point out that most perpetrators are family members or other acquaintances of victims, so the new laws may shift resources away from treatment programs that could help more. Moreover, experts note sex offenders' low recidivism rates and a dramatic drop in child sexual-abuse cases. But with the media giving heavy coverage to the worst cases of abduction and abuse, it's no wonder that lawmakers are willing to approve any punishment or tracking technique that promises to prevent crimes against children.

Hate Groups: Is Extremism on the Rise in the United States?

National crises create opportunities for extremists. Today the global economic crisis now wreaking havoc on millions of American households is hitting while the first black president is in the White House and the national debate over illegal immigration remains unresolved. Already, some far-right extremists are proclaiming that their moment is arriving. Indeed, an annual tally by the Southern Poverty Law Center shows 926 hate groups operating in 2008, a 50 percent increase over the number in 2000. And the Department of Homeland Security concludes that conditions may favor far-right recruitment. But a mix of conservatives and liberal free-speech activists warn that despite concerns about extremism, the administration of Barack Obama should not be intruding on constitutionally protected political debate. Some extremism-monitoring groups say Obama's election showed far-right power is waning, not strengthening. But that equation may change if the economic crisis deepens, the experts caution.

Cyberbullying: Are New Laws Needed to Curb Online Aggression?

Child advocates say a growing epidemic of "cyberbullying"—the use of computers, cell phones, social-networking sites and other technology to threaten or humiliate others—is putting young people at risk, sometimes with deadly consequences. The Centers for Disease Control and Prevention has labeled "electronic aggression" an "emerging public-health problem." Court precedents on school discipline and students' First Amendment rights provide limited guidance to educators grappling with the emerging world of cyber communication, especially transmissions originating off school grounds. Nonetheless, many states and school districts are taking strong steps aimed at curbing cyber abuse. In Congress, bills to provide new funding for online-safety programs have been introduced, but conflicts have arisen over how federal money for such efforts should be spent.

Prostitution Debate: Should the United States Legalize Sex Work?

Prostitution made the front pages recently when Democratic New York Gov. Eliot Spitzer resigned after he was outed as a client of a high-priced escort service. The fall of Spitzer, a fierce foe of prostitution in his previous post as state attorney general, highlighted American ambivalence about the sex industry, which receives little public debate and seems to surface in the media only when high-profile customers are named as clients. Behind the scenes, however, fierce debate rages about the best plan for limiting the harms of prostitution, which include drug addiction and minors being forced into sex work. Anti-prostitution feminists argue that the United States should follow Sweden's example by arresting and jailing johns instead of prostitutes while providing social services to help women leave the sex industry. But other activists argue that only complete decriminalization and recognition of sex work as a form of labor can end the social stigma that leaves prostitutes unprotected from disease and violence.

Child Welfare Reform: Will Recent Changes Make At-Risk Children Safer?

The U.S. child welfare system is designed to protect the nation's children, but in recent years it has been rocked by horror stories of children who were physically and sexually abused and even murdered. More than 900,000 children were maltreated in 2003—and some 1,300 died. But a nationwide reform movement offers hope for the future. Welfare agencies across the country are focusing more on keeping families together and quickly moving the nation's 500,000 foster children into permanent homes. Although the foster care rolls are dropping, unadopted foster teens still must struggle with a lonely transition to adulthood after leaving the system. No state program has passed a federal review, but states are hitting improvement targets in follow-up checks. Meanwhile, social workers continue to complain that they are underpaid and overworked. And Congress is divided over a Bush administration plan that would give states more flexibility in using federal funds but end the guarantee of federal support for every foster child.

Preface

Keeping students up-to-date on timely issues in family and interpersonal violence can be challenging given the range of issues, new research and changing policies regarding children and families. Furthermore, finding readings that are student friendly, accessible and current can be an even greater challenge. Now *CQ Researcher,* CQ Press and SAGE have teamed up to provide a unique selection of articles focused on issues in family and domestic violence, specifically for courses in family violence and working with children and families. This collection aims to promote in-depth discussion, facilitate further research and help students formulate their own positions on crucial issues.

This first edition includes seven up-to-date reports by *CQ Researcher,* an award-winning weekly policy brief that brings complicated issues down to earth. Each report chronicles and analyzes executive, legislative and judicial activities at all levels of government. This collection was carefully crafted to cover a range of issues from domestic violence, sex offenders, hate groups, women's rights, cyberbullying and child welfare reform. All in all, this reader will help your students become better versed on current policy issues and gain a deeper, more critical perspective of timely and important issues.

CQ RESEARCHER

CQ Researcher was founded in 1923 as *Editorial Research Reports* and was sold primarily to newspapers as a research tool. The magazine was renamed and redesigned in 1991 as *CQ Researcher*. Today, students are its primary audience. While still used by hundreds of journalists and newspapers, many of which reprint portions of the reports, the *Researcher's* main subscribers are now high school, college and public libraries. In 2002, *Researcher* won the American Bar Association's coveted Silver Gavel award for magazine excellence for a series of nine reports on civil liberties and other legal issues.

Researcher staff writers—all highly experienced journalists—sometimes compare the experience of writing a Researcher report to drafting a college term paper. Indeed, there are many similarities. Each report is as long as many term papers—about 11,000 words—and is written by one person without any significant outside help. One of the key differences is that writers interview leading experts, scholars and government officials for each issue.

Like students, staff writers begin the creative process by choosing a topic. Working with the *Researcher's* editors, the writer identifies a controversial subject that has important public policy implications. After a topic is selected, the writer embarks on one to two weeks of intense research. Newspaper and magazine articles are clipped or downloaded, books are ordered and information is gathered from a wide variety of sources, including interest groups, universities and the government. Once the writers are well informed, they develop a detailed outline, and begin the interview process. Each report requires a minimum of ten to fifteen interviews with academics, officials, lobbyists and people working in the field. Only after all interviews are completed does the writing begin.

CHAPTER FORMAT

Each issue of *CQ Researcher*, and therefore each selection in this book, is structured in the same way. Each begins with an overview, which briefly summarizes the areas that will be explored in greater detail in the rest of the chapter. The next section chronicles important and current debates on the topic under discussion and is structured around a number of key questions, such as "Should the federal government do more to combat domestic violence?" "Should sex offenders be allowed to live near children?" "Do state and local governments do enough to keep families together?" These questions are usually the subject of much debate among practitioners and scholars in the field.

Hence, the answers presented are never conclusive but detail the range of opinion on the topic.

Next, the "Background" section provides a history of the issue being examined. This retrospective covers important legislative measures, executive actions and court decisions that illustrate how current policy has evolved. Then the "Current Situation" section examines contemporary policy issues, legislation under consideration and legal action being taken. Each selection concludes with an "Outlook" section, which addresses possible regulation, court rulings and initiatives from Capitol Hill and the White House over the next five to ten years.

Each report contains features that augment the main text: two to three sidebars that examine issues related to the topic at hand, a pro versus con debate between two experts, a chronology of key dates and events and an annotated bibliography detailing major sources used by the writer.

ACKNOWLEDGMENTS

We wish to thank many people for helping to make this collection a reality. Tom Colin, managing editor of *CQ Researcher*, gave us his enthusiastic support and cooperation as we developed this edition. He and his talented staff of editors and writers have amassed a first-class library of *Researcher* reports, and we are fortunate to have access to that rich cache. We also wish to thank our colleagues at CQ Press, a division of SAGE and a leading publisher of books, directories, research publications, and Web products on U.S. government, world affairs and communications. They have forged the way in making these readers a useful resource for instruction across a range of undergraduate and graduate courses.

Some readers may be learning about *CQ Researcher* for the first time. We expect that many readers will want regular access to this excellent weekly research tool. For subscription information or a no-obligation free trial of *CQ Researcher*, please contact CQ Press at www.cqpress.com or toll-free at 1-866-4CQ-PRESS (1-866-427-7737).

We hope that you will be pleased by this edition of *Issues for Debate in Family Violence*. We welcome your feedback and suggestions for future editions. Please direct comments to Kassie Graves, Acquisitions Editor, SAGE Publications, 2455 Teller Road, Thousand Oaks, CA 91320, or kassie.graves@sagepub.com.

—The Editors of SAGE

Contributors

Thomas J. Billitteri is a *CQ Researcher* staff writer based in Fairfield, Pennsylvania, who has more than 30 years' experience covering business, nonprofit institutions and public policy for newspapers and other publications. He has written previously for *CQ Researcher* on "Domestic Poverty," "Curbing CEO Pay" and "Mass Transit." He holds a BA in English and an MA in journalism from Indiana University.

Marcia Clemmitt is a veteran social-policy reporter who previously served as editor in chief of *Medicine & Health* and staff writer for *The Scientist*. She has also been a high-school math and physics teacher. She holds a liberal arts and sciences degree from St. John's College, Annapolis, and a master's degree in English from Georgetown University. Her recent reports include "Climate Change," "Health Care Costs," "Cyber Socializing" and "Student Aid."

Karen Foerstel is a freelance writer who has worked for the Congressional Quarterly *Weekly Report* and *Daily Monitor, The New York Post* and *Roll Call,* a Capitol Hill newspaper. She has published two books on women in Congress, *Climbing the Hill: Gender Conflict in Congress* and *The Biographical Dictionary of Women in Congress.* She currently lives and works in London. She has worked in Africa with ChildsLife International, a nonprofit that helps needy children around the world, and with Blue Ventures, a marine conservation organization that protects coral reefs in Madagascar.

Alan Greenblatt is a staff writer at *Governing* magazine. He previously covered elections, agriculture and military spending for *CQ Weekly*, where he won the National Press Club's Sandy Hume Award for political journalism. He graduated from San Francisco State University in 1986 and received a master's degree in English literature from the University of Virginia in 1988. His recent *CQ Researcher* reports include "The Partisan Divide" and "Media Bias."

Peter Katel is a *CQ Researcher* staff writer who previously reported on Haiti and Latin America for *Time* and *Newsweek* and covered the Southwest for newspapers in New Mexico. He has received several journalism awards, including the Bartolomé Mitre Award for coverage of drug trafficking from the Inter-American Press Association. He holds an AB in university studies from the University of New Mexico. His recent reports include "Mexico's Drug War," "Homeland Security" and "Future of the Military."

Pamela M. Prah is a *CQ Researcher* staff writer with several years previous experience at Stateline.org, Kiplinger's Washington Letter and the Bureau of National Affairs. She holds a master's degree in government from Johns Hopkins University and a journalism degree from Ohio University. Her recent reports include "War in Iraq," "Methamphetamines" and "Disaster Preparedness."

Tom Price is a Washington-based freelance journalist who writes regularly for *CQ Researcher*. Previously he was a correspondent in the Cox Newspapers Washington Bureau and chief politics writer for the *Dayton Daily News* and *The Journal Herald*. He is the author of two Washington guidebooks, *Washington, D.C., for Dummies,* and the *Irreverent Guide to Washington, D.C.* His work has appeared in *The New York Times, Time, Rolling Stone* and other periodicals. He earned a bachelor of science in journalism at Ohio University.

Women's Rights

Are Violence and Discrimination Against Women Declining?

Karen Foerstel

Iraqi teenager Du'a Khalil Aswad lies mortally wounded after her "honor killing" by a mob in the Kurdish region of Iraq. No one has been prosecuted for the April 2007 murder, even though a cell-phone video of the incident was posted on the Internet. Aswad's male relatives are believed to have arranged her ritualistic execution because she had dated a boy from outside her religious sect. The United Nations estimates that 5,000 women and girls are murdered in honor killings around the globe each year.

AFP/Getty Images

From *CQ Global Researcher*, May 2008.

She was 17 years old. The blurry video shows her lying in a dusty road, blood streaming down her face, as several men kick and throw rocks at her. At one point she struggles to sit up, but a man kicks her in the face forcing her back to the ground. Another slams a large, concrete block down onto her head. Scores of onlookers cheer as the blood streams from her battered head.[1]

The April 7, 2007, video was taken in the Kurdish area of northern Iraq on a mobile phone. It shows what appear to be several uniformed police officers standing on the edge of the crowd, watching while others film the violent assault on their phones.

The brutal, public murder of Du'a Khalil Aswad reportedly was organized as an "honor killing" by members of her family — and her uncles and a brother allegedly were among those in the mob who beat her to death. Her crime? She offended her community by falling in love with a man outside her religious sect.[2]

According to the United Nations, an estimated 5,000 women and girls are murdered in honor killings each year, but it was only when the video of Aswad's murder was posted on the Internet that the global media took notice.[3]

Such killings don't only happen in remote villages in developing countries. Police in the United Kingdom estimate that up to 17,000 women are subjected to some kind of "honor"-related violence each year, ranging from forced marriages and physical attacks to murder.[4]

But honor killings are only one type of what the international community calls "gender based violence" (GBV). "It is universal," says Taina Bien-Aimé, executive director of the New York-based

Only Four Countries Offer Total Equality for Women

Costa Rica, Cuba, Sweden and Norway receive the highest score (9 points) in an annual survey of women's economic, political and social rights. Out of the world's 193 countries, only 26 score 7 points or better, while 28 — predominantly Islamic or Pacific Island countries — score 3 or less. The United States rates 7 points: a perfect 3 on economic rights but only 2 each for political and social rights. To receive 3 points for political rights, women must hold at least 30 percent of the seats in the national legislature. Women hold only 16.6 percent of the seats in the U.S. Congress. The U.S. score of 2 on social rights reflects what the report's authors call "high societal discrimination against women's reproductive rights."

Status of Women's Rights Around the Globe

What the Ratings Mean:
- **7-9** Offer the most equality for women
- **4-6** Offer moderate equality for women
- **0-3** Offer the least equality for women
- Data not available

Source: Cingranelli-Richards Human Rights Dataset, http://ciri.binghamton.edu/, based on Amnesty International's annual reports and U.S. State Department annual Country Reports on Human Rights. The database is co-directed by David Louis Cingranelli, a political science professor at Binghamton University, SUNY, and David L. Richards, an assistant political science professor at the University of Memphis.

women's-rights group Equality Now. "There is not one country in the world where violence against women doesn't exist."

Thousands of women are murdered or attacked around the world each day, frequently with impunity. In Guatemala, where an estimated 3,000 women have been killed over the past seven years, most involving some

kind of misogynistic violence, only 1 percent of the perpetrators were convicted.[5] In India, the United Nations estimates that five women are burned to death each day by husbands upset that they did not receive sufficient dowries from their brides.[6] In Asia, nearly 163 million females are "missing" from the population — the result of sex-selective abortions, infanticide or neglect.

And since the 1990s some African countries have seen dramatic upsurges in rapes of very young girls by men who believe having sex with a virgin will protect or cure them from HIV-AIDS. After a 70-year-old man allegedly raped a 3-year-old girl in northern Nigeria's commercial hub city of Kano, Deputy Police Chief Suleiman Abba told reporters in January, "Child rape is becoming rampant in Kano." In the last six months of 2007, he said, 54 cases of child rape had been reported. "In some cases the victims are gang-raped."[7]

Epidemics of sexual violence commonly break out in countries torn apart by war, when perpetrators appear to have no fear of prosecution. Today, in Africa, for instance, UNICEF says there is now a "license to rape" in eastern regions of the Democratic Republic of the Congo, where some human-rights experts estimate that up to a quarter of a million women have been raped and often sexually mutilated with knives, branches or machetes.[8] Several of the Congolese rapists remorselessly bragged to an American filmmaker recently about how many women they had gang-raped.[9]

"The sexual violence in Congo is the worst in the world," said John Holmes, the United Nations under secretary general for humanitarian affairs. "The sheer numbers, the wholesale brutality, the culture of impunity — it's appalling."[10]

In some cultures, the female victims themselves are punished. A report by the Human Rights Commission of Pakistan found that a woman is gang-raped every eight hours in that country. Yet, until recently, rape cases could not be prosecuted in Pakistan unless four Muslim men "all of a pious and trustworthy nature" were willing to testify that they witnessed the attack. Without their testimony the victim could be prosecuted for fornication and alleging a false crime, punishable by stoning, lashings or prison.[11] When the law was softened in 2006 to allow judges to decide whether to try rape cases in Islamic courts or criminal courts, where such witnesses are not required, thousands took to the streets to protest the change.[12]

Honor killings are up 400 percent in Pakistan over the last two years, and Pakistani women also live in fear of being blinded or disfigured by "acid attacks" — a common practice in Pakistan and a handful of other countries — in which attackers, usually spurned suitors, throw acid on a woman's face and body.

Women's Suffering Is Widespread

More than two decades after the U.N. Decade for Women and 29 years after the U.N. adopted the Convention on the Elimination of All Forms of Discrimination against Women (CEDAW), gender discrimination remains pervasive throughout the world, with widespread negative consequences for society.

According to recent studies on the status of women today:

- Violence against women is pervasive. It impoverishes women, their families, communities and nations by lowering economic productivity and draining resources. It also harms families across generations and reinforces other violence in societies.
- Domestic violence is the most common form of violence against women, with rates ranging from 8 percent in Albania to 49 percent in Ethiopia and Zambia. Domestic violence and rape account for 5 percent of the disease burden for women ages 15 to 44 in developing countries and 19 percent in developed countries.
- Femicide — the murder of women — often involves sexual violence. From 40 to 70 percent of women murdered in Australia, Canada, Israel, South Africa and the United States are killed by husbands or boyfriends. Hundreds of women were abducted, raped and murdered in and around Juárez, Mexico, over the past 15 years, but the crimes have never been solved.
- At least 160 million females, mostly in India and China, are "missing" from the population — the result of sex-selective abortions.
- Rape is being used as a genocidal tool. Hundreds of thousands of women have been raped and sexually mutilated in the ongoing conflict in Eastern Congo. An estimated 250,000 to 500,000 women were raped during the 1994 genocide in Rwanda; up to 50,000 women were raped during the Bosnian conflict in the 1990s. Victims are often left unable to have children and are deserted by their husbands and shunned by their families, plunging the women and their children into poverty.
- Some 130 million girls have been genitally mutilated, mostly in Africa and Yemen, but also in immigrant communities in the West.
- Child rape has been on the increase in the past decade in some African countries, where some men believe having sex with a virgin will protect or cure them from HIV-AIDS. A study at the Red Cross children's hospital in Cape Town, South Africa, found that 3-year-old girls were more likely to be raped than any other age group.
- Two million girls between the ages of 5 and 15 are forced into the commercial sex market each year, many of them trafficked across international borders.
- Sexual harassment is pervasive. From 40 to 50 percent of women in the European Union reported some form of sexual harassment at work; 50 percent of schoolgirls surveyed in Malawi reported sexual harassment at school.
- Women and girls constitute 70 percent of those living on less than a dollar a day and 64 percent of the world's illiterate.
- Women work two-thirds of the total hours worked by men and women but earn only 10 percent of the income.
- Half of the world's food is produced by women, but women own only 1 percent of the world's land.
- More than 1,300 women die each day during pregnancy and childbirth — 99 percent of them in developing countries.

Sources: "Ending violence against women: From words to action," United Nations, October, 2006, www.un.org/womenwatch/daw/public/VAW_Study/VAW studyE.pdf; www.womankind.org.uk; www.unfp.org; www.oxfam.org.uk; www.ipu.org; www.unicef.org; www.infant-trust.org.uk; "State of the World Population 2000;" http://npr.org; http://asiapacific.amnesty.org; http://news.bbc.co.uk

Negative Attitudes Toward Women Are Pervasive

Negative attitudes about women are widespread around the globe, among women as well as men. Rural women are more likely than city women to condone domestic abuse if they think it was provoked by a wife's behavior.

Location	Percentage of women in selected countries who agree that a man has good reason to beat his wife if:						Women who agree with:	
	Wife does not complete housework	Wife disobeys her husband	Wife refuses sex	Wife asks about other women	Husband suspects infidelity	Wife is unfaithful	One or more of the reasons mentioned	None of the reasons mentioned
Bangladesh city	13.8	23.3	9.0	6.6	10.6	51.5	53.3	46.7
Bangladesh province	25.1	38.7	23.3	14.9	24.6	77.6	79.3	20.7
Brazil city	0.8	1.4	0.3	0.3	2.0	8.8	9.4	90.6
Brazil province	4.5	10.9	4.7	2.9	14.1	29.1	33.7	66.3
Ethiopia province	65.8	77.7	45.6	32.2	43.8	79.5	91.1	8.9
Japan city	1.3	1.5	0.4	0.9	2.8	18.5	19.0	81.0
Namibia city	9.7	12.5	3.5	4.3	6.1	9.2	20.5	79.5
Peru city	4.9	7.5	1.7	2.3	13.5	29.7	33.7	66.3
Peru province	43.6	46.2	25.8	26.7	37.9	71.3	78.4	21.6
Samoa	12.1	19.6	7.4	10.1	26.0	69.8	73.3	26.7
Serbia and Montenegro city	0.6	0.97	0.6	0.3	0.9	5.7	6.2	93.8
Thailand city	2.0	0.8	2.8	1.8	5.6	42.9	44.7	55.3
Thailand province	11.9	25.3	7.3	4.4	12.5	64.5	69.5	30.5
Tanzania city	24.1	45.6	31.1	13.8	22.9	51.5	62.5	37.5
Tanzania province	29.1	49.7	41.7	19.8	27.2	55.5	68.2	31.8

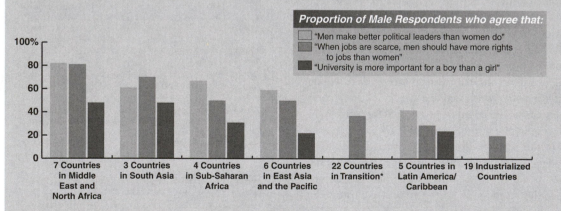

Proportion of Male Respondents who agree that:
- "Men make better political leaders than women do"
- "When jobs are scarce, men should have more rights to jobs than women"
- "University is more important for a boy than a girl"

7 Countries in Middle East and North Africa · 3 Countries in South Asia · 4 Countries in Sub-Saharan Africa · 6 Countries in East Asia and the Pacific · 22 Countries in Transition* · 5 Countries in Latin America/Caribbean · 19 Industrialized Countries

*Countries in transition are generally those that were once part of the Soviet Union.

Sources: World Health Organization, www.who.int/gender/violence/who_multicountry_study/Chapter3-Chapter4.pdf; "World Values Survey," www.worldvaluessruvey.org

But statistics on murder and violence are only a part of the disturbing figures on the status of women around the globe. Others include:

- Some 130 million women have undergone female genital mutilation, and another 2 million are at risk every year, primarily in Africa and Yemen.
- Women and girls make up 70 percent of the world's poor and two-thirds of its illiterate.
- Women work two-thirds of the total hours worked by men but earn only 10 percent of the income.
- Women produce more than half of the world's food but own less than 1 percent of the world's property.
- More than 500,000 women die during pregnancy and childbirth every year — 99 percent of them in developing countries.
- Two million girls between the ages of 5 and 15 are forced into the commercial sex market each year.[13]
- Globally, 10 million more girls than boys do not attend school.[14]

Despite these alarming numbers, women have made historic progress in some areas. The number of girls receiving an education has increased in the past decade. Today 57 percent of children not attending school are girls, compared to two-thirds in the 1990s.[15]

And women have made significant gains in the political arena. As of March, 2008, 14 women are serving as elected heads of state or government, and women now hold 17.8 percent of the world's parliamentary seats — more than ever before.[16] And just three months after the brutal killing of Aswad in Iraq, India swore in its first female president, Pratibha Patil, who vows to eliminate that country's practice of aborting female fetuses because girls are not as valued as boys in India. (*See "At Issue," p. 23*.)[17]

Last October, Argentina elected its first female president, Cristina Fernández de Kirchner,* the second woman in two years to be elected president in South America. Michelle Bachelet, a single mother, won the presidency in Chile in 2006.[18] During her inaugural speech Kirchner

---

* Isabel Martínez Perón assumed the presidency of Argentina on the death of her husband, Juan Perón, in 1974 and served until she was deposed in a coup d'état in 1976; but she was never elected.

admitted, "Perhaps it'll be harder for me, because I'm a woman. It will always be harder for us."[19]

Indeed, while more women than ever now lead national governments, they hold only 4.4 percent of the world's 342 presidential and prime ministerial positions. And in no country do they hold 50 percent or more of the national legislative seats.[20]

"Women make up half the world's population, but they are not represented" at that level, says Swanee Hunt, former U.S. ambassador to Austria and founding director of the Women and Public Policy Program at Harvard's Kennedy School of Government.

While this is "obviously a fairness issue," she says it also affects the kinds of public policies governments pursue. When women comprise higher percentages of officeholders, studies show "distinct differences in legislative outputs," Hunt explains. "There's less funding of bombs and bullets and more on human security — not just how to defend territory but also on hospitals and general well-being."

Today's historic numbers of women parliamentarians have resulted partly from gender quotas imposed in nearly 100 countries, which require a certain percentage of women candidates or officeholders.[21]

During the U.N.'s historic Fourth World Conference on Women — held in Beijing in 1995 — 189 governments adopted, among other things, a goal of 30 percent female representation in national legislatures around the world.[22] But today, only 20 countries have reached that goal, and quotas are often attacked as limiting voters' choices and giving women unfair advantages.[23]

Along with increasing female political participation, the 5,000 government representatives at the Beijing conference — one of the largest gatherings in U.N. history — called for improved health care for women, an end to violence against women, equal access to education for girls, promotion of economic independence and other steps to improve the condition of women around the world.[24]

"Let Beijing be the platform from which our global crusade will be carried forward," Gertrude Mongella, U.N. secretary general for the conference, said during closing ceremonies. "The world will hold us accountable for the implementation of the good intentions and decisions arrived at in Beijing."[25]

AP Photo/Bernat Armangue

Spain's visibly pregnant new Defense minister, Carme Chacón, reviews troops in Madrid on April 14, 2008. She is the first woman ever to head Spain's armed forces. Women hold nine out of 17 cabinet posts in Spain's socialist government, a reflection of women's entrance into the halls of power around the world.

But more than 10 years later, much of the Beijing Platform still has not been achieved. And many question whether women are any better off today than they were in 1995.

"The picture's mixed," says June Zeitlin, executive director of the Women's Environment & Development Organization (WEDO). "In terms of violence against women, there is far more recognition of what is going on today. There has been some progress with education and girls. But the impact of globalization has exacerbated differences between men and women. The poor have gotten poorer — and they are mostly women."

Liberalized international trade has been a two-edged sword in other ways as well. Corporations have been able to expand their global reach, opening new businesses and factories in developing countries and offering women unprecedented employment and economic opportunities. But the jobs often pay low wages and involve work in dangerous conditions because poor countries anxious to attract foreign investors often are willing to ignore safety and labor protections.[26] And increasingly porous international borders have led to growing numbers of women and girls being forced or sold into prostitution or sexual slavery abroad, often under the pretense that they will be given legitimate jobs overseas.[27]

Numerous international agreements in recent years have pledged to provide women with the same opportunities and protections as men, including the U.N.'s Millennium Development Goals (MDGs) and the Convention on the Elimination of All Forms of Discrimination Against Women (CEDAW). But the MDGs' deadlines for improving the conditions for women have either been missed already or are on track to fail in the coming years.[28] And more than 70 of the 185 countries that ratified CEDAW have filed "reservations," meaning they exempt themselves from certain parts.[29] In fact, there are more reservations against CEDAW than against any other international human-rights treaty in history.[30] The United States remains the only developed country in the world not to have ratified it.[31]

"There has certainly been progress in terms of the rhetoric. But there are still challenges in the disparities in education, disparities in income, disparities in health," says Carla Koppell, director of the Cambridge, Mass.-based Initiative for Inclusive Security, which advocates for greater numbers of women in peace negotiations.

"But women are not just victims," she continues. "They have a very unique and important role to play in solving the problems of the developing world. We need to charge policy makers to match the rhetoric and make it a reality. There is a really wonderful opportunity to use the momentum that does exist. I really think we can."

Amidst the successes and failures surrounding women's issues, here are some of the questions analysts are beginning to ask:

Has globalization been good for women?

Over the last 20 years, trade liberalization has led to a massive increase of goods being produced and exported from developing countries, creating millions of manufacturing jobs and bringing many women into the paid workforce for the first time.

"Women employed in export-oriented manufacturing typically earn more than they would have in traditional sectors," according to a World Bank report. "Further, cash income earned by women may improve their status and bargaining power in the family."[32] The report cited a study of 50 families in Mexico that found "a significant proportion of the women reported an improvement in their 'quality of life,' due mainly to their income from working outside their homes, including in (export-oriented) factory jobs."

But because women in developing nations are generally less educated than men and have little bargaining power, most of these jobs are temporary or part-time, offering no health-care benefits, overtime or sick leave.

Women comprise 85 percent of the factory jobs in the garment industry in Bangladesh and 90 percent in Cambodia. In the cut flower industry, women hold 65 percent of the jobs in Colombia and 87 percent in Zimbabwe. In the fruit industry, women constitute 69 percent of temporary and seasonal workers in South Africa and 52 percent in Chile.[33]

Frequently, women in these jobs have no formal contract with their employers, making them even more vulnerable to poor safety conditions and abuse. One study found that only 46 percent of women garment workers in Bangladesh had an official letter of employment.[34]

"Women are a workforce vital to the global economy, but the jobs women are in often aren't covered by labor protections," says Thalia Kidder, a policy adviser on gender and sustainable livelihoods with U.K.-based Oxfam, a confederation of 12 international aid organizations. Women lack protection because they mostly work as domestics, in home-based businesses and as part-time workers. "In the global economy, many companies look to hire the most powerless people because they cannot demand high wages. There are not a lot of trade treaties that address labor rights."

In addition to recommending that countries embrace free trade, Western institutions like the International Monetary Fund and the World Bank during the 1990s recommended that developing countries adopt so-called structural adjustment economic reforms in order to qualify for certain loans and financial support. Besides opening borders to free trade, the neo-liberal economic regime known as the Washington Consensus advocated privatizing state-owned businesses, balancing budgets and attracting foreign investment.

But according to some studies, those reforms ended up adversely affecting women. For instance, companies in Ecuador were encouraged to make jobs more "flexible" by replacing long-term contracts with temporary, seasonal and hourly positions — while restricting collective bargaining rights.[35] And countries streamlined and privatized government programs such as health care and education, services women depend on most.

Globalization also has led to a shift toward cash crops grown for export, which hurts women farmers, who produce 60 to 80 percent of the food for household consumption in developing countries.[36] Small women farmers are being pushed off their land so crops for exports can be grown, limiting their abilities to produce food for themselves and their families.

While economic globalization has yet to create the economic support needed to help women out of poverty, women's advocates say females have benefited from the broadening of communications between countries prompted by globalization. "It has certainly improved access to communications and helped human-rights campaigns," says Zeitlin of WEDO. "Less can be done in secret. If there is a woman who is condemned to be stoned to death somewhere, you can almost immediately mobilize a global campaign against it."

Homa Hoodfar, a professor of social anthropology at Concordia University in Montreal, Canada, and a founder of the group Women Living Under Muslim Laws, says women in some of the world's most remote towns and villages regularly e-mail her organization. "Globalization has made the world much smaller," she says. "Women are getting information on TV and the Internet. The fact that domestic violence has become a global issue [shows globalization] provides resources for those objecting locally."

But open borders also have enabled the trafficking of millions of women around the world. An estimated 800,000 people are trafficked across international borders each year — 80 percent of them women and girls — and most are forced into the commercial sex trade. Millions more are trafficked within their own countries.[37] Globalization has sparked a massive migration of women in search of better jobs and lives. About 90 million women — half of the world's migrants and more than ever in history — reside outside their home countries. These migrant women — often unable to speak the local language and without any family connections — are especially susceptible to traffickers who lure them with promises of jobs abroad.[38]

And those who do not get trapped in the sex trade often end up in low-paying or abusive jobs in foreign factories or as domestic maids working under slave-like conditions.

Female Peacekeepers Fill Vital Roles

Women bring a different approach to conflict resolution.

The first all-female United Nations peacekeeping force left Liberia in January after a year's mission in the West African country, which is rebuilding itself after 14 years of civil war. Comprised of more than 100 women from India, the force was immediately replaced by a second female team.

"If anyone questioned the ability of women to do tough jobs, then those doubters have been [proven] wrong," said U.N. Special Representative for Liberia Ellen Margrethe Løj, adding that the female peacekeepers inspired many Liberian women to join the national police force.[1]

Women make up half of the world's refugees and have systematically been targeted for rape and sexual abuse during times of war, from the 200,000 "comfort women" who were kept as sex slaves for Japanese soldiers during World War II[2] to the estimated quarter-million women reportedly raped and sexually assaulted during the current conflict in the Democratic Republic of the Congo.[3] But women account for only 5 percent of the world's security-sector jobs, and in many countries they are excluded altogether.[4]

In 2000, the U.N. Security Council unanimously adopted Resolution 1325 calling on governments — and the U.N. itself — to include women in peace building by adopting a variety of measures, including appointing more women as special envoys, involving women in peace negotiations, integrating gender-based policies in peacekeeping missions and increasing the number of women at all decision-making levels.[5]

But while Resolution 1325 was a critical step in bringing women into the peace process, women's groups say more women should be sent on field missions and more data collected on how conflict affects women around the world.[6]

"Women are often viewed as victims, but another way to view them is as the maintainers of society," says Carla Koppell, director of the Cambridge, Mass.-based Initiative for Inclusive Security, which promotes greater numbers of women in peacekeeping and conflict resolution. "There must be a conscious decision to include women. It's a detriment to promote peace without including women."

Women often comprise the majority of post-conflict survivor populations, especially when large numbers of men have either fled or been killed. In the wake of the 1994 Rwandan genocide, for example, women made up 70 percent of the remaining population.

And female peacekeepers and security forces can fill vital roles men often cannot, such as searching Islamic women wearing burkas or working with rape victims who may be reluctant to report the crimes to male soldiers.

But some experts say the real problem is not migration and globalization but the lack of labor protection. "Nothing is black and white," says Marianne Mollmann, advocacy director for the Women's Rights Division of Human Rights Watch. "Globalization has created different employment opportunities for women. Migration flows have made women vulnerable. But it's a knee-jerk reaction to say that women shouldn't migrate. You can't prevent migration. So where do we need to go?" She suggests including these workers in general labor-law protections that cover all workers.

Mollmann said countries can and should hammer out agreements providing labor and wage protections for domestic workers migrating across borders. With such protections, she said, women could benefit from the jobs and incomes promised by increased migration and globalization.

Should governments impose electoral quotas for women?

In 2003, as Rwanda struggled to rebuild itself after the genocide that killed at least 800,000 Hutus and Tutsis, the country adopted an historic new constitution that, among other things, required that women hold at least 30 percent of posts "in all decision-making organs."[39]

Today — ironically, just across Lake Kivu from the horrors occurring in Eastern Congo — Rwanda's lower house of parliament now leads the world in female representation, with 48.8 percent of the seats held by women.[40]

"Women bring different experiences and issues to the table," says Koppell. "I've seen it personally in the Darfur and Uganda peace negotiations. Their priorities were quite different. Men were concerned about power- and wealth-sharing. Those are valid, but you get an entirely different dimension from women. Women talked about security on the ground, security of families, security of communities."

In war-torn countries, women have been found to draw on their experiences as mothers to find nonviolent and flexible ways to solve conflict.[7] During peace negotiations in Northern Ireland, for example, male negotiators repeatedly walked out of sessions, leaving a small number of women at the table. The women, left to their own, found areas of common ground and were able to keep discussions moving forward.[8]

"The most important thing is introducing the definition of security from a woman's perspective," said Orzala Ashraf, founder of Kabul-based Humanitarian Assistance for the Women and Children of Afghanistan. "It is not a man in a uniform standing next to a tank armed with a gun. Women have a broader term — human security — the ability to go to school, receive health care, work and have access to

The first all-female United Nations peacekeeping force practices martial arts in New Delhi as it prepares to be deployed to Liberia in 2006.

AP Photo/Mustafa Quraishi

justice. Only by improving these areas can threats from insurgents, Taliban, drug lords and warlords be countered."[9]

[1] "Liberia: UN envoy welcomes new batch of female Indian police officers," U.N. News Centre, Feb. 8, 2008, www.un.org/apps/news/story.asp?NewsID=25557&Cr=liberia&Cr1=.

[2] "Japan: Comfort Women," European Speaking Tour press release, Amnesty International, Oct. 31, 2007.

[3] "Film Documents Rape of Women in Congo," "All Things Considered," National Public Radio, April 8, 2008, www.npr.org/templates/story/story.php?storyId=89476111.

[4] "Ninth Annual Colloquium and Policy Forum," Hunt Alternatives Fund, Jan. 22, 2008, www.huntalternatives.org/pages/7650_ninth_annual_colloquium_and_policy_forum.cfm. Also see Elizabeth Eldridge, "Women cite utility in peace efforts," *The Washington Times*, Jan. 25, 2008, p. A1.

[5] "Inclusive Security, Sustainable Peace: A Toolkit for Advocacy and Action," International Alert and Women Waging Peace, 2004, p. 15, www.huntalternatives.org/download/35_introduction.pdf.

[6] *Ibid.*, p. 17.

[7] Jolynn Shoemaker and Camille Pampell Conaway, "Conflict Prevention and Transformation: Women's Vital Contributions," Inclusive Security: Women Waging Peace and the United Nations Foundation, Feb. 23, 2005, p. 7.

[8] The Initiative for Inclusive Security, www.huntalternatives.org/pages/460_the_vital_role_of_women_in_peace_building.cfm.

[9] Eldridge, *op. cit.*

Before the civil war, Rwandan women never held more than 18 percent of parliament. But after the genocide, the country's population was 70 percent female. Women immediately stepped in to fill the vacuum, becoming the heads of households, community leaders and business owners. Their increased presence in leadership positions eventually led to the new constitutional quotas.[41]

"We see so many post-conflict countries going from military regimes to democracy that are starting from scratch with new constitutions," says Drude Dahlerup, a professor of political science at Sweden's Stockholm University who studies the use of gender quotas. "Today, starting from scratch means including women. It's seen as a sign of modernization and democratization."

Both Iraq and Afghanistan included electoral quotas for women in their new constitutions, and the number of women in political office in sub-Saharan Africa has increased faster than in any other region of the world, primarily through the use of quotas.[42]

But many point out that simply increasing the numbers of women in elected office will not necessarily expand women's rights. "It depends on which women and which positions they represent," says Wendy Harcourt, chair of Women in Development Europe (WIDE), a feminist network in Europe, and editor of *Development*, the journal of the Society for International Development, a global network of individuals and institutions working on development issues. "It's positive, but I don't see yet what it means [in terms of addressing] broader gender issues."

Few Women Head World Governments

Fourteen women currently serve as elected heads of state or government including five who serve as both. Mary McAleese, elected president of Ireland in 1997, is the world's longest-serving head of state. Helen Clark of New Zealand has served as prime minister since 1999, making her the longest-serving female head of government. The world's first elected female head of state was Sirimavo Bandaranaike of Sri Lanka, in 1960.

Current Female Elected Heads of State and Government

Heads of both state and government:

 Gloria Macapagal-Arroyo — President, the Philippines, since 2001; former secretary of Defense (2002) and secretary of Foreign Affairs (2003 and 2006-2007).

 Ellen Johnson-Sirleaf — President, Liberia, since 2006; held finance positions with the government and World Bank.

 Michelle Bachelet Jeria — President, Chile, since 2006; former minister of Health (2000-2002) and minister of Defense (2002-2004).

 Cristina E. Fernández — President, Argentina, since 2007; succeeded her husband, Nestor de Kirchner, as president; former president, Senate Committee on Constitutional Affairs.

 Rosa Zafferani — Captain Regent, San Marino, since April 2008; secretary of State of Public Education, University and Cultural Institutions (2004 to 2008); served as captain regent in 1999; San Marino elects two captains regent every six months, who serve as co-heads of both state and government.

Heads of Government:

 Helen Clark — Prime Minister, New Zealand, since 1999; held government posts in foreign affairs, defense, housing and labor.

 Luísa Días Diogo — Prime Minister, Mozambique, since 2004; held several finance posts in Mozambique and the World Bank.

 Angela Merkel — Chancellor, Germany, since 2005; parliamentary leader of Christian Democratic Union Party (2002-2005).

 Yuliya Tymoshenko — Prime Minister, Ukraine, since 2007; chief of government (2005) and designate prime minister (2006).

 Zinaida Grecianîi — Prime Minister, Moldova, since March 2008; vice prime minister (2005-2008).

Heads of State:

 Mary McAleese — President, Ireland, since 1997; former director of a television station and Northern Ireland Electricity.

 Tarja Halonen — President, Finland, since 2000; former minister of foreign affairs (1995-2000).

 Pratibha Patil — President, India, since 2007; former governor of Rajasthan state (2004-2007).

 Borjana Kristo — President, Bosnia and Herzegovina, since 2007; minister of Justice of Bosniak-Croat Federation, an entity in Bosnia and Herzegovina (2003-2007).

Source: www.guide2womenleaders.com

While Afghanistan has mandated that women hold at least 27 percent of the government's lower house seats and at least 17 percent of the upper house, their increased representation appears to have done little to improve women's rights.[43] Earlier this year, a student journalist was condemned to die under Afghanistan's strict Islamic sharia law after he distributed articles from the Internet on women's rights.[44] And non-governmental groups in Afghanistan report that Afghan women and girls have begun killing themselves in record numbers, burning themselves alive in order to escape widespread domestic abuse or forced marriages.[45]

Having gender quotas alone doesn't necessarily ensure that women's rights will be broadened, says Hoodfar of Concordia University. It depends on the type of quota a government implements, she argues, pointing out that in Jordan, for example, the government has set aside parliamentary seats for the six women who garner the most votes of any other female candidates in their districts — even if they do not win more votes than male candidates.[46] Many small, conservative tribes that cannot garner enough votes for a male in a countrywide victory are now nominating their sisters and wives in the hope that the lower number of votes needed to elect a woman will get them one of the reserved seats. As a result, many of the women moving into the reserved seats are extremely conservative and actively oppose providing women greater rights and freedoms.

And another kind of quota has been used against women in her home country of Iran, Hoodfar points out. Currently, 64 percent of university students in Iran are women. But the government recently mandated that at least 40 percent of university enrollees be male, forcing many female students out of school, Hoodfar said.

"Before, women didn't want to use quotas for politics because of concern the government may try to use it against women," she says. "But women are beginning to look into it and talk about maybe developing a good system."

Quotas can be enacted by constitutional requirements, such as those enacted in Rwanda, by statute or voluntarily by political parties. Quotas also can vary in their requirements: They can mandate the number of women each party must nominate, how many women must appear on the ballot (and the order in which they appear, so women are not relegated to the bottom of the list), or the number of women who must hold government office. About 40 countries now use gender quotas in national parliamentary elections, while another 50 have major political parties that voluntarily use quotas to determine candidates.

Aside from questions about the effectiveness of quotas, others worry about the fairness of establishing quotas based on gender. "That's something feminists have traditionally opposed," says Harcourt.

"It's true, but it's also not fair the way it is now," says former Ambassador Hunt. "We are where we are today through all kinds of social structures that are not fair. Quotas are the lesser of two evils."

Stockholm University's Dahlerup says quotas are not "discrimination against men but compensation for discrimination against women." Yet quotas are not a panacea for women in politics, she contends. "It's a mistake to think this is a kind of tool that will solve all problems. It doesn't solve problems about financing campaigns, caring for families while being in politics or removing patriarchal attitudes. It would be nice if it wasn't necessary, and hopefully sometime in the future it won't be."

Until that time, however, quotas are a "necessary evil," she says.

Women Still Far from Reaching Political Parity

Although they have made strides in the past decade, women hold only a small minority of the world's leadership and legislative posts (right). Nordic parliaments have the highest rates of female representation — 41.4 percent — compared with only 9 percent in Arab countries (below). However, Arab legislatures have nearly tripled their female representation since 1997, and some countries in Africa have dramatically increased theirs as well: Rwanda, at 48.8 percent, now has the world's highest percentage of women in parliament of any country. The U.S. Congress ranks 70th in the world, with 89 women serving in the 535-member body — or 16.6 percent.

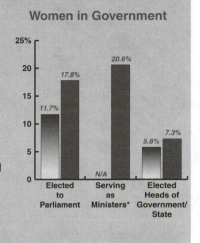

Women in Government

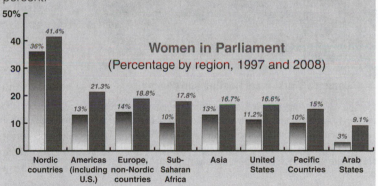

Women in Parliament
(Percentage by region, 1997 and 2008)

* Includes deputy prime ministers, ministers and prime ministers who hold ministerial portfolios.

Sources: Interparliamentarian Union, www.ipu.org/wmn-e/world.htm; State of the World's Children 2007, UNICEF, www.unicef.org/sowc07/; "Worldwide Guide to Women in Leadership" database, www.un.org/womenwatch/daw/csw/41sess.htm.

AP Photo/Rajesh Kumar Singh

National Geographic/Getty Images/Melvyn Goldstein

Women's Work: From Hauling and Churning . . .

Women's work is often back-breaking and monotonous, such as hauling firewood in the western Indian state of Maharashtra (top) and churning yogurt into butter beside Lake Motsobunnyi in Tibet (bottom). Women labor two-thirds of the total hours worked around the globe each year but earn only 10 percent of the income.

Do international treaties improve women's rights?

In recent decades, a variety of international agreements have been signed by countries pledging to improve women's lives, from the 1979 Convention for the Elimination of All Forms of Discrimination Against Women to the Beijing Platform of 1995 to the Millennium Development Goals (MDGs) adopted in 2000. The agreements aimed to provide women with greater access to health, political representation, economic stability and social status. They also focused attention on some of the biggest obstacles facing women.

But despite the fanfare surrounding the launch of those agreements, many experts on women's issues say on-the-ground action has yet to match the rhetoric. "The report is mixed," says Haleh Afshar, a professor of politics and women's studies at the University of York in the United Kingdom and a nonpartisan, appointed member of the House of Lords, known as a crossbench peer. "The biggest problem with Beijing is all these things were stated, but none were funded. Unfortunately, I don't see any money. You don't get the pay, you don't get the job done."

The Beijing Platform for Action, among other things, called on governments to "adjust budgets to ensure equality of access to public sector expenditures" and even to "reduce, as appropriate, excessive military expenditure" in order to achieve the Platform goals.

But adequate funding has yet to be provided, say women's groups.[47] In a report entitled "Beijing Betrayed," the Women's Environment & Development Organization says female HIV cases outnumber male cases in many parts of the world, gender-related violence remains a pandemic and women still make up the majority of the world's poor — despite pledges in Beijing to reverse these trends.[48]

And funding is not the only obstacle. A 2004 U.N. survey revealed that while many countries have enacted laws in recent years to help protect women from violence and discrimination, long-standing social and cultural traditions block progress. "While constitutions provided for equality between women and men on the one hand, [several countries] recognized and gave precedent to customary law and practice in a number of areas . . . resulting in discrimination against women," the report said. "Several countries noted that statutory, customary and religious law coexist, especially in regard to family, personal status and inheritance and land rights. This perpetuated discrimination against women."[49]

While she worries about the lack of progress on the Beijing Platform, WEDO Executive Director Zeitlin says international agreements are nevertheless critical in raising global awareness on women's issues. "They have a major impact on setting norms and standards," she says. "In many countries, norms and standards are very important in setting goals for women to advocate for. We complain about lack of implementation, but if we didn't have the norms and standards we couldn't complain about a lack of implementation."

Like the Beijing Platform, the MDGs have been criticized for not achieving more. While the U.N. says promoting women's rights is essential to achieving the millennium goals — which aim to improve the lives of all the world's populations by 2015 — only two of the eight specifically address women's issues.[50]

One of the goals calls for countries to "Promote gender equality and empower women." But it sets only one measurable target: "Eliminate gender disparity in primary and secondary education, preferably by 2005, and in all levels of education" by 2015.[51] Some 62 countries failed to reach the 2005 deadline, and many are likely to miss the 2015 deadline as well.[52]

Another MDG calls for a 75 percent reduction in maternal mortality compared to 1990 levels. But according to the human-rights group ActionAid, this goal is the "most off track of all the MDGs." Rates are declining at less than 1 percent a year, and in some countries — such as Sierra Leone, Pakistan and Guatemala — maternal mortality has increased since 1990. If that trend continues, no region in the developing world is expected to reach the goal by 2015.[53]

Activist Peggy Antrobus of Development Alternatives with Women for a New Era (DAWN) — a network of feminists from the Southern Hemisphere, based currently in Calabar, Cross River State, Nigeria — has lambasted the MDGs, quipping that the acronym stands for the "Most Distracting Gimmick."[54] Many feminists argue that the goals are too broad to have any real impact and that the MDGs should have given more attention to women's issues.

But other women say international agreements — and the public debate surrounding them — are vital in promoting gender equality. "It's easy to get disheartened, but Beijing is still the blueprint of where we need to be," says Mollmann of Human Rights Watch. "They are part of a political process, the creation of an international culture. If systematically everyone says [discrimination against women] is a bad thing, states don't want to be hauled out as systematic violators."

In particular, Mollmann said, CEDAW has made real progress in overcoming discrimination against women. Unlike the Beijing Platform and the MDGs, CEDAW legally obliges countries to comply. Each of the 185 ratifying countries must submit regular reports to the U.N. outlining their progress under the convention. Several

AP Photo/Sergei Grits

AFP/Getty Images/Ali Burafi

. . . to Gathering and Herding

While many women have gotten factory jobs thanks to globalization of trade, women still comprise 70 percent of the planet's inhabitants living on less than a dollar a day. Women perform a variety of tasks around the world, ranging from gathering flax in Belarus (top) to shepherding goats in central Argentina (bottom).

countries — including Brazil, Uganda, South Africa and Australia — also have incorporated CEDAW provisions into their constitutions and legal systems.[55]

Still, dozens of ratifying countries have filed official "reservations" against the convention, including Bahrain, Egypt, Kuwait, Morocco and the United Arab Emirates, all of whom say they will comply only within the bounds of Islamic sharia law.[56] And the United States has refused to ratify CEDAW, with or without reservations, largely because of conservatives who say it would, among other things, promote abortion and require the government to pay for such things as child care and maternity leave.

AP Photo/Prakash Hatvalne

Indian women harvest wheat near Bhopal. Women produce half of the food used domestically worldwide and 60 to 80 percent of the household food grown in developing countries.

BACKGROUND

'Structural Defects'

Numerous prehistoric relics suggest that at one time matriarchal societies existed on Earth in which women were in the upper echelons of power. Because early societies did not understand the connection between sexual relations and conception, they believed women were solely responsible for reproduction — which led to the worship of female goddesses.[57]

In more modern times, however, women have generally faced prejudice and discrimination at the hands of a patriarchal society. In about the eighth century B.C. creation stories emerged describing the fall of man due to the weakness of women. The Greeks recounted the story of Pandora who, through her opening of a sealed jar, unleashed death and pain on all of mankind. Meanwhile, similar tales in Judea eventually were recounted in Genesis, with Eve as the culprit.[58]

In ancient Greece, women were treated as children and denied basic rights. They could not leave their houses unchaperoned, were prohibited from being educated or buying or selling land. A father could sell his unmarried daughter into slavery if she lost her virginity before marriage. If a woman was raped, she was outcast and forbidden from participating in public ceremonies or wearing jewelry.[59]

The status of women in early Rome was not much better, although over time women began to assert their voices and slowly gained greater freedoms. Eventually, they were able to own property and divorce their husbands. But early Christian leaders later denounced the legal and social freedom enjoyed by Roman women as a sign of moral decay. In the view of the early church, women were dependent on and subordinate to men.

In the 13th century, the Catholic priest and theologian St. Thomas Aquinas helped set the tone for the subjugation of women in Western society. He said women were created solely to be "man's helpmate" and advocated that men should make use of "a necessary object, woman, who is needed to preserve the species or to provide food and drink."[60]

From the 14th to 17th centuries, misogyny and oppression of women took a step further. As European societies struggled against the Black Plague, the 100 Years War and turmoil between Catholics and Reformers, religious leaders began to blame tragedies, illnesses and other problems on witches. As witch hysteria spread across Europe — instituted by both the religious and non-religious — an estimated 30,000 to 60,000 people were executed for allegedly practicing witchcraft. About 80 percent were females, some as young as 8 years old.[61]

"All wickedness is but little to the wickedness of a woman," Catholic inquisitors wrote in the 1480s. "What else is woman but a foe to friendship, an unescapable punishment, a necessary evil, a natural temptation, a desirable calamity. . . . Women are . . . instruments of Satan, . . . a structural defect rooted in the original creation."[62]

Push for Protections

The Age of Enlightenment and the Industrial Revolution in the 18th and 19th centuries opened up job opportunities for women, released them from domestic confines and provided them with new social freedoms.

In 1792 Mary Wollstonecraft published *A Vindication of the Rights of Women*, which has been hailed as "the feminist declaration of independence." Although the book had been heavily influenced by the French Revolution's notions of equality and universal brotherhood, French revolutionary leaders, ironically, were not sympathetic to feminist causes.[63] In 1789 they had refused to accept a Declaration of the Rights of Women when it was presented at the National Assembly. And Jean Jacques Rousseau, one of the philosophical founders of the revolution, had written in 1762:

"The whole education of women ought to be relative to men. To please them, to be useful to them, to make themselves loved and honored by them, to educate them when young, to care for them when grown, to counsel them, to make life sweet and agreeable to them — these are the duties of women at all times, and what should be taught them from their infancy."[64]

As more and more women began taking jobs outside the home during the 19th century, governments began to pass laws to "protect" them in the workforce and expand their legal rights. The British Mines Act of 1842, for instance, prohibited women from working underground.[65] In 1867, John Stuart Mill, a supporter of women's rights and author of the book *Subjection of Women*, introduced language in the British House of Commons calling for women to be granted the right to vote. It failed.[66]

But by that time governments around the globe had begun enacting laws giving women rights they had been denied for centuries. As a result of the Married Women's Property Act of 1870 and a series of other measures, wives in Britain were finally allowed to own property. In 1893, New Zealand became the first nation to grant full suffrage rights to women, followed over the next two decades by Finland, Norway, Denmark and Iceland. The United States granted women suffrage in 1920.[67]

One of the first international labor conventions, formulated at Berne, Switzerland, in 1906, applied exclusively to women — prohibiting night work for women in industrial occupations. Twelve nations signed on to it. During the second Berne conference in 1913, language was proposed limiting the number of hours women and children could work in industrial jobs, but the outbreak of World War I prevented it from being enacted.[68] In 1924 the U.S. Supreme Court upheld a night-work law for women.[69]

In 1946, public attention to women's issues received a major boost when the United Nations created the Commission on the Status of Women to address urgent problems facing women around the world.[70] During the 1950s, the U.N. adopted several conventions aimed at improving women's lives, including the Convention on the Political Rights of Women, adopted in 1952 to ensure women the right to vote, which has been ratified by 120 countries, and the Convention on the Nationality of Married Women, approved in 1957 to ensure that marriage to an alien does not automatically affect the nationality of the woman.[71] That convention has been ratified by only 73 countries; the United States is not among them.[72]

In 1951 The International Labor Organization (ILO), an agency of the United Nations, adopted the Convention on Equal Remuneration for Men and Women Workers for Work of Equal Value, to promote equal pay for equal work. It has since been ratified by 164 countries, but again, not by the United States.[73] Seven years later, the ILO adopted the Convention on Discrimination in Employment and Occupation to ensure equal opportunity and treatment in employment. It is currently ratified by 166 countries, but not the United States.[74] U.S. opponents to the conventions claim there is no real pay gap between men and women performing the same jobs and that the conventions would impose "comparable worth" requirements, forcing companies to pay equal wages to men and women even if the jobs they performed were different.[75]

In 1965, the Commission on the Status of Women began drafting international standards articulating equal rights for men and women. Two years later, the panel completed the Declaration on the Elimination of Discrimination Against Women, which was adopted by the General Assembly but carried no enforcement power.

The commission later began to discuss language that would hold countries responsible for enforcing the declaration. At the U.N.'s first World Conference on Women in Mexico City in 1975, women from around the world called for creation of such a treaty, and the commission soon began drafting the text.[76]

Women's 'Bill of Rights'

Finally in 1979, after many years of often rancorous debate, the Convention on the Elimination of All Forms of Discrimination Against Women (CEDAW) was adopted by the General Assembly — 130 to none, with 10 abstentions. After the vote, however, several countries said their "yes" votes did not commit the support of their governments. Brazil's U.N. representative told the assembly, "The signatures and ratifications necessary to make this effective will not come easily."[77]

Despite the prediction, it took less than two years for CEDAW to receive the required number of ratifications to enter it into force — faster than any human-rights convention had ever done before.[78]

CHRONOLOGY

1700s-1800s *Age of Enlightenment and Industrial Revolution lead to greater freedoms for women.*

1792 Mary Wollstonecraft publishes *A Vindication of the Rights of Women,* later hailed as "the feminist declaration of independence."

1893 New Zealand becomes first nation to grant women full suffrage.

1920 Tennessee is the 36th state to ratify the 19th Amendment, giving American women the right to vote.

1940s-1980s *International conventions endorse equal rights for women. Global conferences highlight need to improve women's rights.*

1946 U.N. creates Commission on the Status of Women.

1951 U.N. International Labor Organization adopts convention promoting equal pay for equal work, which has been ratified by 164 countries; the United States is not among them.

1952 U.N. adopts convention calling for full women's suffrage.

1960 Sri Lanka elects the world's first female prime minister.

1974 Maria Estela Martínez de Perón of Argentina becomes the world's first woman president, replacing her ailing husband.

1975 U.N. holds first World Conference on Women, in Mexico City, followed by similar conferences every five years. U.N. launches the Decade for Women.

1979 U.N. adopts Convention on the Elimination of All Forms of Discrimination against Women (CEDAW), dubbed the "international bill of rights for women."

1981 CEDAW is ratified — faster than any other human-rights convention.

1990s *Women's rights win historic legal recognition.*

1993 U.N. World Conference on Human Rights in Vienna, Austria, calls for ending all violence, sexual harassment and trafficking of women.

1995 Fourth World Conference on Women in Beijing draws 30,000 people, making it the largest in U.N. history. Beijing Platform outlining steps to grant women equal rights is signed by 189 governments.

1996 International Criminal Tribunal convicts eight Bosnian Serb police and military officers for rape during the Bosnian conflict — the first time sexual assault is prosecuted as a war crime.

1998 International Criminal Tribunal for Rwanda recognizes rape and other forms of sexual violence as genocide.

2000s *Women make political gains, but sexual violence against women increases.*

2000 U.N. calls on governments to include women in peace negotiations.

2006 Ellen Johnson Sirleaf of Liberia, Michelle Bachelet of Chile and Portia Simpson Miller of Jamaica become their countries' first elected female heads of state. . . . Women in Kuwait are allowed to run for parliament, winning two seats.

2007 A woman in Saudi Arabia who was sentenced to 200 lashes after being gang-raped by seven men is pardoned by King Abdullah. Her rapists received sentences ranging from 10 months to five years in prison, and 80 to 1,000 lashes. . . . After failing to recognize any gender-based crimes in its first case involving the Democratic Republic of the Congo, the International Criminal Court hands down charges of "sexual slavery" in its second case involving war crimes in Congo. More than 250,000 women are estimated to have been raped and sexually abused during the country's war.

2008 Turkey lifts 80-year-old ban on women's headscarves in public universities, signaling a drift toward religious fundamentalism. . . . Former housing minister Carme Chacón — 37 and pregnant — is named defense minister of Spain, bringing to nine the number of female cabinet ministers in the Socialist government. . . . Sen. Hillary Rodham Clinton becomes the first U.S. woman to be in a tight race for a major party's presidential nomination.

Often described as an international bill of rights for women, CEDAW defines discrimination against women as "any distinction, exclusion or restriction made on the basis of sex which has the effect or purpose of impairing or nullifying the recognition, enjoyment or exercise by women, irrespective of their marital status, on a basis of equality of men and women, of human rights and fundamental freedoms in the political, economic, social, cultural, civil or any other field."

Ratifying countries are legally bound to end discrimination against women by incorporating sexual equality into their legal systems, abolishing discriminatory laws against women, taking steps to end trafficking of women and ensuring women equal access to political and public life. Countries must also submit reports at least every four years outlining the steps they have taken to comply with the convention.[79]

CEDAW also grants women reproductive choice — one of the main reasons the United States has not ratified it. The convention requires signatories to guarantee women's rights "to decide freely and responsibly on the number and spacing of their children and to have access to the information, education and means to enable them to exercise these rights."[80]

While CEDAW is seen as a significant tool to stop violence against women, it actually does not directly mention violence. To rectify this, the CEDAW committee charged with monitoring countries' compliance in 1992 specified gender-based violence as a form of discrimination prohibited under the convention.[81]

In 1993 the U.N. took further steps to combat violence against women during the World Conference on Human Rights in Vienna, Austria. The conference called on countries to stop all forms of violence, sexual harassment, exploitation and trafficking of women. It also declared that "violations of the human rights of women in situations of armed conflicts are violations of the fundamental principles of international human rights and humanitarian law."[82]

Shortly afterwards, as fighting broke out in the former Yugoslavia and Rwanda, new legal precedents were set to protect women against violence — and particularly rape — during war. In 1996, the International Criminal Tribunal in the Hague, Netherlands, indicted eight Bosnian Serb police officers in connection with the mass rape of Muslim women during the Bosnian war, marking the first time sexual assault had ever been prosecuted as a war crime.[83]

Two years later, the U.N.'s International Criminal Tribunal for Rwanda convicted a former Rwandan mayor for genocide, crimes against humanity, rape and sexual violence — the first time rape and sexual violence were recognized as acts of genocide.[84]

"Rape is a serious war crime like any other," said Regan Ralph, then executive director of Human Rights Watch's Women's Rights Division, shortly after the conviction. "That's always been true on paper, but now international courts are finally acting on it."[85]

Today, the International Criminal Court has filed charges against several Sudanese officials for rape and other crimes committed in the Darfur region.[86] But others are demanding that the court also prosecute those responsible for the rapes in the Eastern Congo, where women are being targeted as a means of destroying communities in the war-torn country.[87]

Beijing and Beyond

The U.N. World Conference on Women in Mexico City in 1975 produced a 44-page plan of action calling for a decade of special measures to give women equal status and opportunities in law, education, employment, politics and society.[88] The conference also kicked off the U.N.'s Decade for Women and led to creation of the U.N. Development Fund for Women (UNIFEM).[89]

Five years later, the U.N. held its second World Conference on Women in Copenhagen and then celebrated the end of the Decade for Women with the third World Conference in Nairobi in 1985. More than 10,000 representatives from government agencies and NGOs attended the Nairobi event, believed to be the largest gathering on women's issues at the time.[90]

Upon reviewing the progress made on women's issues during the previous 10 years, the U.N. representatives in Nairobi concluded that advances had been extremely limited due to failing economies in developing countries, particularly those in Africa struggling against drought, famine and crippling debt. The conference developed a set of steps needed to improve the status of women during the final 15 years of the 20th century.[91]

Ten years later, women gathered in Beijing in 1995 for the Fourth World Conference, vowing to turn the rhetoric of the earlier women's conferences into action. Delegates from 189 governments and 2,600

Women Suffer Most in Natural Disasters

Climate change will make matters worse.

In natural disasters, women suffer death, disease and hunger at higher rates then men. During the devastating 2004 tsunami in Asia, 70 to 80 percent of the dead were women.[1] During cyclone-triggered flooding in Bangladesh that killed 140,000 people in 1991, nearly five times more women between the ages of 20 and 44 died than men.[2]

Gender discrimination, cultural biases and lack of awareness of women's needs are part of the problem. For instance, during the 1991 cyclone, Bangladeshi women and their children died in higher numbers because they waited at home for their husbands to return and make evacuation decisions.[3] In addition, flood warnings were conveyed by men to men in public spaces but were rarely communicated to women and children at home.[4]

And during the tsunami, many Indonesian women died because they stayed behind to look for children and other family members. Women clinging to children in floodwaters also tired more quickly and drowned, since most women in the region were never taught to swim or climb trees.[5] In Sri Lanka, many women died because the tsunami hit early on a Sunday morning when they were inside preparing breakfast for their families. Men were generally outside where they had earlier warning of the oncoming floods so they were better able to escape.[6]

Experts now predict global climate change — which is expected to increase the number of natural disasters around the world — will put women in far greater danger than men because natural disasters generally have a disproportionate impact on the world's poor. Since women comprise 70 percent of those living on less than $1 a day, they will be hardest hit by climate changes, according to the Intergovernmental Panel on Climate Change.[7]

"Climate change is not gender-neutral," said Gro Harlem Brundtland, former prime minister of Norway and now special envoy to the U.N. secretary-general on climate change. "[Women are] more dependent for their livelihood on natural resources that are threatened by climate change....With changes in climate, traditional food sources become more unpredictable and scarce. This exposes women to loss of harvests, often their sole sources of food and income."[8]

Women produce 60 to 80 percent of the food for household consumption in developing countries.[9] As drought, flooding and desertification increase, experts say women and their families will be pushed further into poverty and famine.

Women also suffer more hardship in the aftermath of natural disasters, and their needs are often ignored during relief efforts.

In many Third World countries, for instance, women have no property rights, so when a husband dies during a natural disaster his family frequently confiscates the land from his widow, leaving her homeless and destitute.[10] And because men usually dominate emergency relief and response agencies, women's specific needs, such as contraceptives and sanitary napkins, are often overlooked. After floods in Bangladesh in 1998, adolescent girls reported high rates of rashes and urinary tract infections because they had

NGOs attended. More than 30,000 women and men gathered at a parallel forum organized by NGOs, also in Beijing.[92]

The so-called Beijing Platform that emerged from the conference addressed 12 critical areas facing women, from poverty to inequality in education to inadequate health care to violence. It brought unprecedented attention to women's issues and is still considered by many as the blueprint for true gender equality.

The Beijing Conference also came at the center of a decade that produced historic political gains for women around the world — gains that have continued, albeit at a slow pace, into the new century. The 1990s saw more women entering top political positions than ever before. A record 10 countries elected or appointed women as presidents between 1990 and 2000, including Haiti, Nicaragua, Switzerland and Latvia. Another 17 countries chose women prime ministers.[93]

In 2006 Ellen Johnson Sirleaf of Liberia became Africa's first elected woman president.[94] That same year, Chile elected its first female president, Michelle Bachelet, and Jamaica elected Portia Simpson Miller as its first

no clean water, could not wash their menstrual rags properly in private and had no place to hang them to dry.[11]

"In terms of reconstruction, people are not talking about women's needs versus men's needs," says June Zeitlin, executive director of the Women's Environment and Development Organization, a New York City-based international organization that works for women's equality in global policy. "There is a lack of attention to health care after disasters, issues about bearing children, contraception, rape and vulnerability, menstrual needs — things a male programmer is not thinking about. There is broad recognition that disasters have a disproportionate impact on women. But it stops there. They see women as victims, but they don't see women as agents of change."

Women must be brought into discussions on climate change and emergency relief, say Zeitlin and others. Interestingly, she points out, while women are disproportionately affected by environmental changes, they do more than men to protect the environment. Studies show women emit less climate-changing carbon dioxide than men because they recycle more, use resources more efficiently and drive less than men.[12]

"Women's involvement in climate-change decision-making is a human right," said Gerd Johnson-Latham, deputy director of the Swedish Ministry for Foreign Affairs. "If we get more women in decision-making positions, we

The smell of death hangs over Banda Aceh, Indonesia, which was virtually destroyed by a tsunami on Dec. 28, 2004. From 70 to 80 percent of the victims were women.

will have different priorities, and less risk of climate change."[13]

[1] "Tsunami death toll," CNN, Feb. 22, 2005. Also see "Report of High-level Roundtable: How a Changing Climate Impacts Women," Council of Women World Leaders, Women's Environment and Development Organization and Heinrich Boll Foundation, Sept. 21, 2007, p. 21, www.wedo.org/files/Roundtable%20Final%20Report%206%20Nov.pdf.

[2] Ibid.

[3] "Cyclone Jelawat bears down on Japan's Okinawa island," CNN.com, Aug. 7, 2000, http://archives.cnn.com/2000/ASIANOW/east/08/07/asia.weather/index.html.

[4] "Gender and Health in Disasters," World Health Organization, July 2002, www.who.int/gender/other_health/en/genderdisasters.pdf.

[5] "The tsunami's impact on women," Oxfam briefing note, March 5, 2005, p. 2, www.oxfam.org/en/files/bn050326_tsunami_women/download.

[6] "Report of High-level Roundtable," op. cit., p. 5.

[7] "Gender Equality" fact sheet, Oxfam, www.oxfam.org.uk/resources/issues/gender/introduction.html. Also see ibid.

[8] Ibid., p. 4.

[9] "Five years down the road from Beijing: Assessing progress," News and Highlights, Food and Agriculture Organization, June 2, 2000, www.fao.org/News/2000/000602-e.htm.

[10] "Gender and Health in Disasters," op. cit.

[11] Ibid.

[12] "Women and the Environment," U.N. Environment Program, 2004, p. 17, www.unep.org/Documents.Multilingual/Default.asp?DocumentID=468&ArticleID=4488&l=en. Also see "Report of High-level Roundtable," op. cit., p. 7.

[13] Ibid.

female prime minister.[95] Also that year, women ran for election in Kuwait for the first time. In Bahrain, a woman was elected to the lower house of parliament for the first time.[96] And in 2007, Fernández de Kirchner became the first woman to be elected president of Argentina.

Earlier, a World Bank report had found that government corruption declines as more women are elected into office. The report also cited numerous studies that found women are more likely to exhibit "helping" behavior, vote based on social issues, score higher on "integrity tests," take stronger stances on ethical behavior and behave more generously when faced with economic decisions.[97]

"Increasing the presence of women in government may be valued for its own sake, for reasons of gender equality," the report concluded. "However, our results suggest that there may be extremely important spinoffs stemming from increasing female representation: If women are less likely than men to behave opportunistically, then bringing more women into government may have significant benefits for society in general."[98]

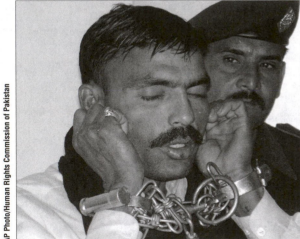

AP Photo/Khalid Tanveer

AP Photo/Human Rights Commission of Pakistan

Honor Killings on the Rise

Women in Multan, Pakistan, demonstrate against "honor killings" in 2003 (top). Although Pakistan outlawed such killings years ago, its Human Rights Commission says 1,205 women were killed in the name of family honor in 2007 — a fourfold jump in two years. Nazir Ahmed Sheikh, a Punjabi laborer (bottom), unrepentantly told police in December 2005 how he slit the throats of his four daughters one night as they slept in order to salvage the family's honor. The eldest had married a man of her choice, and Ahmed feared the younger daughters would follow her example.

CURRENT SITUATION

Rise of Fundamentalism

Despite landmark political gains by women since the late 1990s, violence and repression of women continue to be daily occurrences — often linked to the global growth of religious fundamentalism.

In 2007, a 21-year-old woman in Saudi Arabia was sentenced to 200 lashes and ordered jailed for six months after being raped 14 times by a gang of seven men. The Saudi court sentenced the woman — who was 19 at the time of the attack — because she was alone in a car with her former boyfriend when the attack occurred. Under Saudi Arabia's strict Islamic law, it is a crime for a woman to meet in private with a man who is not her husband or relative.[99]

After public outcry from around the world, King Abdullah pardoned the woman in December. A government spokesperson, however, said the king fully supported the verdict but issued the pardon in the "interests of the people."[100]

Another Saudi woman still faces beheading after she was condemned to death for "witchcraft." Among her accusers is a man who claimed she rendered him impotent with her sorcery. Despite international protest, the king has yet to say if he will pardon her.[101]

In Iraq, the rise of religious fundamentalism since the U.S. invasion has led to a jump in the number of women being killed or beaten in so-called honor crimes. Honor killings typically occur when a woman is suspected of unsanctioned sexual behavior — which can range from flirting to "allowing" herself to be raped. Her relatives believe they must murder her to end the family's shame. In the Kurdish region of Iraq, the stoning death of 17-year-old Aswad is not an anomaly. A U.N. mission in October 2007 found that 255 women had been killed in Iraqi Kurdistan in the first six months of 2007 alone — most thought to have been murdered by their communities or families for allegedly committing adultery or entering into a relationship not sanctioned by their families.[102]

The rise of fundamentalism is also sparking a growing debate on the issue of women wearing head scarves, both in Iraq and across the Muslim world. Last August Turkey elected a conservative Muslim president whose wife wears a head scarf, signaling the emergence of a new ruling elite that is more willing to publicly display religious beliefs.[103] Then in February, Turkey's parliament voted to ease an

80-year ban on women wearing head scarves in universities, although a ban on head scarves in other public buildings remains in effect.

"This decision will bring further pressure on women," Nesrin Baytok, a member of parliament, said during debate over the ban. "It will ultimately bring us Hezbollah terror, al Qaeda terror and fundamentalism."[104]

But others said lifting the ban was actually a victory for women. Fatma Benli, a Turkish women's-rights activist and lawyer, said the ban on head scarves in public buildings has forced her to send law partners to argue her cases because she is prohibited from entering court wearing her head scarf. It also discourages religiously conservative women from becoming doctors, lawyers or teachers, she says.[105]

Many women activists are quick to say that it is unfair to condemn Islam for the growing abuse against women. "The problem women have with religion is not the religion but the ways men have interpreted it," says Afshar of the University of York. "What is highly negative is sharia law, which is made by men. Because it's human-made, women can unmake it. The battle now is fighting against unjust laws such as stoning."

She says abuses such as forced marriages and honor killings — usually linked in the Western media to Islamic law — actually go directly against the teachings of the *Koran*. And while the United Nations estimates that some 5,000 women and girls are victims of honor killings each year, millions more are abused and killed in violence unrelated to Islam. Between 10 and 50 percent of all women around the world have been physically abused by an intimate partner in their lifetime, studies show.[106]

"What about the rate of spousal or partner killings in the U.K. or the U.S. that are not called 'honor killings'?" asks Concordia University's Hoodfar. "Then it's only occasional 'crazy people' [committing violence]. But when it's present in Pakistan, Iran or Senegal, these are uncivilized people doing 'honor killings.' "

And Islamic fundamentalism is not the only brand of fundamentalism on the rise. Christian fundamentalism is also growing rapidly. A 2006 Pew Forum on Religion and Public Life poll found that nearly one-third of all Americans feel the Bible should be the basis of law across the United States.[107] Many women's-rights activists say Christian fundamentalism threatens women's rights, particularly with regard to reproductive issues. They also condemn the Vatican's opposition to the use of condoms, pointing

Pakistani acid attack survivors Saira Liaqat, right, and Sabra Sultana are among hundreds, and perhaps thousands, of women who are blinded and disfigured after being attacked with acid each year in Pakistan, Bangladesh, India, Cambodia, Malaysia, Uganda and other areas of Africa. Liaqat was attacked at age 18 during an argument over an arranged marriage. Sabra was 15 when she was burned after being married off to an older man who became unsatisfied with the relationship. Only a small percentage of the attacks — often perpetrated by spurned suitors while the women are asleep in their own beds — are prosecuted.

out that it prevents women from protecting themselves against HIV.

"If you look at all your religions, none will say it's a good thing to beat up or kill someone. They are all based on human dignity," says Mollmann of Human Rights Watch. "[Bad things] are carried out in the name of religion, but the actual belief system is not killing and maiming women."

In response to the growing number of honor-based killings, attacks and forced marriages in the U.K., Britain's Association of Chief Police Officers has created an honor-based violence unit, and the U.K.'s Home Office is drafting an action plan to improve the response of police and other agencies to such violence. Legislation going into effect later this year will also give U.K. courts greater guidance on dealing with forced marriages.[108]

Evolving Gender Policies

This past February, the U.N. Convention on the Elimination of All Forms of Discrimination Against Women issued a report criticizing Saudi Arabia for its repression of women. Among other things, the report attacked Saudi Arabia's ban on women drivers and its

AP Photo/Light Press/Alex de Jesus

Female farmworkers in Nova Lima, Brazil, protest against the impact of big corporations on the poor in March 2006, reflecting the increasing political activism of women around the globe.

system of male guardianship that denies women equal inheritance, child custody and divorce rights.[109] The criticism came during the panel's regular review of countries that have ratified CEDAW. Each government must submit reports every four years outlining steps taken to comply with the convention.

The United States is one of only eight countries — among them Iran, Sudan and Somalia — that have refused to ratify CEDAW.[110] Last year, 108 members of the U.S. House of Representatives signed on to a resolution calling for the Senate to ratify CEDAW, but it still has not voted on the measure.[111] During a U.N. vote last November on a resolution encouraging governments to meet their obligations under CEDAW, the United States was the lone nay vote against 173 yea votes.[112]

American opponents of CEDAW — largely pro-life Christians and Republicans — say it would enshrine the right to abortion in *Roe v. Wade* and be prohibitively expensive, potentially requiring the U.S. government to provide paid maternity leave and other child-care services to all women.[113] They also oppose requirements that the government modify "social and cultural patterns" to eliminate sexual prejudice and to delete any traces of gender stereotypes in textbooks — such as references to women's lives being primarily in the domestic sector.[114] Many Republicans in Congress also have argued that CEDAW would give too much control over U.S. laws to the United Nations and that it could even require the legalization of prostitution and the abolition of Mother's Day.[115]

The last time the Senate took action on CEDAW was in 2002, when the Senate Foreign Relations Committee, chaired by Democratic Sen. Joseph Biden of Delaware, voted to send the convention to the Senate floor for ratification. The full Senate, however, never took action. A Biden spokesperson says the senator "remains committed" to the treaty and is "looking for an opportune time" to bring it forward again. But Senate ratification requires 67 votes, and there do not appear to be that many votes for approval.

CEDAW proponents say the failure to ratify not only hurts women but also harms the U.S. image abroad. On this issue, "the United States is in the company of Sudan and the Vatican," says Bien-Aimé of Equality Now.

Meanwhile, several countries are enacting laws to comply with CEDAW and improve the status of women. In December, Turkmenistan passed its first national law guaranteeing women equal rights, even though its constitution had addressed women's equality.[116] A royal decree in Saudi Arabia in January ordered an end to a long-time ban on women checking into hotels or renting apartments without male guardians. Hotels can now book rooms to women who show identification, but the hotels must register the women's details with the police.[117] The Saudi government has also said it will lift the ban on women driving by the end of the year.[118]

And in an effort to improve relations with women in Afghanistan, the Canadian military, which has troops stationed in the region, has begun studying the role women play in Afghan society, how they are affected by military operations and how they can assist peacekeeping efforts. "Behind all of these men are women who can help eradicate the problems of the population," said Capt. Michel Larocque, who is working with the study. "Illiteracy, poverty, these things can be improved through women."[119]

In February, during the 52nd session of the Commission on the Status of Women, the United Nations kicked off a new seven-year campaign aimed at ending violence against women. The campaign will work with international agencies, governments and individuals to increase funding for anti-violence campaigns and pressure policy makers around the world to enact legislation to eliminate violence against women.[120]

But women's groups want increased U.N. spending on women's programs and the creation of a single unified

Should sex-selective abortions be outlawed?

YES

Nicholas Eberstadt
Henry Wendt Chair in Political Economy,
American Enterprise Institute Member,
President's Council on Bioethics

Written for *CQ Global Researcher,* April 2008

The practice of sex-selective abortion to permit parents to destroy unwanted female fetuses has become so widespread in the modern world that it is disfiguring the profile of entire countries — transforming (and indeed deforming) the whole human species.

This abomination is now rampant in China, where the latest census reports six boys for every five girls. But it is also prevalent in the Far East, South Korea, Hong Kong, Taiwan and Vietnam, all of which report biologically impossible "sex ratios at birth" (well above the 103-106 baby boys for every 100 girls ordinarily observed in human populations). In the Caucasus, gruesome imbalances exist now in Armenia, Georgia and Azerbaijan; and in India, the state of Punjab tallies 126 little boys for every 100 girls. Even in the United States, the boy-girl sex ratio at birth for Asian-Americans is now several unnatural percentage points above the national average. So sex-selective abortion is taking place under America's nose.

How can we rid the world of this barbaric form of sexism? Simply outlawing sex-selective abortions will be little more than a symbolic gesture, as South Korea's experience has shown: Its sex ratio at birth continued a steady climb for a full decade after just such a national law was passed. As long as abortion is basically available on demand, any legislation to abolish sex-selective abortion will have no impact.

What about more general restrictions on abortion, then? Poll data consistently demonstrate that most Americans do not favor the post-*Roe* regimen of unconditional abortion. But a return to the pre-*Roe* status quo, where each state made its own abortion laws, would probably have very little effect on sex-selective abortion in our country. After all, the ethnic communities most tempted by it are concentrated in states where abortion rights would likely be strongest, such as California and New York.

In the final analysis, the extirpation of this scourge will require nothing less than a struggle for the conscience of nations. Here again, South Korea may be illustrative: Its gender imbalances began to decline when the public was shocked into facing this stain on their society by a spontaneous, homegrown civil rights movement.

To eradicate sex-selective abortion, we must convince the world that destroying female fetuses is horribly wrong. We need something akin to the abolitionist movement: a moral campaign waged globally, with victories declared one conscience at a time.

NO

Marianne Mollmann
Advocacy Director, Women's Rights
Division, Human Rights Watch

Written for *CQ Global Researcher,* April 2008

Medical technology today allows parents to test early in pregnancy for fetal abnormalities, hereditary illnesses and even the sex of the fetus, raising horrifying questions about eugenics and population control. In some countries, a growing number of women apparently are terminating pregnancies when they learn the fetus is female. The resulting sex imbalance in countries like China and India is not only disturbing but also leads to further injustices, such as the abduction of girls for forced marriages.

One response has been to criminalize sex-selective abortions. While it is tempting to hope that this could safeguard the gender balance of future generations, criminalization of abortion for whatever reason has led in the past only to underground and unsafe practices. Thus, the criminalization of sex-selective abortion would put the full burden of righting a fundamental wrong — the devaluing of women's lives — on women.

Many women who choose to abort a female fetus face violence and exclusion if they don't produce a boy. Some see the financial burden of raising a girl as detrimental to the survival of the rest of their family. These considerations will not be lessened by banning sex-selective abortion. Unless one addresses the motivation for the practice, it will continue — underground.

So what is the motivation for aborting female fetuses? At the most basic level, it is a financial decision. In no country in the world does women's earning power equal men's. In marginalized communities in developing countries, this is directly linked to survival: Boys may provide more income than girls.

Severe gaps between women's and men's earning power are generally accompanied by severe forms of gender-based discrimination and rigid gender roles. For example, in China, boys are expected to stay in their parental home as they grow up, adding their manpower (and that of a later wife) to the family home. Girls, on the other hand, are expected to join the husbands' parental home. Thus, raising a girl is a net loss, especially if you are only allowed one child.

The solution is to remove the motivation behind sex-selective abortion by advancing women's rights and their economic and social equality. Choosing the blunt instrument of criminal law over promoting the value of women's lives and rights will only serve to place further burdens on marginalized and often vulnerable women.

agency addressing women's issues, led by an under-secretary general.[121] Currently, four different U.N. agencies address women's issues: the United Nations Development Fund for Women, the International Research and Training Institute for the Advancement of Women (INSTRAW), the Secretary-General's Special Advisor on Gender Issues (OSAGI) and the Division for the Advancement of Women. In 2006, the four agencies received only $65 million — a fraction of the more than $2 billion budget that the U.N.'s children's fund (UNICEF) received that year.[122]

"The four entities that focus on women's rights at the U.N. are greatly under-resourced," says Zeitlin of the Women's Environment & Development Organization. "If the rhetoric everyone is using is true — that investing in women is investing in development — it's a matter of putting your money where your mouth is."

Political Prospects

While the number of women leading world governments is still miniscule compared to their male counterparts, women are achieving political gains that just a few years ago would have been unthinkable.

While for the first time in U.S. history a woman is in a tight race for a major party's nomination as its candidate for president, South America — with two sitting female heads of state — leads the world in woman-led governments. In Brazil, Dilma Rousseff, the female chief of staff to President Luiz Inacio Lula da Silva, is the top contender to take over the presidency when da Silva's term ends in 2010.[123] In Paraguay, Blanca Ovelar was this year's presidential nominee for the country's ruling conservative Colorado Party, but she was defeated on April 20.[124]

And in Europe, Carme Chacón was named defense minister of Spain this past April. She was not only the first woman ever to head the country's armed forces but also was pregnant at the time of her appointment. In all, nine of Spain's 17 cabinet ministers are women.

In March, Pakistan's National Assembly overwhelmingly elected its first female speaker, Fahmida Mirza.[125] And in India, where Patil has become the first woman president, the two major political parties this year pledged to set aside one-third of their parliamentary nominations for women. But many fear the parties will either not keep their pledges or will run women only in contests they are unlikely to win.[126]

There was also disappointment in Iran, where nearly 600 of the 7,000 candidates running for parliament in March were women.[127] Only three won seats in the 290-member house, and they were conservatives who are not expected to promote women's rights. Several of the tallies are being contested. Twelve other women won enough votes to face run-off elections on April 25; five won.[128]

But in some countries, women running for office face more than just tough campaigns. They are specifically targeted for violence. In Kenya, the greatest campaign expense for female candidates is the round-the-clock security required to protect them against rape, according to Phoebe Asiyo, who served in the Kenyan parliament for more than two decades.[129] During the three months before Kenya's elections last December, an emergency helpdesk established by the Education Centre for Women in Democracy, a nongovernmental organization (NGO) in Nairobi, received 258 reports of attacks against female candidates.[130]

The helpdesk reported the attacks to police, worked with the press to ensure the cases were documented and helped victims obtain medical and emotional support. Attacks included rape, stabbings, threats and physical assaults.[131]

"Women are being attacked because they are women and because it is seen as though they are not fit to bear flags of the popular parties," according to the center's Web site. "Women are also viewed as guilty for invading 'the male territory' and without a license to do so!"[132]

"All women candidates feel threatened," said Nazlin Umar, the sole female presidential candidate last year. "When a case of violence against a woman is reported, we women on the ground think we are next. I think if the government assigned all women candidates with guns...we will at least have an item to protect ourselves when we face danger."[133]

Impunity for Violence

Some African feminists blame women themselves, as well as men, for not doing enough to end traditional attitudes that perpetuate violence against women.

"Women are also to blame for the violence because they are the gatekeepers of patriarchy, because whether educated or not they have different standards for their sons and husbands [than for] their daughters," said Njoki Wainaina, founder of the African Women Development

Communication Network (FEMNET). "How do you start telling a boy whose mother trained him only disrespect for girls to honor women in adulthood?"[134]

Indeed, violence against women is widely accepted in many regions of the world and often goes unpunished. A study by the World Health Organization found that 80 percent of women surveyed in rural Egypt believe that a man is justified in beating a woman if she refuses to have sex with him. In Ghana, more women than men — 50 percent compared to 43 percent — felt that a man was justified in beating his wife if she used contraception without his consent.[135] (*See survey results, p. 4.*)

Such attitudes have led to many crimes against women going unpunished, and not just violence committed during wartime. In Guatemala, no one knows why an estimated 3,000 women have been killed over the past seven years — many of them beheaded, sexually mutilated or raped — but theories range from domestic violence to gang activity.[136] Meanwhile, the government in 2006 overturned a law allowing rapists to escape charges if they offered to marry their victims. But Guatemalan law still does not prescribe prison sentences for domestic abuse and prohibits abusers from being charged with assault unless the bruises are still visible after 10 days.[137]

In the Mexican cities of Chihuahua and Juárez, more than 400 women have been murdered over the past 14 years, with many of the bodies mutilated and dumped in the desert. But the crimes are still unsolved, and many human-rights groups, including Amnesty International, blame indifference by Mexican authorities. Now the country's 14-year statute of limitations on murder is forcing prosecutors to close many of the unsolved cases.[138]

Feminists around the world have been working to end dismissive cultural attitudes about domestic violence and other forms of violence against women, such as forced marriage, dowry-related violence, marital rape, sexual harassment and forced abortion, sterilization and prostitution. But it's often an uphill battle.

After a Kenyan police officer beat his wife so badly she was paralyzed and brain damaged — and eventually died — media coverage of the murder spurred a nationwide debate on domestic violence. But it took five years of protests, demonstrations and lobbying by both women's advocates and outraged men to get a family protection bill enacted criminalizing domestic violence. And the bill passed only after legislators removed a provision outlawing

marital rape. Similar laws have languished for decades in other African legislatures.[139]

But in Rwanda, where nearly 49 percent of the elected representatives in the lower house are female, gender desks have been established at local police stations, staffed mostly by women trained to help victims of sexual and other violence. In 2006, as a result of improved reporting, investigation and response to rape cases, police referred 1,777 cases for prosecution and convicted 803 men. "What we need now is to expand this approach to more countries," said UNIFEM's director for Central Africa Josephine Odera.[140]

Besides criticizing governments for failing to prosecute gender-based violence, many women's groups also criticize the International Criminal Court (ICC) for not doing enough to bring abusers to justice.

"We have yet to see the investigative approach needed to ensure the prosecution of gender-based crimes," said Brigid Inder, executive director of Women's Initiatives for Gender Justice, a Hague-based group that promotes and monitors women's rights in the international court.[141] Inder's group released a study last November showing that of the 500 victims seeking to participate in ICC proceedings, only 38 percent were women. When the court handed down its first indictments for war crimes in the Democratic Republic of the Congo last year, no charges involving gender-based crimes were brought despite estimates that more than 250,000 women have been raped and sexually abused in the country. After an outcry from women's groups around the world, the ICC included "sexual slavery" among the charges handed down in its second case involving war crimes in Congo.[142]

The Gender Justice report also criticized the court for failing to reach out to female victims. It said the ICC has held only one consultation with women in the last four years (focusing on the Darfur conflict in Sudan) and has failed to develop any strategies to reach out to women victims in Congo.[143]

OUTLOOK

Economic Integration

Women's organizations do not expect — or want — another international conference on the scale of Beijing. Instead, they say, the resources needed to launch such a

Seaweed farmer Asia Mohammed Makungu in Zanzibar, Tanzania, grows the sea plants for export to European companies that produce food and cosmetics. Globalized trade has helped women entrepreneurs in many developing countries improve their lives, but critics say it also has created many low-wage, dangerous jobs for women in poor countries that ignore safety and labor protections in order to attract foreign investors.

conference would be better used to improve U.N. oversight of women's issues and to implement the promises made at Beijing.

They also fear that the growth of religious fundamentalism and neo-liberal economic policies around the globe have created a political atmosphere that could actually set back women's progress.

"If a Beijing conference happened now, we would not get the type of language or the scope we got 10 years ago," says Bien-Aimé of Equity Now. "There is a conservative movement, a growth in fundamentalists governments — and not just in Muslim countries. We would be very concerned about opening up debate on the principles that have already been established."

Dahlerup of Stockholm University agrees. "It was easier in the 1990s. Many people are afraid of having big conferences now, because there may be a backlash because fundamentalism is so strong," she says. "Neo-liberal trends are also moving the discourse about women toward economics — women have to benefit for the sake of the economic good. That could be very good, but it's a more narrow discourse when every issue needs to be adapted into the economic discourse of a cost-benefit analysis."

For women to continue making gains, most groups say, gender can no longer be treated separately from broader economic, environmental, health or other political issues. While efforts to improve the status of women have historically been addressed in gender-specific legislation or international treaties, women's groups now say women's well-being must now be considered an integral part of all policies.

Women's groups are working to ensure that gender is incorporated into two major international conferences coming up this fall. In September, the Third High-Level Forum on Aid Effectiveness will be hosted in Accra, Ghana, bringing together governments, financial institutions, civil society organizations and others to assess whether assistance provided to poor nations is being put to good use. World leaders will also gather in November in Doha, Qatar, for the International Conference on Financing for Development to discuss how trade, debt relief and financial aid can promote global development.

"Women's groups are pushing for gender to be on the agenda for both conferences," says Zeitlin of WEDO. "It's important because . . . world leaders need to realize that it really does make a difference to invest in women. When it comes to women's rights it's all micro, but the big decisions are made on the macro level."

Despite decades of economic-development strategies promoted by Western nations and global financial institutions such as the World Bank, women in many regions are getting poorer. In Malawi, for example, the percentage of women living in poverty increased by 5 percent between 1995 and 2003.[144] Women and girls make up 70 percent of the world's poorest people, and their wages rise more slowly than men's. They also have fewer property rights around the world.[145] With the growing global food shortage, women — who are the primary family caregivers and produce the majority of crops for home consumption in developing countries — will be especially hard hit.

To help women escape poverty, gain legal rights and improve their social status, developed nations must rethink their broader strategies of engagement with developing countries. And, conversely, female activists say, any efforts aimed at eradicating poverty around the world must specifically address women's issues.

In Africa, for instance, activists have successfully demanded that women's economic and security concerns be addressed as part of the continent-wide development plan known as the New Partnership for Africa's Development (NEPAD). As a result, countries participating in NEPAD's peer review process must now show they are taking measures to promote and protect women's rights. But, according to Augustin Wambo, an agricultural specialist at the NEPAD secretariat, lawmakers now need to back up their pledges with "resources from national budgets" and the "necessary policies and means to support women."[146]

"We have made a lot of progress and will continue making progress," says Zeitlin. "But women's progress doesn't happen in isolation to what's happening in the rest of the world. The environment, the global economy, war, peace — they will all have a major impact on women. Women all over world will not stop making demands and fighting for their rights."

NOTES

1. http://ballyblog.wordpress.com/2007/05/04/warning-uncensored-video-iraqis-stone-girl-to-death-over-loving-wrong-boy/.

2. Abdulhamid Zebari, "Video of Iraqi girl's stoning shown on Internet," Agence France Presse, May 5, 2007.

3. *State of the World Population 2000*, United Nations Population Fund, Sept. 20, 2000, Chapter 3, "Ending Violence against Women and Girls," www.unfpa.org/swp/2000/english/ch03.html.

4. Brian Brady, "A Question of Honour," *The Independent on Sunday*, Feb. 10, 2008, p. 8, www.independent.co.uk/news/uk/home-news/a-question-of-honour-police-say-17000-women-are-victims-every-year-780522.html.

5. Correspondence with Karen Musalo, Clinical Professor of Law and Director of the Center for Gender & Refugee Studies at the University of California Hastings School of Law, April 11, 2008.

6. "Broken Bodies, Broken Dreams: Violence Against Women Exposed," United Nations, July 2006, http://brokendreams.wordpress.com/2006/12/17/dowry-crimes-and-bride-price-abuse/.

7. Various sources: www.womankind.org.uk, www.unfpa.org/gender/docs/studies/summaries/reg_exe_summary.pdf, www.oxfam.org.uk. Also see "Child rape in Kano on the increase," IRIN Humanitarian News and Analysis, United Nations, www.irinnews.org/report.aspx?ReportId=76087.

8. "UNICEF slams 'licence to rape' in African crisis," Agence France-Press, Feb. 12, 2008.

9. "Film Documents Rape of Women in Congo," "All Things Considered," National Public Radio, April 8, 2008, www.npr.org/templates/story/story.php?storyId=89476111.

10. Jeffrey Gettleman, "Rape Epidemic Raises Trauma Of Congo War," *The New York Times*, Oct. 7, 2007, p. A1.

11. Dan McDougall, "Fareeda's fate: rape, prison and 25 lashes," *The Observer*, Sept. 17, 2006, www.guardian.co.uk/world/2006/sep/17/pakistan.theobserver.

12. Zarar Khan, "Thousands rally in Pakistan to demand government withdraw rape law changes," The Associated Press, Dec. 10, 2006.

13. *State of the World Population 2000, op. cit.*

14. Laura Turquet, Patrick Watt, Tom Sharman, "Hit or Miss?" ActionAid, March 7, 2008, p. 10.

15. *Ibid.*, p. 12.

16. "Women in Politics: 2008" map, International Parliamentary Union and United Nations Division for the Advancement of Women, February 2008, www.ipu.org/pdf/publications/wmnmap08_en.pdf.

17. Gavin Rabinowitz, "India's first female president sworn in, promises to empower women," The Associated Press, July 25, 2007. Note: India's first female prime minister was Indira Ghandi in 1966.

18. Monte Reel, "South America Ushers In The Era of La Presidenta; Women Could Soon Lead a Majority of Continent's Population," *The Washington Post*, Oct. 31, 2007, p. A12. For background, see Roland Flamini, "The New Latin America," *CQ Global Researcher*, March 2008, pp. 57-84.

19. Marcela Valente, "Cristina Fernandes Dons Presidential Sash," Inter Press Service, Dec. 10, 2007.

20. "Women in Politics: 2008" map, *op. cit.*

21. *Ibid.*; Global Database of Quotas for Women, International Institute for Democracy and Electoral Assistance and Stockholm University, www.quotaproject.org/country.cfm?SortOrder=Country.

22. "Beijing Betrayed," Women's Environment and Development Organization, March 2005, p. 10, www.wedo.org/files/gmr_pdfs/gmr2005.pdf.

23. "Women in Politics: 2008" map, *op. cit.*

24. Gertrude Mongella, address by the Secretary-General of the 4th World Conference on Women, Sept. 4, 1995, www.un.org/esa/gopher-data/conf/fwcw/conf/una/950904201423.txt. Also see Steven Mufson, "Women's Forum Sets Accord; Dispute on Sexual Freedom Resolved," *The Washington Post*, Sept. 15, 1995, p. A1.

25. "Closing statement," Gertrude Mongella, U.N. Division for the Advancement of Women, Fourth World Conference on Women, www.un.org/esa/gopher-data/conf/fwcw/conf/una/closing.txt.

26. "Trading Away Our Rights," Oxfam International, 2004, p. 9, www.oxfam.org.uk/resources/policy/trade/downloads/trading_rights.pdf.

27. "Trafficking in Persons Report," U.S. Department of State, June 2007, p. 7, www.state.gov/g/tip/rls/tiprpt/2007/.

28. Turquet, *et al.*, *op. cit.*, p. 4.

29. United Nations Division for the Advancement of Women, www.un.org/womenwatch/daw/cedaw/.

30. Geraldine Terry, *Women's Rights* (2007), p. 30.

31. United Nations Division for the Advancement of Women, www.un.org/womenwatch/daw/cedaw/.

32. "The impact of international trade on gender equality," The World Bank PREM notes, May 2004, http://siteresources.worldbank.org/INTGENDER/Resources/premnote86.pdf.

33. Thalia Kidder and Kate Raworth, " 'Good Jobs' and hidden costs: women workers documenting the price of precarious employment," *Gender and Development*, July 2004, p. 13.

34. "Trading Away Our Rights," *op. cit.*

35. Martha Chen, *et al.*, "Progress of the World's Women 2005: Women, Work and Poverty," UNIFEM, p. 17, www.unifem.org/attachments/products/PoWW2005_eng.pdf.

36. Eric Neumayer and Indra de Soys, "Globalization, Women's Economic Rights and Forced Labor," London School of Economics and Norwegian University of Science and Technology, February 2007, p. 8, http://papers.ssrn.com/sol3/papers.cfm?abstract_id=813831. Also see "Five years down

the road from Beijing — assessing progress," *News and Highlights*, Food and Agriculture Organization, June 2, 2000, www.fao.org/News/2000/000602-e.htm.

37. "Trafficking in Persons Report," *op. cit.*, p. 13.

38. "World Survey on the Role of Women in Development," United Nations, 2006, p. 1, www.un.org/womenwatch/daw/public/WorldSurvey2004-Women&Migration.pdf.

39. Julie Ballington and Azza Karam, eds., "Women in Parliament: Beyond the Numbers," International Institute for Democracy and Electoral Assistance, 2005, p. 155, www.idea.int/publications/wip2/upload/WiP_inlay.pdf.

40. "Women in Politics: 2008," *op. cit.*

41. Ballington and Karam, *op. cit.*, p. 158.

42. *Ibid.*, p. 161.

43. Global Database of Quotas for Women, *op. cit.*

44. Jerome Starkey, "Afghan government official says that student will not be executed," *The Independent*, Feb. 6, 2008, www.independent.co.uk/news/world/asia/afghan-government-official-says-that-student-will-not-be-executed-778686.html?r=RSS.

45. "Afghan women seek death by fire," BBC, Nov. 15, 2006, http://news.bbc.co.uk/1/hi/world/south_asia/6149144.stm.

46. Global Database for Quotas for Women, *op. cit.*

47. "Beijing Declaration," Fourth World Conference on Women, www.un.org/womenwatch/daw/beijing/beijingdeclaration.html.

48. "Beijing Betrayed," *op. cit.*, pp. 28, 15, 18.

49. "Review of the implementation of the Beijing Platform for Action and the outcome documents of the special session of the General Assembly entitled 'Women 2000: gender equality, development and peace for the twenty-first century,' " United Nations, Dec. 6, 2004, p. 74.

50. "Gender Equality and the Millennium Development Goals," fact sheet, www.mdgender.net/upload/tools/MDGender_leaflet.pdf.

51. *Ibid.*

52. Turquet, *et al.*, *op. cit.*, p. 16.

53. *Ibid.*, pp. 22-24.

54. Terry, *op. cit.*, p. 6.

55. "Inclusive Security, Sustainable Peace: A Toolkit for Advocacy and Action," International Alert and Women Waging Peace, 2004, p. 12, www.huntalternatives.org/download/35_introduction.pdf.

56. "Declarations, Reservations and Objections to CEDAW," www.un.org/womenwatch/daw/cedaw/reservations-country.htm.

57. Merlin Stone, *When God Was a Woman* (1976), pp. 18, 11.

58. Jack Holland, *Misogyny* (2006), p. 12.

59. *Ibid.*, pp. 21-23.

60. Holland, *op. cit.*, p. 112.

61. "Dispelling the myths about so-called witches" press release, Johns Hopkins University, Oct. 7, 2002, www.jhu.edu/news_info/news/home02/oct02/witch.html.

62. The quote is from the *Malleus maleficarum* (*The Hammer of Witches*), and was cited in "Case Study: The European Witch Hunts, c. 1450-1750," *Gendercide Watch*, www.gendercide.org/case_witch-hunts.html.

63. Holland, *op. cit.*, p. 179.

64. Cathy J. Cohen, Kathleen B. Jones and Joan C. Tronto, *Women Transforming Politics: An Alternative Reader* (1997), p. 530.

65. *Ibid.*

66. Holland, *op. cit*, p. 201.

67. "Men and Women in Politics: Democracy Still in the Making," IPU Study No. 28, 1997, http://archive.idea.int/women/parl/ch6_table8.htm.

68. "Sex, Equality and Protective Laws," *CQ Researcher*, July 13, 1926.

69. The case was *Radice v. People of State of New York*, 264 U. S. 292. For background, see F. Brewer, "Equal Rights Amendment," *Editorial Research Reports*, April 4, 1946, available at *CQ Researcher Plus Archive*, www.cqpress.com.

70. "Short History of the CEDAW Convention," U.N. Division for the Advancement of Women, www.un.org/womenwatch/daw/cedaw/history.htm.

71. U.N. Women's Watch, www.un.org/womenwatch/asp/user/list.asp-ParentID=11047.htm.

72. United Nations, http://untreaty.un.org/ENGLISH/bible/englishinternetbible/partI/chapterXVI/treaty2.asp.

73. International Labor Organization, www.ilo.org/public/english/support/lib/resource/subject/gender.htm.

74. *Ibid.*

75. For background, see "Gender Pay Gap," *CQ Researcher*, March 14, 2008, pp. 241-264.

76. "Short History of the CEDAW Convention" *op. cit.*

77. "International News," The Associated Press, Dec. 19, 1979.

78. "Short History of the CEDAW Convention" *op. cit.*

79. "Text of the Convention," U.N. Division for the Advancement of Women, www.un.org/women-watch/daw/cedaw/cedaw.htm.

80. Convention on the Elimination of All Forms of Discrimination against Women, Article 16, www.un.org/womenwatch/daw/cedaw/text/econvention.htm.

81. General Recommendation made by the Committee on the Elimination of Discrimination against Women No. 19, 11th session, 1992, www.un.org/womenwatch/daw/cedaw/recommendations/recomm.htm#recom19.

82. See www.unhchr.ch/huridocda/huridoca.nsf/(Symbol)/A.CONF.157.23.En.

83. Marlise Simons, "For First Time, Court Defines Rape as War Crime," *The New York Times*, June 28, 1996, www.nytimes.com/specials/bosnia/context/0628warcrimes-tribunal.html.

84. Ann Simmons, "U.N. Tribunal Convicts Rwandan Ex-Mayor of Genocide in Slaughter," *Los Angeles Times*, Sept. 3, 1998, p. 20.

85. "Human Rights Watch Applauds Rwanda Rape Verdict," press release, Human Rights Watch, Sept. 2, 1998, http://hrw.org/english/docs/1998/09/02/rwanda1311.htm.

86. Frederic Bichon, "ICC vows to bring Darfur war criminals to justice," Agence France-Presse, Feb. 24, 2008.

87. Rebecca Feeley and Colin Thomas-Jensen, "Getting Serious about Ending Conflict and Sexual Violence in Congo," Enough Project, www.enoughproject.org/reports/congoserious.

88. "Women; Deceived Again?" *The Economist*, July 5, 1975.

89. "International Women's Day — March 8: Points of Interest and Links with UNIFEM," UNIFEM New Zealand Web site, www.unifem.org.nz/IWDPointsofinterest.htm.

90. Joseph Gambardello, "Reporter's Notebook: Women's Conference in Kenya," United Press International, July 13, 1985.

91. "Report of the World Conference to Review and Appraise the Achievements of the United Nations Decade for Women: Equality Development and Peace," United Nations, 1986, paragraph 8, www.un.org/womenwatch/confer/nfls/Nairobi1985report.txt.

92. U.N. Division for the Advancement of Women, www.un.org/womenwatch/daw/followup/background.htm.

93. "Women in Politics," Inter-Parliamentary Union, 2005, pp. 16-17, www.ipu.org/PDF/publications/wmn45-05_en.pdf.

94. "Liberian becomes Africa's first female president," Associated Press, Jan. 16, 2006, www.msnbc.msn.com/id/10865705/.

95. "Women in the Americas: Paths to Political Power," *op. cit.*, p. 2.

96. "The Millennium Development Goals Report 2007," United Nations, 2007, p. 12, www.un.org/millenniumgoals/pdf/mdg2007.pdf.

97. David Dollar, Raymond Fisman, Roberta Gatti, "Are Women Really the 'Fairer' Sex? Corruption and Women in Government," The World Bank, October 1999, p. 1, http://siteresources.worldbank.org/INTGENDER/Resources/wp4.pdf.

98. *Ibid.*

99. Vicky Baker, "Rape victim sentenced to 200 lashes and six months in jail; Saudi woman punished for being alone with a man," *The Guardian*, Nov. 17, 2007, www.guardian.co.uk/world/2007/nov/17/saudiarabia.international.

100. Katherine Zoepf, "Saudi King Pardons Rape Victim Sentenced to Be Lashed, Saudi Paper Reports," *The New York Times*, Dec. 18, 2007, www.nytimes.com/2007/12/18/world/middleeast/18saudi.html.

101. Sonia Verma, "King Abdullah urged to spare Saudi 'witchcraft' woman's life," *The Times* (Of London), Feb. 16, 2008.

102. Mark Lattimer, "Freedom lost," *The Guardian*, Dec. 13, 2007, p. 6.

103. For background, see Brian Beary, "Future of Turkey," *CQ Global Researcher*, December, 2007, pp. 295-322.

104. Tracy Clark-Flory, "Does freedom to veil hurt women?" *Salon.com*, Feb. 11, 2008.

105. Sabrina Tavernise, "Under a Scarf, a Turkish Lawyer Fighting to Wear It," *The New York Times*, Feb. 9, 2008, www.nytimes.com/2008/02/09/world/europe/09benli.html?pagewanted=1&sq=women&st=nyt&scp=96.

106. Terry, *op. cit.*, p. 122.

107. "Many Americans Uneasy with Mix of Religion and Politics," The Pew Forum on Religion and Public Life, Aug. 24, 2006, http://pewforum.org/docs/index.php?DocID=153.

108. Brady, *op. cit.*

109. "Concluding Observations of the Committee on the Elimination of Discrimination against Women: Saudi Arabia," Committee on the Elimination of Discrimination against Women, 40th Session, Jan. 14-Feb. 1, 2008, p. 3, www2.ohchr.org/english/bodies/cedaw/docs/co/CEDAW.C.SAU.CO.2.pdf.

110. Kambiz Fattahi, "Women's bill 'unites' Iran and US," BBC, July 31, 2007, http://news.bbc.co.uk/2/hi/middle_east/6922749.stm.

111. H. Res. 101, Rep. Lynn Woolsey, http://thomas.loc.gov/cgi-bin/bdquery/z?d110:h.res.00101.

112. "General Assembly Adopts Landmark Text Calling for Moratorium on Death Penalty," States News Service, Dec. 18, 2007, www.un.org/News/Press/docs//2007/ga10678.doc.htm.

113. Mary H. Cooper, "Women and Human Rights," *CQ Researcher*, April 30, 1999, p. 356.

114. Christina Hoff Sommers, "The Case against Ratifying the United Nations Convention on the Elimination of All Forms of Discrimination against Women," testimony before the Senate Foreign Relations Committee, June 13, 2002, www.aei.org/publications/filter.all,pubID.15557/pub_detail.asp.

115. "CEDAW: Pro-United Nations, Not Pro-Woman" press release, U.S. Senate Republican Policy Committee, Sept. 16, 2002, http://rpc.senate.gov/_files/FOREIGNje091602.pdf.

116. "Turkmenistan adopts gender equality law," BBC Worldwide Monitoring, Dec. 19, 2007.

117. Faiza Saleh Ambah, "Saudi Women See a Brighter Road on Rights," *The Washington Post*, Jan. 31, 2008, p. A15, www.washingtonpost.com/wp-dyn/content/article/2008/01/30/AR2008013003805.html.

118. Damien McElroy, "Saudi Arabia to lift ban on women drivers," *The Telegraph*, Jan. 1, 2008.

119. Stephanie Levitz, "Lifting the veils of Afghan women," *The Hamilton Spectator* (Ontario, Canada), Feb. 28, 2008, p. A11.

120. "U.N. Secretary-General Ban Ki-moon Launches Campaign to End Violence against Women," U.N. press release, Feb. 25, 2008, http://endviolence.un.org/press.shtml.

121. "Gender Equality Architecture and U.N. Reforms," the Center for Women's Global Leadership and the Women's Environment and Development Organization, July 17, 2006, www.wedo.org/files/Gender%20Equality%20Architecture%20and%20UN%20Reform0606.pdf.

122. Bojana Stoparic, "New-Improved Women's Agency Vies for U.N. Priority," Women's eNews, March 6, 2008, www.womensenews.org/article.cfm?aid=3517.

123. Reel, *op. cit.*

124. Eliana Raszewski and Bill Faries, "Lugo, Ex Bishop, Wins Paraguay Presidential Election," Bloomberg, April 20, 2008.

125. Zahid Hussain, "Pakistan gets its first woman Speaker," *The Times* (of London), March 20, p. 52.

126. Bhaskar Roy, "Finally, women set to get 33% quota," *Times of India*, Jan. 29, 2008.

127. Massoumeh Torfeh, "Iranian women crucial in Majlis election," BBC, Jan. 30, 2008, http://news.bbc.co.uk/1/hi/world/middle_east/7215272.stm.

128. "Iran women win few seats in parliament," Agence-France Presse, March 18, 2008.

129. Swanee Hunt, "Let Women Rule," *Foreign Affairs*, May-June 2007, p. 109.

130. Kwamboka Oyaro, "A Call to Arm Women Candidates With More Than Speeches," Inter Press Service, Dec. 21, 2007, http://ipsnews.net/news.asp?idnews=40569.

131. Education Centre for Women in Democracy, www.ecwd.org.

132. *Ibid.*

133. Oyaro, *op. cit.*

134. *Ibid.*

135. Mary Kimani, "Taking on violence against women in Africa," *AfricaRenewal*, U.N. Dept. of Public Information, July 2007, p. 4, www.un.org/ecosocdev/geninfo/afrec/vol21no2/212-violence-aganist-women.html.

136. Correspondence with Karen Musalo, Clinical Professor of Law and Director of the Center for Gender & Refugee Studies, University of California Hastings School of Law, April 11, 2008.

137. "Mexico and Guatemala: Stop the Killings of Women," Amnesty International USA Issue Brief, January 2007, www.amnestyusa.org/document.php?lang=e&id=engusa20070130001.

138. Manuel Roig-Franzia, "Waning Hopes in Juarez," *The Washington Post*, May 14, 2007, p. A10.

139. Kimani, *op. cit.*

140. *Ibid.*

141. "Justice slow for female war victims," *The Toronto Star*, March 3, 2008, www.thestar.com/News/GlobalVoices/article/308784p.

142. Speech by Brigid Inder on the Launch of the "Gender Report Card on the International Criminal Court," Dec. 12, 2007, www.iccwomen.org/news/docs/Launch_GRC_2007.pdf

143. "Gender Report Card on the International Criminal Court," Women's Initiatives for Gender Justice,

November 2007, p. 32, www.iccwomen.org/publications/resources/docs/GENDER_04-01-2008_FINAL_TO_PRINT.pdf.

144. Turquet, *et al.*, *op. cit.*, p. 8.

145. Oxfam Gender Equality Fact Sheet, www.oxfam.org.uk/resources/issues/gender/introduction.html.

146. Itai Madamombe, "Women push onto Africa's agenda," *AfricaRenewal*, U.N. Dept. of Public Information, July 2007, pp. 8-9.

BIBLIOGRAPHY

Books

Holland, Jack, *Misogyny: The World's Oldest Prejudice*, Constable & Robinson, 2006.
The late Irish journalist provides vivid details and anecdotes about women's oppression throughout history.

Stone, Merlin, *When God Was a Woman*, Harcourt Brace Jovanovich, 1976.
The book contends that before the rise of Judeo-Christian patriarchies women headed the first societies and religions.

Terry, Geraldine, *Women's Rights*, Pluto Press, 2007.
A feminist who has worked for Oxfam and other non-governmental organizations outlines major issues facing women today — from violence to globalization to AIDS.

***Women and the Environment*, UNEP, 2004.**
The United Nations Environment Programme shows the integral link between women in the developing world and the changing environment.

Articles

Brady, Brian, "A Question of Honour," *The Independent on Sunday*, Feb. 10, 2008, p. 8.
"Honor killings" and related violence against women are on the rise in the United Kingdom.

Kidder, Thalia, and Kate Raworth, " 'Good Jobs' and hidden costs: women workers documenting the price of precarious employment," *Gender and Development*, Vol. 12, No. 2, p. 12, July 2004.
Two trade and gender experts describe the precarious working conditions and job security experienced by food and garment workers.

Reports and Studies

"Beijing Betrayed," *Women's Environment and Development Organization*, **March 2005, www.wedo.org/files/gmr_pdfs/gmr2005.pdf.**
A women's-rights organization reviews the progress and shortcomings of governments in implementing the commitments made during the Fifth World Congress on Women in Beijing in 1995.

"The Millennium Development Goals Report 2007," *United Nations*, **2007, www.un.org/millenniumgoals/pdf/mdg2007.pdf.**
International organizations demonstrate the progress governments have made — or not — in reaching the Millennium Development Goals.

"Trafficking in Persons Report," *U.S. Department of State*, **June 2007, www.state.gov/documents/organization/82902.pdf.**
This seventh annual report discusses the growing problems of human trafficking around the world.

"The tsunami's impact on women," *Oxfam briefing note*, **March 5, 2005, www.oxfam.org/en/files/bn050326_tsunami_women/download.**
Looking at how the 2004 tsunami affected women in Indonesia, India and Sri Lanka, Oxfam International suggests how governments can better address women's issues during future natural disasters.

"Women in Politics," *Inter-Parliamentary Union*, **2005, www.ipu.org/PDF/publications/wmn45-05_en.pdf.**
The report provides detailed databases of the history of female political representation in governments around the world.

Ballington, Julie, and Azza Karam, "Women in Parliament: Beyond the Numbers," *International Institute for Democracy and Electoral Assistance*, **2005, www.idea.int/publications/wip2/upload/WiP_inlay.pdf.**
The handbook provides female politicians and candidates information and case studies on how women have overcome obstacles to elected office.

Chen, Martha, Joann Vanek, Francie Lund, James Heintz, Renana Jhabvala and Christine Bonner, "Women, Work and Poverty," *UNIFEM,* **2005, www .unifem.org/attachments/products/PoWW2005_eng .pdf.**
The report argues that greater work protection and security is needed to promote women's rights and reduce global poverty.

Larserud, Stina, and Rita Taphorn, "Designing for Equality," *International Institute for Democracy and Electoral Assistance,* **2007, www.idea.int/publications/ designing_for_equality/upload/Idea_Design_low .pdf.**

The report describes the impact that gender quota systems have on women's representation in elected office.

Raworth, Kate, and Claire Harvey, "Trading Away Our Rights," *Oxfam International,* **2004, www .oxfam.org.uk/resources/policy/trade/downloads/ trading_rights.pdf.**
Through exhaustive statistics, case studies and interviews, the report paints a grim picture of how trade globalization is affecting women.

Turquet, Laura, Patrick Watt and Tom Sharman, "Hit or Miss?" *ActionAid,* **March 7, 2008.**
The report reviews how governments are doing in achieving the U.N.'s Millennium Development Goals.

For More Information

Equality Now, P.O. Box 20646, Columbus Circle Station, New York, NY 10023; www.equalitynow.org. An international organization working to protect women against violence and promote women's human rights.

Global Database of Quotas for Women; www.quotaproject.org. A joint project of the International Institute for Democracy and Electoral Assistance and Stockholm University providing country-by-country data on electoral quotas for women.

Human Rights Watch, 350 Fifth Ave., 34th floor, New York, NY 10118-3299; (212) 290-4700; www.hrw.org. Investigates and exposes human-rights abuses around the world.

Hunt Alternatives Fund, 625 Mount Auburn St., Cambridge, MA 02138; (617) 995-1900; www.huntalternatives.org. A private foundation that provides grants and technical assistance to promote positive social change; its Initiative for Inclusive Security promotes women in peacekeeping.

Inter-Parliamentary Union, 5, Chemin du Pommier, Case Postale 330, CH-1218 Le Grand-Saconnex, Geneva, Switzerland; +(4122) 919 41 50; www.ipu.org. An organization of parliaments of sovereign states that

maintains an extensive database on women serving in parliaments.

Oxfam International, 1100 15th St., N.W., Suite 600, Washington, DC 20005; (202) 496-1170; www.oxfam.org. Confederation of 13 independent nongovernmental organizations working to fight poverty and related social injustice.

U.N. Development Fund for Women (UNIFEM), 304 East 45th St., 15th Floor, New York, NY 10017; (212) 906-6400; www.unifem.org. Provides financial aid and technical support for empowering women and promoting gender equality.

U.N. Division for the Advancement of Women (DAW), 2 UN Plaza, DC2-12th Floor, New York, NY 10017; www .un.org/womenwatch/daw. Formulates policy on gender equality, implements international agreements on women's issues and promotes gender mainstreaming in government activities.

Women's Environment & Development Organization (WEDO), 355 Lexington Ave., 3rd Floor, New York, NY 10017; (212) 973-0325; www.wedo.org. An international organization that works to promote women's equality in global policy.

Domestic Violence

2

Do Teenagers Need More Protection?

Pamela M. Prah

Supporters of tougher domestic-violence legislation demonstrate in Columbia, S.C., on April 27, 2005. Congress recently reauthorized the Violence Against Women Act, adding more funding for youth programs and prevention.

AP Photo/Mary Ann Chastain

From *CQ Global Researcher*, January 2006.

Domestic violence doesn't seem to get much attention until a celebrity comes along like O. J. Simpson, the former football star and admitted wife beater who was accused of murdering his ex-wife and her male companion in a fit of jealous rage. Also grabbing headlines was the case of Lorena Bobbitt, the abused Virginia woman who cut off her husband's penis while he slept.*

Yet, on a typical day in the United States, three women are murdered by their spouses, ex-spouses or partners — and thousands more are raped or injured.[1]

They are women like Yvette Cade, 31, from Clinton, Md., who was doused with gasoline and set on fire by her estranged husband. And Jessica Wickiewicz, of Garden City, N.Y., whose boyfriend started punching and kicking her when she was a senior in high school. And Maria, a pregnant 15-year-old from Los Angeles whose boyfriend hit her so hard when she was pregnant that she had to have her baby delivered by cesarean.[2]

Violence against women has been reported since ancient Roman times and has been commonplace in America since Colonial times. But in the last decade, the rate of domestic violence against women has dropped more than 50 percent.[3] And the number of men

---

* Simpson was acquitted of the murders of Nicole Brown Simpson and her friend Ronald Goldman, but in a civil trial he was found liable for their deaths and ordered to pay the Goldman family $8.5 million in compensatory damages. A jury in Manassas, Va., acquitted Bobbitt of malicious wounding in January 1994.

Partner Violence Against Women Plummeted

The number of female victims of so-called intimate-partner violence dropped nearly 50 percent — from 1.1 million incidents in 1993 to 588,490 incidents in 2001. Women make up 85 percent of all victims of abuse by either a spouse or ex partner.

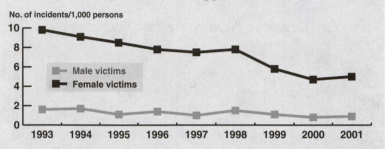

Rates of Non-Fatal Violence by an Intimate Partner*
(per 1,000 persons of each gender; includes rape, sexual assault, robbery and simple or aggravated assault)

* Intimate partners include current or former spouses, boyfriends or girlfriends.

Source: Bureau of Justice Statistics, U.S. Department of Justice, February 2003

murdered by their wives, girlfriends and former partners has declined even more dramatically — by some 70 percent since 1976.

Many experts credit the changes to the billions of dollars spent in recent years on shelters, hotlines and legal help for victims and training sessions for police, prosecutors and judges. With more help available, abused women, in particular, recognized they no longer had to resort to violence to get out of a bad relationship.

Despite the positive trends, experts say the true scope of the domestic-violence problem is hard to gauge, because researchers and government agencies use different definitions for the term. Fourteen states, for example, do not include dating violence as a form of domestic violence. Nonetheless, the latest figures from the Department of Justice (DOJ) show more than 588,000 women and more than 100,000 men were physically assaulted, raped or robbed by their "intimate partners" in 2001.[4] And more than 1 million women are stalked.[5]

Researchers are now finding that young people ages 16 to 24 are most at risk.[6] Some teens are exposed to violence at the hands of their parents, while others are young parents themselves and are beating each other and/or their children.

Moreover, teen-dating violence is more prevalent than most parents suspect, since young people usually do not tell their parents about the abuse. Wickiewicz, for example, blamed her high school bruises on cheerleading and hid them under baggy jeans. "It was all a big secret," she said.[7]

While girls and women are much more likely to suffer at the hands of a loved one, men and boys are often victims as well. For 13 years, for example, Karen Gillhespy of Marquette, Mich., brutally abused her husband. Indeed, she broke his ribs, ripped patches of his hair out, beat him with a baseball bat and scratched, bit and kicked him — but he never hit back or filed charges.[8]

In fact, a federal study showed that high school boys are nearly as likely as girls to get hit, slapped or physically hurt by their partners. After surveying youths in Chicago, Dallas, Milwaukee, San Diego and Washington, D.C., the study found that 10 to 17 percent of girls are hit by their boyfriends, and almost the same number of boys — 10 to 15 percent — are abused by their girlfriends.[9]

The fact that researchers are studying dating violence reflects the recent sea change in how the nation views and deals with domestic violence. Forty years ago, there were no shelters or hotlines for battered women. Police often responded to a domestic-violence call by telling the batterer, typically a man, to walk around the block to cool off. Doctors and health-care providers rarely screened their patients for domestic violence.

But the women's liberation movement of the 1970s shined a spotlight on domestic violence — triggering a wave of state laws dealing with the problem. Much later, the 1994 Violence Against Women Act (VAWA) provided billions of federal dollars to help victims of domestic violence, including funds for legal services and for building local shelters.

The sweeping law — which Congress expanded in December 2005 — also created the National Domestic Violence Hotline and made it a federal crime to cross state lines with the intent of stalking or committing domestic violence. VAWA funding has been used to set up domestic-violence courts as well as specially trained "response teams" to deal with sexual-assault victims.

"Although violent crime has decreased nationwide, it still devastates the lives of many women," says Diane M. Stuart, director of the DOJ's Office on Violence Against Women, who in the 1980s ran a shelter for battered women in Utah. "We have much more work to do."

Today 2,000 shelters provide refuge for victims and information on how to obtain restraining orders against their abusers. Rape-victim advocates offer support in many hospitals, and state courthouses often provide special programs to help guide victims through the legal process.

Businesses also are becoming active on the domestic-violence front, partly because it's the right thing to do and partly because domestic violence costs society, particularly employers. Victims annually lose nearly 8 million days of work, the equivalent of more than 32,000 full-time jobs.[10] In 1995, researchers estimated that domestic violence costs the country more than $5.8 billion — more than $8.3 billion in today's dollars — primarily for medical and mental health care.[11]

In 2005 the DOJ formally kicked off the president's Family Justice Center Initiative, modeled after a San Diego program that brings legal and social services under one roof with victim-support and counseling programs. At the one location, victims can undergo forensic exams, obtain legal advice and even restraining orders against their abusers, speak with a chaplain and meet with a victim's advocate.

"It's a one-stop process. Everything that a person who has been victimized needs is right there," says Stuart.

Advocates and women's groups hope the recent VAWA expansion will usher in a new era that focuses on preventing domestic violence from ever beginning in the first place, rather than treating the victims and punishing the abusers afterward.

"Many programs today focus on helping adult victims, and prevention has a lesser emphasis, if it is addressed at all," says Esta Soler, president of the Family Violence Prevention Fund, an advocacy group that sponsors

Simple Assault Is Most Common Crime

Nearly three-quarters of the intimate-partner crimes against women and nearly half of those against men were simple assaults.

Types of Violence by Intimate Partners

Violent Crime	No. of female victims	Rate/1,000 females	No. of male victims	Rate/1,000 males
Simple Assault	421,550	3.6	50,310	0.5
Aggravated Assault	81,140	0.7	36,350	0.3
Robbery	44,060	0.4	16,570	0.1
Rape/Sexual Assault	41,740	0.4	---	---
Total	588,490		103,230	

Source: Bureau of Justice Statistics, U.S. Department of Justice, February 2003

campaigns, in partnership with the Advertising Council, to raise awareness about family violence. She says adolescents, young adults and the poor particularly need more attention.

Prevention is key because children who grow up in homes where domestic violence or dating violence occur are more likely to become victims or perpetrators of domestic or dating violence themselves.[12] Abuse also tends to lead to other problems. Young people and adults abused by their spouses or partners are more likely to abuse alcohol or drugs, suffer from eating disorders and engage in risky behavior, such as having unprotected sex. They also are more apt to have mental and physical health problems that make it difficult for them to hold jobs.

Some fathers'-rights and conservative groups, however, say many domestic-violence programs demonize men and promote a feminist and leftist agenda. "The Violence Against Women Act is gender-driven politics being operated through the public purse," says Michael McCormick, executive director of the American Coalition for Fathers and Children. "We're spending nearly $1 billion a year to reinforce in the public's mind that men are indiscriminately attacking women."

As Congress, researchers and advocates debate how best to combat domestic violence, here are some of the questions being asked:

Should the federal government do more to combat domestic violence?

Women's groups say federal programs have contributed to remarkable gains in curtailing domestic violence,

A high-school student in New York state submitted the winning poster in a statewide contest to increase awareness of teen-dating violence.

sexual assault and stalking. But they say the programs should be expanded to provide more housing options and focus more on prevention. Meanwhile, some fathers'-rights and conservative groups say the programs at the local level that get funds from the federal government demonize men and promote a radical feminist agenda.

In the decade after Congress passed the Violence Against Women Act in 1994, domestic violence dropped more than 50 percent, according to government figures. "VAWA has had a huge impact," says Jill Morris, public policy director of the National Coalition Against Domestic Violence. "It has changed attitudes. It's a great success."

Besides providing billions of dollars to help victims of domestic violence and sexual assault, VAWA forced the issue out into the open. "People are now talking about it in newspapers and in Congress," Morris says.

While lauding VAWA, the coalition and other women's groups say more federal funds should be targeted to help minorities, the disabled, the elderly, victims in rural areas, Native Americans, young people, gays and immigrants who fear being deported. And rape crisis centers should be guaranteed additional federal funds to help counsel victims of sexual assault.

Several states, including Illinois, Massachusetts and Pennsylvania, have waiting lists of sexual assault victims needing counseling, and in many states "rural areas have no services at all," said Mary Lou Leary, executive director of the National Center for Victims of Crime.[13]

Victims also need more housing options, say advocates. "Homelessness does not cause domestic violence, but rather the opposite," according to Lynn Rosenthal, president of the National Network to End Domestic Violence. Half of homeless women and children are fleeing domestic violence, and 38 percent of domestic-violence victims become homeless at some point in their lives, she estimated.[14]

Advocates say victims who live in public housing need protection from their abusers — and sometimes from their landlords. A 39-year-old North Carolina woman, for example, was evicted from her apartment because she was "too loud" after her ex-boyfriend shot her and she jumped from her apartment's second-story balcony to escape his attack.[15] A Michigan woman was evicted because of "criminal activity" in her apartment after her ex-boyfriend returned and attacked her.

Conservative and fathers'-rights groups, however, say VAWA ignores men who are abused. The Safe Homes for Children and Families Coalition and other groups want to rename the law as the Family Violence Prevention Act. They also have pressed for new VAWA language making clear that the law includes programs for men.

"It's a blatant lie to say that new language is not necessary," says David Burroughs, legislative consultant to the coalition. Burroughs says he was denied a VAWA grant because his proposal targeted men and also was rejected for a federal grant to pay for hotel stays for male victims wanting to leave their homes for a cooling-off period. He helped mount a billboard campaign at the Wilmington, Del., Amtrak station to remind Sen. Joseph Biden Jr., D-Del. — lead sponsor of VAWA — that men are abuse victims, too.

VAWA advocates argue, however, that all of the law's provisions are gender neutral. "Nothing in the act denies services, programs, funding or assistance to male victims of violence," says Morris.

Government figures show women overwhelmingly are the victims of domestic violence, with men making up only 15 percent of the victims.[16] But men's groups say more than 100 studies show that men and women are equally likely to initiate domestic violence, adding that 99 percent of the federal funding should not go to programs that help only women.

Abused men have a hard time finding legal help and shelters — services that get federal funds under VAWA, Burroughs says. About 20 percent of the victims who apply for free legal services are men, but they receive less than 1 percent of the pro bono services, he says, adding that only a handful of domestic-violence shelters nationwide are open to men.

VAWA should be scrapped altogether, says McCormick of the American Coalition for Fathers and Children, although he acknowledges, "the political reality is that it's not going to be withdrawn." The coalition opposes violence against anyone, but McCormick says VAWA funds "a one-sided agenda driven by people who really don't want to see families stay together," namely, feminists and left-wing organizations.

VAWA breaks up families and increases the number of fatherless children, McCormick says, because it funds programs that push couples into divorce instead of trying to get the victim and abuser into counseling.

Lisa Scott, a Bellevue, Wash., attorney specializing in family law, agrees. "VAWA is not about stopping violence," Scott wrote. "It is about greedy special interests slopping at the federal trough, perpetuating gender supremacy for women. If proponents were truly concerned about helping victims, they would demand that all intervention and funding be gender neutral and gender inclusive."[17]

Are judges and police doing enough to protect domestic-violence victims?

Forty years ago, a wife beater would not be arrested unless police actually saw the incident or had a warrant. Police and judges would routinely dismiss the problem as a "family matter."

Things have changed, particularly in the last decade, as police officers, judges and prosecutors have received VAWA-funded training on how to deal with domestic violence. But women's advocates say much still needs to be changed, both in the courtroom and on the police beat.

For instance, Yvette Cade might never have been burned if Judge Richard Palumbo had not dismissed her request for a protective order against her estranged husband. Three weeks later Mrs. Cade's husband walked into the store where she worked, poured gasoline on her and set her on fire. Cade suffered third-degree burns over much of her body. Advocates said Palumbo has a pattern of dismissing temporary protective orders and making flip remarks about domestic violence.* In one instance, he told an abused woman to speak up, even though he had been told her husband had attacked her and crushed her voice box.[18]

"There are judges, for whatever reason, who still don't get it," says Billie Lee Dunford-Jackson, co-director of the Family Violence Project at the National Council on Juvenile and Family Court Judges. But, she quickly adds, "most judges now readily recognize [domestic violence] as a crime and will take steps to protect the victim."

She points to intensive three-day training sessions for judges that the National Judicial Institute on Domestic Violence has sponsored since 1998, largely funded by VAWA. Judges are taught what makes a batterer batter, why victims stay and how to identify and overcome their own biases and blinders when it comes to the problem.

Nationwide, more than 300 judicial systems have established specially designed "domestic-violence courts."[19] Some states have created courts that handle only domestic violence, while others have staff trained who provide support to victims, Dunford-Jackson explains. New York uses both approaches, with more than 30 domestic-violence courts plus special units that include victims' advocates and staff members who monitor those convicted of domestic violence to ensure they are complying with the terms of their sentence.

Law students also are getting training. As of 2003, most law schools offered educational programming on domestic violence, says Robin R. Runge, director of the American Bar Association's Commission on Domestic Violence.

However, there are still gaps in the system. Most states require volunteers on domestic violence hotlines to complete 40 to 50 hours of training but don't require

---

* Palumbo's actions led to his temporary removal from the bench and reassignment to administrative duties on Oct. 26, 2005.

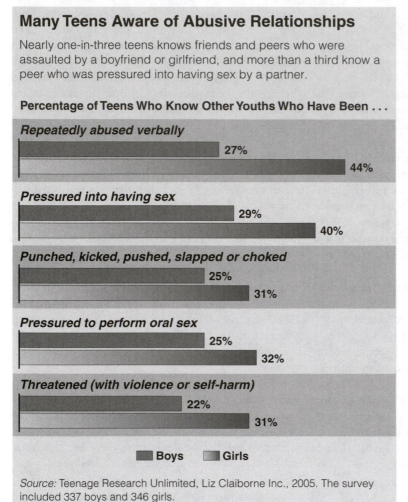

Many Teens Aware of Abusive Relationships

Nearly one-in-three teens knows friends and peers who were assaulted by a boyfriend or girlfriend, and more than a third know a peer who was pressured into having sex by a partner.

Percentage of Teens Who Know Other Youths Who Have Been . . .

Repeatedly abused verbally
27%
44%

Pressured into having sex
29%
40%

Punched, kicked, pushed, slapped or choked
25%
31%

Pressured to perform oral sex
25%
32%

Threatened (with violence or self-harm)
22%
31%

■ Boys ■ Girls

Source: Teenage Research Unlimited, Liz Claiborne Inc., 2005. The survey included 337 boys and 346 girls.

training for police, judges or lawyers. Even with VAWA, 80 percent of domestic-violence victims are without lawyers to guide them through the process, Runge says. "We've seen the difference having lawyers available" can make, she says. For example, lawyers can help abused women file the legal paperwork more quickly to obtain protection orders, which prohibit their abusers from coming into contact with them.

However, some men's groups say the training given to judges, police and attorneys reinforces the notion that only women are victims. "They are being taught garbage," says Burroughs, of the Safe Homes for Children and Families Coalition.

Some conservatives also argue that women who seek help from domestic-violence legal programs get an edge in their custody or divorce proceedings. VAWA "has little to do with violence and much to do with divorce court," family-law attorney Scott wrote.[20] McCormick of the American Coalition for Fathers and Children says abused women who turn to shelters do not get counseling first but instead are directed to the courthouse to get a restraining order, which helps them in a divorce or child custody case because judges will view the man as abusive and dangerous even if he is not.

Meanwhile, feminists and some domestic-violence experts are backing away from the "mandatory arrest" laws that they pushed states to enact 20 years ago. At least 23 states require police officers to make an arrest when responding to a domestic-violence complaint. But police on the scene often cannot tell the victim from the aggressor, so they arrest both.

States began passing mandatory-arrest laws after a 1984 Minnesota study found that few people arrested under such laws repeated their crimes. But researcher Lawrence Sherman says that states acted too hastily after his first study. His follow-up research showed that mandatory arrests only work in middle-class communities with low unemployment rates, but for some reason, he says, "the new findings got buried."

The new findings showed that unemployed people or those without ties to the community have less to lose by getting arrested and often become angrier. In such cases, mandatory arrest "causes more violence than it prevents," according to Sherman, director of the Jerry Lee Center on Criminology at the University of Pennsylvania.

In any event, even when mandatory-arrest laws are in effect, many police officers are reluctant to respond quickly to domestic-violence cases because they are considered so potentially dangerous, with either the abuser or the victim — or both — liable to turn on the officer. Although studies have yet to prove that family disputes are more dangerous to police officers than other incidents, so many officers believe it to be true they often wait for backup before responding to such calls.[21]

However, John Terrill, a spokesman for the National Association of Police Organizations, denies that police treat domestic violence any differently than other cases and supports mandatory-arrest laws.

Some women's groups say a June 2005 U.S. Supreme Court decision undercut efforts to beef up enforcement of mandatory-arrest laws and restraining orders. In *Town of Castle Rock, Colorado v. Gonzales*, the court ruled that a woman did not have the right to sue a police department for failing to enforce a court-ordered restraining order against her husband.[22] Women's groups fear that police departments now will have less incentive to aggressively enforce such orders.

"Mandatory restraining orders aren't worth the paper they're printed on if police officers are not required to enforce them," said Eleanor Smeal, president of the Feminist Majority Foundation. The organization said the decision jeopardizes women's lives and potentially lets police departments off the hook for failing to enforce mandatory orders.[23]

Terrill says police "try to the best of their ability to enforce restraining orders," but sometimes they "get pushed down on the list" of calls police officers must handle. "You can't keep an officer stationed outside the door 24 hours a day."

Should the government do more to protect teens?

The recent expansion of VAWA provides millions of dollars to help teen victims of domestic violence, including dating violence.

Female Teens at Risk for Partner Violence

Females ages 16-24 were the most vulnerable to intimate-partner violence in 1999.

Number of Women Abused by Intimate Partners, 1999*
(by age)

No. of Victims: 12-15: 9,000; 16-19: 119,630; 20-24: 144,100; 25-34: 182,070; 35-49: 194,380; 50 or older: 21,030

* Includes assault, robbery and rape/sexual assault
Source: Bureau of Justice Statistics, U.S. Department of Justice, 2001

Dating violence represents an "epidemic of monumental proportions" among today's youth, says Juley Fulcher, director of public policy at Break the Cycle, a Los Angeles-based group that provides information and legal help to young people experiencing domestic violence. Fulcher points to Justice Department data showing that girls and young women between the ages of 16 and 24 experience the highest rate of non-fatal "intimate-partner" violence, or attacks by a spouse, partner or former spouse or partner — 16 incidents per 1,000 women in this age group compared to six incidents per 1,000 for all women.[24]

"Not enough attention has been paid to finding ways to stop the intimate-partner violence that pervades and sometimes shapes the lives of adolescents and young adults," says Soler, of the Family Violence Prevention Fund.

In 2005, a Gallup survey found that one-in-eight teens ages 13 to 17 knows someone in an abusive relationship with a boyfriend or girlfriend.[25] Another 2005 youth survey, commissioned by Liz Claiborne Inc., the clothing maker, found that one-in-three 13-to-18-year-olds had a friend or peer who had been hit, punched, kicked or slapped by a partner.[26] And up

Safe Homes for Children and Families Coalition

Members of the Safe Homes for Children and Families Coalition call for changes in the Violence Against Women Act during a rally at the U.S. Supreme Court in July 2005. Congress in December 2005 addressed some of their concerns.

programs to educate people working with teens on how to recognize, respond to and provide services to teen victims of domestic and dating violence. Women's groups also wanted middle and high schools to train teachers, coaches and administrators to recognize and address issues related to dating violence and sexual assault.

"Teens must be taught what is healthy and what is not, and services must be offered to help them through this transition," says Fulcher, noting that many teens are dating for the first time and are unsure of the differences between a healthy relationship and an abusive one. A 2003 federal study of schools in Alabama, Idaho, Oklahoma and Utah found that between 11 and 16 percent of female students — and between 4.5 and 7 percent of males — reported being forced to have intercourse.[28]

Fulcher and other women's groups want the federal government to pay for education programs that involve courts, law-enforcement agencies and youth-based community groups. Only a handful of states — Minnesota, Oklahoma, Utah, Washington and Wyoming — allow minors ages 16 and older to petition for an order of protection without an adult, according to the National Coalition Against Domestic Violence. Moreover, only one county in the United States — Santa Clara, Calif. — has a domestic-violence court just for juveniles.

VAWA already provides grants to reduce sexual assault, rape and other violent crimes on college campuses. "There isn't a university in the country that doesn't have this problem," says Stuart, of the Office on Violence Against Women. Some universities, for example, provide information to all incoming freshmen about sexual assault and other crimes, she says. The programs also "help universities understand that a rape or sexual assault on campus isn't something that can be handled within the university," she says. "It's a crime."

Stuart says she would also like to see secondary schools become more involved, allowing community leaders to come into the schools to share their expertise.

But McCormick, of the American Coalition for Fathers and Children, says the federal government is already too deeply involved in private matters and that talk of domestic violence in the classroom "is not in line with public education." He is particularly concerned that the "education" would in fact be "propaganda" that

to 18 percent said their partners had threatened to harm themselves if the couple broke up, making the victim feel trapped.

In many cases, teens exposed to violence have fewer options than adults. Many shelters for battered women do not admit their teenage sons. And few shelters accommodate teenage mothers and their children. Teen mothers can be particularly vulnerable to domestic violence. A 2001 study found that a quarter of teen mothers experience violence by their boyfriends or husbands before, during or just after their pregnancies.[27]

Advocates successfully pushed Congress in 2005 to revise the Violence Against Women Act to provide federal money for new programs targeting teens, including

reinforces feminists groups' one-sided message that men are always the perpetrators.

Burroughs, of the Safe Homes for Children and Families Coalition, says domestic violence is an appropriate topic for schools, even though many school boards may be reluctant to address it because it is a family-related issue and involves sex and sexuality. "We'd be doing young people a favor by teaching them what healthy relationships are," he says, as long as the education doesn't "inject bias" that only women are victims.

BACKGROUND

Women as Property

Well into the 19th century, U.S. laws were influenced by the 1768 English "rule of thumb" law, which allowed a husband to beat his wife as long as the stick was no thicker than his thumb.[29]

Early in America's history, women were viewed as the property of men, much like children or slaves, who could be punished physically for not obeying orders. The Mississippi Supreme Court in 1824 upheld a husband's right to use corporal punishment on his wife, even as women were fighting for equal rights and the right to vote.

Suffrage and temperance movement leaders in the 19th and early 20th centuries saw wife beating as one of society's scourges. The first women's-rights convention was held in Seneca, N.Y., in 1848, and by the 1870s, wife beating was becoming unacceptable, at least legally. In 1871, courts in Alabama and Massachusetts overturned the right of a husband to beat his wife. This change coincided with growing concern over child abuse, which expanded to women's issues.

Maryland became the first state to outlaw wife beating, in 1883, but it took the turbulent 1960s and the women's movement of the 1970s to fundamentally change how Americans viewed domestic violence.[30]

The race riots, violent protests and assassinations of President John F. Kennedy, Sen. Robert F. Kennedy, D-N.Y., and the Rev. Martin Luther King Jr. during the 1960s prompted creation of the President's Commission on the Causes and Prevention of Violence. The panel's national survey gave researchers invaluable — and troubling — data. For instance, about a quarter of all adult men said they

Former NFL star O. J. Simpson was revealed as a wife beater during his trial for the murders of his ex-wife Nicole Brown Simpson and her friend Ronald Goldman. Simpson was acquitted but in a civil trial was found liable for their deaths and ordered to pay the Goldman family $8.5 million.

could think of circumstances in which it was acceptable for spouses to hit one another.[31]

While abhorring violence in the streets, many Americans still viewed domestic violence as a private matter between family members. For example, after a young woman in New York City named Kitty Genovese was stabbed repeatedly in an alley in 1964 — and her neighbors ignored her screams — many concluded that Americans had become inured to violence. But upon closer examination, the witnesses said they didn't get involved because they thought it was a man beating his wife and felt it wasn't their business to get involved.[32]

Police and judges also were reluctant to intervene in family matters that turned violent. For example, in 1967 the International Association of Police training manual said that "in dealing with family disputes, arrest should be exercised as a last resort."

Slow Progress

The women's-rights movement of the 1970s helped to change such attitudes about handling domestic violence. It led to establishment of telephone hotlines, support groups and shelters for rape victims — all of which helped battered women admit that they were being beaten at home. The first shelter for battered women opened in 1974 in St. Paul, Minn., and the National Organization for Women created a task force to examine wife beating in 1975.

The judicial and law-enforcement communities also began to step in. In 1977 Oregon became the first state to enact a mandatory-arrest law for domestic-violence incidents. The next year Minnesota became the first state to allow domestic-violence arrests without warrants. By 1980, all but six states had domestic-violence laws. And in 1981, Massachusetts and New Jersey supreme courts ruled that a husband could be criminally liable for raping his wife.

But progress was slow. By the mid-1980s, 22 states still barred police from making arrests without a warrant in domestic-violence cases unless an officer had actually witnessed the battering.

In many cases, police departments beefed up their domestic-violence activities in order to protect against lawsuits. In 1984, a jury awarded a $2.3 million judgment against the Torrington, Conn., police department for failing to protect a woman and her son from her husband's repeated violence.[33] Indeed, while the police were at her house, Tracy Thurman's husband stabbed her 13 times and broke her neck, leaving her partially paralyzed.

That same year, Congress passed the Family Violence Prevention and Services Act and the Victims of Crime Act, which, for the first time, provided money for states to set up shelters for battered women and a national, toll-free hotline for victims of domestic violence. The amount of money provided, however, was "but a trickle," wrote Richard J. Gelles, now dean of the School of Social Work at the University of Pennsylvania and an expert in the field.[34]

By 1987, more than half of the nation's major police departments had adopted "pro-arrest" policies requiring officers to make arrests in domestic-violence cases unless they could document a good reason not to.

Two widely reported cases in the 1980s dispelled the notion that domestic violence affected only the poor or uneducated. In 1985, President Ronald Reagan forced the resignation of John Fedders, a top official at the Securities and Exchange Commission, when Fedders' wife cited 18 years of repeated beatings as grounds for divorce.

Two years later, New York City lawyer Joel Steinberg was convicted of beating his 8-year-old adopted daughter Lisa to death.* During the trial it was also disclosed that Steinberg also routinely beat his companion, Hedda Nussbaum, who hadn't tried to stop the child's abuse. Photos of Nussbaum's badly injured face and vacant stare introduced the nation to "battered women's syndrome," suffered by women living in abusive relationships. Its symptoms include loss of self-esteem, fear, passivity and isolation.

While data suggest that fewer battered women are resorting to violence against their abusers, no one really knows how many women are in prison today for killing or assaulting their abusive partners, says Sue Osthoff, director of the Philadelphia-based National Clearinghouse for the Defense of Battered Women. Recent Justice Department data don't track how many violent crimes committed by women involve spouses or intimates, although a 1991 Justice Department survey of 11,800 female prisoners found that nearly 20 percent were incarcerated for a violent offense committed against an intimate.

Only 125 battered women from 23 states have received clemency since 1978, according to the clearinghouse. Osthoff says many governors and pardon boards are leery of giving battered women a break on their sentences because much of the public opposes early releases for anyone convicted of violent crimes, including battered women. In addition, many believe victims could have avoided violence by turning to today's array of domestic-violence programs.

In the early 1990s the medical community got more involved in domestic violence. The Joint Commission on Accreditation of Hospitals in 1991 required that all emergency room personnel be trained in identifying battered women. The next year the American Medical Association (AMA) and the U.S. surgeon general encouraged the screening of all women patients for domestic abuse.

Few medical organizations, however, supported requiring health-care workers to report patients who were apparent

---

* Charlotte Fedders was granted a divorce in 1985. In 1987 John Fedders sought a financial share of his ex-wife's book about her experiences, *Shattered Dreams,* which became a made-for-TV movie; a circuit court judge rejected Fedders' claim. He was never criminally prosecuted and still practices law in Washington. Steinberg was convicted of first-degree manslaughter in 1989 and sentenced to up to 25 years in prison; he was released in 2004. Murder charges against Hedda Nussbaum were dropped after prosecutors concluded she had been too severely battered to protect Lisa. She now works at My Sisters' Place, an organization that helps battered women.

CHRONOLOGY

19th Century *Family violence becomes an issue for charitable organizations. By the 1870s, most states declare wife beating illegal, but there are few services and no shelters to help battered women.*

1824 Mississippi Supreme Court says a husband can beat his wife.

1871 Courts in Alabama and Massachusetts overturn the right of a husband to beat his wife.

1960s *Most police and judges view marital violence as a private affair. In most areas, a husband cannot be arrested for wife beating unless police see the incident or have a warrant.*

1967 International Association of Chiefs of Police training manual says arrests should be made only as a last resort in family disputes.

1970s *Feminist movement identifies spousal assault and rape as major women's issues, and shelters for battered women are established.*

1971 First hotline for battered women is started in St. Paul, Minn.

1977 Oregon becomes first state to require mandatory arrests in domestic-violence incidents.

1978 Minnesota becomes first state to allow arrests without warrants in domestic-violence incidents.

1980s *All states pass domestic-violence legislation, and most mandate or permit the arrest of batterers.*

1981 Massachusetts and New Jersey supreme courts say a husband can be charged with raping his wife.

1984 Congress passes Family Violence Prevention and Services Act and the Victims of Crime Act, providing federal funds for domestic-violence programs and shelters.

1985 President Ronald Reagan forces John Fedders, a top Securities and Exchange Commission attorney, to resign after his wife cites 18 years of repeated beatings as grounds for divorce. . . . U.S. surgeon general identifies domestic violence as a major health problem.

1990s *High-profile celebrity cases focus on domestic violence, leading to a new federal law providing money for services to help victims and train officials to deal with domestic violence.*

1991 Joint Commission on Accreditation of Hospitals in 1991 requires emergency-room personnel to be trained to identify battered women.

1992 American Medical Association and surgeon general suggest that all women patients be screened for domestic abuse.

1994 Spousal assault gets national attention during the trial of Lorena Bobbitt, a battered woman who cut off her sleeping husband's penis. . . . O. J. Simpson, a sports broadcaster and former football star, is charged with murdering his estranged wife and a male companion. Bobbitt and Simpson are both acquitted.

1994 Congress passes Violence Against Women Act (VAWA), establishing community-based programs for domestic violence, training for police and court officials and a national 24-hour hotline for battered women. The law also makes it a federal crime to cross state lines to commit domestic violence.

2000s *Supreme Court limits the types of lawsuits domestic-violence victims can file; Congress targets dating violence and prevention.*

2000 Supreme Court says victims of rape and domestic violence cannot sue attackers in federal court. . . . Congress reauthorizes VAWA to include dating violence and stalking.

2005 Supreme Court says a domestic-violence victim cannot sue a police department for failing to enforce a restraining order. . . . Congress updates VAWA to include teen dating and more prevention funds.

Domestic Violence Gets Military's Attention

Master Sgt. William Wright strangled his 32-year-old wife, Jennifer Gail, and buried her in a shallow grave in a North Carolina field. She was among four wives killed in a six-week period in 2002 by their husbands, all soldiers stationed at Fort Bragg, N.C. Three had recently returned from fighting in Afghanistan.[1]

The murders drew considerable media attention and prompted the Pentagon to modify its handling of domestic violence, says Anita Sanchez, spokeswoman for the Miles Foundation, a Connecticut-based advocacy group that deals with domestic violence in the military.

Among other things, the military started requiring troops returning from long deployments to complete a mental health checklist — promptly dubbed the "don't kill your wife survey" by troops. They quickly learned "what to check" to avoid raising red flags, Sanchez says, adding that few services are provided for families on what to expect from their returning soldiers. And with so many troops in Iraq and Afghanistan, many military families are strained and anxious.

Even before the four slayings, concern about domestic violence in the military had prompted lawmakers on Capitol Hill to require the Pentagon to establish a Defense Task Force on Domestic Violence. Established in 1999, it issued several reports and some 200 recommendations before disbanding in 2003.

Maj. Michael Shavers, a Pentagon spokesman, says the Defense Department has made "substantial progress" implementing the task force's recommendations and improving the military's response to domestic violence. For example, the department has funded 22 domestic-violence training conferences over the past two years for commanding officers, judge advocates, law-enforcement personnel, victims' advocates, chaplains, health-care providers and fatality-review team members. The Pentagon also is working with the Family Violence Prevention Fund and the National Domestic Violence Hotline to develop public-awareness campaigns encouraging the military community "to take a stand against domestic violence," Shavers says.

In the last five years, the Miles Foundation reports a dramatic spike in its caseload. In October 2001, the foundation was handling 50 cases a month. Now it has 147 a week, Sanchez says, attributing the increase to greater public awareness of the issue as well as to the confidentiality and privacy the foundation can offer that the military cannot.

Military life, by its very nature, is stressful, making some family members especially vulnerable to domestic violence. Frequent relocations and high unemployment for military spouses, for example, make them more dependent on their service-member partner for income, health care and housing. Moreover, long deployments can cause some soldiers to worry that their spouses are having extramarital affairs. And easy

victims of domestic violence to the police or social services, as they are required to do in cases of suspected child abuse.

"Reporting does not ensure that a victim will have access to necessary resources and safeguards, nor does it guarantee prosecution, punishment or rehabilitation of abusers," says Peggy Goodman, director of violence-prevention resources at East Carolina University's Brody School of Medicine in Greenville, N.C. "In fact, [reporting] can further escalate an abusive situation and further endanger the life of the patient," she says. Thus, she says the American College of Emergency Physicians, the AMA and the American College of Obstetrics and Gynecology all oppose mandatory reporting by health-care workers.

The 1990s also ushered in a series of domestic-violence cases that either involved celebrities or made celebrities out of the parties involved because the trials were televised. In 1992, heavyweight boxer Mike Tyson was convicted

of raping an 18-year-old beauty-pageant contestant, drawing national attention to date rape. A year later, the issue of spousal assault got national attention when Bobbitt cut off her husband's penis with a knife.

Then, in 1994, O. J. Simpson was arrested and charged with murdering his ex-wife, Nicole Brown Simpson, and her friend, Ronald Goldman. Simpson had pleaded no contest in 1989 to charges that he beat his wife and was fined $700 and sentenced to two years' probation. Police records also showed that Mrs. Simpson had frequently made emergency calls to police to report that her husband was beating her.

Congress Acts

Experts say the Simpson case helped prod Congress to approve the Violence Against Women Act in 1994, which proponents call a turning point in the fight against

access to weapons also has been shown to be a risk factor in domestic-violence homicides.

Abuse victims in military families are often reluctant to report incidents of abuse because they know it could jeopardize the spouse's career, along with the family's paycheck, housing and health care.

"Imagine, in the civilian world, that calling a local shelter or confiding in your doctor automatically caused your batterer's employer to find out about his acts of violence and abuse," Judith E. Beals, a member of the Defense Task Force on Domestic Violence, wrote in the group's 2003 report.[2]

Victims' advocates say, however, that in recent years the military has lagged behind the nation in dealing with domestic violence. When the military created its Family Advocacy Programs (FAP) more than 20 years ago, the programs were considered progressive. But over time, experts say, FAP stayed the same while the civilian world changed the way it dealt with domestic violence.

In terms of domestic-violence programs, "the military today is where the country was in the 1980s," Sanchez says. For example, in the 1980s, many civilian hospitals were beginning to make sure they had registered nurses on staff — called SANEs (sexual assault nurse examiners) — trained to examine sexual-assault victims. But Camp Lejeune, a big Marine Corps base in North Carolina, didn't get its first SANE until 2002, Sanchez says. Until recently, sexual-assault victims on some military bases had to be transferred to civilian hospitals to obtain treatment.

Advocates had hoped to persuade Congress in 2005 to add military-specific provisions to the Violence Against Women Act but were told the bill would have to go through the Armed Services and other committees with jurisdiction over military issues, possibly delaying or derailing the entire bill.

Meanwhile, the DOD and the Justice Department's Office on Violence Against Women in 2005 kicked off two domestic-violence demonstration projects that use the "coordinated community response" approach. The projects involve the U.S. Army at Fort Campbell, Ky., and the communities of Hopkinsville, Ky., and Clarksville, Tenn., and the U.S. Navy and the city of Jacksonville, Fla. The projects are expected to provide "lessons learned" and serve as a guide for other military installations.

"There really isn't a set model for coordinating the military and civilian response to domestic-violence incidents, so hopefully we can create one," said Connie Sponsler-Garcia, the Military Projects Coordinator and coordinator of the Jacksonville project.[3]

---

[1] Fox Butterfield, "Wife Killings at Fort Reflect Growing Problem in Military," *The New York Times,* July 29, 2002, p. A9, and "Rash of Wife Killings at Ft. Bragg Leaves the Base Wondering Why," The Associated Press, July 27, 2002.

[2] Judith E. Beals, "The Military Response to Victims of Domestic Violence," 2003. The report comes from the Battered Women's Justice Project, which provides technical advice to the Department of Justice's Office on Violence Against Women.

[3] Kaylee LaRocque, "New Program Will Help Navy Deal with Domestic Violence Cases," *Navy NewsStand,* March 4, 2005.

domestic violence. President Bill Clinton, who as a child had witnessed his own mother being beaten by his stepfather, was a strong supporter of VAWA, which was attached to Clinton's crime bill.

The legislation reworked several areas of federal criminal law. It created penalties for stalking or domestic abuse in which an abuser crossed a state line and then physically harmed the victim in the course of a violent crime. VAWA also set new rules of evidence specifying that a victim's past sexual behavior generally was not admissible in federal civil or criminal cases regarding sexual misconduct. The law also allowed rape victims to demand that their alleged assailants be tested for HIV, the virus that causes AIDS.

VAWA encouraged local governments to create "coordinated community responses" bringing together criminal-justice agencies, social-services systems and local shelters

and other nonprofits. The strategy is often called the "Duluth model," after the northern Minnesota city where it was developed over a 15-year period. Researchers say the ideal coordinated community response should also involve health-care providers, child-protection services, local businesses, the media, employers and clergy. Health-care providers, in particular, can be important since doctors, nurses and emergency-room workers may see and treat women who don't or can't seek other kinds of assistance.

States in the 1990s also began experimenting with ways to help victims and alternatives to penalizing perpetrators. New Haven, Conn., for example, launched a pilot program that included weekend jail stays combined with counseling. The approach allowed offenders to keep their jobs while remaining behind bars on weekends, when batterers often drink and become abusive. Illinois and Oregon were among the states that put domestic-violence counselors in welfare

Killings of Men Dropped

The number of men killed by so-called intimates dropped by 71 percent between 1976 and 2001.* Experts say women now feel they don't have to resort to violence because there are safer shelters and tougher laws to protect them from domestic violence.

No. Killed

Women and Men Killed by Intimates

Male
Female

1976 1978 1980 1982 1984 1986 1988 1990 1992 1994 1996 1998 2000 2002

* "Intimates" includes spouses, ex-spouses, boyfriends and girlfriends.

Source: Bureau of Justice Statistics, U.S. Department of Justice, 2003.

high court's ruling did not affect any VAWA grant programs.[35]

Although the VAWA amendments passed in 2000 with nearly unanimous support, the law had its share of critics. Most of the criticism came from those who complained that violence was a problem of both men and women but that VAWA addressed only the needs of female victims.

CURRENT SITUATION

Reworking VAWA

Working until the early-morning hours of Dec. 17, 2005, Congress updated and expanded VAWA, kicking off several new initiatives, including a focus on young people and prevention.

Sen. Biden, the lead sponsor of both the original VAWA and the 2005 updated law, called passage of the new bill "a major victory," saying it "provides cities and towns with the tools they need to combat domestic violence, assist victims and go after abusers when it occurs."[36]

The updated legislation sets aside federal grant money for programs that help teen domestic-violence victims — including those in abusive dating relationships — and focuses more on children exposed to domestic violence at home. It also provides funds to combat domestic violence, sexual assault and dating violence in middle and high schools and expands services for rape victims and rape crisis centers, homeless-youth shelters and homes for runaways.

Targeting federal funds to younger victims "makes sense since we know that the highest rates of intimate-partner violence affect those in the 16-to-24 age group," says Kiersten Stewart, director of public policy at the Family Violence Prevention Fund, which lobbied Congress to enact the original Violence Against Women Act and many of the key revisions in 2005.

Stewart lauded Congress for continuing existing domestic-violence programs and for adding new ones, particularly those that focus on young people. "We're very pleased," she says.

offices. Washington became the first state to allow battered women to set up confidential addresses their abusers couldn't locate.

Congress updated VAWA in 2000, adding "dating violence" to the definition of domestic violence and urging grant programs to address it. The revised law also created penalties for anyone traveling across state lines with the intent to kill, injure, harass or intimidate a spouse or intimate partner. The revised law also laid out special rules for battered immigrant spouses and their children, allowing them to remain in the United States. Under the old law, battered immigrant women could be deported if they left their abusers, who usually are their sponsors for residency and citizenship in the United States.

Also in 2000, the U.S. Supreme Court invalidated portions of the law permitting victims of rape and domestic violence to sue their attackers in federal court for damages. Ruling in *United States v. Morrison*, the justices said those provisions were unconstitutional under the Commerce and Equal Protection clauses. Victims could still bring damage suits in state courts. In addition, the court said, such violence does not substantially affect interstate commerce and noted that the Equal Protection clause is directed at government actions, not private. The

The updated VAWA also includes money for programs to help domestic-abuse victims who are over age 60. It is difficult to say how many older Americans are abused, neglected or exploited, in large part because the problem remains "greatly hidden," says the National Center on Elder Abuse, a Washington, D.C., group that receives funds from the U.S. Administration on Aging. A 1998 federal study estimated that in 1996 some 450,000 Americans 60 and over were victims of physical, emotional or sexual abuse, neglect or financial exploitation. In 90 percent of the cases, a family member was the perpetrator, the study found.[37]

Experts fear that as the U.S. population ages, the number of elder-abuse cases will grow. "It's a hidden epidemic," Daniel Reingold, president and chief executive officer of the Hebrew Home for the Aged in Riverdale, N.Y., told *AARP* magazine.[38] That's largely because older victims are ashamed to report the abuse, because they feel they are old enough to know better than to be victimized. Reingold compares the current attention to elder abuse to the domestic-violence and child-abuse movements 25 years ago.

The expanded VAWA also funds programs to educate health-care professionals on how to identify and serve victims of domestic violence. A 2005 report from researchers at Harvard Medical School found that nearly one-third of doctors surveyed fail to document patients' reports of domestic violence, and only 10 percent offer information about domestic abuse to their patients.[39]

The National Network to End Domestic Violence says VAWA's new housing provisions are of particular importance, since 92 percent of homeless women have experienced severe physical or sexual abuse. The new law protects victims of domestic violence or stalking from being evicted from public housing and provides grants for transitional housing for domestic-violence victims.

"The reauthorization of VAWA shows that Congress recognizes domestic violence as a devastating social problem," said network President Rosenthal.[40]

The updated law fails to make the Violence Against Women Act gender neutral, as some men's groups had requested, but contains language specifying that men can't be discriminated against. Rep. James Sensenbrenner Jr., R-Wis., chairman of the House Judiciary Committee and

---

Is Your Relationship Healthy or Abusive?

Break the Cycle, a nonprofit organization helping young people create lives free of abuse, suggests teens ask themselves the following questions to determine if their relationships are healthy. If teens answer yes to any of these questions, they may be in an abusive or potentially abusive relationship, the organization says.

Does the person I am with:

Get extremely jealous or possessive?

Accuse me of flirting or cheating?

Constantly check up on me or make me check in?

Tell me how to dress or how much makeup to wear?

Try to control what I do or whom I see?

Try to keep me from seeing or talking to my family and friends?

Have big mood swings — being angry and yelling at me one minute, and the next being sweet and apologetic?

Make me feel nervous or like I'm "walking on eggshells?"

Put me down or criticize me and make me feel like I can't do anything right or that no one else would want me?

Threaten to hurt me?

Threaten to hurt my friends or family?

Threaten to commit suicide or hurt himself or herself because of me?

Threaten to hurt my pets or destroy my things?

Yell, grab, push, shove, shake, punch, slap, hold me down, throw things or hurt me in any way?

Break things or throw things when we argue?

Pressure or force me into having sex or going farther than I want to?

Source: Break the Cycle, www.breakthecycle.org

Innovative Programs Fight Domestic Violence

A host of programs around the country are dedicated to fighting and preventing domestic violence. Among those that have been found to work well are:

- **Coaching Boys into Men** — This program from the Family Violence Prevention Fund recognizes the mentoring role coaches have with their athletes and provides training tools to encourage disciplined and respectful behaviors. (www.endabuse.org) A similar effort comes from New York Yankees' Manager Joe Torre, who founded the Joe Torre Safe at Home Foundation to prevent others from suffering as he did as a child. Growing up, he stayed away from home, fearful of his own father, who abused his mother. (www.joetorre.org)

- **Cut it Out** — Originally a statewide program created by The Women's Fund of Greater Birmingham and the Alabama Coalition Against Domestic Violence, this program went national in 2003, training hair salon professionals to recognize the signs of domestic abuse and to encourage suspected victims to get help. The project is cosponsored by *Southern Living At Home* magazine, the National Cosmetology Association and Clairol Professional. (www.cutitout.org)

- **Domestic Violence Prevention Enhancement and Leadership Through Alliances (DELTA)** — These state demonstration projects get funds from the U.S. Centers for Disease Control and Prevention to focus on preventing violence between intimate partners. A program at John Dickenson High School in Wilmington, Del., involves an interactive play for ninth-graders, weekly "healthy relationship" lessons during health class and a weekly after-school club called "Teens Talking About Relationships." Delaware Gov. Ruth Ann Minner (D) awarded the club the 2004 Outstanding Youth Volunteer Service Award. (www.cdc.gov/ncipc/DELTA/default.htm)

- **Family Justice Center, San Diego, Calif.** — Opened in 2002, this program provides "one-stop shopping" for legal, social service and some medical services in downtown San Diego, avoiding the need for abuse victims to go to different locations on different days. It is considered the gold standard for a compact community with good access to mass transit. But researchers have found that such programs are not as efficient for rural areas or spread-out cities that are more auto-dependent. It's a model for President Bush's Family Justice Center program. (www.familyjustice-center.org)

- **Greenbook Demonstration Initiative** — Named for the report's green cover, this program was launched in 2001 and brings a closer collaboration between child-abuse and domestic-violence services. The project took place in six counties: San Francisco and Santa Clara counties in California; Grafton County, N.H.; St. Louis County, Mo.; El Paso County, Colo.; and Lane County, Ore. Among the key lessons from the Greenbook project: Mothers should not be accused of neglect for being victims of domestic violence, and separating battered mothers and children should be the alternative of last resort.[1] (www.thegreenbook.info/)

- **Judicial Oversight Demonstration Initiative** — This Justice Department program, which began in 1999, establishes closer working relationships between the courts, police departments, district attorneys' offices, probation departments and batterer intervention and victim services. The program was launched in Milwaukee, Wis., Dorchester, Mass., and Ann Arbor, Mich. (www.vaw.umn.edu/documents/1jod/1jod.html)

- **Victim Intervention Program (VIP)** — This program at Parkland Hospital at the University of Texas in Dallas provides staff caseworkers to help determine the health-care and social-service needs of patients who are victims of abuse and provides referrals for other services. Ellen Taliaferro, an emergency physician, founded the program in 1999. (www.parklandhospital.com)

---

[1] "The Greenbook Demonstration Initiative: Interim Evaluation Report," Caliber Associates, Education Development Center and the National Center for State Courts, Dec. 16, 2004.

AT ISSUE

Did Congress improve the Violence Against Women Act?

YES
JILL J. MORRIS
Public Policy Director, National Coalition Against Domestic Violence

NO
MICHAEL MCCORMICK
Executive Director, American Coalition for Fathers and Children

Written for the *CQ Researcher*, January 2006

Written for the *CQ Researcher*, January 2006

Since Congress passed the bipartisan and groundbreaking Violence Against Women Act (VAWA) in 1994, the criminal-justice and community-based responses to domestic violence, dating violence, sexual assault and stalking have significantly improved. Ten years of successful VAWA programs have helped new generations of families and justice professionals understand that society will not tolerate these crimes.

Congress improved VAWA when it reauthorized it in December 2005. Since 1994, lawmakers have authorized more than $5 billion for states and local programs under VAWA. This relatively small amount has had a huge impact on local communities. For example, the number of women murdered by an intimate partner declined by 22 percent between 1993 and 2001. Also, more women came forward to report being abused in 1998 than in 1993.

VAWA is not only good social policy but also sound fiscal policy. A 2002 university study found that money spent to reduce domestic violence between 1995 and 2000 saved nearly 10 times the potential costs of responding to these crimes. The study estimated that $14.8 billion was saved on medical, legal and other costs that arise from responding to domestic violence. On an individual level, VAWA saved an estimated $159 per victim.

VAWA has fostered community-coordinated responses that for the first time brought together the criminal-justice system, social services and private, nonprofit organizations. With VAWA reauthorized, our local communities can continue to provide life-saving services such as rape prevention and education, victim witness assistance, sexual-assault crisis intervention and legal assistance.

Additionally, VAWA grants help reduce violent crimes on college campuses and provide services for children who witness violence, transitional housing, supervised visitation centers and programs for abused seniors and victims with disabilities.

The updated VAWA will expand programs to fill unmet needs, such as fostering a more community-based response system and addressing housing discrimination, preventing violence, promoting healthy relationships and engaging male allies to encourage positive roles for young men and boys.

The 2005 reauthorization of VAWA was one of the few pieces of legislation that was overwhelmingly supported by members of Congress on both sides of the aisle. Together, Democrats and Republicans agreed that passing VAWA showed that Congress was willing to recommit federal resources to programs that save lives, save money and help future generations of Americans live free from violence.

Violence perpetrated against others should be unacceptable regardless of the initiator's sex. But as many lawmakers privately confide, the Violence Against Women Act (VAWA) is not good law. Unfortunately, it has become the third rail of politics: Legislators acknowledge that it is political suicide to oppose passage of the bill. As one chief of staff aptly stated, "You do not want to be one of the few congressmen returning to your district having voted against this legislation, regardless of your reservations."

As a result, VAWA funds a political agenda that addresses domestic violence from a myopic viewpoint. It expands government encroachment into the private sphere of citizens' lives without adequate safeguards to those running afoul of the law and the domestic-violence industry.

Congress had a chance to address the law's shortcomings but failed to do so. For example, therapeutic approaches aimed at preserving the relationship and developing conflict-resolution skills still receive lower priority than law enforcement and relationship-dissolution options. This focus is at odds with stated public-policy objectives of building and maintaining strong, intact families. Congress should have changed this policy and did not.

Congress was correct to include language making clear that VAWA programs cannot discriminate against male victims, but it is still too early to tell whether male victims and their children will indeed get the help they need. Men and their children are not recognized as an underserved population, even though numerous studies indicate men are likely to be victims and suffer injury 15-30 percent of the time.

Even further, Congress made the right move by mandating that the Government Accountability Office study the issue, including the extent to which men are victims of domestic violence. This study will be balanced and give a better idea of how many men are abused and have access to services.

The biggest problem, however, is that VAWA does not recognize the role women play in domestic violence. The updated VAWA reinforces and statutorily codifies the notion that women are victims and men are abusers — a sure-fire way to assure half-baked solutions to a multi-faceted problem. This simplistic view of domestic violence ignores the vast storehouse of data indicating a small minority of both men and women are equally likely to initiate and engage in domestic violence.

Until such fundamental concerns are addressed, VAWA will continue to support a one-sided approach to dealing with domestic violence. Gender politics has no business being funded through the public purse.

Break the Cycle

Youths from Los Angeles plan programs to publicize and prevent domestic violence against teens at a meeting of Break the Cycle's Youth Voices program.

lead VAWA sponsor in the House, said after the bill's passage that the reauthorization "specifies that programs addressing these problems can serve both female and male victims."[41]

It is widely speculated on Capitol Hill that gay men, who have been excluded from men's groups, could be the biggest beneficiaries of making sure VAWA funds help abused men. While numbers are hard to come by, domestic-violence groups say gays are frequent victims of abuse. "Clearly, it would benefit gay men if the act was gender neutral," Sean Cahill, director of the National Gay and Lesbian Task Force's Policy Institute, told *CQ Weekly.*[42]

McCormick, of the American Coalition for Fathers and Children, is still troubled that the updated law focuses too much on the criminal aspect of domestic violence and not the social problems associated with it. "It still resorts to the nuclear option of blowing up a family," arresting and incarcerating someone who could be falsely accused without even seeing whether counseling could keep the family together, he says.

But McCormick says he's glad the new law authorizes the Government Accountability Office to study the issue, including the extent to which men, women, youths and children are victims of domestic violence, dating violence, sexual assault and stalking. The study will be balanced and provide a better idea of how many men are abused and have access to services, McCormick says.

Finding What Works

While Congress debated reworking VAWA, the Bush administration's Office on Violence Against Women was launching the president's Family Justice Center Initiative. Fifteen centers will get federal funds to provide one-stop help for victims, including legal, medical and social services.

In 2005 family-justice centers opened in Brooklyn, N.Y.; Bexar County, Texas; Alameda County, Calif.; Ouachita Parish, La., and Nampa, Idaho. Additional centers are slated to open in 2006 in St. Louis, Tulsa, Boston and Tampa. The DOJ's Stuart says the centers are examples of approaches that are working. (*See sidebar, p. 50.*)

Meanwhile, 14 states are working with the U.S. Centers for Disease Control and Prevention (CDC) to prevent domestic violence in the so-called DELTA (Domestic Violence Prevention Enhancement and Leadership Through Alliances) program.*

Each state project is a little different, since domestic violence and social programs differ from state to state, says Corinne Graffunder, branch chief of the CDC's National Center for Injury Prevention and Control. She says all 14 are innovative because they focus on prevention, not treating the victim or punishing the perpetrator. "That is new," she says.

In Valdez, Alaska, for example, the DELTA program is developing a healthy-relationships curriculum for the local high school. Mayor Bert Cottle proclaimed December 2005 as "White Ribbon Campaign Month" and encouraged all citizens, particularly men, to wear white ribbons in support of preventing domestic violence. And Dane County, Wis., provides programs and discussions for young men about sexual assault and domestic violence. The CDC expects to be able to evaluate the effectiveness of the programs in about three years, Graffunder says.

In New York state, Republican Gov. George Pataki and his wife Libby have spearheaded campaigns targeting teen-dating violence, including a statewide contest in which students were invited to submit posters, songs and music videos to raise awareness of the problem's seriousness. As part of Domestic Violence Awareness month in October 2005, New York kicked off its new "If It Doesn't Feel Right, It Probably Isn't" education campaign and distributed information packets — including copies of the 2005 winning poster — to all high schools in the state. (*See photo, p. 38.*)

---

* The 14 states are Alaska, California, Delaware, Florida, Kansas, Michigan, Montana, New York, North Carolina, North Dakota, Ohio, Rhode Island, Virginia and Wisconsin.

"This campaign will serve as a powerful platform to raise awareness about teen dating violence and will let all of New York's teens know that there are resources available to help if they are suffering from abuse," Pataki said.[43]

States also are using welfare offices to help victims of domestic violence, but the efforts have been spotty. Studies have indicated that up to 50 percent of welfare recipients are, or have been, victims of domestic violence and all but three states — Maine, Oklahoma and Ohio — screen welfare recipients for signs of domestic violence. Most states will waive some federal welfare rules pertaining to work, the five-year lifetime limit on cash assistance and child-support requirements for victims of domestic violence. But a recent Government Accountability Office report found that state requirements varied widely and that few welfare recipients received waivers.[44]

The Center for Impact Research, a Chicago anti-poverty research group, found that workers in a local welfare office "overwhelmingly" did not refer welfare recipients to domestic-violence services, says Lise McKean, the center's deputy director. Part of the problem was a cumbersome form that welfare recipients had to fill out and overburdened caseworkers who didn't have the time or interest to pursue the matter.

"The vision of the [welfare] office as the public agency with access to poor women that can identify individuals living with domestic violence and help them gain access to domestic violence services may be unrealistic," the center concluded.[45]

Rather than welfare offices, McKean suggests putting domestic-violence services at employment-service agencies — an approach the center tried in Houston, Chicago and Seattle.[46] Having a domestic-violence counselor on site was key, she says. The case manager did not have to worry whether clients would follow up because the manager could escort them directly to the counselor. Plus, adding domestic violence to a case manger's list of concerns was not a big burden since a specialist was available to handle it.

Experts say domestic violence also should be addressed in marriage and responsible-fatherhood programs. Recent federally funded research found that many of the widely available marriage-education programs were designed and tested with middle-income, college-educated couples and do not address domestic violence.[47]

Some states, such as New York, argue that programs designed to encourage healthy relationships have the positive benefit of reducing the likelihood of both physical and emotional abuse. The Oklahoma Marriage Initiative addresses domestic violence implicitly by focusing on communication and conflict resolution and has recently created a handout telling couples how to identify domestic violence and where to obtain help.[48]

Businesses and nonprofits also are stepping in. Liz Claiborne Inc., Break the Cycle and the Education Development Center, Inc., have created curriculums for ninth- and 10th-graders on dating violence. And 19 schools are participating in the "Love is not abuse" program, which formally began in October 2005.

"Our hope is that this curriculum will help educate teens on how to identify all forms of relationship abuse and understand what types of actions are and are not acceptable in a healthy dating relationship," said Jane Randel, vice president of corporate communications at Liz Claiborne.[49] (*See questionnaire, p. 49.*)

Kraft Foods has sponsored several studies, including the Center for Impact Research's project that looked at how domestic violence affects women's job training and employment.[50] Verizon Wireless has donated more than $8 million to shelters and prevention programs nationwide. Kaiser Permanente has stepped up its efforts to train counselors to perform domestic-violence evaluations and provides resources for patients who need help. The Blue Shield of California Foundation offers free consultations to any employer in California interested in setting up a domestic-violence prevention program in the workplace.[51]

OUTLOOK

Focus on Prevention

Most experts say the country has made significant headway in viewing domestic violence as a crime instead of merely a private family matter. But most agree that more focus should be placed on prevention.

"True primary prevention is the next real area on the horizon," says the CDC's Graffunder.

"We're just now beginning to scratch the surface," says Soler, of the Family Violence Prevention Fund. "We can't just intervene after the fact."

"All the recent emphasis has been on the criminal aspect of domestic violence," says Jeffrey L. Edelson, director of the Minnesota Center Against Violence and Abuse at the University of Minnesota. "This is a public health epidemic" that must be tackled in both the courts and public health agencies. "The prevention piece is important."

Until now, prevention has not been a top priority because the immediate concern has been helping victims in crisis and making sure batterers were held accountable and got counseling, says Graffunder. And, she adds, while advocates fighting domestic violence like to envision a day when violence no longer destroys families and lives, "We still have a lot of work to do."

Research and funding still lag behind the needs, advocates say. "We have a pretty good idea what works, but we need documentation by researchers to back it up," says Stuart, of the Justice Department's Office on Violence Against Women. For example, she says, research is particularly lacking on stalking. "Right now, it's hidden. We really don't know how much stalking is out there."

Dunford-Jackson, of the Family Violence Project, also sees a dearth of data. She says judges are always asking for statistics on successful programs and techniques. "We're still in the infancy of domestic-violence research," she says.

Researchers expect to know more from the CDC's DELTA prevention programs once results are in. Advocates are also trying to figure out best practices from several other demonstration projects, such as the "Greenbook" program that provides closer collaboration between child-custody and domestic-violence agencies.

Burroughs of the Safe Homes for Children and Families Coalition is confident that in the coming years male victims of domestic violence will get more attention and federal funds. Soler of the Family Violence Prevention Fund likewise sees a bigger role ahead for men — as major players in prevention.

"Men — as fathers, coaches, teachers and mentors — are in a unique position to influence the attitudes and behaviors of young boys," Soler says. The Family Violence Prevention Fund has two major initiatives aimed at boys, Founding Fathers and Coaching Boys Into Men, which are funded by foundations and private donors.

Fulcher of Break the Cycle says it's critical that more prevention programs target teens. "Now is the time to tell the youth of our nation that we are done pretending, that we will lead them into healthy adulthoods, that we won't tolerate violence and neither should they."

Advocates, however, worry that the budget crunch in Washington caused by Hurricane Katrina and the war in Iraq will mean less money for state and local social and domestic-violence programs, jeopardizing the progress made so far.

"As resources are strained, the decisions that people have to make at the local, community and state levels just get harder and harder," says the CDC's Graffunder. "Prevention doesn't traditionally fare well in those environments."

NOTES

1. U.S. Department of Justice, Bureau of Justice Statistics, "Intimate Partner Violence, 1993-2001," February 2003.

2. Prepared testimony of Juley Fulcher and Victoria Sadler before the U.S. Senate Judiciary Committee, July 19, 2005; Allison Klein and Ruben Castaneda, "Md. Burn Victim Told Judge of Fears," *The Washington Post*, Oct. 13, 2005, p. B7 (Cade); Pat Burson, "The Dark Side of Dating," *Los Angeles Times*, June 20, 2005, p. F6 (Wickiewicz).

3. U.S. Department of Justice, Bureau of Justice Statistics, "Family Violence Statistics," June 12, 2005.

4. U.S. Department of Justice, *op. cit.*, February 2003.

5. Testimony of Diane M. Stuart, director, U.S. Department of Justice Office on Violence Against Women before Senate Judiciary Committee, July 19, 2005.

6. Family Violence Prevention Fund, "Promoting Prevention, Targeting Teens: An Emerging Agenda to Reduce Domestic Violence," 2003.

7. Burson, *op. cit.*

8. Becky Beaupre, "Spotlight on female abuser: For 13 years, he never hit her back," *The Detroit News*, April 20, 1997.

9. Centers for Disease Control and Prevention, "Youth Risk Behavior Surveillance — United States 2003," *Surveillance Summaries*, May 21, 2004.

10. Centers for Disease Control and Prevention, National Center for Injury Prevention and Control, "Intimate Partner Violence: Fact Sheet," updated October 2005.

11. Wendy Max, *et al.*, "The economic toll of intimate partner violence against women in the United States," *Violence and Victims 2004*; 19(3), pp. 259-72.

12. Miriam K. Ehrensaft and Patricia Cohen, "Intergenerational Transmission of Partner Violence: A 20-Year Prospective Study," *Journal of Consulting and Clinical Psychology*, Vol. 71, No. 4, August 2003, pp. 741-753.

13. Prepared testimony, Senate Judiciary Committee, July 19, 2005.

14. Prepared testimony of Lynn Rosenthal, president, National Network to End Domestic Violence, Senate Judiciary Committee, July 19, 2005.

15. *Ibid.*

16. U.S. Department of Justice, *op. cit.*, February 2003.

17. Lisa Scott, "Pending federal DV law has little to do with violence and much to do with divorce court, attorney says," *The Liberator*, fall 2005.

18. Allison Klein and Ruben Castaneda, "Character in a Courtroom Drama," *The Washington Post*, Nov. 17, 2005, p. B1.

19. Kristin Little, "Specialized Courts and Domestic Violence," National Center for State Courts, May 2003.

20. Scott, *op. cit.*

21. Harvey Wallace, *Family Violence: Legal, Medical and Social Perspectives* (2002, 3rd ed.), p. 221.

22. *Town of Castle Rock v. Gonzales*, 542 U.S. ___ (2005).

23. "Supreme Court Decision Weakening Restraining Orders Short-Shrifted in the News," *Feminist Daily News Wire*, June 28, 2005.

24. U.S. Department of Justice, Bureau of Justice Statistics, "Special Report: Intimate Partner Violence and Age of Victim, 1993-1999," 2001.

25. Gallup Poll, "Adolescents Not Invulnerable to Abusive Relationships," May 24, 2005.

26. "Liz Claiborne Inc. Omnibuzz Topline Findings: Teen Relationship Abuse Research," February 2005; www.loveisnotabuse.com.

27. Sally Leidermann and Cair Almo, "Interpersonal Violence and Adolescent Pregnancy: Prevalence and Implications for Practice and Policy," Center for Assessment and Policy Development and National Organization on Adolescent Pregnancy, Parenting and Prevention, 2001.

28. Centers for Disease Control and Prevention, *op. cit.*, May 21, 2004.

29. Background drawn from Richard J. Gelles and Claire Pedrick Cornell, *Intimate Violence in Families* (1990) and Harvey Wallace, *Family Violence* (2002).

30. For background see Sarah Glazer, "Violence Against Women," *CQ Researcher*, Feb. 26, 1993, pp. 169-192.

31. Gelles and Cornell, *op. cit.*, p. 39.

32. *Ibid.*

33. *Thurman v. City of Torrington*, 595 F.Supp. 1521 (Conn. 1984).

34. Gelles and Cornell, *op. cit.*

35. *United States v. Morrison*, 529 U.S. 598 (2000).

36. Statement, Dec. 19, 2005.

37. "National Elder Abuse Incidence Study, Final Report," Administration for Children and Families and the Administration on Aging, U.S. Department of Health and Human Services, September 1998; www.aoa.gov/eldfam/Elder_Rights/Elder_Abuse/ABuseReport_Full.pdf.

38. David France, "And Then He Hit Me," *AARP The Magazine*, January/February 2006, p. 81.

39. Megan Gerber, "How and why community hospital clinicians document a positive screen for intimate partner violence: a cross-sectional study," *BMC Family News*, Vol. 6, p. 48, Nov. 19, 2005.

40. Statement, Dec. 17, 2005.

41. *Congressional Record*, Dec. 17, 2005, p. H12122.

42. Jill Barshay, "Men on the Verge of Domestic Abuse Protection," *CQ Weekly*, Sept. 5, 2005, p. 2276.

43. Press release, Office of New York Gov. George Pataki, "Governor Promotes Awareness of Teen Dating Violence," Sept. 23, 2005.

44. Government Accountability Office, "TANF: State Approaches to Screening for Domestic Violence Could Benefit from HHS Guidance," August 2005.

45. Center for Impact Research, "Less Than Ideal: The Reality of Implementing a Welfare-to-Work Program for Domestic Violence Victims and Survivors in Collaboration with the TANF Department," February 2001.

46. Lise McKean, Center for Impact Research, "Addressing Domestic Violence as a Barrier to Work," October 2004.

47. Government Accountability Office, *op. cit.*

48. *Ibid.*

49. Liz Claiborne Inc., "Love is not abuse" curriculum, Oct. 11, 2005.

50. McKean, *op. cit.*

51. Available at www.endabuse.org/workplace/display .php?DocID=33018.

BIBLIOGRAPHY

Books

Gelles, Richard J., *Intimate Violence in Families,* SAGE Publications, 3rd ed., 1997.
Gelles, the then-dean of the University of Pennsylvania's School of Social Work, looks at the myths that hinder understanding of family violence, such as the belief that domestic violence is a lower-class phenomenon.

Gosselin, Denise Kindschi, *Heavy Hands, An Introduction to the Crimes of Domestic Violence,* Prentice-Hall, 2000.
A Massachusetts State Police trooper who developed domestic-violence prevention courses for Western New England College examines different kinds of family violence and legal responses, with each chapter providing review questions on domestic violence.

Wallace, Harvey, *Family Violence, Legal, Medical and Social Perspectives,* 3rd ed., Allyn & Bacon, 2002.
The director of California State University's Justice Center examines medical and legal responses to domestic violence, particularly among homosexuals and rural victims.

Articles

Beaupre, Becky, "Spotlight on female abuser: For 13 years, he never hit her back," and "No place to run for male victims of domestic abuse," *The Detroit News*, April 20, 1997.
Male victims of domestic violence are sometimes turned away from aid agencies.

Burson, Pat, "The Dark Side of Dating," *Los Angeles Times*, June 20, 2005, p. F6.
The author examines teen-dating violence, giving examples of teens in abusive relationships and how few turn to their parents for help.

Young, Cathy, "Ending Bias in Domestic Assault Law," *The Boston Globe*, July 25, 2005, p. A11.
A libertarian *Reason* magazine editor argues that the Violence Against Women Act helped enshrine a one-sided approach to family violence and that it should be more gender neutral.

Reports and Studies

"Full Report of the Prevalence, Incidence, and Consequences of Violence against Women: Findings from the National Violence Against Women Survey," U.S. Department of Justice, November 2000; www.ncjrs.org/ txtfiles1/nij/183781.txt.
The survey quantifies the pervasiveness of domestic violence and its impact on women and society.

"The Greenbook Demonstration Initiative: Interim Evaluation Report," Caliber Associates, Education Development Center and the National Center for State Courts, Dec. 16, 2004.
An innovative pilot program aims to improve coordination between public agencies that deal with domestic violence and child welfare.

"Intimate Partner Violence: Fact Sheet," National Center for Injury Prevention and Control, U.S. Centers for Disease Control and Prevention, updated October 2005.
This backgrounder includes the latest research on domestic violence.

"Intimate Partner Violence, 1993-2001," Bureau of Justice Statistics, U.S. Department of Justice, February 2003.
A federal domestic-violence study looks at abusive relationships involving spouses, boyfriends, girlfriends and ex-spouses and partners.

"Less Than Ideal: The Reality of Implementing a Welfare-to-Work Program for Domestic Violence Victims and Survivors in Collaboration with the TANF Department," February 2001, and "Addressing Domestic Violence as a Barrier to Work," October 2004, Center for Impact Research.
Providing domestic-violence services at welfare agencies does little to help battered women, but putting such services

in employment agencies can be beneficial because they help battered women achieve economic independence.

"Liz Claiborne Inc. Omnibuzz Topline Findings: Teen Relationship Abuse Research," February 2005, www .loveisnotabuse.com.
A survey sponsored by the clothing manufacturer shows that more than half of teens surveyed knew friends who had been physically, sexually or verbally abused.

"Promoting Prevention, Targeting Teens: An Emerging Agenda to Reduce Domestic Violence," Family Violence Prevention Fund, 2003.

An advocacy group concludes that the next generation of work in the domestic-violence field must target teens and young parents and emphasize prevention.

Ehrensaft, Miriam, and Patricia Cohen, "Intergenerational Transmission of Partner Violence: A 20-Year Prospective Study," *Journal of Consulting and Clinical Psychology,* **Vol. 71, No. 4, August 2003, pp. 741-753.**
Children raised in homes where domestic or dating violence occurs are more likely to become victims or perpetrators of such violence.

For More Information

American Coalition for Fathers and Children, 1718 M St., N.W., Suite 187, Washington, DC 20036; (800) 978-3237; www.acfc.org. Argues that the Violence Against Women Act destroys families and funds an anti-male, profeminist ideological agenda.

Break the Cycle, P.O. Box 64996, Los Angeles, CA 90064; (888) 988-TEEN; www.breakthecycle.org. An advocacy group that educates and empowers youth to build lives and communities free from dating violence and domestic abuse.

Family Violence Prevention Fund, 383 Rhode Island St., Suite 304, San Francisco, CA 94103-5133; (415) 252-8900; www.endabuse.org. Sponsors education campaigns on family violence and was instrumental in lobbying Congress to enact the Violence Against Women Act.

National Coalition Against Domestic Violence, 1633 Q St., N.W., Suite 210, Washington, DC 20009; (202) 745-121; www.ncadv.org. Serves as a national information and referral center for battered women and their children as well as the public, media and allied agencies and organizations.

National Network to End Domestic Violence, 660 Pennsylvania Ave., S.E., Suite 303, Washington, DC 20003; (202) 543-5566; www.nnedv.org. Represents state domestic-violence coalitions and lobbies for stronger domestic-violence measures.

National Resource Center on Domestic Violence, (800) 537-2238; www.nrcdv.org. Provides comprehensive

information and resources, policy development and assistance to enhance community response to and prevention of domestic violence.

National Sexual Violence Resource Center, 123 N. Enola Dr., Enola, PA 17025; (877) 739-3895; www.nsvrc.org. Provides information and technical assistance to local and national organizations and the public.

Safe Homes for Children and Families Coalition, 185 Springfield Dr., North East, MD 21901; (410) 392-8244. Advocates for gender-neutral federal legislation regarding domestic violence.

Stalking Resource Center, 2000 M St., N.W., Suite 480, Washington, DC 20036; (800) 394-2255); www.ncvc.org/ src. Part of the National Center for Victims of Crime; serves as an information clearinghouse and peer-to-peer exchange program on stalking.

U.S. Centers for Disease Control and Prevention, National Center for Injury Prevention and Control, Mailstop K65, 4770 Buford Highway, N.E., Atlanta, GA 30341-3724; (770) 488-1506; www.cdc.gov/ViolencePrevention/ intimatepartnerviolence/index.html. Studies ways to prevent intimate-partner and sexual violence.

U.S. Department of Justice, Office on Violence Against Women, 800 K St., N.W., Suite 920, Washington, DC 20530; (202) 307-6026; www.usdoj.gov. Handles legal and policy issues regarding violence against women and administers Violence Against Women Act grants.

Sex Offenders

Will Tough, New Laws Do More Harm Than Good?

Alan Greenblatt

3

Jessica Lunsford's death last year led some two-dozen states to enact versions of "Jessica's Law," which requires more thorough tracking of sex offenders and stricter sentences. Congress also enacted a law this year that will prod states to track sex offenders more closely. Contrary to popular belief, sex offenders have relatively low recidivism rates, and family members, not strangers, are responsible for most reported sex crimes against children.

From *CQ Global Researcher*, September 2006.

Getty Images/Citrus County Sheriff's Department

Kerry Skora thinks there are worse things than being known as a murderer.

Sex offenders still face penalties after they serve their sentences — including some that don't even apply to murderers. That's why Skora didn't want to be labeled as a sex offender when he was released from an Illinois prison this year after serving 15 years for a murder he committed at age 19. But because his victim was 16, that's how state law categorized him, even though his crime did not involve sex.

And in Illinois sex offenders have to register their whereabouts with police and are not allowed to live within 500 feet of schools or other public places where children gather — making it hard to find a place to live. Miami Beach, Iowa City and many other cities and states have similar laws.

"It's more like banishment than a zoning restriction," says Roxanne Lieb, executive director of the Washington State Institute for Public Policy. "There isn't any other group in society where we banish them. You could commit a double murder and come back and live somewhere, or be a three-time drug dealer, but not a sex offender."

The Illinois legislature agreed with Skora's complaint that it was unfair to tar him as a sex offender just because his victim was a minor. The state created a new registry for non-sexual violent criminals. The fact that sex offenders are subject to even more intense scrutiny than murderers demonstrates just how seriously lawmakers are taking the problem of sex crimes against children.

It's not hard to figure out their motivation. Sex crimes against children are among the most heinous imaginable. "Surely there can

Child Sexual Abuse Dropped Significantly

The rate of identified sexual abuse of children in the United States fell by 50 percent from 1991 to 2004. David Finkelhor, director of the Crimes Against Children Research Center, thinks the declines may be linked to greater awareness about child maltreatment, improved parenting and more effective treatment for family and mental health problems, including psychiatric medications.

Child Sexual-Abuse Rates in the United States
(based on substantiated reports)

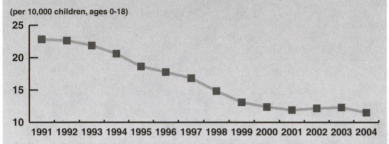

(per 10,000 children, ages 0-18)

Note: The data come from state child-protection agencies and cover offenses against children committed primarily by parents and other caretakers; they do not typically cover sex crimes against children committed by strangers.

Source: Crimes Against Children Research Center, University of New Hampshire, 2006

be no crime that inspires greater anguish among the general public than sexual crimes, especially violent sexual offenders," writes Karen J. Terry, an associate professor at the City University of New York's John Jay College of Criminal Justice.[1]

The media have made several especially terrifying crimes into continuing national nightmares, vividly and repeatedly portraying both the victim and the crime. A case in point is the rape and murder of 6-year-old Colorado beauty queen JonBenet Ramsey a decade ago. After an Atlanta, Ga., man, John Mark Karr, said he killed the child, he was arrested in Thailand and brought back to the United States. However, police said his DNA didn't match that found in her underwear, and he was not charged.

But there have been numerous other high-profile cases that have shocked the public and prompted increased legislative action. Last year, 9-year-old Jessica Marie Lunsford was abducted from her Florida home by a convicted sex offender, sexually assaulted and buried alive. Since then, two-dozen states have enacted versions of "Jessica's Law," which requires more thorough

tracking of released sex offenders through means such as DNA samples, ankle bracelets and GPS (global positioning system) devices.

California voters are expected to approve a particularly strict version of the law in November. Congress also enacted a law this year that will prod states to track sex offenders more closely.

"When you have someone taking a 9-year-old child and burying her alive, it just calls out for a legislative response," says Lieb.

What is particularly troubling about a case such as Jessica's, say those calling for stricter laws, is that her alleged assailant had a long criminal record, including sexual offenses. (The trial of John Evander Couey has not been able to proceed because it was impossible to seat an impartial jury in the county in which the crime occurred.)

"Whatever it takes to track these sex offenders must be done, because rehabilitation tends not to happen," says Stacie D. Rumenap, executive director of Stop Child Predators, which lobbies for passage of Jessica's Law in every state.

But Terry and other experts on deviancy dispute the frequently heard claim that sex offenders have a particularly high rate of recidivism. Tracking every sex offender — or even, as in Skora's case, many non-sexual offenders — is a distraction, they argue, from concentrating attention on those who are most dangerous and most likely to commit more crimes.

"We have 41,000 names on our [sex offenders] registry," said Allison Taylor, executive director of the Texas Council on Sex Offender Treatment. "If we could take our money and focus it on the 10 percent or so who are most likely to re-offend, we could make great progress."[2]

Although a Gallup Poll last year found that more Americans are "very concerned" about child molesters than violent crime in general or even terrorism, the rates of sex crimes against children have actually dropped significantly since the early 1990s.[3] What's more, such crimes are far more likely to be committed by a family member or someone else previously known to the victim than by a stranger. (*See chart, p. 65.*)

In fact, strangers are responsible for only 7 percent of reported cases of juvenile sex crimes, according to the Justice Department. Thirty-four percent are victimized by their own families, and 59 percent of cases occur among friends.[4] According to the National Center for Missing and Exploited Children, only about 115 out of 260,000 children kidnapped each year are snatched by strangers.[5]

"We're doing a disservice, essentially, with most of the legislation we're seeing right now around sex offenders," says Alisa Klein, public-policy consultant with the Association for the Treatment of Sexual Abusers. "We're creating this myth that if we just know who the identified sex offenders are, you can keep your children safe."

Some of the layers of sex-offender laws passed over the past decade do seem to conflict with each other. For instance, the recent rigid zoning restrictions are leading some sex offenders to lie about their whereabouts or to drop off law enforcement's radar entirely, undercutting the effectiveness of registration and community-notification requirements.

But once anti-sex-offender legislation comes to a vote following an emotionally charged crime, the voices of skeptics are barely heard. "Everyone knew some parts of the bill were flawed," says Republican Georgia state Rep. John Lunsford, referring to the state's new zoning restrictions passed in April, parts of which have already been found to be unconstitutional. "Once it reached the floor, you were either voting for the perverts or voting for your constituency."

Tough, new sex-offender laws tend to pass unanimously, or nearly so. If there are flaws in some of the approaches, advocates for the get-tough approach say, that is only more reason to keep working to strengthen them. If many sex offenders are slipping between the cracks, for instance, that makes it all the more necessary to ensure compliance through GPS or other methods.

Few Sex Offenders Rearrested for Sex Crimes

Less than 4 percent of the sex offenders released from prison in the U.S. in 1994 were reconvicted of a new sex crime within three years of their release. Sexual assault is considered an underreported crime, however, and actual recidivism rates may be higher than indicated below. Studies of released sex offenders over longer periods of time show greater recidivism rates.

Recidivism Measure	Percentage of Released Sex Offenders		
	Child Molesters	Rapists	Statutory Rapists
Within 3 years following release:			
Rearrested for any new sex crime	5.1%	5.0%	5.0%
Reconvicted for any new sex crime	3.5%	3.2%	3.6%

Source: "Recidivism of Sex Offenders Released From Prison in 1994," Bureau of Justice Statistics, November 2003

The new federal law makes failure to register a felony and offers states money to buy GPS systems. "We track library books better than we do sex offenders," complained Republican Florida Rep. Mark Foley, one of the bill's sponsors.[6]

And if most sex offenders are family members or other close acquaintances of children, that's still no reason not to try to protect children against violent and predatory criminals, such as the one who killed Jessica Lunsford.

"It's not about the overall rate, it's about wanting to make sure that events like this don't occur," says Lieb.

As the debate about the best way to prevent child molestation rages on, here are some of the questions people are debating:

Should sex offenders be allowed to live near children?

In May, Jim L'Etoile lost his job as director of California's Parole and Community Services Division because of his handling of sex offenders. It's not that he lost track of too many of them, or that they committed new crimes under his supervision. His mistake was placing 23 "high-risk" sex offenders — those considered most likely to commit repeat crimes — in hotels and motels within a few miles of Disneyland.

That placement showed "a total lack of common sense," says Democratic state Rep. Rudy Bermudez, a

Sex Abuse Still Haunts Catholic Church

The Rev. Francisco Xavier Ochoa, a Catholic priest in Santa Rosa, Calif., confessed to local church officials on April 28 that he had kissed a 12-year-old boy and offered him $100 to do a striptease. Ochoa also admitted to other incidents with boys elsewhere in earlier years. But in defiance of California law, church authorities failed to report Ochoa immediately to the police, instead waiting until May 1. In the meantime, Ochoa fled to Mexico.

"I made an error in judgment by waiting to report Rev. Ochoa's admissions," Bishop Daniel Walsh wrote in an August letter to parishioners. "I should have acted immediately and not delayed."

The bishop's apology didn't satisfy the Sonoma County Sheriff's Department, which recommended on Aug. 25 that criminal charges be filed against Walsh. It would be the first time a U.S. Catholic Church official faces criminal prosecution for failing to report sexual abuse.[1]

The Catholic Church has arguably been damaged more by child sex-abuse scandals than any other institution in American life. The scandal appeared to peak in 2002, when the U.S. Conference of Catholic Bishops announced a sweeping set of reform measures intended to curb abuse and protect children.[2]

Since that time, legal settlements with victims of priestly abuse have forced dioceses in Tucson, Spokane and Portland, Ore., to declare bankruptcy, while many other dioceses have sold property to pay the bills. Abuse-related church expenses peaked last year at $467 million.[3]

The 2002 reforms call for priests and other parish officials, as well as the laity and children, to undergo regular training in spotting and preventing sexual abuse of children. The program includes educational videos, workshops and the development of a common language and policy for confronting people whose behavior is questionable, such as saying, "It's parish policy not to give long, lingering hugs to small children."

These efforts are subject to regular audits, and "the church urges that anyone who has been abused by a priest or deacon or person of authority report the abuse immediately and that the person be removed from their position," says Sister Mary Ann Walsh, spokeswoman for the bishops' conference.

"The church has addressed the problem very aggressively," she said. "We're horrified by it."

But critics of the church complain that Catholic leaders, while paying lip service to the problem, have failed to live up to their own promises. "The gap between what the bishops say publicly and what they do privately has never been greater," says David Clohessy, national director of the Survivor Network of Those Abused by Priests. "The reforms they've adopted since 2002 are essentially like speed limits, but no cops."

Several recent incidents suggest the church has not learned from the earlier round of scandals, in which its leadership allowed known molesters to continue working with children. In Chicago, the Rev. Daniel McCormack was allowed to continue in his ministry for four months after allegations surfaced that he had abused three boys. After a stinging audit, Cardinal Francis George said in March that he was "most truly sorry . . . for the tragedy of allowing children to be in the presence of a priest against whom a current accusation of sexual abuse has been made."[4]

That same week, New Hampshire's attorney general released an audit saying the church had failed to make sure

former parole officer. "When you place high-risk sex offenders where children are, you're almost violating the laws by putting children in harm's way."

Communities around the country don't want sex offenders living anywhere near children. They may not have attractions as glamorous as Disneyland, but 17 states and dozens, if not hundreds, of local governments have banned registered sex offenders from living near public places where children can be expected to gather, such as schools.

"I've had folks say, 'I don't want them anywhere in my town,' " says Charles Olney, a researcher at the U.S. Department of Justice's Center for Sex Offender Management. "Everyone wants these folks somewhere else."

As Democratic Miami Beach Mayor David Dermer puts it, "If you have a child, do you want a registered sex offender living next to you? Do you feel comfortable with that?"

His city passed an ordinance last year to block sex offenders from living within 2,500 feet of any school,

all those who work with children pass criminal background checks. To get the state to agree to drop a criminal investigation, the church had to agree to conduct the background checks. And the church has lobbied hard against legislation in several states to extend the statute of limitations for bringing sex-abuse complaints.[5]

Even the National Review Board, a lay committee created in 2002 to investigate sex abuse, has sharply criticized church leaders. The board's chairman, a former governor, compared bishops to the mafia, while a former leader said the bishops had "manipulated" the group and had been far from forthcoming.[6]

At the local level, church officials say that the new policies and education programs are starting to take root. "I don't tend to use superlatives very often, but I think this is a program that is going to change lives," says Helen Osman, communications director for the diocese of Austin, describing the church's education efforts for children. "As far as sexual abuse, no one has reported anything to us."

Former Los Angeles Catholic priest Michael Wempe, right, was sentenced in May to three years in prison for child abuse.

AP Photo/Nick Ut

Meanwhile, critics charge that the bishops remain impervious to outside oversight, relying too heavily on self-audits by dioceses to ensure compliance with the church's own rules and legal settlements, such as the one in New Hampshire that required thorough background checks.

"As long as there is that structure, with no checks and balances," says Clohessy, "with no oversight and no consequences for wrongdoing, there will continue to be sex crimes and cover-ups."

---

[1] John Cote, "Catholic Bishop May Face Jail," *San Francisco Chronicle*, Aug. 26, 2006, p. B1.

[2] For background, see Kenneth Jost, "Sexual Abuse and the Clergy," *CQ Researcher*, May 3, 2002, pp. 393-416.

[3] Rachel Zoll, "Costs Soar as Clergy Sex Abuse Cases Rise," Associated Press, March 31, 2006.

[4] T.R. Reid, "Catholic Leaders Fight Legislation on Suits," *The Washington Post*, April 1, 2006, p. A10.

[5] *Ibid.*

[6] Joe Feuerhard, "Review Board Head Charges Bishops 'Manipulated' Sex Abuse Panel and Withheld Information," *National Catholic Reporter Online*, May 11, 2004.

---

public bus stop, day-care center, park "or other place where children regularly congregate." For all practical purposes, no sex criminals can live anywhere in the city. "The whole city is basically covered by this," Dermer says. "As far as I'm concerned, it worked well."

Others worry that so-called proximity restrictions amount to an unfair extra dose of punishment brought against offenders who already have served their sentences. A federal judge has blocked a portion of Georgia's law, finding it unconstitutional to force sex offenders to

move — even if the crimes they committed occurred many years earlier — when school bus stops are rerouted close to their homes.

Because of such concerns, 11 of the 17 states with proximity laws offer exemptions to those who lived within the buffer zones before the new laws were passed, according to Wayne A. Logan, a law professor at the College of William and Mary.

Even critics of the residency restrictions agree that convicted sex offenders should not be allowed to work in jobs, such as teaching, that would bring them into close proximity with children. It's dangerous when predators are able to establish relationships with children and build a level of trust that they can exploit. Most sex crimes, after all, are perpetrated by someone known to the victim. (*See chart, p. 65.*)

But offenders' ability to establish such relationships has nothing to do with where they live, critics of the restrictions say. Criminals don't have to live near arcades or playgrounds to visit them. "Schools, parks and playgrounds aren't a factor in most sex-abuse cases," says Jill S. Levenson, a human-services professor and researcher at Lynn University, in Fort Lauderdale, Fla., who has coauthored studies of sex-offender residency restrictions.

"It sounds good in theory," Levenson continues, "but the big problem with residency restrictions, aside from the fact that there's no evidence that they work, is that they push sex offenders from cities into rural areas so they're more difficult to track and monitor and are farther from social services and psychiatric services." Those are factors associated with increased recidivism, not lower recidivism, Levenson says.

"When you ostracize these individuals, they're taken away from social-network support, job opportunities and family," says Logan, who is preparing a book on offender-registration laws. In one instance, 21 sex offenders wound up grouped together in a cheap motel outside of Cedar Rapids, Iowa, because they had been, in effect, banished from within the city limits.[7] The fact that some sex offenders are being forced either into homelessness or into living arrangements with their ostracized peers may make them less likely to stay on the straight-and-narrow.

"Yes, it's an inconvenience — some folks will have to move," said Republican state Rep. Jerry Keen, majority leader of the Georgia House and sponsor of the state's proximity law. "But if you weigh that argument against the overall impact, which is the safety of children, most folks would agree this is a good thing."[8]

The foundation for residency restrictions on sex offenders was laid more than a decade ago, in 1994, when Congress required states to compel convicted sex offenders to register their addresses with local police. The requirement helped parole and probation officers supervise and monitor their charges. Two years later, "Megan's

Law" required communities to provide citizens with information on sex offenders in their midst. The law was named in honor of Megan Kanka, a 7-year-old New Jersey child raped and murdered in 1994 by a convicted sex offender who lived across the street, Jesse Timmendequas.

But some critics of the proximity laws — including some prosecutors and law-enforcement officials — are now worried that the buffer-zone approach also may erode the effectiveness of the registry and community-notification requirements. If it becomes too difficult for sex offenders to find an affordable place to live, they may change residences without notifying authorities, register false addresses or simply disappear, making it harder for law enforcement to do its job.

In Chicago, for example, more than 75 percent of the addresses given by 81 sex offenders were found to be bogus.[9] In Iowa, the number of sex offenders who are unaccounted for on the state's list of 6,000 offenders has doubled since a statewide residence law took effect last September.[10] "The truth is that we're starting to lose people," said Don Vrotsos, chief deputy of the Dubuque County sheriff's office.[11] The Iowa County Attorneys Association has called for a repeal of the banishment law.

"You have to be very careful with those sorts of laws because we don't know if they're going to help, and they may hurt," says Carlos Cuevas, an assistant professor at Northeastern University's College of Criminal Justice.

Should sex offenders receive harsher punishments?

James Jenkins says he's "all for castration for certain sex offenders. It would do a lot to prevent recidivism and [reduce] the amount of money we have to spend on treatment centers."

Jenkins should know. He was sent to a sex-offender treatment center after he molested three young girls. Before being sent to the institution, Jenkins castrated himself with a razor. "Castration has done precisely what I wanted it to do," Jenkins said. "I have not had any sexual urges or desires in over two years. My mind is finally free of the deviant sexual fantasies I used to have about young girls."[12]

Eight states allow either for chemical or surgical castration. It's one sign among many that over the past decade states and local communities have decided they need to toughen their laws against sex offenders.

In the wake of the community-notification requirements passed a decade ago, nearly half the states now have passed versions of Jessica's Law, which requires more aggressive tracking of sex offenders through use of GPS (global positioning system) technology.

"You see the continual need for more pieces of the pie — tougher law enforcement and greater community awareness," says Rumenap, of Stop Child Predators. "We need to keep our children safe."

Anti-sex-offender laws rarely encounter much political resistance. Both houses of the Washington state legislature, for instance, earlier this year passed mandatory 25-year prison sentences for some sex offenders without a dissenting vote.

"In Oklahoma, we have no sympathy for those who would harm our children. We've increased penalties across the board for all forms of sex abuse against children," says Democratic Gov. Brad Henry, who signed a law in June imposing the death penalty on certain repeat offenders who have abused children.

Oklahoma became the fifth state to impose the death penalty for sex crimes against children. (South Carolina had enacted its law one day earlier.)

The U.S. Supreme Court ruled in 1977 that the death penalty was disproportionate in cases involving the rape of adults, and thus amounted to "cruel and unusual punishment," which is banned by the Eighth Amendment. The court has not ruled on a death-penalty case involving an offense against a child.[13]

Lieb, of the Washington State Institute for Public Policy, says the new laws serve an important purpose — not just by imposing harsher sentences but in raising public awareness about sex crimes. "Personally, I think it's a very valuable change in our society. It's recognition of the harm," she says. "There's no doubt, looking at sex offenders who have committed horrific crimes and gotten out, the thing you would most wish for is that they got a longer sentence."

Most Victims Know Their Attacker

The vast majority of sexual-assault victims are attacked by family members or acquaintances, not strangers.

Offenders (by percentage)

Victim Age	Family Member	Acquaintance	Stranger
All Victims	26.7%	59.6%	13.8%
Juveniles	34.2	58.7	7.0
0-5 years old	48.6	48.3	3.1
6-11	42.4	52.9	4.7
12-17	24.3	66.0	9.8
Adults			
18-24	9.8	66.5	23.7
24+	12.8	57.1	30.1

Source: "Sexual Assault of Young Children as Reported to Law Enforcement: Victim, Incident, and Offender Characteristics," Bureau of Justice Statistics, U.S. Department of Justice, July 2000

But Lieb questions laws that raise the level of punishment for sex offenses above those for murder, as in Washington. "There's been research that shows if you set mandatory sentences too high, then prosecutors won't file those charges, and judges and juries won't convict," she says.

It's not only a question of whether the legal system will apply the most rigorous penalties, says R. Karl Hanson, a psychologist and a corrections researcher with Public Safety and Emergency Preparedness Canada, that country's main public safety agency. Victims invariably find the court process a challenge, he says, and they are sometimes especially reluctant to press charges when the perpetrator is a relative or someone known to them, as is the case more often than not. Studies from the 1990s showed that 73 percent of molestation victims don't report the crime if the perpetrator is a relative or step-parent, while 70 percent don't report an acquaintance.[14] Children sometimes fear further harm as a result of reporting.

"The consequences may be harsher than the victim wants," Hanson says. "Many victims of sexual assault don't necessarily want a big punishment — they just want it to stop. Sometimes they're afraid to disclose the crime because it's their uncle who will have to go away forever."

President George W. Bush shakes hands with John Walsh after signing the Adam Walsh Child Protection and Safety Act on July 27; Mrs. Walsh is at left. Six-year-old Adam was murdered in 1981 after being abducted from a suburban shopping mall in Florida. John Walsh later became host of "America's Most Wanted" and a leader in the push for victims' rights.

Becky Rogers Martin, a Republican state representative in South Carolina, also has concerns that police and prosecutors may not enforce laws that they don't believe fit the crime. "Lots of times we'll put in real strict penalties so that even if they're cut down they'll still serve real time," she says. "But our concern was that if we made it so strict, they wouldn't take it seriously."

Others warn that longer sentences or even the death penalty won't act as a successful deterrent to crime. "People think it's effective because they confuse deterrence with retribution," says Murray A. Straus, a sociologist at the University of New Hampshire. "That doesn't mean that punishment never works as a deterrent. It does — but it has a very high failure rate."

"Offenders are going to become more aware that society doesn't want to deal with them on the street," says Christopher J. Murphy, deputy chief of the adult probation and parole department in Montgomery County, Pa. "But the majority of sex offenders that I've dealt with didn't think they were going to be caught to begin with."

Many criminologists also are concerned that contemporary laws dealing with sex offenders often lump them together broadly as a group. In some cases, men who were teenagers when found guilty of statutory rape may be subjected to the same kinds of living restrictions and community-notification requirements as older men who repeatedly molested young children. Even putting aside the question of fairness, they say, this amounts to a wasteful dilution of effort. Keeping track of hundreds of sex offenders is hard.

"We tend to put all sex offenders under one umbrella, and these laws are applied to them equally," says Terry, of the John Jay College of Criminal Justice.

"We often apply the resources to the punishment rather than to the treatment," she continues. "Personally, I think that there should be more of a focus on treatment."

Can sex offenders be rehabilitated?

Many of the most disturbing violations of children in recent times have been perpetrated by repeat offenders. The suspect in the case of Jessica Lunsford, the Florida girl whose kidnap, rape and murder has prompted half the states to pass stricter tracking requirements, is a previously convicted sex offender who had failed to register with police.

The idea that someone could molest children and then be set free to commit the same crime again — or an even more violent crime — is a central motivation behind the current push toward more stringent punishments and tracking.

"The problem with this type of crime is that the rate of recidivism is high," contends Rumenap, of Stop Child Predators.

Referring to "To Catch a Predator," the NBC "Dateline" series that investigates men who use the Internet to troll for minors, Rumenap says, "That show has been on five or six times, and they're getting some of the same sex offenders showing up time and again."

Determining the true rate of recidivism among sex offenders, though, is one of the most contentious points within the policy debate surrounding the issue. Some studies indicate that rates of recidivism among sex offenders are actually lower than for people who commit other violent crimes or property crimes.

A study by the Justice Department's Bureau of Justice Statistics found that only 5.3 percent of sex offenders (defined as men who had committed rape or sexual assault) were rearrested for another sex crime within three years after their release from prison in 15 states. That was far below the 68 percent rearrest rate for non-sex offenders, 25 percent of whom were resentenced to prison for new crimes.[5]

A broader and widely cited Canadian study found that within five years of release 14 percent of sex offenders were brought up on new charges for a sexual offense. After 20 years of release, 73 percent of sex offenders had not been charged with another sexual offense.[16]

"It's hard to argue that all sex offenders will inevitably re-offend," says psychologist Hanson, coauthor of the Canadian study. "On average, the overall recidivism rate is lower than for general offenders, but they are more at risk for committing new sex offenses."

Ernie Allen, president of the National Center for Missing and Exploited Children, disputes the idea that recidivism studies prove that sex offenders are relatively unlikely to strike again. Just because they aren't brought up again on charges doesn't mean they haven't perpetrated more crimes, he argues.

"Recidivism research measures crimes reported to law enforcement that result in arrest and conviction," Allen writes. "But according to the Justice Department, crimes against children are the most underreported of all crimes. Researchers estimate that one-in-five girls and one-in-10 boys will be sexually victimized in some way before they reach adulthood. Yet only one-in-three will tell anybody about it."[17]

Even those who believe that most sex offenders are unlikely to strike again concede that such criminals will never entirely shed their destructive impulses. But they say that the behavior of many sex offenders can be managed, just as incurable diseases such as diabetes can be managed.

"We don't talk about it in terms of a cure," says Levenson, of the Center for Offender Rehabilitation and Education. "Some may always be attracted to children, but they can certainly learn to control that and not act on it."

Many Victims Are Under Age 6

One of every seven victims of sexual assault (14 percent) reported to law-enforcement agencies was under age 6, and more than a third of all victims were under 12.

Ages of Sexual-Assault Victims
(1991-1996)

Victim Age	All Sexual Assault	Forcible Rape	Forcible Sodomy	Sexual Assault With Object	Forcible Fondling
0-5	14.0%	4.3%	24.0%	26.5%	20.2%
6-11	20.1	8.0	30.8	23.2	29.3
12-17	32.8	33.5	24.0	25.5	34.3
18-24	14.2	22.6	8.7	9.7	7.7
25-34	11.5	19.6	7.5	8.3	5.0
34+	7.4	12.0	5.1	6.8	3.5

Source: "Sexual Assault of Young Children as Reported to Law Enforcement: Victim, Incident, and Offender Characteristics," Bureau of Justice Statistics, U.S. Department of Justice, July 2000

Hanson says crunching the data from 17 different studies about sex-offender management shows a five-year recidivism rate of 10 percent for those who had undergone some form of treatment, compared with a 17 percent rate for those who hadn't. "The evidence suggests that those offenders who go to treatment are less likely to re-offend than those who don't," he says. "That may be partly because the more cooperative offenders are more likely to go."

Trying to sort out which criminals are going to be more compliant is just one of the tricks involved in successful sex-offender management. Criminologists say that sex offenders are more heterogeneous than other types of violent criminals, with a wider range of age and education.

They also vary widely in terms of their tendencies toward violence. For that reason, management programs need to be tailored to take into account particular offending patterns and proclivities. A program that works for a middle-aged offender, for instance, won't work for a teenager.

"If you have sex offender-specific treatment, it can work, for those offenders who want to take advantage of it," says Murphy, the Pennsylvania probation official. "Unfortunately, you don't know which ones are which."

BACKGROUND

Cycles of Concern

Throughout the 20th century, the legal and political response to sex offenders has evolved through a series of cycles. At certain junctures, horrific crimes have sparked stepped-up efforts to combat the problem. Over time, however, as tensions ease, more liberal approaches come into fashion, such as a greater focus on rehabilitation. But then some new and shocking event shakes society's complacency, and tougher laws again sweep the land.

A series of "Jack the Ripper" serial-murder cases in several states drew public attention during the early 1900s, some of which involved child molestation. The killings led to a widespread belief that sex crimes were perpetrated by a deviant person from outside the community. "It is always the crime of a mentally unbalanced, feeble-minded person," editorialized *The New York Times* in 1915. "Moral degenerates are easily discoverable without waiting until acts of violence put them in the category of harming children."[18]

Reflecting such concerns, police began to investigate men with suspicious collections of photographs of children, believing they might mark a potential "ripper." And most states between 1905 and 1915 passed new laws for sex offenders that imposed open-ended sentences. By 1921, New York state permitted offenders considered mentally defective to be imprisoned for life (overseen by a doctor rather than a warden), regardless of whether they had been convicted of a crime.

"Failure to require actual conviction on a specific charge reflected the therapeutic assumption that no real harm could come from merely being diagnosed and treated medically, and the social assumption that merely being charged demonstrated that a person was a troublemaker of some kind," writes Philip Jenkins, a historian and religious-studies professor at Pennsylvania State University, in his 1998 book *Moral Panic*.[19]

The twin mixing of civil and criminal penalties and penology with treatment would remain the legal model for decades. The social and political climate shifted during the 1920s, however, and by the end of the decade charges of offenses against morality and chastity had plummeted. Police and the media turned their attention to Prohibition and the culture of gangsters, while a National Commission on Law Observance and Enforcement barely mentioned sex crimes in its 1931 report on pressing criminal-justice issues.

The period's relative quiet was disturbed by the 1934 apprehension of Albert Fish, who was charged with the murder, mutilation and cannibalism of Grace Budd, a 12-year-old from White Plains, N.Y. Fish had experimented with numerous perverse activities, which he recorded in his diaries. His shocking trial exposed the public to the outer reaches of sexual deviancy, engendering the sense that dangerous perverts were on the loose and waiting to strike. Fish's execution preceded by three months that of Bruno Hauptmann, who had kidnapped and killed the infant son of aviation pioneer Charles Lindbergh. Their stories often jostled for space on the front pages of the nation's newspapers and "may have encouraged readers to see the generalized danger to children in sexually explicit terms," Jenkins writes.[20]

The Fish case and several other notorious crimes over the next decade put sex offenders squarely back on the radar of both media and law enforcement. In the years following World War II, 15 states established commissions to study the problem. In a widely quoted article — "How Safe Is Your Daughter?" — FBI Director J. Edgar Hoover asserted, "The most rapidly increasing type of crime is perpetrated by degenerate sex offenders," and his agency distributed posters urging children to be wary of strangers and not to accept rides from them.[21] A third of Americans surveyed agreed with the proposition that "prison is too good for sex criminals. They should be publicly whipped or worse."[22]

More than half the states passed so-called sexual-psychopath statutes allowing dangerous offenders to be held for treatment for indeterminate periods (the Pennsylvania statute authorized a sentence of "one day to life").[23] "The sexual psychopath gets locked up, and that's the end of it," said a Wisconsin administrator.[24] The statutes assumed that psychopaths were compulsive and would progress naturally from one type of crime to something worse, so they were broadly defined. Swept into the dragnet were not just rapists and molesters but also those charged with "public masturbation (without indecent exposure)"; "the following of a white female by a Negro"; and "a non-aggressive homosexual convicted of passing bad checks."[25]

CHRONOLOGY

1940s–1970s *Ineffective civil-commitment statutes lead to a backlash against tough sex-offender laws.*

1949 During "horror week" in November, three young girls across the country are raped and murdered or left to die. In response, 15 states establish commissions to study the sex-offender problem.

1955 After nearly 20 states pass laws allowing sexual-psychopaths to be held indefinitely, the population of state mental hospitals reaches 550,000, more than double the total 25 years earlier.

1974 Congress passes the Child Abuse Prevention and Treatment Act, mandating the reporting and investigation of abuse allegations.

1975 U.S. Supreme Court rules there is no constitutional basis for confining mental patients unless they present an immediate danger to themselves or their communities.

1980s–1990s *Sex crimes, particularly those against children, re-emerge as a major legislative concern.*

1981 Two members of Congress are accused of having sex with teenage congressional pages.

1982 Wayne B. Williams is convicted for two out of a string of 23 murders of children that shocked Atlanta from 1979 to 1981.

1990 Washington state passes a law that becomes a model for other states, requiring dangerous sex offenders to register with police and reopening the possibility of civil commitment following prison sentences. . . . After six years of criminal trials in California, there are no convictions in the McMartin preschool case, in which a teacher and administrator had been accused of ritual sex abuse involving hundreds of children despite a lack of physical evidence.

1992 The number of reported child sex-abuse cases peaks at about 150,000.

1993 Polly Klaas and Jacob Wetterling, pre-teens who were abducted and either killed or presumed dead, spark massive public interest, leading to the pictures of missing children appearing on milk cartons and further legislation against sex offenders.

1994 As part of a larger crime bill, Congress passes the Jacob Wetterling Act, requiring sex offenders to register their whereabouts with police. . . . New Jersey becomes the first state to pass "Megan's Law," requiring community notification when a sex offender lives in the area; it honors murdered 7-year-old Megan Kanka.

1996 Congress passes a federal version of Megan's Law requiring all states to enact sex-offender registries or forfeit law-enforcement grants. . . . California requires chemical castration of offenders twice convicted of child molestation. . . . JonBenet Ramsey, a 6-year-old beauty queen, is found murdered and sexually assaulted in her home in Boulder, Colo., on Dec. 26.

2000s *Congress and the states crack down further on sex offenders, despite declining rates of such crimes.*

2002 Bringing a year of scandal to a close, the U.S. Conference of Catholic Bishops adopts sweeping new sex-abuse prevention policies that mandate education in each diocese and call for tougher action against priests accused of pedophilia or other sex offenses involving children.

2005 Jessica Lunsford, a 9-year-old Florida girl, is abducted, sexually assaulted and buried alive. In response, two-dozen states enact "Jessica's Law," requiring stricter tracking of convicted sex offenders. . . . In all, states pass more than 100 new sex-offender laws, the most ever in a given year.

2006 U.S. marshals lead a 27-state dragnet from April 17-23 that nabs 1,102 wanted sex offenders. . . . On June 9 Oklahoma becomes the fifth state to approve the death penalty for sex offenders. . . . A U.S. district judge rules on June 29 that portions of Georgia's residence-restriction law, passed in April, are unconstitutional. . . . President Bush on Aug. 27 signs the Adam Walsh Act, requiring sex offenders to provide DNA samples and states to maintain offender registries on the Internet and impose criminal penalties for offenders who fail to register. . . . On Nov. 7 California voters are expected to approve a strict version of Jessica's Law, imposing mandatory minimum sentences on convicted sex offenders.

Online Predators Worry Experts

Kids who spent this past summer camping at Island Lake in Starrucca, Pa., were encouraged to write about their experiences online but not to say exactly where they were. Camp officials were worried about Internet sex predators.

Many camps have banned the use of their names or logos from Web pages and blogs set up by campers. Some even ban digital cameras from their grounds. "The information that kids share today often is personal and private information that allows predators to track them down," said Peg Smith, chief executive officer of the American Camp Association.[1]

Of course, children and youth don't have to go away to camp to make their presence known on the Internet. Social-networking sites such as MySpace and Facebook have loads of information about millions of children and youths — their names, their photographs, their diaries and pet peeves and favorite songs — even their eating habits and relative tendency to motion sickness.[2]

All of that is rich material for sex predators, who typically try to "groom" potential victims by getting to know them and building up trusting relationships. "The social-networking sites have become, in a sense, a happy hunting ground for child predators," says Rep. Michael G. Fitzpatrick, R-Pa.

Fitzpatrick's Deleting Online Predators Act passed the House, 410-15, on July 26.[3] The bill would ban access to chat rooms and a variety of online forums in public schools and libraries. Some groups, such as the American Library Association, say that it could have the effect of blocking students from finding information on legitimate sites, such as Yahoo, that host legitimate social forums.

Congress has tried for years to fashion laws that would protect children from the perils of the Internet. The Communications Decency Act of 1996 made it a crime to transmit "patently offensive" material over the Internet in a way that would be accessible to minors. The Supreme Court struck the law down the next year on free-speech grounds, however.

But the court in 2003 upheld the Children's Internet Protection Act of 2000, which requires libraries that accept federal funds to install anti-pornography filtering software. "The interest in protecting young library users from material inappropriate for minors is legitimate," Justice Anthony Kennedy wrote.[4]

Justice Department officials have grown particularly concerned about Internet pornography because, says a senior counsel at the Department of Justice, "the price of admission" for access to some pornography sites may be images of child sex abuse that in many cases may be

No Constitutional Basis

Although sexual-psychopath laws continued to be passed into the 1960s, they drew increasing criticism for being overly broad and for violating ordinary rules of due process. A consultant for New Jersey's sex-offender commission said that prosecutors came to view them "merely as a useful tool to be employed or avoided in accordance with their own convenience."[26]

Sexual-psychopath laws soon became completely ineffective or were nullified in most of the states that had passed them. (Only about 200 offenders a year were committed annually by the end of the 1950s.[27]) Sociologist Edwin H. Sutherland wrote in 1950, "The concept of the 'sexual psychopath' is so vague that . . . the states which have enacted such laws make little or no use of them."[28]

In a backlash against the earlier panic, judges and legislators during the 1960s and early '70s sharply curtailed forced civil commitments and indeterminate sentencing for several psychopaths. Many media accounts of sex crimes turned their focus to miscarriages of justice or racial bias.

This shift in attitudes was exemplified by sociologists who began to claim that rape was an overreported phenomenon and that women seldom resisted their assailants, instead filing complaints only after they'd been jilted or abandoned. And the professional literature of the era also downplayed the damaging effects of molestation on children. "In every way," Jenkins writes, "scholarship of this era presented the plight of the abuse victim in language that seems stunningly callous to modern ears."[29]

The courts began to afford more protection to defendants. In the famous *Miranda* case, which involved a sex

homemade — suggesting that "mere possession of child porn may indicate a dangerous person."

Internet companies had resisted calls from the Bush administration that they share more information about their users with law-enforcement agencies, citing privacy concerns. But five leading Internet service providers, including AOL, Yahoo and Microsoft, announced in June that they will jointly build a database of child-pornography images and develop tools to help law enforcement prevent their distribution.[5]

A large percentage of those who possess illicit images of children, says the Justice official, who asked not to be named, may actually be offenders or contact children. "The Internet is a wonderful connector," he says, "but it brings dark alleys and dangerous places into your home, putting deviants together with their prospective victims."

As part of its Project Safe Childhood initiative, the Justice Department has stepped up its investigation and coordination of "enticement cases" in which predators contact children through the Internet and arrange to meet with them in person. NBC has broadcast an occasional series called "To Catch a Predator" that has resulted in nearly 100 arrests.[6]

According to a study released last month by the University of New Hampshire's Crimes Against Children Research Center, about 13 percent of children ages 10 to 17 have been solicited online for sexual activity or conversations. That was down from a total of 19 percent five years earlier. Researchers attributed the drop to warnings and education campaigns.

But "the most serious kinds of sexual solicitations, those in which solicitors make offline contact with young children, did not decline."[7]

Larry D. Rosen, a psychologist at California State University-Dominguez Hills and an expert on Internet socializing, says that sites such as MySpace are not "inherently scary or dangerous," but can, in fact, be healthy ways for teens to develop a sense of community and their own identity.

The major issue he found in a recent study is that "parents simply ignore their children's activities on MySpace. This is particularly striking, given that through the media parents are convinced that MySpace is ripe with sexual predators."[8]

[1] Pam Belluck, "Young People's Web Postings Worry Summer Camp Directors," *The New York Times*, June 22, 2006, p. A16.

[2] For background, see Marcia Clemmitt, "Cyber Socializing," *CQ Researcher*, July 28, 2006, pp. 625-648.

[3] Kathryn A. Wolfe, "Minors' Use of Social Web Sites at Schools and Libraries Targeted," *CQ Weekly*, July 31, 2006, p. 2125.

[4] Jan Crawford Greenburg, "Justices Back Porn Filters at Libraries," *Chicago Tribune*, June 24, 2003, p. 1.

[5] The Associated Press, "Internet Firms to Step Up Child-Porn Fight," *Los Angeles Times*, June 27, 2006, p. C7.

[6] Julia Rawe, "How Safe is MySpace?" *Time*, July 3, 2006, p. 34.

[7] "Youth Online Exposed to More Porn But Fewer Sexual Solicitations, According to New Study," University of New Hampshire press release, Aug. 9, 2006.

[8] Larry D. Rosen, "Adolescents in MySpace: Identity Formation, Friendship and Sexual Predators," June 2006; www.csudh.edu/psych/Adolescents%20in%20MySpace%20-%20Executive%20Summary.pdf.

offender, the Supreme Court found in 1966 that police had to respect the due-process rights of defendants or forfeit evidence they'd acquired. In subsequent years, courts rejected indeterminate sentencing, the confinement of mental patients who posed no immediate danger to themselves or others and sexual-psychopath statutes that set an impossibly high bar for release.

Mandatory Reporting

But even as the courts were reflecting the notion that child molestation was not a significant problem, the broader societal pendulum was once again swinging back toward fear about the issue. The feminist movement joined with conservatives to draw attention to problems of rape, incest and child abuse, generating renewed media interest and prompting legislative action. In 1974, Congress passed the Child Abuse Prevention and Treatment Act, which mandated the reporting and investigation of abuse allegations and provided matching funds to states that identified abused children and prosecuted abusers. This led to the creation of an infrastructure of agencies, both public and private, devoted to investigating mistreatment.

The advent of mandated reporting swelled abuse statistics. States began to ease physical-evidence requirements, and the number of reported rapes — which had been 22,467 in 1965 — quadrupled to more than 100,000 by 1990.[30] The media also began to report that huge numbers of children — as many as 100,000 — were caught up in pornography rings. Although the figures were largely uncorroborated, increased attention to child pornography and abuse meant that actual incidents were more likely to be reported, which in turn stimulated further investigation and legislation. Sex-abuse claims

AP Photo

Twelve-year-old Polly Klaas was murdered after being kidnapped at knife-point from her home in Petaluma, Calif., by Richard Allen Davis, who is now awaiting execution at San Quentin Prison.

AP Photo/Nick Ut

Peggy McMartin Buckey was cleared in the infamous McMartin preschool case in 1990 after testimony indicated false allegations of an abusive sex ring at the Los Angeles school had been the result of inappropriate coaching of witnesses by police and social workers.

increased by a factor of 18 between 1976 and 1985, while various surveys indicated that upwards of 20 percent of Americans had been sexually abused as children.

States throughout the 1980s made it easier for children to testify in abuse cases, lifting the obligation that victims — or survivors, as they were becoming known — had to face defendants against whom they were testifying. In a series of rulings in the early 1990s, the Supreme Court made clear that it would favor child protection over established constitutional assumptions about the rights of defendants. In 1992, the court ruled that hearsay testimony offered by doctors, police or family could be offered in lieu of forcing a child to testify.[31]

Studies of treatment programs conducted in the 1970s and '80s found no evidence of reduced recidivism. But therapists and others dealing with sex offenders made important strides during the 1980s, developing cognitive-behavioral therapy programs and relapse training. "Offenders were finally trained to recognize and manage their fantasies and behavior that could not be cured," writes Terry, of the John Jay College of Criminal Justice.[32] In the 1990s, the use of polygraphs also strengthened sex-offender management, offering insights into offenders' honesty (or lack thereof) about their behavior between sessions.

However, shocking cases garnered much more public attention than rehabilitation methods. In the infamous McMartin preschool case in Manhattan Beach, Calif., sensational allegations of satanic sex rituals at the school ultimately proved false. As the case dragged on throughout the 1980s, it became clear that the allegations had been the result of inappropriate coaching of testimony by police and social workers after initial complaints had been brought by a delusional woman. Fear of satanic and ritual sex rings led to other instances in which children who had been coached began, as with the Salem witch trials of the 17th century, to direct charges against investigators once they ran out of other adults they could plausibly accuse.[33] (The validity of repressed or "recovered" memories of abuse that emerged under therapeutic intervention also came into question.[34])

"Part of the problem is that you had really little kids — 3, 4 and 5 years old — and people interviewing them who had almost no awareness of children's suggestibility," says John E.B. Myers, director of the criminal-justice program at the University of the Pacific's McGeorge School of Law.

But other cases were real enough and again focused attention on "stranger danger." In 1989, Earl K. Shriner assaulted and mutilated a 7-year-old boy in Washington state. Shriner had a long criminal record and, while in prison, had designed a van he intended to use for abducting, torturing and killing children. After it became clear that authorities had released an offender who clearly meant to do more harm, the legislature, under enormous pressure to act, in 1990 required dangerous sex offenders to register with police. The law also allowed the state to detain an offender past his release date pending a hearing on civil commitment. (As a *New York Times* headline explained, "Strategy on Sex Crimes Is Prison, Then Prison."[35])

The Washington law drew questions about its constitutionality but nonetheless became a model for at least 16 other state laws, as well as federal legislation enacted in 1994. Before 1994, only five states required sex offenders to register their addresses.

That year, 7-year-old Megan Kanka was raped and strangled. Within weeks, the New Jersey legislature had passed a statute modeled on Washington state's, with the added requirement that police notify neighbors and schools about high-risk offenders in their community. "Megan's Law" had been passed in 35 other states by the time Congress enacted its version in 1996.

CURRENT SITUATION

New Legislation

The pace of sex-offender legislation has never been quicker than it is today. In 2005, 45 states passed more than 150 sex-offender laws, according to the National Conference of State Legislatures. That was the most ever passed in a single year and twice the amount of legislation in 2004.

States have kept up the pace, joined by federal lawmakers. Congress this summer passed the Adam Walsh Child

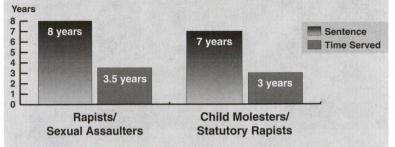

Average Molester Serves Three Years

Convicted child molesters who were released from prison in 1994 were sentenced to about seven years in prison, on average, but served an average of about three years. Rapists and sexual assaulters served slightly longer before release.

Note; The data are based on 9,691 rapists and 4,295 molesters released in 1994 in 15 states (Ariz., Calif., Del., Fla., Ill., Md., Mich., Minn., N.J., N.Y., N.C., Ohio, Ore., Texas, Va.)

Source: "Recidivism of Sex Offenders Released From Prison in 1994," Bureau of Justice Statistics, November 2003

Protection and Safety Act, requiring states to maintain publicly accessible offender registries on the Internet, in effect creating a national registry. The new law also requires that sex offenders provide DNA samples and be subject to more frequent in-person verification of their homes and workplaces. Offenders who don't register or update their information are subject to 10-year prison terms, and those who commit violent crimes while registered face five-year minimum sentences. The law also imposes a 30-year minimum sentence for those who have sex with a child younger than 12.[36]

President Bush signed the bill into law on July 27, the 25th anniversary of the murder of the 6-year-old boy, who was abducted while shopping with his mother in Hollywood, Fla. His killer has never been found. Adam was the son of John Walsh, who became a victims'-rights advocate and host of the TV show "America's Most Wanted." "This may be the toughest piece of child-protection legislation in 25 years," Walsh said.

The U.S. Department of Justice has also made fighting sex offenders a top priority. The Adam Walsh Act authorized the department's Project Safe Childhood program, launched earlier this year, which seeks to combat Internet predators by providing grants to states and

operation "targeted the worst of the worst," said U.S. Attorney General Alberto R. Gonzales.[37]

At the state level, the signature sex-offender law of the last two years is Jessica's Law, after Jessica Lunsford, a 9-year-old Florida girl who was abducted, raped and buried alive in 2005. Two-dozen states have passed versions of Jessica's Law, which generally imposes mandatory minimum sentences of 25 years on some categories of offenders and requires those who have committed specific sex crimes to wear satellite-tracking devices for life.

California voters are expected to overwhelmingly pass a strict version of Jessica's Law in November. In addition to a minimum-sentencing requirement (25 years for child rapists) and satellite tracking, the measure would bar offenders from living within 2,000 feet of schools and increase prison terms for a variety of crimes, including possession of child pornography and Internet luring.

A Florida State University study released this year of more than 75,000 offenders placed on home confinement found that those who were tracked by GPS were 90 percent less likely to abscond or re-offend, compared with those who were not electronically monitored.[38]

"We will not mess around with those who mess with our children," Gov. Arnold Schwarzenegger, R-Calif., said in June. "We will find them. We will put them in jail. And we will keep them there."[39] Schwarzenegger's opponent for re-election, Democratic state Treasurer Phil Angelides, has also endorsed the initiative.

The California Legislative Analyst's Office has estimated that Jessica's Law could cost the state $200 million annually after 10 years because of the cost of electronic monitoring and extra parole officers. "It costs an awful lot of money, and it's going to have virtually no effect," said Ron Kokish, a spokesman for the California Coalition on Sexual Offending, a group of treatment providers, public defenders and probation officers.[40]

Such groups have had a hard time getting heard in most legislative debates. In Prince George's County, Md., the public-defender's office lobbied against state legislation requiring GPS tracking and bans on rapists and child molesters from school grounds. The office had no success with its arguments that the GPS technology is uncertain and that it may not be practical to notify churches and schools every time an offender moves. "The problem I'm having is that this is such an emotional issue," said Public Defender Brian C. Denton. "I mean, no one's for sex offenders."[41]

False Confession in Ramsey Case

The sensational sexual assault and murder of 6-year-old beauty queen JonBenet Ramsey, of Boulder, Colo., in December 1996 focused suspicion on her parents, John and Patricia, holding a reward poster. John Mark Karr, a teacher from Atlanta, Ga., confessed to the crime after his recent arrest in Thailand, but DNA testing indicated he was not the killer, and he was not charged.

coordinating federal, state and local law enforcement agencies. "This is an area where effective government is not an option — we *must* be effective," says a DOJ senior counsel.

As part of an annual dragnet in April, the U.S. Marshals Service rounded up 1,102 people wanted for violent sex crimes or for failing to register as a sex offender. The

Should California voters approve Jessica's Law?

YES

Stacie D. Rumenap
Executive Director, Stop Child Predators

NO

Carleen R. Arlidge
President, California Attorneys for Criminal Justice

Written for *CQ Researcher*, September 2006

With more than 560,000 registered sex offenders in the United States (over 100,000 of them living in California) it should come as no surprise that one-in-five girls and one-in-10 boys are sexually exploited.

In Florida last year a registered sex offender with arrests for sexual assault and fondling a minor was accused of abducting, molesting and burying alive 9-year-old Jessica Lunsford. In Idaho, a twice-convicted registered sex offender was charged with kidnapping and molesting 8-year-old Sasha Groene, molesting and murdering her brother and killing the rest of the family. And these are just a couple of examples of the horrific crimes committed against our nation's children.

As these examples make clear, sex offenders are often released back into society too soon. According to the Justice Department's Bureau of Justice Statistics, the average sentence imposed on a child molester released in 1994 was seven years, although the average offender was released after serving only three — despite the fact that sex offenders are four times more likely than other criminals to commit a sexual offense.

Fortunately for the voters of California, they have the opportunity to protect their children by voting "yes" this November on Proposition 83, "Jessica's Law." Proposition 83 increases penalties for violent sex offenders to 25 years to life in prison and requires lifelong tracking of sex offenders upon release — with costs of the monitoring system paid by the offender. Proposition 83 also bans sex offenders from living within 2,000 feet of any school or park and allows prosecutors to classify possession of child pornography as a felony.

Some critics may argue that mandatory sentencing takes away judicial discretion. As recent court cases demonstrate, however, such discretion is not always in the public's best interest.

In Vermont this past January, Judge Edward Cashman came under fire for handing out a light sentence to a man who confessed to repeatedly raping a young girl over a four-year period. More recently, Judge Kristine Cecava of Nebraska placed a five-foot-one-inch man convicted of sexually assaulting a 12-year-old girl on probation rather than giving him prison time because she was afraid of what might happen to him in jail.

At the very least, mandatory sentencing ensures that judicial indiscretion will not put predatory criminals immediately back on the streets.

We cannot afford another Jessica Lunsford tragedy. It is time for California to join the 24 states that have already passed Jessica's Law by voting "yes" on Proposition 83.

Excerpted from *California Voter Information Guide*, Aug. 14, 2006

Proposition 83 would cost taxpayers an estimated $500 million but will not increase our children's safety. Instead, by diluting law-enforcement resources, the initiative would actually reduce most children's security while increasing the danger for those most at risk.

The initiative proposes to monitor every registered sex offender on the misguided theory that each is likely to re-offend against strangers. But law-enforcement experience shows that when sex registrants re-offend, their targets are usually members of their own household. This proposition would do nothing to safeguard children in their own homes, even though they are most at risk.

Second, the proposition would not focus on the real problem — dangerous sex offenders — but would instead waste limited resources tracking persons who pose no risk. The new law would create an expensive tracking system for thousands of registrants who were convicted of minor, non-violent offenses, perhaps years or decades ago. Law-enforcement's resources should be directed toward high-risk individuals living in our neighborhoods.

Proposition 83 would have other dangerous, unintended consequences. The proposition's monitoring provisions would be least effective against those posing the greatest danger. Obviously, dangerous offenders would be the least likely to comply, so the proposed law would push the more serious offenders underground, where they would be less effectively monitored by police. In addition, by prohibiting sex offenders from living within 2,000 feet of a park or school, the initiative would force many offenders from urban to rural areas with smaller police forces. A high concentration of sex offenders in rural neighborhoods will not serve public safety.

Prosecutors in the state of Iowa know from sad experience that this type of residency restriction does not work. In 2001, Iowa adopted a similar law, but now the association of county prosecutors says that it does not provide the protection that was originally intended and that the cost of enforcing the requirement and unintended effects on families of offenders warrant replacing the restriction with more effective protective measures.

Residency restrictions do not reduce sex offenses against children or improve children's safety. Residency restrictions will not be effective against 80 to 90 percent of the sex crimes against children because those crimes are committed by a relative or acquaintance of the child. Residency restrictions cause sex registrants to disappear from the registration system.

The laws also cause unwarranted disruption to the innocent families of ex-offenders.

Getty Images/Jeff Topping

A newly installed facial-recognition camera linked to a Sheriff's Department database of registered sex offenders monitors Royal Palms Middle School, near Phoenix, Ariz., in December 2003. The school removed its two cameras last year after no suspects were spotted entering the school after two years.

Another popular type of legislation, however, appears to be attracting increasingly louder criticism. Seventeen states and numerous localities have passed such laws, which prohibit sex offenders from living near schools, parks, playgrounds and other places where children congregate.

For supporters, it only makes sense to try to protect children from sexually violent predators. 'This is something that is taking root all over the country," said state Rep. Keen, sponsor of a Georgia proximity law enacted in April. "People are putting a premium on the safety of kids."[42]

But critics say residency-restriction laws are counterproductive. In states where they have taken effect, such as Iowa, there is already evidence that sex offenders are no longer registering. (Groups that follow the issue generally estimate that approximately 100,000 of the 550,000 known sex offenders nationwide have absconded, or gone missing.) The Iowa County Attorneys Association favors repeal of the law.

In addition to the problem of offenders who abscond, critics say, offenders who comply but are forced to move because their homes are located too near to schools or other facilities that serve children often must go to rural areas with fewer support services. "We know that for people who have a tendency to violence, if they have no support or basic comforts, that really creates an incredibly heightened risk for re-offense," says Klein of the Association for the Treatment of Sexual Abusers.

Vigilantism also has been a problem. Last Easter, a Canadian man shot two registered sex offenders in their Maine homes after tracking them down via the state's sex-offender registry Web site. One had been convicted as a sexual predator. The other was 17 when he was arrested for being in a relationship with a 15-year-old girl. The state temporarily took down its registry after the shootings.[43]

Where to Put Ex-Offenders?

With sex offenders facing either legal banishment or, in many cases, community ostracism and protests, it's become tough to know where to put them once they get out of prison. In Colorado, there has been talk of creating a separate town for sex offenders. In Solano County, east of the San Francisco Bay area, California corrections officials have resorted to letting a few sex offenders sleep on cots in a parole office due to a lack of other options.[44]

Perhaps the most controversial approach has been the revival in some states of permanent or semi-permanent civil commitment — holding offenders involuntarily in mental institutions and similar facilities. In an echo of the sexual-psychopath laws of the 1930s, 17 states now allow prisoners to be held for evaluation and treatment after serving their sentences. At the end of 2004, nearly 3,500 prisoners nationwide were being held, according to the Washington State Institute for Public Policy.

Civil commitment is expensive, costing in the neighborhood of $100,000 per year per inmate. In January, Gov. Tim Pawlenty, R-Minn., proposed borrowing $44.6 million to build a 400-bed locked residential building.[45] Republican New York Gov. George E. Pataki has proposed turning an upstate, rural prison into a civil-commitment facility, with a $130 million price tag.[46]

In addition to cost concerns, civil-commitment laws have drawn frequent legal challenge. The U.S. Supreme Court upheld a Kansas law in 1997, saying the state can commit individuals who are likely to engage in predatory acts of violence due to mental abnormality or personality disorder. But the court narrowed states' latitude in 2002, saying they must prove offenders have "serious difficulty" controlling their behavior before they can be committed.[47]

Several other recent sex-offender laws have drawn legal scrutiny. A U.S. district judge found a portion of the Georgia residency-restriction law unconstitutional in June. Iowa's proximity law also was struck down by a district judge in 2004, but an appeals court subsequently ruled that sex-offenders' rights were superseded by the state's compelling interest in protecting its citizens.

In general, concern about citizens' safety has led courts to be tolerant of recent crackdown laws. Some of the laws would seem to violate the Constitution's ex post facto clause — which prohibits laws that impose new punishments for crimes committed prior to the law's passage — such as requiring men who committed sex crimes years earlier to wear satellite-tracking ankle bracelets. Others would seem to violate the double-jeopardy rule — meaning the state can't punish an offender twice for the same crime — such as subjecting an offender to a sanity hearing and civil commitment after his prison term. In general, the courts have held that such laws are regulatory, rather than punitive, and within the state's charge of maintaining public safety.

The return to indefinite civil commitment troubles Lieb, of the Washington State Institute for Public Policy, who has favored other tough, new punishments. "When I read historical articles, in some ways it's disturbing," she says. "You see the same thing going on. It's taught me a certain amount of patience."

Opponents of the contemporary crackdown, however, are happy that the Adam Walsh Act calls for the attorney general to study different containment and treatment methods. They hope that a thorough look at modern treatment techniques will reveal the value of providing programs to offenders who can benefit from them. For instance, juvenile offenders have lower recidivism rates than adult offenders if they undergo treatment, but they tend increasingly to be lumped in with the adults under many of the new laws.

Treatment programs tend to be underfunded, particularly in prison settings. Many officials are skeptical of

AP Photo/Jeff Roberson

Kerry Skora served 15 years for murder but was labeled as a sex offender after his release because his victim had been a minor. Skora's complaint about the policy led the Illinois legislature to create a new registry for non-sexually violent criminals.

them, recalling their poor record in early studies and noting that some of the most notorious offenders were treatment failures. In the current environment, though, treatment and rehabilitation are bound to be greeted with more skepticism than stricter punishment.

Approximately 60 to 70 percent of sex offenders are given either probation or a combination of jail and probation, with nearly 90 percent of those required to participate in treatment. But there aren't enough programs to go around and even fewer available in prisons, reports John Jay College criminologist Terry. "The politicians, community and media alike tend to focus only on the risk-management failures of this group of offenders, thereby presenting the supervision agencies as largely ineffective," she writes.[48]

New York Assembly Speaker Sheldon Silver, for instance, proposed legislation this year to require at least two years of treatment for all prisoners incarcerated for a felony sex offense and continued treatment upon release. That measure failed. But the legislature expanded the categories of offenders whose registration information had to be made available to the public while greatly extending the length of time offenders would have to remain on registries. Lawmakers also increased penalties for sexual assaults against children and lengthened the statute of limitations on sex crimes.

OUTLOOK

Tougher Laws?

The rate of reported sex crimes against children continues to be low compared to the levels reached 15 years ago. Experts say the tougher laws could be starting to have an effect — either through deterrence or by simply keeping more offenders behind bars or under surveillance. In addition, there has been a 400 percent increase in sex-offender convictions over the past decade. Sex crimes against adults are stable. The attention paid to sex crimes in the wake of high-profile cases has made communities more aware and perhaps more vigilant in keeping children safe.

For some, that's not entirely a good thing. Aside from the incidents of vigilante violence — like Connecticut man charged with stabbing his 2-year-old daughter's alleged molester on Aug. 29 — some observers worry that people are not equipped to deal with the amount of information now available about sex offenders in their midst. The number of Internet searches looking for neighboring sex offenders, for instance, spikes every year around Halloween (several states have made it illegal for registered offenders to hand out candy).

"If I read [online] there's a sex offender in the community, give me some guidance on what I ought to be doing about it," says Fred Berlin, an associate professor of psychiatry at Johns Hopkins University who has been treating sex offenders for 25 years. "That's not happening in a universal way."

Others worry that since sex crimes are overwhelmingly perpetrated by people previously known to the child, all of these laws that try to insulate children from strangers will have the unwarranted effect of making parents feel falsely secure. Moreover, most sex crimes perpetrated by strangers are the work of first-time offenders, against whom background checks, registries and residence restrictions offer no protection.

"Teaching our children about stranger danger sends them the wrong message if that's the only message we give," said Robert Schilling, lead detective in the Seattle Police Department's Sex and Kidnapping Offender unit. "Parents get the idea that Internet predators and strangers in the bushes are who sex offenders are. They don't realize that is one out of thousands. The message has to change."[49]

But fear of sex crimes is likely to extend the push for increasingly strict laws. In California, for instance, the number of forcible rapes dropped by nearly 23 percent from 1999 to 2004 while other sex felonies remained flat, according to the state attorney general's office. Nevertheless, California voters are expected to overwhelming approve one of the toughest sex-offender laws in the nation come November.

"The benefit of having laws like these in all 50 states is that there's no place for sex offenders to hide," says Rumenap, of Stop Child Predators.

The current cycle of anti-sex-offender lawmaking, which extends back for more than 20 years, is already longer than any other such cycle during the 20th century and shows no signs of abating. "There's certainly a movement for longer sentences, often life sentences," says John Jay College criminologist Terry. "Instead of cognitive-behavioral treatment, we're moving toward more chemical castration. There's a move in many states toward civil-commitment laws where they don't already have them."

Beyond the debate about the wisdom and effectiveness of sex-offender legislation, which will certainly be gauged carefully in the coming years, it's clearly one issue that will not go away. "It's not likely state policymakers are going to come up with a solution that will eliminate these problems," says Lieb, of the Washington State Institute for Public Policy.

NOTES

1. Karen J. Terry, *Sexual Offenses and Offenders* (2006), p. xv.

2. Mark Memmott, "Girl's Death Raises Question About Tracking of Sex Offenders," *USA Today*, March 25, 2005, p. 4A.

3. "The Greatest Fear," *The Economist*, Aug. 26, 2005, p. 24.

4. Howard N. Snyder, "Sexual Assault of Young Children as Reported to Law Enforcement: Victim, Incident, and Offender Characteristics," Bureau of Justice Statistics, U.S. Department of Justice, July 2000, p. 10; available at www.ojp.usdoj.gov/bjs/pub/pdf/saycrle.pdf.

5. Tara Bahrampour, "Discovering a World Beyond the Front Yard," *The Washington Post*, Aug. 27, 2006, p. C1.

6. Wendy Koch, "States Get Tougher With Sex Offenders," *USA Today*, May 24, 2006, p. 1A.

7. Lee Rood, "Residency Law Creates Clusters of Sex Offenders," *Des Moines Register*, January 29, 2006, p. 1A.

8. Jenny Jarvie, "Suit Targets Sex Offender Law," *Los Angeles Times*, July 2, 2006, p. A24.

9. Charles Sheehan, "Sex Offenders Slip Away," *Chicago Tribune*, March 31, 2006, p. 1.

10. Ellen Perlman, "Where Will Sex Offenders Live?" *Governing*, June 2006, p. 54.

11. Monica Davey, "Iowa's Residency Rules Drive Sex Offenders Underground," *The New York Times*, March 15, 2006, p. A1.

12. Candade Rondeaux, "Can Castration Be a Solution for Sex Offenders?" *The Washington Post*, July 5, 2006, p. B1.

13. Adam Liptak, "Death Penalty in Some Cases of Child Sex Is Widening," *The New York Times*, June 10, 2006, p. 9. The case is *Coker v. Georgia*, 433 U.S. 584 (1977).

14. Terry, *op. cit.*, p. 17.

15. Patrick A. Langan, Erica L. Schmitt and Matthew R. Durose, "Recidivism of Sex Offenders Released From Prison in 1994," Bureau of Justice Statistics, November 2003; www.ojp.usdoj.gov/bjs/pub/pdf/rsorp94.pdf.

16. Andrew J.R. Harris and R. Karl Hanson, "Sex Offender Recidivism: A Simple Question," Public Safety and Emergency Preparedness Canada User Report 2004-03; available at http://ww2.psepc-sppcc.gc.ca/publications/corrections/pdf/200403-2_e.pdf.

17. Ernie Allen, "We Need Stronger Tools for Tracking Sex Offenders," *The Washington Post*, Sept. 14, 2005, p. A30.

18. Quoted in Philip Jenkins, *Moral Panic* (1998), p. 37.

19. *Ibid.*, p. 37.

20. *Ibid.*, p. 50.

21. J. Edgar Hoover, "How Safe Is Your Daughter?" *American Magazine*, July 1947, p. 32.

22. Elizabeth H. Pleck, *Domestic Tyranny* (1987), p. 121.

23. Terry, *op. cit.*, p. 28.

24. Quoted in Gladys Schultz, *How Many More Victims?* (1965), p. 210.

25. Jenkins, *op. it.*, p. 86.

26. Paul Tappan, *The Habitual Sex Offender* (1950), p. 15.

27. Jenkins, *op. cit.*, p. 86

28. Edwin H. Sutherland, "The Diffusion of Sexual Psychopath Laws," *American Journal of Sociology 56*, 1950, p. 142.

29. Jenkins, *op. cit.*, p. 103.

30. *Ibid.*, p. 127.

31. David G. Savage, "Justices Shield Child Victims in Abuse Cases," *Los Angeles Times*, Jan. 16, 1992, p. A3.

32. Terry, *op. cit.*, p. 142.

33. Jenkins, *op. cit.*, p. 166.

34. Terry, *op. cit.*, p. 33.

35. Robb London, "Strategy on Sex Crimes Is Prison, Then Prison," *The New York Times*, Feb. 8, 1991, p. B16.

36. Seth Stern, "Law Enacted to Strengthen Penalties Against Child Molesters," *CQ Weekly*, July 29, 2006, p. 2116.

37. The Associated Press, "1,102 Sex Offenders Rounded up in 27-State Dragnet," *The Washington Post*, April 28, 2006, p. A2.

38. Wendy Koch, "More Sex Offenders Tracked by Satellite," *USA Today*, June 7, 2006, p. 3A.

39. John Maurelius, "Governor Pushes Anti-Crime Agenda," *The San Diego Union-Tribune*, June 30, 2006, p. B1.

40. Jordan Rau, "A Bid to Toughen Stance on Sex Offenses," *Los Angeles Times*, Feb. 19, 2006.

41. Matthew Mosk, "A Lone Voice Against Sex Offender Bill," *The Washington Post*, March 25, 2006, p. B1.

42. Jarvie, *op. cit.*

43. Judy Harrison, "2 men slain in Milo, Corinth; Suspect from Canada kills himself in Boston," *Bangor Daily News*, April 17, 2006, p. A1.

44. Jenifer Warren, "Sex Offender Housing Scarce," *Los Angeles Times*, May 31, 2006, p. A1.

45. John Q. La Fond and Bruce J. Winick, "Doing More Than Their Time," *The New York Times*, May 21, 2006, p. 14:23.

46. "A Place for Sex Offenders," *The New York Times*, Jan. 22, 2006, p. 14:11.

47. Jan Crawford Greenburg, "Justices Set Higher Bar for Detention," *Chicago Tribune*, Jan. 23, 2002, p. 8. The cases are *Kansas v. Hendricks*, 521 U.S. 346 (1997) and *Kansas v. Crane*, 534 U.S. 407 (2002).

48. Terry, *op. cit.*, p. 142.

49. Natalie Singer, "'Stranger Danger' Emphasis Misguided," *Seattle Times*, May 23, 2006, p. B1.

BIBLIOGRAPHY

Books

Jenkins, Philip, *Moral Panic: Changing Concepts of the Child Molester in America*, Yale University Press, 1998.
A Pennsylvania State University historian shows how periods of concern have been followed by periods of neglect throughout the 20th century.

La Fond, John Q., *Preventing Sexual Violence: How Society Should Cope With Sex Offenders*, American Psychological Association, 2005.
A University of Missouri law professor says laws enacted since 1990 are based on false assumptions and present data in an effort to persuade professionals in the field to focus on risk-management programs.

Terry, Karen J., *Sexual Offenses and Offenders: Theory, Practice, and Policy*, Wadsworth, 2006.
A John Jay College criminologist offers a comprehensive survey of current data and policy regarding sex offenders.

Articles

"The Greatest Fear," *The Economist*, Aug. 26, 2006, p. 24.
The British magazine concludes that American fear of sex crimes is disproportionate.

Koch, Wendy, "States Get Tougher With Sex Offenders," *USA Today*, May 24, 2006, p. 1A.
Both Congress and the states are working on stricter penalties for sex offenders.

Jarvie, Jenny, "Suit Targets Sex Offender Law," *Los Angeles Times*, July 2, 2006, p. A24.
A U.S. district judge rules that part of a Georgia law restricting where sex offenders can live is unconstitutional.

Liptak, Adam, "Death Penalty in Some Cases of Child Sex Is Widening," *The New York Times*, June 10, 2006, p. 9.
Oklahoma and South Carolina join three other states in imposing the death penalty on repeat sex offenders.

Perlman, Ellen, "Where Will Sex Offenders Live?" *Governing*, June 2006, p. 54.
State and local laws are making it harder for sex criminals to find places to live, which in turn hampers law enforcement's ability to do its job effectively.

Rau, Jordan, "A Bid to Toughen Stance on Sex Offenses," *Los Angeles Times*, Feb. 19, 2006, p. B1.
California voters will decide whether to stiffen penalties against sex offenders, but the experience of other states with similar laws cautions against certain success.

Rondeaux, Candace, "Can Castration Be a Solution for Sex Offenders?" *The Washington Post*, July 5, 2006, p. B1.
A sex criminal who castrated himself argues that the method eliminates unhealthy sexual desires, but others wonder whether it's effective or constitutional.

Stern, Seth, "Law Enacted to Strengthen Penalties Against Child Predators," *CQ Weekly*, July 29, 2006, p. 2116.
President Bush signs a law that creates a national sex-offender registry and toughens penalties for sex crimes against children.

Turner, Joseph, "Bill Ups Required Sex Felon Sentence," *The [Tacoma] News Tribune*, **March 5, 2006, p. B1.**
The Washington state legislature unanimously approves longer sentences for sex offenders.

Reports and Studies

Finkelhor, David, and Lisa M. Jones, "Explanations for the Decline in Child Sexual Abuse Cases," Juvenile Justice Bulletin, Office of Juvenile Justice and Delinquency Prevention, U.S. Department of Justice, January 2004.
The authors, from the Crimes Against Children Research Center at the University of New Hampshire, say multiple factors are involved in a 40 percent reduction in child sex-abuse cases between 1992 and 2000, including a particular focus on preventing this form of child maltreatment.

Harris, Andrew J.R., and R. Karl Hanson, "Sex Offender Recidivism: A Simple Question," Public Safety and Emergency Preparedness Canada User Report 2004-03.
Data from 10 follow-up studies of adult, male sex offenders indicate that most do not reoffend sexually and that first-time offenders are much less likely to sexually reoffend than those with previous sex crime convictions.

Langan, Patrick A., Erica L. Schmitt and Matthew R. Durose, "Recidivism of Sex Offenders Released From Prison in 1994," Bureau of Justice Statistics, November 2003.
A study of 9,691 prisoners released from prisons in 15 states in 1994 finds that 5.3 percent of them were rearrested for another sex crime within three years of release.

Snyder, Howard N., "Sexual Assault of Young Children as Reported to Law Enforcement: Victim, Incident, and Offender Characteristics," Bureau of Justice Statistics, U.S. Department of Justice, July 2000.
Crimes against juveniles represent a large majority of sex-abuse cases handled by law enforcement. One-in-seven victims is under age 7, and more than a third of cases involved a victim under 12.

For More Information

Association for the Treatment of Sexual Abusers, 4900 S.W. Griffith Dr., Suite 274, Beaverton, OR 97005; (503) 643-1023; www.atsa.com. A nonprofit, interdisciplinary organization that fosters research, develops practice guidelines and promotes professional education in the field of sex-offender evaluation and treatment.

Bureau of Justice Statistics, U.S. Department of Justice, 810 Seventh St., N.W., Washington, DC 20531; (202) 307-0765; www.ojp.usdoj.gov/bjs/welcome.html. A primary source for crime statistics; collects, analyzes and publishes information on crime and criminal offenders.

Center for Sex Offender Management, 8403 Colesville Rd., Suite 720, Silver Spring, MD 20910; (301) 589-9383; www.csom.org. A group supported by the U.S. Department of Justice that works to improve means of managing adult and juvenile sex offenders who are not incarcerated.

National Center for Missing and Exploited Children, 699 Prince St., Alexandria, VA 22314; (202) 274-3900; www.missingkids.com. A nonprofit group that works to prevent child abduction and sexual exploitation.

Stop Child Predators, 601 Thirteenth St., N.W., Suite 930 South, Washington, DC 20005; (202) 234-0090; www.stopchildpredators.org. An advocacy group promoting more diligent tracking of sex offenders and greater protection of victims' rights.

4

Hate Groups

Is Extremism on the Rise in the United States?

Peter Katel

Richard Poplawski, 22, faces murder charges in Pittsburgh after allegedly shooting and killing three police officers on April 4, 2009. Three weeks earlier, Poplawski, who is tattooed on his chest with what he reportedly described as an "Americanized" Nazi eagle, apparently posted an anti-Semitic message on Stormfront, a neo-Nazi Web site. The number of active hate groups in the nation has jumped to 926 groups — a 50 percent increase — since 2000.

From *CQ Global Researcher*, May 2009.

Two police officers drove up to a brick house in the middle-class Pittsburgh neighborhood of Stanton Heights on April 4, responding to an emergency call from a woman about her 22-year-old son. "I want him gone," Margaret Poplawski told a 911 operator.[1]

She also said that he had weapons, but the operator failed to share that crucial information with the police, who apparently took no special precautions in responding. Seconds after officers Stephen J. Mayhle and Paul J. Sciullo walked into the house, Richard Poplawski opened fire, killing both men. He then shot and killed Eric Kelly, a policeman outside the house. After a four-hour standoff, Poplawski surrendered.[2] Hours after that, the Anti-Defamation League and a *Pittsburgh Post-Gazette* reporter traced a March 13 Web post by Poplawski to the neo-Nazi Web site Stormfront.

"The federal government, mainstream media and banking system in these United States are strongly under the influence of — if not completely controlled by — Zionist interest," the post said. "An economic collapse of the financial system is inevitable, bringing with it some degree of civil unrest if not outright balkanization of the continental U.S., civil/revolutionary/racial war. . . . This collapse is likely engineered by the elite Jewish powers that be in order to make for a power and asset grab."[3]

Obsessions with Jewish conspiracy, racial conflict and looming collapse of the political and social order have long festered in the extreme outposts of U.S. political culture. While extremists typically become active in times of social and economic stress, Timothy McVeigh, the Oklahoma City bomber, struck in 1995 during a

Hate Groups Active in All But Two States

Hate groups were active in all the states except Hawaii and Alaska in 2008, according to the Southern Poverty Law Center. Iowa, California, Texas and Mississippi had the largest concentrations of groups.

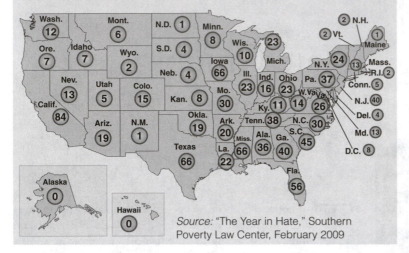

Source: "The Year in Hate," Southern Poverty Law Center, February 2009

relatively tranquil, prosperous time. (*See "Background," p. 94.*)

Now, law enforcement officials warn, dire conditions throughout the country have created a perfect storm of provocations for right-wing extremists. In the midst of fighting two wars, the country is suffering an economic crisis in which more than 5 million people have lost their jobs, while the hypercharged debate over immigration — and the presence of about 12 million illegal immigrants — continues unresolved.[4]

"This is the formula — the formula for hate," says James Cavanaugh, special agent in charge of the Bureau of Alcohol, Tobacco, Firearms and Explosives (ATF) Nashville, Tenn., division and a veteran investigator of far-right extremists. "Everything's aligning for them for hate."

The Department of Homeland Security (DHS) drew a similar conclusion in early April, adding a concern over the apparent rekindling of extremist interest in recruiting disaffected military veterans.

"The consequences of a prolonged economic downturn . . . could create a fertile recruiting environment for right-wing extremists and even result in confrontations between such groups and government authorities," the DHS said.[5]

The election of Barack Obama as the nation's first African-American president also could prompt an extremist backlash. "Obama is going to be the spark that arouses the white movement," the Detroit-based National Socialist Movement* — considered a leading neo-Nazi organization — announced on its Web site.[6]

But the Obama effect will be negligible among hardcore, violent extremists, says an ex-FBI agent who worked undercover in right-wing terrorist cells in the early 1990s. "They're in an alternative universe," says Mike German, author of the 2007 book *Thinking Like a Terrorist*, and now a policy counselor to the American Civil Liberties Union on national-security issues. "When you believe the American government is the puppet of Israel, whether Obama is the face of the government instead of George W. Bush makes little difference."

Indeed, says Columbia University historian Robert O. Paxton, the Obama victory demonstrated that the country's worrisome conditions haven't sparked widespread rejection of the political system — the classic catalyst for major upsurges of extremism. "Sure, we have a black president, but if the Right were really at the door, we wouldn't have elected him," says Paxton, a leading scholar of European fascism. (*See sidebar, p. 92.*)

Still, Paxton and others caution that the sociopolitical effects of the economic crisis may take a while to hit. The Montgomery, Ala.-based Southern Poverty Law Center (SPLC), which tracks the Ku Klux Klan and other "hate groups," reports activity by 926 such groups in 2008, a 50 percent increase over the number in 2000.[7] "That is a real and a significant rise," says Mark Potok, director of the center's Intelligence Project. Despite the increased activity, the center says there's nothing approaching a mass movement. Moreover, drawing connections between extremist

---

* "Nazi" is the German-language contraction of "National Socialist."

organizations and hate crimes can be complicated.

"Most hate crimes are not committed by members of organized hate groups," says Chip Berlet, senior analyst for Political Research Associates of Somerville, Mass., who has been writing about the far right for a quarter-century. "These groups help promote violence through their aggressive rhetoric. But you're more likely to be victim of hate crime from a neighbor."

For example, three young men from Staten Island, N.Y., charged with beating a 17-year-old Liberian immigrant into a coma on presidential election night last year were not accused of membership in anything more than a neighborhood gang. Their victim, who also lives on Staten Island, said his attackers, one of them Hispanic, yelled "Obama" as they set on him.[8]

Mental health problems also may play a role in such violence, not all of which is inspired by hate rhetoric. In the single deadliest attack on immigrants in memory, Jiverly Wong is charged with killing 13 people (and then himself) at an immigrants' service center in Binghamton, N.Y., one day before Poplawski's alleged killings in Pittsburgh. Eleven of Wong's victims were immigrants, like Wong, a native of Vietnam. Wong left a note in which he complained of his limited English-speaking ability and depicted himself as a victim of police persecution.[9]

But in other recent cases in which immigrants were targeted, the alleged shooters did invoke far-right views. Keith Luke, 22, who lived with his mother in the Boston suburb of Brockton, was charged in January with killing a young woman, shooting and raping her sister and killing a

Dozens of Extremist Events Planned This Summer

More than two dozen gatherings of white extremists will be held around the nation this summer, according to the Anti-Defamation League. Many are being held in traditional Ku Klux Klan (KKK) strongholds in the South and Midwest by groups such as the KKK, National Socialist Movement and Christian Identity organizations.

Upcoming Extremist Events in the United States
(Partial list, May-October)

Location	Event
Russelville, Ala.	Courthouse rally organized by Church of the National Knights of the Ku Klux Klan.
Odessa, Mo.	Paramilitary training organized by the Missouri Militia.
Phoenix, Ariz.	Gathering organized by neo-Nazi Nationalist Coalition Arizona with invitations to members of Stormfront, a hate Web site.
York County, Pa.	Open meeting of the neo-Nazi National Socialist Movement for current and interested members.
Marshall, Texas	KKK cookout on private property organized by the United White Knights.
Las Vegas, Nev.	Workshop organized by Paper Advantage, a sovereign citizen group advocating right-wing anarchy.
Champaign County, Ohio	Paramilitary training with the Unorganized Militia of Champaign County.
Burlington, N.C.	Conference organized by the neo-Confederate North Carolina Chapter of League of the South.
New Albany, Miss.	KKK rally at county courthouse followed by a gathering and cross-burning on private property.
Dawson Springs, Ky.	Annual Nordic Fest white power rally organized by the Imperial Klans of America.
Oceana and Muskegon counties, Mich.	Camping trip organized by the white-supremacist forum White Pride Michigan.
Schell City, Mo.	National youth conference organized by Church of Israel, whose followers practice Christian Identity, a racist and anti-Semitic religion.
Jackson, Miss.	Annual national conference of racist group Council of Conservative Citizens.
Sandpoint, Idaho	Weekend conference organized by America's Promise Ministries, practitioners of Christian Identity.
Pulaski, Tenn.	Weekend gathering commemorating the birthday of Nathan Bedford Forrest — the first KKK leader — including a march, cross-burning and fellowship.

Source: Anti-Defamation League

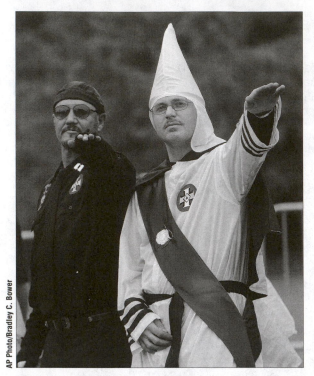

AP Photo/Bradley C. Bower

Members of the World Order of the Ku Klux Klan, one of scores of Klan groups in the United States, rally on Sept. 2, 2006, at Gettysburg National Military Park, site of a decisive Civil War battle.

72-year-old man — all immigrants from Cape Verde. His planned next stop, police said, was a synagogue. Luke, whom one law enforcement source described as a "recluse," allegedly told police he was "fighting extinction" of white people.[10]

A similar motive was expressed by a 60-year-old Destin, Fla., man charged with killing two Chilean students and wounding three others, all visiting Florida as part of a cultural-exchange program. Shortly before the killings, Dannie Roy Baker had asked a neighbor, "Are you ready for the revolution?" And last summer, he had sent e-mails to Walton County Republican Party officials — who forwarded them to the sheriff's office. One said, in part, "The Washington D.C. Dictators have already confessed to rigging elections in our States for their recruiting dictators to overthrow us with foreign illegals here."[11]

Some immigrant advocates say such comments indicate that extremists are exploiting resentment of immigrants in the hope of stirring up more attacks.

"It is the perfect vehicle, particularly with the decline of the economy," says Eric Ward, national field director of the Chicago-based Center for New Community, which works with immigrants. "With American anxiety building, they hope that they can use immigrants as scapegoats to build their movement."

"Illegals are turning America into a third-world slum," says one of a series of leaflets distributed in the New Haven, Conn., area in early March by North-East White Pride (NEWP). "They come for welfare, or to take our jobs and bring with them drugs, crime and disease."

The NEWP Web site carries the cryptic slogan, "Support your local 1488." In neo-Nazi code, "88" represents "Heil Hitler," words that begin with the eighth letter in the alphabet. And "14" stands for an infamous, 14-word racist dictum: "We must secure the existence of our people and a future for white children." Its author was the late David Lane, a member of the violent neo-Nazi organization, The Order, who died in prison in 2007.[12]

The Order, whose crimes included the murder of a Jewish radio talk-show host in Denver in 1984, sprang from the far-right milieu, as did Oklahoma City bomber McVeigh. And a source of inspiration in both cases was a novel glorifying genocide of Jews and blacks, *The Turner Diaries*, authored by the late William Pierce, founder of the neo-Nazi National Alliance, based in West Virginia.[13]

Pierce's death from cancer in 2002 was one of a series of developments that left a high-level leadership vacuum in the extremist movement. One of those trying to fill it is Billy Roper, 37, chairman of White Revolution, a group based in Russellville, Ark. Roper predicts that racial-ethnic tensions will explode when nonstop immigration from Latin America forces the violent breakup of the United States.

"We're at a pre-revolutionary stage, where it's too late to seek recompense through the political process, and too early to start shooting," Roper says.

As police and scholars monitor extremist groups, here are some of the key questions they are asking:

Could the election of a black president and the nation's economic crisis spark a resurgence of far-right political activity or violence?

The precedent-shattering nature of Obama's presidency could provide enough of a spark for racist reaction, some extremism experts argue. Others question whether that's enough to propel significant numbers of people into outright rejection of the political system, even amid the nation's economic turbulence. They note that organized racist violence against African-Americans was already fading by the late 1960s, after civil rights had become the law of the land.

Nonetheless, at least some members of the far right are reacting. Shortly before the presidential election last year, federal agents charged an 18-year-old from Arkansas and a 20-year-old from Tennessee with plotting to kill Obama after first killing 88 black people, beheading 14 of them — apparent references to the "88" and "14" codes. The father of one of the young men said the alleged plans were no more than "a lot of talk." According to the SPLC, the 20-year-old, Daniel Cowart, had been a probationary member of a new and active skinhead organization, Supreme White Alliance, though the organization said he'd been expelled before the alleged murder plot was conceived.[14]

Michael Barkun, a professor of political science at Syracuse University, says older extremists may see Obama's election as a big favor to their movement. "They tend to think of it as a great recruiting tool," says Barkun, who specializes in political and religious extremism. "My sense is that from their point of view, they would see it as a continuation of what they regard as the marginalization of the white population: 'See, we were right all along.' "

But extremists may be disappointed, Barkun adds, given how the election itself showed the extent to which racism has weakened. Still, the economic crisis offers recruiting possibilities to extremists, because millions of people are suffering its effects. "I would be surprised if the economic crisis did not produce some very nasty side effects," he says, citing the pseudo-constitutional interpretations adopted by the "Posse Comitatus" movement that flourished in the 1980s. "Certainly some of the

fringe legal doctrines on the far right lend themselves to exploitation here."*

Yet for a segment of U.S. society, Obama's election is already stoking the fires of rage, says another veteran observer of the far right. Michael Pitcavage, investigative research director for the Anti-Defamation League, says that immediately after the election, extremists with MySpace pages started including the slogan, "I have no president."

These are anecdotal signs, Pitcavage acknowledges. But he notes that at least one president in the recent past did prompt an extreme reaction on the far right. "The election of Bill Clinton, I would call one of the secondary causes of the resurgence of right-wing extremism in the 1990s," he says. Clinton's Vietnam War draft avoidance and his evasive acknowledgement of past drug use aroused enormous anger among extremists (as among mainstream conservatives), Pitcavage says — sentiments that expanded into conspiracist views after a violent confrontation between federal law enforcement officers and a heavily armed religious group in Waco, Texas.

But at least one right-wing writer on racial issues says that in his circles Obama's presidency has had little effect. "We have always had sophisticated readers whose views of the world are not going to be knocked askew by some unforeseen political event," says Jared Taylor, editor of *American Renaissance*, a magazine based in Oakton, Va., a Washington suburb. "Though I don't wish to detract at all from the symbolic importance of a non-white American president, it's very much part of a predictable sequence. Readers of *American Renaissance* don't necessarily approve of the idea of a black president, but it's not something that wakes them up to something they weren't aware of before." Taylor greeted Obama's election with an article headlined, "Transition to Black Rule?"[15]

Taylor's magazine opposes all anti-discrimination and affirmative-action laws but doesn't espouse violence. However, attendees at the magazine's annual conference in 2006 included well-known extremists, including

---

* Posse Comitatus means "power of the county," a phrase that adherents used to denote the supposed illegitimacy of the federal government. The Posse Comitatus Act of 1878 was passed to remove the U.S. Army from domestic law enforcement activities.

David Duke. When the former Louisiana Klan leader raised the issue of Jewish influence, a Jewish attendee walked out. Taylor later wrote that he would never exclude Jews, adding, "Some people in the [*American Renaissance*] community believe Jewish influence was decisive in destroying the traditional American consensus on race. Others disagree."[16]

As for the ailing economy, Taylor says it hasn't been helping his publication. "We haven't seen any sort of sudden leap in subscribers," he says. "If anything, the economic conditions are bad for us because we're a non-profit organization. We depend on contributions; people have less to contribute."

Still, the sociopolitical consequences of the economic crisis transcend financial problems at individual outposts of right-wing opinion.

Cavanaugh, the longtime ATF official, is one of many who sees the global economic meltdown as an echo of the crisis in Germany's Weimar Republic in the 1920s and early '30s, which enabled Hitler's National Socialist Party to come to power.

"This is how they recruited," says Cavanaugh. "Nazism was founded on blaming the Jewish people for the economic crisis." In today's United States, Cavanaugh hypothesizes, extremists could try to make immigrants the group responsible for the crisis.

But Cavanaugh doubts that Obama's presidency, per se, appeals to extremists. Many of them view the conventional political system as the "Zionist Occupation Government," or ZOG. "The president has done more to unite the country — you can feel it," he says. "That doesn't help hate groups get stronger. They can rail against any president, and they have. Any president to them is the head of ZOG."

Are immigrants in danger from extremist violence?

Black Americans have been far and away the major targets of 20th-century extremist violence.

But organized racist violence, from cross-burning to bombings, lynching and assassinations of black community leaders or white civil rights supporters, has faded from the scene, despite episodic hate crimes that sometimes target Jews as well as blacks.

Obama's election demonstrated the extent to which the black-white divide in American life has narrowed.

Indeed, when it comes to arousing political passion, race has been replaced by illegal immigrants, who number an estimated 12 million in the United States.[17]

"Black people are here, and no one is talking about deporting them," says Taylor of *American Renaissance*. "Immigration is a current and constant flow that is, in my view, only building up problems and conflict for the future, and that's a process that could be stopped. That is why it is much more a subject of political interest."

Bipartisan congressional legislation to provide a "path to citizenship" — restrictionists prefer the term "amnesty" — for illegal immigrants stalled during the George W. Bush administration.

Aside from mainstream political debate over the solution to illegal immigration, immigrant advocates say they're worried that violence against Latinos — or brown-skinned people thought to be immigrants — is on the rise. According to the most recent FBI statistics, there were 830 attacks of various kinds on Hispanics in 2007. By comparison, 1,087 attacks were made on homosexuals, who are also frequent targets of hate speech.[18] In 2000, there were 557 reported attacks on Hispanics compared to 1,075 attacks against homosexuals.[19]

But both conservatives and liberals take a dim view of those FBI statistics. Marcus Epstein, a conservative anti-immigration activist who draws a line between his views and those of extremists, criticizes the FBI categorization scheme for using the ethnic term "Hispanic" only for crime victims. Offenders, by contrast, are listed only by race, so "Hispanic" doesn't appear. The result, he argues, is that statistics are skewed so that any Hispanic hate-crime perpetrators are statistically invisible. (The FBI says that the agency "does not agree" that its categories "render the data invalid for statistical purposes.")

Epstein, executive director of The American Cause, a conservative organization founded by political commentator and immigration restrictionist Pat Buchanan, is particularly concerned about illegal immigrants with criminal records committing further crimes. He cites the case of Manuel Cazares, who turned himself in to police in Hannibal, Mo., in March, saying he'd killed an ex-girlfriend and a male friend of hers. Cazares, a Mexican citizen, was in the United States illegally, but police hadn't checked his status, although federal immigration authorities said his name wasn't in their database.[20] "Illegal immigrants kill American citizens — that greatly outweighs the number of crimes committed by right-wing white Americans against immigrants," Epstein says.

He cites a statistical analysis by Edwin S. Rubinstein, an economic consultant in Indianapolis and former senior fellow at the Hudson Institute, a conservative think tank. Writing on the VDare Web site, which opposes immigration except by white people, Rubinstein, while acknowledging that national data on crime and ethnicity are thin, extrapolated from California and national figures to estimate that in any given year illegal immigrants "could kill 2.6 persons per day across the U.S."[21]

The vast majority of violent crimes fall within city and state jurisdictions, not all of which collect data on ethnicity. Mark Hugo Lopez, associate director of the Pew Hispanic Center, and co-author of a recent report on Hispanics and federal crime, says, "The reason that we used federal statistics is that those are the cleanest data." The Pew study showed that 70 percent of Latino offenders were non-citizens, and that 3.1 percent of all Latino convicts were sentenced for crimes of violence, including murder.[22]

Others warn that hate crime statistics aren't reliable where immigrants are concerned. "One of the difficulties we have is getting certain communities to report hate crime," said Brian Levin, director of the Center for the Study of Hate and Extremism at California State University, San Bernardino. Illegal immigrants are especially reluctant, says Levin, in a widely shared observation.[23]

In any event, supercharged rhetoric from extremists has ratcheted up fear among immigrants and their advocates. Ward of the Center for New Community says that recent episodes of violence targeting immigrants reflect a general hostility toward immigrants that he's sensing on the street. For example, he says, following an organizational meeting in Wilmer, Minn., a town in the meat-processing factory belt of the upper Midwest, "A woman pulls up behind a car of our field people and starts screaming racial epithets."

Though of little significance by itself, Ward says it reflects an atmosphere that reminds him of "things I saw in the 1980s and '90s during the rise of the neo-Nazi movement." He adds, "These kinds of incidents, I would call an early warning of what will be the backlash."

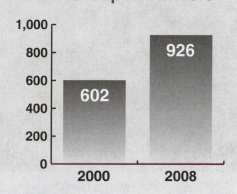

Hate Groups Increased by 50 Percent

The number of hate groups active in the United States — including skinheads, the Ku Klux Klan and neo-Nazis — increased more than a 50 percent from 2000 to 2008.

Hate Groups in the U.S.

Source: "The Year in Hate," Southern Poverty Law Center, February 2009

Immigration restrictionists argue that their political foes are whipping up passions in an effort to create the appearance that Latinos in general and immigrants in particular face growing danger.

"All hate crimes are abominable, and any decent person would oppose them no matter who the target is," says Ira Mehlman, national media director of the Federation for American Immigration Reform (FAIR), which advocates restricting immigration. "But they are hyping the statistics on hate crimes. Hate crimes against Hispanics are much fewer in actual number than attacks against gays or Jews, who represent much smaller percentages of the population."

Hard-core extremists still rank Jews as their No. 1 enemy, says Pitcavage at the Anti-Defamation League, which was formed in 1913 to combat anti-Semitism.

Some of the most horrific hate crimes are committed by "mission offenders," or mentally ill people who hear

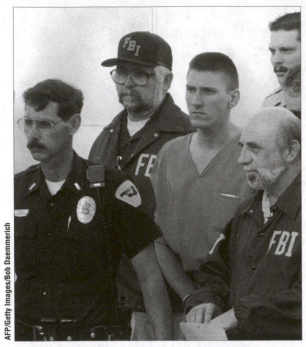

AFP/Getty Images/Bob Daemmerich

Oklahoma City bomber Timothy McVeigh, a neo-Nazi Army veteran, was executed in 2001 for killing 168 people, including 19 children, at the Murrah Federal Building. While extremists typically become active in times of social and economic stress, McVeigh struck in 1995 during a period of relative tranquility.

voices that command them to rid the world of a particular set of evildoers, Pitcavage says.[24] While they may target Jews — and those are often some of the most horrific crimes — "racial/ethnic targets" — including Latinos and immigrants in general — do run a risk from hate crime because they're "more visually identifiable and thus better targets of opportunity," he says.

Is right-wing and extremist speech encouraging hate crimes?

The killings of three Pittsburgh police officers intensified the ongoing debate over free speech and its consequences. Some liberal and left-wing commentators saw Richard Poplawski's horrific crime as an outgrowth, at least in part, of the far-right conspiracy culture that had influenced him, judging by his Web posts. In addition, they say, his rage had been stoked by conservative commentators. Still, the Pittsburgh reporter who helped trace those posts argues in the online magazine *Slate*

that the writings reveal more inner torment than ideology.

Journalist Dennis B. Roddy wrote that Poplawski also posted to a non-racist conspiracist site — Infowars, which describes its politics as libertarian. There, the alleged cop-killer "seemed to find . . . a bridge from the near-mainstream to a level of paranoid obsession in search of an explanation for his life's failures. For that, one does not need an ideology, just an inclination."[25]

Nevertheless, Roddy acknowledges that Poplawski complained on Infowars that the site neglected race. Other commentators insisted that Poplawski's posts follow a clear pattern. "Poplawski's black-helicopter and anti-Semitic ravings put him at the outer edge of the right," wrote Gary Kamiya, executive editor of *Salon*, a liberal online magazine. "But his paranoid fear that Obama was going to take away his AK-47 is mainstream among conservatives . . . fomented by the NRA and echoed by right-wing commentators from Lou Dobbs to Limbaugh."[26]

Kamiya doesn't propose limiting free-speech rights, but he does argue that extreme anti-Obama and gun-rights rhetoric is bound to produce more episodes like the Pittsburgh shootings.

The U.S. Supreme Court has ruled that even hate-filled racist speechmaking is protected by the First Amendment. In 1969, the court overturned the terrorism-advocacy conviction of an Ohio Ku Klux Klan leader who'd given a speech including a call to "send the Jews back to Israel," and to "bury the niggers." The court ruled unanimously that the government may not "forbid or proscribe advocacy of the use of force or of law violation except where such advocacy is directed to inciting or producing imminent lawless action."[27]

Worries about the effects of vicious and hyperbolic speech haven't only come from the left. In 2005, Freedom House, a human-rights advocacy organization then headed by former CIA director James Woolsey, a neo-conservative, issued a report accusing the government of Saudi Arabia of disseminating "hate propaganda" — targeting Christians, Jews and converts from Islam — in religious publications sent to mosques.[28]

In late March, an American writer of Arab descent wrote on a conservative Web site that American Muslims who get their news on satellite TV from the Middle East are, in effect, being brainwashed into a pro-jihadist

CHRONOLOGY

1930s-1960s *Attempts to create U.S. versions of European fascism fail, but far-right activists build smaller organizations after World War II.*

1934 The Rev. Charles Coughlin ("Father Coughlin") gains a nationwide following for denouncing President Franklin D. Roosevelt and Jews.

1941-1942 Coughlin is forced off the air and another far-right leader, William Dudley Pelley, is sent to prison for sedition.

1952 Anti-Semite Gerald L.K. Smith fails to persuade the Republican Party to link communism and Jews.

1958 John Birch Society is founded.

1963 Ku Klux Klan members bomb a black church in Birmingham, Ala., killing four young girls.

1967 American neo-Nazi leader George Lincoln Rockwell is killed by an embittered ex-aide.

1969 U.S. Supreme Court rules that a Ku Klux Klan leader's denunciations of blacks and Jews are constitutionally protected speech.

1970s-1980s *Anti-government and anti-Jewish organizations turn to violence, most often against police officers, who are seen as agents of the "Zionist Occupation Government."*

1971 Anti-Semitic, Christian Identity activist William Potter Gale formulates the doctrine underlying the radically anti-government Posse Comitatus movement, which by 1976 has at least 12,000 members, according to the FBI.

1978 *The Turner Diaries,* a genocide fantasy by neo-Nazi William Pierce (pseudonym: Andrew Macdonald), is published.

1983 Posse Comitatus leader Gordon Kahl kills two federal marshals in North Dakota, later dies in a shootout with federal agents in Arkansas.

1984 The Order, a small extremist group inspired by *The Turner Diaries,* murders a Jewish talk-show host in Denver who had denounced racism. . . . The group's founder is killed later in a shootout in Washington state.

1988 A federal jury in Arkansas acquits 14 right-wing extremists, including five members of The Order, on sedition and other charges.

1990s *Extremist violence climaxes in armed confrontations with federal officers.*

1992 An attempt to arrest survivalist and Christian Identity proponent Randy Weaver in Ruby Ridge, Idaho, ends with the deaths of a marshal and Weaver's wife and young son.

1993 Extremist leaders gather in Estes Park, Colo., to plan cooperation with less-threatening groups. . . . Federal siege of the Branch Davidian religious-cult compound in Waco, Texas, leads to deaths of more than 80 people. . . . Extremists depict Ruby Ridge and Waco as examples of government ruthlessness. . . . Outrage at government helps build "patriot militia" movement.

1995 Timothy McVeigh, an extremist military veteran inspired by *The Turner Diaries,* detonates truck bomb outside Alfred P. Murrah Federal Building in Oklahoma City, killing 168 people. . . . Militia membership declines.

2000s *Extremist movement erodes further following 9/11 attacks and the removal of major figures by death and imprisonment, but economic crisis ignites fears of a resurgence.*

2001 McVeigh executed by lethal injection.

2004 Richard Butler, influential leader of Idaho-based "Aryan Nations," dies of natural causes.

2005 Up-and-coming extremist leader Matthew Hale, founder of World Church of the Creator, is sentenced to 40 years for conspiracy to commit murder.

2009 Homeland Security Department warns extremists could exploit economic crisis as a recruiting opportunity; critics blast department for focusing on ideology rather than criminal acts.

Concern About Extremism Rising in Europe

Czech Republic expels ex-Klan leader David Duke.

Memories of the horrific consequences of far-right extremism remain strong in Europe. Yet nearly 65 years after the Nazi Holocaust, the extreme right has been gaining ground in parts of the continent, prompting worries that ultranationalism is on the upswing.

"The possibilities for a rise of the far right in the light of the financial and economic crisis are there," Anton Pelinka, a professor of politics at Central European University in Budapest, Hungary, told *The Guardian*, a leading British newspaper.[1]

So far, the European far right is advancing further — at the polls and in the expansion of illegal neo-Nazi organizations — than in the United States. But the gains by European extremists give heart to their U.S. counterparts, who have long maintained ties to Europe, though some European governments do their best to disrupt the relationships. In April, the Czech Republic expelled ex-Ku Klux Klan leader David Duke, a neo-Nazi, who had been invited by an extremist Czech group to lecture in Prague and Brno.

And the British government announced in early May that it had barred — among others — Don Black, founder of the Stormfront Web site, from entering Britain.

Duke's aborted visit notwithstanding, transatlantic ties may have frayed somewhat following the 2002 death of William Pierce. The American neo-Nazi leader had been traveling regularly to Europe for meetings, says Mark Potok, Intelligence Project director at the Southern Poverty Law Center, in Birmingham, Ala. But even if Duke fails to take Pierce's place as emissary to the Old World, American far-right Web sites commonly post links to extremist Web sites and news from Europe.[2]

The news is plentiful. In Austria, the country's two far-right parties together won 29 percent of the vote in national parliamentary elections last year. One of the parties had been founded by Jörg Haider, who died in a car crash shortly after the vote. Haider made his brand of politics a major force by combining salesmanship, xenophobic opposition to immigration and appeals to the Nazi heritage of Adolf Hitler's country of birth.

Haider had been forced to quit as a provincial governor in 1991 (he was reelected in 1999) after praising Hitler's "orderly employment program." And in 1995 he praised Waffen SS veterans as "decent men of character who remained faithful to their ideals."[3]

Indicators of the growing strength of extremism extend into Germany and Britain as well as parts of the former Soviet bloc. In Russia, where ultranationalist groups, including neo-Nazis, are part of the political landscape, there were at least 85 systematic killings of migrant workers from Central Asia, as well as others seen as ethnically non-Slavic, in 2008, according to the Sova Center, a Moscow-based hate crime-monitoring group. The victims included a migrant worker from Tajikistan who was beheaded. Human-rights advocates who denounce these killings have been threatened with death themselves.[4]

Violence isn't limited to Russia. In late 2008, the police chief of Passau, a Bavarian town with a strong neo-Nazi presence, was stabbed following his 2008 order to open the grave of a former Nazi who had been buried with an illegal Swastika flag.[5]

The attack took place against a backdrop of increasing violence by German neo-Nazi organizations. A German newspaper reported that violent crimes originating in the extremist right increased by 15 percent during the first 10 months of 2008. And a government research institute reported that a greater segment of male teenagers — 5

outlook. "We must never underestimate the power of hate propaganda," Nonie Darwish wrote, "because, quite simply, it works. Believe it or not, if you grow up hearing 'holy' cursing day in and day out, it can feel and sound normal, justified and even good." Darwish didn't call for banning the transmissions.[29]

But the more explosive recent disputes over speech arise from the immigration conflict. At the center of the controversy are radio and cable TV commentators like Glenn Beck, of Fox News. In June 2007 (before he had joined Fox), Beck read on his radio program a fake commercial for "Mexinol" — a fuel produced from the bodies of illegal immigrants from Mexico.[30]

"We have a butt load of illegal aliens in our country," said the fake ad, which was ascribed to Evil Conservative Industries. "With Mexinol, your raw materials come to you in a seemingly never-ending stream." Beck tried to put some distance between himself and the ad's authors,

percent — were involved in neo-Nazi groups than in mainstream politics in 2007-2008. In formerly communist-ruled eastern Germany, nearly 10 percent of youths participated in far-right groups.[6]

Throughout Western Europe, the enormous growth of immigrant populations, especially from Muslim countries, has provided the biggest boost to right-wing parties — from traditional conservative groups to neo-Nazis — over the past two decades.

However, the European far right's growth isn't uniform. In France, Jean-Marie Le Pen, an apologist for Nazism who was one of the pioneers of the post-World War II extreme right, saw his National Front party win only 4.3 percent of the vote in parliamentary elections in 2007.[7] Analysts said that President Nicolas Sarkozy effectively co-opted Le Pen's anti-immigration politics, though without the ethnic and religious extremism. In 2002, Le Pen had finished second in the first round of the presidential race.[8]

Le Pen's counterparts across the English Channel are showing more success. The British National Party (BNP) is seen by some British politicians as likely to win the most votes in an election in June to choose European Parliament representatives. BNP leaders portray their party as defending the country against non-white immigrants. Pro-immigrant policies "have made white Britons second-class citizens," the party says.[9]

Meanwhile, the BNP is trying to play down its historic anti-Semitism. Party leader Nick Griffin wrote in 2007 that taking an "Islamophobic" stance "is going to produce on average much better media coverage than . . . banging on about 'Jewish power.' "[10]

That purely tactical shift notwithstanding, others in the European political world argue that old-school anti-Semitism is flourishing — on the left as well as the right — often disguised as opposition to Israeli policies.

"The extravagant rhetoric of the demagogic left and right is gaining ground, and the most obvious manifestation is the return of anti-Semitism as an organizing ideology," Dennis MacShane, a Labor Party member of Parliament, wrote in late 2008. "As jobs are lost and welfare becomes meaner and leaner, the politics of blaming the outsider can only grow."[11]

[1] Quoted in Kate Connolly, "Haider is our Lady Di," *The Guardian*, Oct. 18, 2008, p. A29. For background, see Sarah Glazer, "Anti-Semitism in Europe," *CQ Global Researcher*, June 2008, pp. 149-181.

[2] For example, see "Stormfront forum, international," www.storm front.org/forum/forumdisplay.php?f=18; Kinism.net — Occidental Christianity, http://kinism.net/; The French Connection, http://iamthewitness.com/; League of American Patriots, http://leagueap.org/wordpress/?page_id=17.

[3] Quoted in Matt Schudel, "Jörg Haider; Politician Made Far-Right Party a Force in Austria," *The Washington Post*, Oct. 12, 2008, p. C8.

[4] Michael Schwirtz, "Migrant Worker Decapitated in Russia," *The New York Times*, Dec. 13, 2008; Luke Harding, "Putin's worst nightmare: Their mission is to cleanse Russia of its ethnic 'occupiers,'" *The Observer* magazine (U.K.), Feb. 8, 2009, p. 32; "Neo-Nazis threaten to murder journalists in Russia," Committee to Protect Journalists, Feb. 11, 2009, http://cpj.org/2009/02/neo-nazis-threaten-to-murder-journalists-in-russia.php.

[5] Nicholas Kulish, "Ancient City's Nazi Past Seeps Out After Stabbing," *The New York Times*, Feb. 12, 2009, p. A18; "Police Chief Long Reviled by NPD Leadership," *Spiegel Online International*, Dec. 19, 2008, www.spiegel.de/international/germany/0,1518,597645,00.html.

[6] *Ibid.*; and "German teens drawn to neo-Nazi groups — study," Reuters, March 17, 2009, http://in.reuters.com/article/worldNews/idINIndia-38554620090317.

[7] In 2008, Le Pen was fined 10,000 Euros for having called the Nazi occupation of France "not especially inhumane, even if there were a number of blunders." Quoted in "Le Pen fined over war comments," *The Irish Times* (Reuters), Feb. 9, 2008, p. A10.

[8] Adam Sage, "Hard-up National Front sells office to immigrants," *The Times* (London), Aug. 13, 2008, p. A37.

[9] "Immigration — time to say ENOUGH!" British National Party, undated, http://bnp.org.uk/policies-2/immigration. Also see Andrew Grice, "The BNP are now a bigger threat than ever," *The Independent* (London), April 10, 2009, p. A12.

[10] Quoted in Matthew Taylor, "BNP seeks to bury antisemitism and gain Jewish votes in Islamophobic campaign," *The Guardian* (London), April 10, 2008, p. A17.

[11] Denis MacShane, "Europe's Jewish Problem," *Newsweek*, International Edition, Dec. 15, 2008, p. 0.

though in a lighthearted tone. "I don't even know if that's conservative," he said, chuckling. "That would be . . . psychotic, perhaps?"[31]

Last year, Janet Murguía, president of the National Council of La Raza, a leading Hispanic organization, cited the segment in calling for cable channels "to clean up the rhetoric of their own commentators or take them out of their chairs." She argued that much of the commentary by the hosts and some of their guests spurred anti-immigrant violence. "When free speech transforms into hate speech, we've got to draw that line."[32]

Epstein of The American Cause argues that Murguía is trying to "muzzle" free speech. The painful reality of the nation's economic crisis, not anti-immigrant rhetoric — explains more about anti-Hispanic violence, he says.

"People should not hold an individual Hispanic responsible for the fact that wages are being depressed, and they can't get a job, or that schools are overcrowded, that there's an increase in crime in the community," he says. "But that's the reason these people are lashing out. In the few cases of [violence], they're responding to the problems that immigration causes."

Epstein argues that mainstream anti-immigration groups like FAIR provide a legitimate channel for citizens who favor limiting immigration to express their views. "If there was no one actually speaking for Americans, they're going to turn to more radical groups," he says. Epstein posts his writings on the VDare Web site but says he doesn't agree with all the views expressed on the site, some of them virulently racist.

A recent post by one contributor argued that hiring people of South Asian Indian ancestry guaranteed "corruption and ethnocentric discrimination"; another opined that hiring better public school teachers and firing less competent ones means "on net, firing blacks and hiring whites." And another contributor attacked "the cultural pollution of our 'entertainment industry,' which promotes diversity, multiculturalism and white demoralization."[33]

Cavanaugh of the ATF says he's aware that a constellation of legal organizations provide moral backing even for violent actions. In the civil rights days, such groups were known as the "white-collar Klan," he says. "They support people who will go out and do those things."

But, he says, free speech is free speech. "Is it illegal?" he asks rhetorically. "It's awful, but I can't do much about awful, and I shouldn't be able to."

BACKGROUND

Building Movements

Extreme-right political movements reached their peak in the 1930s in the United States and abroad. Adolf Hitler came to power in Germany in 1933. Benito Mussolini, originator of the term "fascism," who began his rule of Italy in 1922, soon forged an alliance with Hitler. Other far-right movements triumphed in Central Europe. The United States, of course, never succumbed to totalitarian rule. But the American extreme right did command a sizable sector of public opinion.[34]

As in Germany and elsewhere (though not to a major extent in Italy), hatred of Jews played a key role in the American right-wing mobilization, with communists and socialists close behind on the enemies list.

Henry Ford, founder of the Ford Motor Co., actively spread anti-Semitism in the 1920s, using a newspaper that he owned, the *Dearborn Independent*, to publish vast amounts of propaganda about a Jewish plot for world domination.[35]

After Ford withdrew from public anti-Semitic activity under pressure from Jewish organizations and the U.S. government, other leaders emerged. Gerald L. K. Smith, a minister and failed political candidate allied with hate-mongers, denounced President Franklin D. Roosevelt (FDR) and African-Americans as well as Jews. William Dudley Pelley led the fascist Silver Legion — the "Silver Shirts" — which dedicated itself mainly to marches and other publicity-seeking events expressing hatred of Jews, blacks and all minorities.

The Rev. Charles Coughlin, a Roman Catholic priest, known as "Father Coughlin," soared to national prominence and influence through radio broadcasts from his church outside Detroit. At first a Roosevelt supporter, the "radio priest" by 1934 was raging against FDR and the Jews, on whom he blamed the Great Depression.

After the United States entered World War II, the Catholic Church and the federal government forced Coughlin off the air. Pelley was convicted in 1942 of sedition and intent to cause insurrection in the military and was sentenced to 15 years in prison.[36]

By war's end, American fascism as a mass movement had ended. But a core of committed activists kept the far right alive, spurred on by the Cold War against the Soviet Union and the first stirrings of the civil rights movement.[37]

As public opposition to communism grew, Smith preached that Jews and communists were one and the same and that the Holocaust never occurred.

The founding of the John Birch Society in 1958 marked the reemergence of conspiratorial, far-right views — minus the anti-Semitism — in respectable society. Birch Society doctrine viewed the United Nations as a communist organization. Founder Robert Welch, an executive in his brother's candy company, went further, calling President Dwight D. Eisenhower "a dedicated, conscious agent of the communist conspiracy."[38]

Welch's wild accusation stoked outrage in the political mainstream. President Harry S. Truman reportedly called the Birch Society "the Ku Klux Klan, without nightshirts."[39]

By the mid-1960s, the Klan — established in 1866 in Pulaski, Tenn. — had become the center of extremist resistance to the civil rights movement. Members and ex-members of the secret organization carried out some of the most notorious crimes of the era, including the 1963 bombing of the 16th Street Baptist Church in Birmingham, Ala., in which four young girls were killed; the assassination of civil rights leader Medgar Evers in Jackson, Miss., that same year; the murder of three civil rights workers in 1964 in Neshoba County, Miss.; and the killing of another civil rights worker in Alabama in 1965.[40]

Anti-civil rights violence ebbed after enactment of the Voting Rights Act in 1965. From then on, the extremist right became steadily more influenced by neo-Nazism. George Lincoln Rockwell, founder of the American Nazi Party, pioneered the white-nationalist trend. The former Navy pilot and World War II veteran was shot and killed by a dismissed follower in 1967.[41]

Rockwell had been a mentor to William Pierce, a former university physics professor who in 1974 founded the National Alliance, which became a major influence in the extremist right. Pierce became nationally notorious in the 1990s as author of *The Turner Diaries*, which laid out a scenario for white genocide of blacks, Jews and "race traitors" — a process led by a secret brotherhood known as The Order, which sets events in motion by blowing up FBI headquarters with a truck bomb.

The first open sign of a Klan-Nazi nexus was the 1979 killing in broad daylight of five Communist Workers Party members who were starting an anti-Klan march in Greensboro, N.C., in 1979.

Fighting and Killing

Less visibly, another trend was under way. An extreme anti-government and anti-Jewish movement founded in 1971 by William Potter Gale began growing, especially in the West and Midwest. Posse Comitatus ("Power of the County") held that the federal government was con-stitutionally illegitimate. For example, county justices of the peace held legal supremacy over the U.S. Supreme Court, according to Posse ideology, and federal currency was invalid.[42]

Posse alienation went far deeper. An anti-Semitic reli-gious doctrine known as "Christian Identity" exerted deep

influence on many Posse leaders and members, including Gale (despite his own definitively proved Jewish descent, which he denied). The doctrine — rejected by all mainstream Christian denominations — holds that white people are the genuine descendants of the Biblical Hebrews. That is, they're God's chosen people, and Jews and blacks are the devil's spawn. By 1976, the FBI estimated Posse membership at 12,000 to 50,000, not including sympathizers.

Posse Comitatus played a major role in raising the level of far-right extremism to a fever pitch in the last two decades of the 20th century. In the early 1980s, economic crisis gripped the Farm Belt, bringing a wave of foreclosures. The Posse launched a major recruiting drive, preaching that Jewish bankers were to blame for the falling grain prices and land values that brought many farmers to ruin.

One Posse tactic was to flood the federal court system with amateur lawsuits to cancel farmers' loan obligations, on the grounds that the loans were illegal. When authorities enforced foreclosure orders, trouble sometimes erupted.

In 1983, Gordon Kahl, a Christian Identity Posse activist who had served a prison term for tax evasion, killed two federal marshals following a meeting to recruit members in North Dakota. Kahl fled and was killed three months later in a gunfight with federal agents in Arkan-sas. Kahl became a martyr in extremist circles.

An almost identical episode took place the next year near Cairo, Neb., when a Posse sympathizer, Arthur Kirk, was killed in a shootout with state police officers serving foreclosure papers. Before the shooting started, Kirk denounced Jews, bankers and the Israeli intelligence agency, Mossad, to officers trying to get him to surrender.[43]

Ideology aside, some farmers who accepted help from the Posse were trying to survive financial crisis. Another group formed in the 1980s dedicated itself purely to violence.

The Order (its name borrowed from *The Turner Dia-ries*) vowed to strike the "Zionist Occupation Government" in defense of "White America." Robert Mathews founded the small group with eight other men in the early 1980s. By 1983, The Order had begun committing armed rob-beries to raise money. In 1984, the group assassinated a Denver radio talk-show host, Alan Berg, who was Jewish, and had argued with racists on the air. Later that same year, the group robbed an armored car of $3.6 million.

Mathews died in a shootout with federal agents on Whidbey Island, near Seattle, in December 1984.

In 1985, 23 surviving members of the group went to trial or pleaded guilty to racketeering charges, with most receiving sentences of 40 to 100 years. David Lane later was sentenced to 150 years in a separate trial for participating in Berg's murder.[44]

Federal prosecutors in Fort Smith, Ark., failed, however to convict Lane and 13 other extremists of sedition in 1988. They'd been charged with plotting to overthrow the government and set up a separate white nation in the Pacific Northwest.[45]

That same year, in that very region, an upsurge of anti-minority violence by skinheads claimed the life of Ethiopian immigrant Mulugeta Seraw, who was bludgeoned to death with a baseball bat by the East Side White Pride gang. Three years later, Tom Metzger, an infamous San Diego extremist, was found responsible for the death, along with others, on the grounds that his White Aryan Resistance group had incited the group who killed Seraw. The verdict, in a civil suit brought by the SPLC, required Metzger and his codefendants to pay $12.5 million to Seraw's family.[46]

Explosion and Aftermath

The violence that marked the 1980s intensified in the '90s, sparked by the botched 1992 arrest of survivalist and Christian Identity adherent Randy Weaver for failing to appear in court on a gun-law charge. (He'd been given the wrong court date.) Weaver had holed up with his family in remote Ruby Ridge, in northern Idaho, which had become a center for the extreme right and was home to Christian Identity leader Richard Butler.[47]

When federal marshals attempted to arrest Weaver, who had not been involved in previous violence, a gunfight broke out in which Weaver's son and a marshal were killed; later, during a siege of the family's cabin, an FBI sniper killed Weaver's wife. Weaver surrendered and was sentenced to 18 months in prison.[48]

FBI handling of the case was widely considered a fiasco, and worse. But on the far right, a more ominous view prevailed: Ruby Ridge seemed to validate conspiracist fears of government violence against gun owners and opponents of the "New World Order" — far-right code for U.N.-controlled global government.

Months after Ruby Ridge, Christian Identity preacher Peter Peters organized a meeting of about 150 extremists at Estes Park, Colo. In a keynote speech, Louis Beam, a former leader of the Texas Klan and one of those acquitted in the Arkansas sedition case, outlined a strategy of "leaderless resistance" — formation of small cells of committed activists without central direction. A Vietnam veteran, Beam also spoke of the need for "camouflage" — the ability to blend in the public's eye the more committed groups of resistance "with mainstream 'kosher' associations that are generally seen as harmless."[49]

Similarly, others at the meeting advocated uniting with less extreme groups to form a broad anti-government movement.[50]

Meanwhile, a related development had just shocked the mainstream political establishment. David Duke, a former Klan leader who hadn't renounced his anti-black or anti-Jewish views, won the 1991 Republican primary for Louisiana governor. (He went on to lose the general election.)[51]

Following the Estes Park conclave, "militias" sprang up around the country, especially in the rural Midwest and West. Ideas animating the movement included survivalism, gun-rights defense and — among many members, but not all — far-right conspiracy theories. Among those who passed through militia circles was a U.S. Army veteran of the 1990-1991 Persian Gulf War, Timothy McVeigh.

But before McVeigh's name hit the headlines, a series of events near Waco, Texas, would seize national attention and electrify the far right. Members of the Branch Davidian religious cult, led by a fiery preacher named David Koresh, fired on ATF agents attempting to search for guns and ammunition believed to be stored at the Davidians' compound; four agents were killed. On April 19, 1993, after a 51-day siege, FBI agents moved on the compound with tanks. In the conflagration that resulted, Koresh and about 80 other Davidians died, including many children.

A widespread suspicion that FBI teargas canisters started the fire became a certainty on the far right. In those circles, Waco stood as evidence of government ruthlessness. Koresh, who had followed the Weaver case closely, probably wouldn't have been surprised. "Koresh spoke to me frequently on the phone about Ruby Ridge," says Special Agent Cavanaugh of the ATF, who negotiated with the Branch Davidian leader during the siege. Koresh and his top aide "were well-versed in everything that happened there and were spitting out 'New World Order' crackpot conspiracy theories."

In 2000, an outside counsel to the Justice Department concluded that the canisters hadn't started the fire but that Davidians themselves ignited it.[52]

But by then, April 19 had become notorious for another reason. On April 19, 1995, McVeigh detonated a bomb in a rented truck he parked in front of the Alfred P. Murrah Federal Building in Oklahoma City, killing 168 people, including 19 children. Arrested hours later after a traffic stop, McVeigh was later often described as a lone wolf. But, among other activities, he had sold *The Turner Diaries* at gun shows, which were popular with militia members and with extremists in general.

"McVeigh was not a lone extremist; instead, he was trained to make himself look like a lone extremist," wrote former FBI agent German. "It's a right-wing terrorism technique that comes complete with written instruction manuals."[53]

The bombing — for which McVeigh was executed in 2001 — made *Turner Diaries* author Pierce and his National Alliance notorious. But the bombing also saw a steep decline in militia membership, as those without a high level of commitment to extremist politics dropped away.

More blows followed. Pierce died of cancer in 2002. Two years later Butler died; earlier he had lost his Idaho compound after losing a civil lawsuit filed by the Southern Poverty Law Center.[54]

Then, in 2005, Matthew Hale, 33, considered an up-and-coming extremist leader as head of the World Church of the Creator, was sentenced to 40 years in federal prison for conspiring to kill a federal judge. Since his imprisonment, extremist-watchers say, no charismatic leader has emerged from the extremist world.

CURRENT SITUATION

Hate in April

Hitler was born in April, which marks the beginning of the public rally season for right-wing extremists, and for opponents who mount counterdemonstrations.[55]

This year promises to be a busy one for haters. In April alone, 32 conferences, celebrations, militia training sessions and other events were planned by neo-Nazi, Klan, Christian Identity and related organizations in 22 states,

according to the Anti-Defamation League; dozens more events are scheduled into October.[56]

The list includes Hitler birthday commemorations in Illinois and North Carolina and a march by robed Klan members in Pulaski, Tenn., where Confederate veterans founded the Klan.

Counterdemonstrators showed for an NSM rally of about 70 members the day before at the Gateway Arch in St. Louis, Mo. No one was arrested, but the two groups yelled at each other and traded "Heil Hitler" salutes and raised-middle-finger retorts. A second group of counterdemonstrators organized by the ADL held a "rally for respect" at a nearby site.[57]

Commenting on the NSM rally, Lewis Reed, president of the St. Louis Board of Aldermen, said, "It's sad that there are still people today, in 2009, that only want to divide the races and breed hate."[58]

Yet neo-Nazi rallies, at least in major metropolitan areas, typically don't draw big crowds of extremists. In Skokie, Ill., a Chicago suburb with a large Jewish population — including Holocaust survivors — the opening of a state holocaust museum in April drew a neo-Nazi demonstration — of seven people. Twelve thousand people attended the opening ceremony, where former President Bill Clinton spoke.[59]

This year's rally season began with a snag. "East Coast White Unity" and "Volksfront" ("Peoples' Front" in German) had planned to meet in Boston over the April 11 weekend. But after the Boston Anti-Racist Coalition told the Veterans of Foreign Wars (VFW) about the nature of the "Patriot's Day" rally, the VFW withdrew permission to use their hall. Instead, the event was held at an American Legion Hall in Loudon, N.H.[60]

"These racist speakers, bands and their supporters will always have to walk on egg shells and face the very real prospect of their events being exposed to the general public, wherever and whenever they rear their ugly heads," the coalition said in a post on an anarchist Web site.[61]

But Roper of White Revolution replied, "Because a venue, or two, or three, has cancelled on us due to the efforts of anti-white, communist and Jewish activists, the event has not been cancelled and will go on," he said. "We plan for such eventualities in depth."[62]

For its part, One People's Project, an anti-supremacist organization, says it infiltrates neo-Nazi and Klan groups to find out about planned events in time to organize

'Fascism' Label Comes in Handy for Critics

But respected writers say it's a legitimate — if unlikely — concern.

Accompanying today's worries about an extremist resurgence are fears that the United States could, if economic conditions worsen, embrace fascism — the totalitarian ideology that modern hate groups champion.

But the concern focuses on the federal government itself, not fringe, neo-Nazi organizations. Indeed, some of President Barack Obama's foes are calling him a fascist, the same label some had applied to President George W. Bush.

The labeling would seem to show once again that "fascist" is one of the most loosely applied — and handy — terms in the political lexicon. Nevertheless, fascism isn't foreign to the United States, even though the word comes from 1920s Italy. Italian dictator Benito Mussolini coined "fascismo" to name the violence-glorifying, socialist-hating and ultranationalist movement he formed after World War I, appropriating a term then used for militant political groups of all stripes.[1]

Notwithstanding those Italian roots, Robert Paxton, one of the leading historians of the European far right, wrote that the first fascist group in history may have been the Ku Klux Klan. "By adopting a uniform . . . as well as by their techniques of intimidation and their conviction that violence was justified in the cause of their group's destiny," wrote Paxton, a Virginia native, "the first version of the Klan in the defeated American South was arguably a remarkable preview of the way fascist movements were to function in interwar Europe."[2]

But Paxton, an emeritus professor of social science at Columbia University, dismisses the attempt to label Obama fascist as a desperation move. "When there's a popular figure and you can't get a grip on opposing him, you call him a fascist," he says. "As opposed to Hitler and Mussolini in uniform, shrieking into microphones and juicing up the nationalism of crowds, Obama is a calm, reasonable person whose basic drives have all been toward bolstering democracy and the rule of law."

Obama's extreme critics insist otherwise. Obama heads a "Gestapo government," conservative blogger David Limbaugh (brother of radio commentator Rush Limbaugh) told a radio interviewer. And *The American Spectator*, a conservative magazine, likened Obama's economic policies to those of Mussolini.[3]

The author of the *Spectator* piece, senior editor Quinn Hillyer, added that he wouldn't go so far as to compare Obama's administration to that of Adolf Hitler, whose version of fascism turned out far deadlier than the Italian original. Still, he wrote, "The comparison of today's situation to that of Italian fascism is no mere scare tactic but a serious concern."[4]

In calling Obama a fascist, critics may simply be hoping for better results than they got when they tried pinning the "socialist" label on him during and after the 2008 presidential campaign. "We've so overused the word 'socialism' that it no longer has the negative connotation it had 20 years ago, or even 10 years ago," Sal Anuzis, former chairman of the Michigan Republican Party, told *The New York Times*. "Fascism — everybody still thinks that's a bad thing."[5]

To be sure, only a small minority accepts "fascist" as a compliment. But aiming it at a politician after first denouncing him as a leftist seems an odd tactic, given fascists' historic hatred of socialists.[6]

But that seemed to bother Obama's foes as little as the fact that they were borrowing from the vocabulary that some critics of the Bush administration used in 2001-2008.

The liberal group MoveOn.org, for instance, created an ad in 2004 that tried to connect Bush to Hitler, intoning: "A nation warped by lies. Lies fuel fear. Fear fuels aggression. Invasion. Occupation. What were war crimes in 1945 is foreign policy in 2003."[7]

Liberal author Naomi Wolf made a similar case in her book *The End of America*, published toward the end of the Bush administration.[8]

countermobilizations. "We can't keep on allowing groups like the Klan, Aryan Nations, National Alliance, National Vanguard and the National Socialist Movement to hold society at-large hostage," Daryle Lamont Jenkins of One People's Project said.[63]

On April 19, 2008, 30 to 40 members of the National Socialist Movement (NSM) rallied in Washington for an anti-immigration march from the National Mall to the U.S. Capitol. They were greeted by raucous counterdemonstrators, five of whom were arrested for allegedly assaulting police officers with pepper spray and a pole.[64]

White supremacist gatherings don't tend to be large affairs. Roper told a reporter by phone from the New Hampshire event that 200 people were participating,

"The Nazis rose to power in a living, if battered, democracy," Wolf wrote. "Dictators can rise in a weakened democracy even with a minority of popular support."[9]

Drawing in part from Paxton's most recent book on fascism, Wolf argued that erosions of civil liberties under the Bush administration paralleled events in Italy and Germany as Mussolini and Hitler moved toward totalitarian rule.

Followers of the neo-Nazi NPD party stand defiantly near a "Berlin against Nazis" poster during a demonstration in Berlin on May 1, 2009. Anti-immigration neo-Nazis and skinheads often clash with anti-fascists on May Day in Germany.

Hitler upon winning election as chancellor in 1933. "You can draw some parallels — with care," he says. "The focus should be on steps away from the rule of law."

Still, Paxton discourages complacency. "In three years, if we're not out of this mess, we could see something that would call itself the patriotic party or the minutemen, a symbol that has a nice nationalistic resonance," he says. "It would sweep up all the discontented from the left and the right; it would be light

But these arguments leave out the widespread loss of faith in democracy, and the state of near-civil war that served as the backdrop to the rise of fascism in Italy and Germany, Paxton says.

By contrast, Americans opposed to Bush expressed their discontent within the system, by voting in Obama, Paxton notes. And the political climate even before that, when Wolf was writing, didn't begin to approach the Italian and German precedents. "In the collection of preconditions, you need something worse," he says. "A lost war, big-time national humiliation — we might get there, but we're not quite there yet — and a sense that our existing way of doing politics isn't working. And then power moving to the streets, with paramilitary organizations. I don't see any of that."

Paxton does agree that the detention and intelligence-gathering policies adopted after the Sept. 11, 2001, terrorist attacks could be compared with early moves by

on ideology. The immigration issue would be a very plausible gathering point for some sort of movement like this."

---

[1] Robert O. Paxton, *The Anatomy of Fascism* (2004), pp. 4-5.

[2] *Ibid.*, p. 49.

[3] Quinn Hillyer, "Il Duce, Redux?" *The American Spectator*, April 2, 2009, http://spectator.org/archives/2009/04/02/il-duce-redux. Limbaugh quoted in Carla Marinucci and Joe Garofoli, "Fascist? Socialist? Attacks on Obama take a shrill tone," *San Francisco Chronicle*, April 9, 2009, p. A1.

[4] Hillyer, *op. cit.*

[5] Quoted in John Harwood, "But Can Obama Make the Trains Run on Time?" *The New York Times*, April 20, 2009, www.nytimes.com/2009/04/20/us/politics/20caucus.html?scp=1&sq=fascism&st=cse.

[6] Paxton, *op. cit.*, pp. 60-67.

[7] Marinucci and Garofoli, *op. cit.*

[8] Naomi Wolf, *The End of America: Letters of Warning to a Young Patriot, A Citizen's Call to Action* (2007).

[9] *Ibid.*, pp. 39-40.

---

making it one of the bigger events of its type. But no independent confirmation was available.

In 2005, Roper organized a protest demonstration outside an event in Boston commemorating the 60th anniversary of the liberation of Nazi death camps. Police and counterprotesters far outnumbered Roper and his dozen or so demonstrators.[65]

However, on occasion, supremacists' crowds have been bigger, and violence has erupted. In 2002, about 60 supporters of the now-imprisoned Matthew Hale's World Church of the Creator gathered in York, Pa., where a former mayor and eight others had been charged in the 1969 death of a black woman during a racially charged riot. Several hundred counterprotesters fought with Hale's supporters in the city streets, as police tried to separate the groups. Twenty-five people were arrested.[66]

However, in April of that year, only about 30 to 40 neo-Nazis showed up in York for a Hitler's birthday celebration.[67]

Free Speech, Hate Speech

Some conservatives are attacking the Department of Homeland Security (DHS) examination of far-right extremism as a barely disguised attack on political foes of the Obama administration.

"One of the most embarrassingly shoddy pieces of propaganda I'd ever read out of DHS," thundered conservative blogger Michelle Malkin. Others in the conservative blogosphere shared her view that the report tried to tie conservatives to extremists.[68] Homeland Security Secretary Janet Napolitano later responded that the agency is on "the lookout for criminal and terrorist activity but we do not — nor will we ever — monitor ideology or political beliefs."[69]

The report noted that extremists are especially interested in recruiting veterans, an observation that triggered angry criticism from some veterans' organizations (see below). In essence the 14-page assessment holds that economic turmoil, the election of a black president and a growing number of veterans — whom right-wing extremists have a documented interest in recruiting — are creating a climate in which far-right extremism could flourish again. Specifically, the report said the DHS "assesses that right-wing extremist groups' frustration over a perceived lack of government action on illegal immigration has the potential to incite individuals or small groups toward violence." But any such violence would likely be "isolated" and "small-scale."[70]

Though critics later said the DHS failed to distinguish between extremists and mainstream political advocates, the report did try to draw that line. Debates on gun rights and other constitutional issues are often intense — but perfectly legal, the report said. "Violent extremists," it added, "may attempt to co-opt the debate and use the controversy as a radicalization tool."[71]

But Berlet of Political Research Associates argues that the report itself crosses into the potentially unconstitutional territory of monitoring ideological trends.

"The government should not be in the business of undermining radical ideas," he says. "As citizens we have

a responsibility to challenge rhetoric that demonizes and scapegoats, but I don't think the First Amendment allows the government to be in that battle."

Despite attacks from the left as well as right, some commentators defended the report against its critics. "This DHS assessment was begun more than a year ago, before Barack Obama was even nominated," blogger Charles Johnson — a political independent who had been popular with conservative critics of Islam — wrote on his influential "Little Green Footballs" site. "It was not done at the behest of the Obama administration. . . . The DHS report is not intended to target anyone but the most extreme elements of the far right, and it's depressing to see so many bloggers jumping to totally unwarranted conclusions."[72]

Reaction to the document may have been especially intense because it followed closely on an uproar that greeted disclosure of a report on the "Modern Militia Movement" in Missouri. It was produced by a "fusion center," one of 70 around the country that were set up by law enforcement agencies after Sept. 11 to ensure that intelligence is shared between federal, state and local officers. The report mostly summarized information on extremist activities in the 1990s and outlined some ideas said to be circulating now on the far right.[73]

But the report lumped together extremists and mainstream political activists with no violent inclinations. "Militia members most commonly associate with third-party political groups," the report said, going on to name supporters of 2008 libertarian presidential candidate Bob Barr, Constitution Party candidate Chuck Baldwin and Rep. Ron Paul, R-Texas, who ran for the Republican Party presidential nomination.[74]

"This smacks of totalitarian regimes of days gone by," said Baldwin, one of many to react furiously to the document.[75]

Within weeks, the Missouri State Highway Patrol had apologized to the three politicians and replaced the head of the fusion center.[76]

Not all critics came from the right. "This is part of a national trend where intelligence reports are turning attention away from people who are actually doing bad things to people who are thinking thoughts that the government, for whatever reason, doesn't like," former FBI agent German told The Associated Press.[77]

The ACLU, where German is now a policy counselor, noted that the North Central Texas Fusion System had produced a report in February that tied former Rep. Cynthia McKinney and former U.S. Attorney General Ramsey Clark to "far left groups" that allegedly sympathize with the Iranian-backed Hezbollah militia of Lebanon and other armed movements in the Middle East.[78]

Fusion centers, German said, are an "equal opportunity infringer" on civil rights of citizens on the right and the left.[79]

Indeed, DHS says that it produced a report earlier this year on left-wing extremists. That report soon leaked out as well. The document forecast a rise in cyber-attacks aimed at businesses, especially those deemed to be violators of animal rights.[80]

Extremism-watchers, for their part, greeted the DHS report as an echo of their own conclusions. "This Homeland Security report reinforces our view that the current political and economic climate in the United States is creating the right conditions for a rise in extremist activity," said Potok of the SPLC.[81]

But one of the center's most ferocious left-wing critics, writer Alexander Cockburn, ridiculed that reasoning, accusing the center of "fingering militiamen in a potato field in Idaho" instead of "attacking the roots of Southern poverty, and the system that sustains that poverty as expressed in the endless prisons and death rows across the South, disproportionately crammed with blacks and Hispanics."[82]

Fights are also continuing over broadcasters' commentaries. In Boston, radio station WTKK-FM suspended right-wing radio talk-show host Jay Severin after he responded to the influenza outbreak with comments including: "So now, in addition to venereal disease and the other leading exports of Mexico — women with mustaches and VD — now we have swine flu." Mexicans, he said, are "the world's lowest of primitives."[83]

Franklin Soults, a spokesman for Massachusetts Immigrant and Refugee Advocacy Coalition, called Severin's language "dehumanizing."

Severin himself referred questions to his lawyer, George Tobia, who told the *Boston Globe* that he expected the broadcaster to be back on the air soon. "But I don't know when."[84]

Recruiting Veterans

Discharged from the U.S. Marine Corps after being arrested for allegedly taking part in armed robberies at two hotels in Jacksonville, N.C., a former lance corporal now faces prosecution for allegedly threatening President Obama's life.

Kody Brittingham, 20, who served in the 2nd Tank Battalion, 2nd Marine Division, was indicted in February for the alleged threat by a federal grand jury in Raleigh, N.C. An unnamed federal law enforcement official told the Jacksonville (N.C.) *Daily News* that the charge followed discovery of a journal in Brittingham's barracks at Camp Lejeune in which he laid out a plan to kill Obama, who at that point hadn't yet been inaugurated. Investigators reportedly also found white-supremacist literature among Brittingham's possessions.[85]

How plausible the alleged assassination plans were is not clear. But the arrest did reawaken concerns about white-supremacist and neo-Nazi recruitment of men with military training, especially those with combat experience (Brittingham, however, had never served overseas).

Those concerns aren't limited to extremist-watchers from advocacy organizations. An FBI report last year counted 203 individuals with "confirmed or claimed" military experience who had been spotted in extremist groups since the Sept. 11 attacks, which effectively marked the beginning of a period in which hundreds of thousands of military personnel began acquiring battlefield experience.[86]

Those 203 individuals represent a minuscule fraction of the country's 23.8 million veterans or 1.4 million active-duty personnel, the report acknowledged.[87]

The recent DHS assessment discussed extremist groups' interest in recruiting veterans, only to prompt outraged reaction from some veterans' organizations and some politicians. "To characterize men and women returning home after defending our country as potential terrorists is offensive and unacceptable," House Republican leader John Boehner of Ohio said in a press release. The Department of Homeland Security owes our veterans an apology."[88]

In discussing extremists' interest in veterans, the FBI said that neo-Nazis were not discouraged by the small number of vets who might be responsive to recruiting pitches.

"The prestige which the extremist movement bestows upon members with military experience grants them the potential for influence beyond their numbers," said the report, which is marked "unclassified/for official use only/law enforcement sensitive." The report, now available

Is anti-immigration rhetoric provoking hate crimes against Latinos?

YES
Mark Potok
Director, Intelligence Project, Southern Poverty Law Center

Written for *CQ Researcher*, April 2009

Across the board, nativist organizations in America have angrily denounced those who suggest that demonizing rhetoric leads to hate violence. One of them even recently issued a press release criticizing the "outrageous behavior" of groups like the Southern Poverty Law Center that propose such a link and "provide no proof whatsoever."

Nativist organizations take the remarkable position that hate speech directed against Latino immigrants has no relationship at all to hate crime — not even the utterly false allegations that Latinos are secretly planning to hand the American Southwest over to Mexico, are far more criminal than others, are bringing dread diseases to the United States, and so on.

In addition to defying common sense, that head-in-the-sand approach completely ignores the statements that are typically made by hate criminals during their attacks.

Take the case of Marcelo Lucero, who was allegedly murdered by a gang of white teenagers in the Long Island town of Patchogue, N.Y., last November. Prosecutors say the suspects told detectives they regularly went "beaner jumping" — beating up Latinos — and that they used racial epithets during the attack. "Let's go find some Mexicans to [expletive] up," one said beforehand, according to *Newsday*.

Nativist groups use the fact that we don't know precisely where the teens' fury comes from to deny it was related to nativist demonization. But just because it's not possible to pinpoint the exact source of their racial anger — rhetoric from nativist groups, their parents, local anti-immigrant politicians, or pundits — does not mean it magically popped into the assailants' minds.

There is also hard evidence to back up the link between demonization and violence. According to FBI statistics, anti-Latino hate crimes went up 40 percent between 2003 and 2007 — the very same period that saw a remarkable proliferation of nativist rhetoric.

Experts agree that there is a link. "Racist rhetoric and dehumanizing images inspire violence perpetrated against innocent human beings," says Jack Levin, a nationally known hate crime expert at Northeastern University. "It's not just the most recent numbers. It's the trend over a number of years that lends credibility to the notion that we're seeing a very real and possibly dramatic rise in anti-Latino hate incidents."

Ignoring the role that demonization plays in such violence is a surefire way to generate more of it. Marcelo Lucero's murder is only the latest in a sad list of violent incidents inspired by ugly rhetoric that will certainly grow longer.

NO
Marcus Epstein
Executive Director, The American Cause

Written for *CQ Researcher*, April 2009

Last year, Barack Obama accused broadcasters Lou Dobbs and Rush Limbaugh of "feeding a kind of xenophobia." He added that their broadcasts were a "reason why hate crimes against Hispanic people doubled last year."

Obama's facts and logic are plain wrong. The FBI found only 745 anti-Latino hate crimes nationwide in 2007, down from 770 in 2006. In fact anti-Hispanic hate crimes per capita dropped 18 percent over the last decade.

Most of these hate crimes were for minor offenses, such as graffiti or name-calling, with only 145 aggravated assaults, two murders and no rapes in 2007. To put this in perspective, former Hudson Institute economist Ed Rubenstein estimates illegal aliens murder at least 949 people a year.

There is also no evidence that hate crimes are motivated by the immigration-control movement. Those who claim there's a connection cannot point to a single, significant commentator or politician who has advocated violence against Latinos. Nor can they find a single hate crime committed by their followers.

Although whites are the vast majority of listeners of conservative talk radio and television, they committed only 52 percent of hate crimes against Latinos — a percentage well below their proportion of 66 percent of the population. Moreover, Los Angeles County classified 42 percent of black-on-Hispanic hate crimes as "gang related." This is not to suggest that blacks cannot be racist, but that they are unlikely to be influenced by the purveyors of supposed anti-immigrant rhetoric.

The 2008 murder of José Osvaldo Sucuzhanay in Brooklyn by blacks who targeted him because they mistook him as gay was denounced as a significant anti-Hispanic, anti-immigrant hate crime by all New York politicians and by *The New York Times*. Even when they were at large, the race of the killers was rarely mentioned.

Groups like the Southern Poverty Law Center that perpetuate misconceptions about anti-Latino hate crimes make no secret of their goals. They want supporters of immigration control silenced because, in the words of La Raza president Janet Murguía, "We have to draw the line on freedom of speech, when freedom of speech becomes hate speech."

These organizations run relentless smear campaigns accusing virtually all opponents of illegal immigration — no matter how nuanced or tempered — of hate speech that must not be allowed on the airwaves, in print, or in front of Congress.

Before we abandon our core democratic principles of free speech and open debate in the name of stopping hate crimes, we should at least get our facts straight.

online, has circulated among journalists and nongovernmental specialists.[89]

Among a handful of specific cases, the FBI noted that two privates in the elite Army 82nd Airborne Division received six-year prison sentences for attempting to sell body armor and other equipment in 2007 to an undercover agent posing as a white-supremacist movement member. And in 2005, a former Army intelligence analyst who'd been convicted of a firearms violation founded a skinhead group that reportedly advocated training members in firearms, knife-fighting, close-quarters combat and "house sweeps."[90]

The FBI intelligence assessment followed an investigation by the SPLC. In 2006 the center published a detailed report that quoted neo-Nazi vets, a supremacist who had renounced the extremist cause, as well as a Defense Department investigator. Extremists "stretch across all branches of service, they are linking up across the branches once they're inside, and they are hard-core," investigator Scott Barfield told the SPLC. "We've got Aryan Nations graffiti in Baghdad."[91]

Worries about a neo-Nazi presence in the military had surfaced years before U.S. troops were deployed to Iraq and Afghanistan. The trigger was the random murder in 1995 of a black man and woman in Fayetteville, N.C., by two soldiers in the elite Army 82nd Airborne Division, whose home base is nearby Fort Bragg. In the uproar that followed, 22 members of the 82nd — including those arrested for the killing — were found by the Army to have extremist ties.[92]

But far-right efforts to penetrate the Armed Forces apparently continued. The SPLC published excerpts from a 1999 article in the *National Alliance* magazine by an Army Special Forces veteran who urged young supremacists to sign up. "Light infantry is your branch of choice," he wrote, "because the coming race war, and the ethnic cleansing to follow, will be very much an infantryman's war. It will be house-to-house, neighborhood-by-neighborhood, until your town or city is cleared and the alien races are driven into the countryside where they can be hunted down and 'cleansed.' "[93]

Supremacists who enlisted were told to stay undercover: "Do not — I repeat, do not — seek out other skinheads. Do not listen to skinhead 'music.' Do not keep 'racist' or 'White-supremacist tracts' where you live. During your service you will be subjected to a constant barrage of equal opportunity drivel. . . . Keep your mouth shut."[94]

Members of the National Socialist Movement demonstrate on the grounds of the U.S. Capitol on April 19, 2008. Fifteen years earlier, on another April 19, a fire during an FBI siege at the Branch Davidian compound outside Waco, Texas, killed David Koresh and about 80 followers, including many children.

OUTLOOK
Guns in Holsters

The possibility that far-right extremists will emerge from the margins is as uncertain as the course of today's economic crisis, veteran analysts say.

For their part, extremists including Roper of White Revolution harbor no doubt that the medium-term future will see the outbreak of major racial and ethnic violence accompanying the breakup of the United States. "A lot of people might think it's impossible, but if you had gone to those same people in 1980 and told them the Berlin Wall was going to fall and the Soviet Union was going to collapse without a single missile being launched, they would have thought that was impossible too," Roper says.

Others would argue that U.S. society and government have firmer foundations than the Soviet system, which came to power in 1917 and sustained itself first by mass terror and then by mass repression.

In any event, the consensus among monitors of the far right is that extremist intensity hasn't even reached the level of the 1990s — the point at which the extremist movement "goes from red-hot to white-hot," as Pitcavage of the ADL puts it.

A key indicator of the latter stage is the discovery of major conspiracies or actual large-scale attacks, such as the Oklahoma City bombing. "In the 1980s and mid-'90s, a variety of white-supremacist or anti-government extremist groups had huge plots — start a white revolution, break off part of the country, hit military targets," Pitcavage says. "What they shared was an elaborate large-scale conception, often far larger than actual capabilities. If we start seeing some more of these we will know that things are starting to go white-hot again."

The present crisis is too new to suddenly spawn a new wave of high-intensity extremism, Pitcavage adds. "Movements don't start overnight," he says. "It takes a while for people to experience these things and form a reaction to them."

But Barkun at Syracuse University says today's conditions are far more alarming than those of the "white-hot" years. War and global economic crisis alone open the possibility of a new extremism paradigm, he says.

"We're in an economic situation which is so dire and so long-lasting that it will have social and political effects," Barkun says. "Things may develop along entirely novel lines that don't necessarily arise out of pre-existing groups, or that can readily be placed along the right-wing continuum, where the extreme right and the extreme left come together."

He adds that he hasn't seen any evidence of this taking place. However, left-right extremes have met before, at least elsewhere. Mussolini's early fascist movement took in former socialists like him. The "socialist" in Germany's National Socialist (Nazi) Party did express some — short-lived — opposition to capitalism. Attempts by some European far-rightists to co-opt left-wing anarchists represent an attempt to revive that tradition.

Also up in the air, to Barkun and others, is whether America's tradition of racial conflict will reassert itself in a country whose demography has been transformed from the old, white majority-black minority pattern.

One effect of the growing Latino political presence likely will be an accommodation by the Republican Party, where most support for tougher immigration control has centered, says Potok of the Southern Poverty Law Center. The result would be that white, non-Hispanic voters alienated by demographic change fall away from the conventional political system. "When that happens, a lot of these people would just go home, but some percentage of them would go into that extremist world," he speculates. "For them, there's no way out of a multiracial system. So it's 'Let's go off and start our own country.' "

On the organizational side, Potok theorizes, the absence of major, controlling figures, such as Pierce of the National Alliance and Butler of Aryan Nations, may be a danger sign. "I understand that a lot of really scary people, like The Order, came out of the Alliance," he says, adding that some extremist leaders have a history of depicting a need for violence only at some indefinite point in the future. "Leaders ultimately have the effect of holding people back: 'We're going to kill the Jews, but keep your guns in your holsters.' "

NOTES

1. Quoted in Jonathan D. Silver, "911 Operator Failed to Warn About Weapons," *Pittsburgh Post-Gazette*, April 7, 2009, p. A1. Unless otherwise indicated, all details of this event are drawn from *Post-Gazette* articles published April 5-8, 2009.

2. Quoted in Michael A. Fucco, "Deadly Ambush Claims the Lives of 3 City Police Officers," *Pittsburgh Post-Gazette*, April 5, 2009, p. A1.

3. Quoted in Dennis B. Roddy, "On Web: Racism, Anti-Semitism, Warnings," *Pittsburgh Post-Gazette*, April 7, 2009, p. A1.

4. "The Employment Situation: March 2009," U.S. Bureau of Labor Statistics, April 3, 2009, www.bls.gov/news.release/empsit.nr0.htm; Jeffrey Passel and D'Vera Cohn, "Trends in Unauthorized Immigration," Pew Hispanic Center, Oct. 2, 2008, http://pewhispanic.org/reports/report.php?ReportID=94. *CQ Researcher* has published reports on immigration going back to the early 1920s. Three of the most recent are: Reed Karaim, "America's Border Fence," Sept. 19, 2008, pp. 745-768; Alan Greenblatt, "Immigration Debate," Feb. 1, 2008, pp. 97-120; and Peter Katel, "Real ID," May 4, 2007, pp. 385-408.

5. "Rightwing Extremism: Current Economic and Political Climate Fueling Resurgence in Radicalization and Recruitment," Homeland Security Department, April 7, 2009, http://images.logicsix.com/DHS_RWE.pdf.

6. "Why Obama is Good for Our Movement," National Socialist Movement, undated, www.nsm88.org/activities/why obama is good for our movement

.html. See also Alan Greenblatt, "Race in America," *CQ Researcher*, July 11, 2003, pp. 593-624.

7. David Holthouse, "The Year in Hate," Intelligence Report, Southern Poverty Law Center, spring 2009, www.splcenter.org/intel/intelreport/article .jsp?aid=1027. For background, see Kenneth Jost, "Hate Crimes," *CQ Researcher*, Jan. 8, 1993, pp. 1-24.

8. Tom Hays, "Feds charge 3 men in election bias attacks," The Associated Press, Jan. 7, 2009; Christine Hauser and Colin Moynihan, "Three Are Charged in Attacks on Election Night," *The New York Times*, Jan. 8, 2009, p. A25.

9. Manny Fernandez and Javier C. Hernandez, "Binghamton Victims Shared a Dream of Living Better Lives," *The New York Times*, April 5, 2009, www.nytimes.com/2009/04/06/nyregion/06victims .html?scp=7&sq=Jiverly Binghamton&st=cse; Al Baker and Liz Robbins, "Police Had Few Contacts With Killer," *The New York Times*, April 7, 2009.

10. Quoted in Jessica Fargen, "Sicko Kill Plot Emerges," *Boston Herald*, Jan. 23, 2009, p. 5; Milton J. Valencia, "Father of attacked Brockton sisters calls for justice," *Boston Herald*, Jan. 24, 2009, p. B3.

11. Quoted in Melissa Nelson, "FL man acted oddly before Chilean students' deaths," The Associated Press, March 13, 2009.

12. "Hate on Display: A Visual Database of Extremist Symbols, Logos and Tattoos," ADL, undated, www .adl.org/hate_symbols/numbers_14-88.asp. For a Web site filled with praise for Lane see www.freethe-order.org/dlrip.html.

13. Jeffrey Gettleman, "William L. Pierce, 68; Ex-Rocket Scientist Became White Supremacist," *Los Angeles Times*, July 24, 2002, p. B10.

14. Quoted in John Krupa, "Teen in plot lists drinking as his job," *Arkansas Democrat-Gazette*, Oct. 29, 2008; see also Holthouse, *op. cit.*

15. Jared Taylor, "Transition to Black Rule," *American Renaissance*, Nov. 14, 2008, www.amren.com/ mtnews/archives/2008/11/transition_to_b.php.

16. Jared Taylor, "Jews and American Renaissance," *American Renaissance*, May 2006, www.amren.com/ mtnews/archives/2006/04/jews_and_americ.php.

17. Passel and Cohn, *op. cit.*

18. "Hate Crime Statistics, Victims, 2007," FBI, www .fbi.gov/ucr/hc2007/table_07.htm.

19. *Ibid.*

20. Jim Salter, "Mo. town outraged over killings, illegal immigrant," The Associated Press, March 20, 2009; "Hannibal murder suspect is illegal alien," The Associated Press, March 4, 2009.

21. Edwin S. Rubinstein, "Illegals kill a dozen a day?" *VDare*, Jan. 12, 2007, www.vdare.com/rubenstein/ 070112_nd.htm.

22. Mark Hugo Lopez and Michael T. Light, "A Rising Share: Hispanics and Federal Crime," Pew Hispanic Center, Feb. 18, 2009, p. 4, http://pewhispanic .org/files/reports/104.pdf.

23. Quoted in Sarah Burge, "Hate Crimes Continue Their Rise in Riverside County," *Press-Enterprise* (Riverside, Calif.), July 20, 2006, p. B1. See also Denes Husty III, "Crime vs. Hispanics up," *The News-Press* (Fort Myers, Fla.) Feb. 11, 2007, p. A1, and Troy Graham, "Hate Crime Statistics Belie Truth," *Daily Press* (Newport News, Va.), Jan. 30, 2000, p. A1.

24. "A Local Prosecutor's Guide For Responding to Hate Crimes," American Prosecutors Research Institute, undated, www.ndaa.org/pdf/hate_crimes.pdf.

25. Dennis B. Roddy, "An Accused Cop Killer's Politics," *Slate*, April 10, 2009, www.slate.com/id/2215826/.

26. Gary Kamiya, "They're coming to take our guns away," *Salon.com*, April 7, 2009, www.salon.com/ opinion/kamiya/2009/04/07/richard_poplowski.

27. Quoted in Adam Liptak, "The Nation: Prisons to Mosques; Hate Speech and the American Way," *The New York Times*, Jan. 11, 2004. The Supreme Court decision is *Brandenburg v. Ohio*, 395, U.S. 444 (1969).

28. Quoted in Katherin Clad, "Group cites Saudi 'hate' tracts," *The Washington Times*, Jan. 29, 2005, p. A1.

29. Nonie Darwish, "Muslim Hate," *FrontPageMagazine. com*, March 25, 2009, www.frontpagemag.com/ Articles/Read.aspx?GUID=A629F1F3-BBBA-420-D-8C31-D340A577A083.

30. "Glen Beck joins Fox News," Reuters, Oct. 16, 2008, www.reuters.com/article/televisionNews/id USTRE49G0NW20081017.

31. Eric Boehlert and Jamison Foser," On radio show, Beck read 'ad' for refinery that turns Mexicans into fuel," *County Fair blog*, Media Matters for America, June 29, 2007, (audio clip is posted), http://media-matters.org/items/200706290010.

32. Ariel Alexovich, "A Call to End Hate Speech," *The New York Times*, *The Caucus blog*, Feb. 1, 2008, http://thecaucus.blogs.nytimes.com/2008/02/01/a-call-to-end-hate-speech/?scp=1&sq=murguia%20hate%20speech&st=Search; "President and CEO Janet Murguia's Remarks at the Wave of Hope press briefing," National Council of La Raza, Jan. 31, 2008, www.nclr.org/content/viewpoints/detail/50389/.

33. Steve Sailer, "What Obama hasn't figured out yet," *Vdare*, April 27, 2009, http://blog.vdare.com/archives/2009/04/27/what-obama-hasnt-figured-out-yet-better-teachers-means-___/; Patrick Cleburne, "More Indians means more . . .," *Vdare*, April 19, 2009, http://blog.vdare.com/archives/2009/04/19/more-indians-means-more-fill-in-blank/; Cooper Sterling, "Tom Tancredo at American University: Maybe It Is About Race," *Vdare*, March 14, 2009, www.vdare.com/sterling/090314_tancredo.htm.

34. Unless otherwise indicated this subsection draws on Robert O. Paxton, *The Anatomy of Fascism* (2004); William E. Leuchtenburg, *Franklin D. Roosevelt and the New Deal* (1963); and Chip Berlet and Matthew N. Lyons, *Right-Wing Populism in America: Too Close for Comfort* (2000); Daniel Levitas, *The Terrorist Next Door: The Militia Movement and the Radical Right* (2002).

35. See Binjamin Segel, *A Lie and a Libel: The History of the Protocols of the Elders of Zion* (1996). For an article in the *Dearborn Independent* that takes the Protocols as fact, see Henry Ford and the editors of the *Dearborn Independent*, " 'Jewish Protocols' Claim Partial Fulfillment," www.churchoftrueisrael .com/Ford/original/ij12.html.

36. Biographical sketch in "William Dudley Pelley Collection," University of North Carolina at Asheville, D. H. Ramsey Library, http://toto.lib .unca.edu/findingaids/mss/pelley/default_pelley_william_dudley.htm.

37. Unless otherwise indicated, this subsection draws on Levitas, *op. cit.*; and Berlet and Lyons, *op. cit.*

38. Quoted in *ibid.*, p. 180.

39. Quoted in Thomas M. Storke, "How Some Birchers Were Birched," *The New York Times*, Dec. 10, 1961.

40. See Shaila Dewan, "Revisiting '64 Civil Rights Deaths, This Time in a Murder Trial," *The New York Times*, June 12, 2005, p. A26; Manuel Roig-Franzia, "Reopened Civil Rights Cases Evoke Painful Past," *The New York Times*, Jan. 10, 2005, p. A1. For background on the KKK, see the following *Editorial Research Reports*, predecessor to *CQ Researcher*: K. Lee, "Ku Klux Klan," July 10, 1946; W.R. McIntyre, "Spread of Terrorism and Hatemongering," Dec. 3, 1958; H.B. Shaffer, "Secret Societies and Political Action," May 10, 1961; R.L. Worsnop, "Extremist Movements in Race and Politics," March 31, 1965; S. Stencel, "The South: Continuity and Change," March 7, 1980, and M.H. Cooper, "The Growing Danger of Hate Groups," May 12, 1989.

41. Fred P. Graham, "Rockwell, U.S. Nazi, Slain," *The New York Times*, Aug. 26, 1967.

42. Except where otherwise indicated, this subsection is drawn from Levitas, *op. cit.*, and James Ridgeway, *Blood in the Face: The Ku Klux Klan, Aryan Nations, Nazi Skinheads, and the Rise of a New White Culture* (1990).

43. Wayne King, "Right-Wing Extremists Seek to Recruit Farmers," *The New York Times*, Sept. 20, 1985, p. A13. See also "Arthur Kirk: Kirk & Radical Farm Groups," nebraskastudies.org, undated, www .nebraskastudies.org/1000/frameset_reset.html?www .nebraskastudies.org/1000/stories/1001_0112.html.

44. "Supremacists Sentenced," *The Washington Post*, Dec. 4, 1987; "Five White Supremacists Get Long Prison Terms," *Los Angeles Times*, Feb. 7, 1986, p. A41; "40-Year Sentences Given to 5 in White-Supremacist Group," *The New York Times* (The Associated Press), Feb. 8, 1986, p. A17.

45. "13 Supremacists Are Not Guilty of Conspiracies," *The New York Times*, April 8, 1988, p. A14.

46. Richard A. Serrano, "Metzger Must Pay $5 Million in Rights Death," *Los Angeles Times*, Oct. 23, 1990, p. A1.

47. Elaine Woo, "Richard Butler, 86; Supremacist Founded the Aryan Nations," *Los Angeles Times*, Sept. 9, 2004, p. B8.

48. David Johnston with Stephen Labaton, "F.B.I. Shaken by Inquiry Into Idaho Siege," *The New York Times*, Nov. 25, 1993, p. A1.

49. Louis Beam, "Leaderless Resistance," February 1992, www.louisbeam.com/leaderless.htm. See also "Militias," in Peter Knight, ed., *Conspiracy Theories in American History: An Encyclopedia* (2003), pp. 467-476.

50. Leonard Zeskind, "Armed and Dangerous," *Rolling Stone*, Nov. 2, 1995.

51. Megan K. Stack, "Duke Admits Bilking Backers," *Los Angeles Times*, Dec. 19, 200, p. A22.

52. Susan Schmidt, "Investigation Clears Agents at Waco," *The Washington Post*, July 22, 2000, p. A1. See also "Final Report to the Deputy Attorney General Concerning the 1993 Confrontation at the Mt. Carmel Complex," John C. Danforth, Special Counsel, Nov. 8, 2000, www.apologeticsindex.org/pdf/finalreport.pdf.

53. Mike German, *Thinking Like a Terrorist: Insights of a Former FBI Undercover Agent* (2007), p. 71.

54. Woo, *op. cit.*; "William Pierce, 69, Neo-Nazi Leader, Dies," *The New York Times*, July 24, 2002, p. A16.

55. "Hitler's birthday was April 20, 1889. Unwelcome distinction as Hitler's birthday burdens Austrian town," *The Globe and Mail* (Toronto), (Reuters), April 20, 1989.

56. "Schedule of Upcoming Extremist Events: 2009," regularly updated, www.adl.org/learn/Events_2001/events_2003_flashmap.asp.

57. Steve Giegerich, "Angry words fill air at neo-Nazi rally," *St. Louis Post-Dispatch*, April 19, 2009, p. A4.

58. Quoted in *ibid*.

59. Lisa Black, "Holocaust museum opens to 'fight capacity for evil,'" *Chicago Tribune*, April 20, 2009, p. A8.

60. Padraig Shea," Spurned by Hub hall, supremacist group holds rally in N.H.," *The Boston Globe*, April 12, 2009, p. B3; "White supremacists' event shifted to N.H.," UPI, April 12, 2009.

61. "We shut down the fascists!" Boston Anti-Racist Coalition, April 8, 2009, www.anarkismo.net/article/12633.

62. Billy Roper, "One If By Land, Two If By Sea," *White Revolution*, April 8, 2009, http://whiterevolution.com.

63. "Ku Klux Klan Coming to Your Town?" *The Tennessee Tribune* (Nashville), July 6, 2006, p. C8.

64. "Arrests, fights break out at neo-Nazi march," wtop.com, April 19, 2009, www.wtop.com/?sid=1389944&nid=25. Video available at Albert Xavier Barnes, "The Arrests, Counter-Demo," undated, www.truveo.com/The-Arrests-Counter-Demo-NSM-March-on-DC-19/id/3760920024.

65. Brooke Donald, "Two arrested outside Boston Holocaust gathering," The Associated Press, May 9, 2005.

66. R. Scott Rappold, "Mobs clash in York," *York Sunday News*, Jan. 13, 2002 , p. A1.

67. Marc Levy, "White supremacist rally sparsely attended," The Associated Press, April 22, 2002.

68. Michelle Malkin, "Confirmed: The Obama DHS hit job on conservatives is real," michellemalkin.com, April 14, 2009, http://michellemalkin.com/2009/04/14/confirme-the-obama-dhs-hit-job-on-conservatives-is-real/. See also Stephen Gordon, "Homeland Security document targets most conservatives and libertarians in the country," *The Liberty Papers* (blog), April 12, 2009, www.the-libertypapers.org/2009/04/12/homeland-security-document-targets-most-conservatives-and-libertarians-in-the-country.

69. Quoted in "Napolitano defends report on right-wing extremist groups," CNN, April 15, 2009, www.cnn.com/2009/POLITICS/04/15/extremism.report/.

70. "Rightwing Extremism. . . .," *op. cit.*, p. 5.

71. *Ibid.*, p. 6.

72. "About That DHS Report on Right-Wing Extremism," *Little Green Footballs*, April 14, 2009, http://littlegreenfootballs.com/article/33364_About_That_DHS_Report_on_Right-Wing_Extremism.

73. "The Modern Militia Movement," MIAC [Missouri Information Analysis Center] Strategic Report, Feb. 20, 2009, pp. 3-4, www.scribd.com/doc/13290698/ The-Modern-Militia-MovementMissouri-MIAC-Strategic-Report-20Feb09-; David A. Lieb, "Analysis: Militia report unites ACLU, Republicans," The Associated Press, April 6, 2009.

74. "Modern Militia Movement," *op. cit.*

75. Chad Livengood, "Agency apologizes for militia report on candidates," *Springfield* (Mo.) *News-Leader*, p. A1.

76. Chris Blank, "Mo. Patrol names new leader for information center," The Associated Press, April 6, 2009.

77. Quoted in Lieb, *op. cit.*

78. Quoted in "Prevention Bulletin," North Central Texas Fusion System, Feb. 19, 2009, p. 4, www.privacylives.com/wp-content/uploads/2009/03/ texasfusion_021909.pdf.

79. Quoted in Lieb, *op. cit.*

80. "Leftwing Extremists Likely to Increase Use of Cyber Attacks over the Coming Decade," Department of Homeland Security, Jan. 26, 2009, www.fas.org/irp/eprint/leftwing.pdf.

81. Quoted in "Homeland Security: Economic, Political Climate Fueling Extremism," Southern Poverty Law Center, April 15, 2009.

82. Quoted in *ibid.* Alexander Cockburn, "King of the Hate Business," *The Nation*, May 18, 2009, www .thenation.com/doc/20090518/cockburn.

83. Quoted in David Abel, "WTKK-FM suspends Severin for derogatory comments about Mexicans," *The Boston Globe*, April 30, 2009, www.boston .com/news/local/breaking_news/2009/04/_jay_ severin.html.

84. Quoted in *ibid.*

85. Lindell Kay, "U.S. charges former Marine with making a threat against Obama," *Jacksonville Daily News*, Feb. 27, 2009, www2.journalnow.com/ content/2009/feb/27/us-charges-former-marine-with-making-a-threat-agai.

86. "White Supremacist Recruitment of Military Personnel since 9/11," FBI, Counterterrorism Division, July 7, 2008, http://wikileaks.org/wiki/ FBI:_White_Supremacist_Recruitment_of_ Military_Personnel_2008.

87. *Ibid.*

88. "Boehner: Homeland Security Report Characterizing Veterans as Potential Terrorists is 'Offensive and Unacceptable,' " press release, April 15, 2009, http://republicanleader.house.gov/News/ DocumentSingle.aspx?DocumentID=122567.

89. "White Supremacist Recruitment . . . ," *op. cit.* See also Jim Popkin, "White-power groups recruiting from military," "Deep Background — NBC News Investigates," July 16, 2008, http://deepback-ground.msnbc.msn.com/archive/2008/07/ 16/1202484.aspx.

90. "White Supremacist Recruitment," *op. cit.*

91. David Holthouse, "A Few Bad Men," *Intelligence Report*, Southern Poverty Law Center, July 7, 2006, www.splcenter.org/intel/news/item.jsp?pid=79.

92. Art Pine, "Ft. Bragg Troops Restricted After Swastikas Are Painted," *Los Angeles Times*, July 17, 1996, p. A9; William Branigin and Dana Priest, "3 White Soldiers Held in Slaying of Black Couple," *The Washington Post*, Dec. 9, 1995, p. A1.

93. "Planning a Skinhead Infantry," sidebar to "A Few Bad Men," *op. cit.*, www.splcenter.org/intel/news/ item.jsp?sid=21.

94. *Ibid.*

BIBLIOGRAPHY

Books

Berlet, Chip, and Matthew N. Lyons, *Right-Wing Populism in America: Too Close For Comfort,* **Guilford Press, 2000.**
Longtime analysts of the far right chronicle the long history of a movement that's larger than right-wing extremism.

German, Mike, *Thinking Like a Terrorist,* **Potomac Books, 2007.**
A former FBI agent recounts his undercover assignments in violent, far-right cells while arguing for government focus on law-breaking, not ideology.

Levitas, Daniel, *The Terrorist Next Door: The Militia Movement and the Radical Right,* **St. Martin's Press, 2002.**
The life of Posse Comitatus founder William Potter Gale provides the framework for an independent scholar's detailed history of domestic militias.

Paxton, Robert O., *The Anatomy of Fascism,* **Alfred A. Knopf, 2004.**
A leading scholar of the European extreme right distinguishes between its historic relics and the elements that survive.

Raspail, Jean, *The Camp of the Saints,* **Charles Scribner's Sons, 1975.**
Popular on the far right, this novel by a well-known French writer anticipates the fervent opposition to immigration from developing countries by depicting it as an invasion that will topple Western democratic societies.

Ridgeway, James, *Blood in the Face: Ku Klux Klan, Aryan Nations, Nazi Skinheads, and the Rise of a New White Culture,* **Thunder's Mouth Press, 1990.**
Journalist Ridgeway's prescient book includes documentary extremist material.

Articles

Blow, Charles M., "Pitchforks and Pistols," *The New York Times,* **April 3, 2009, www.nytimes .com/2009/04/04/opinion/04blow.html.**
A columnist argues that apocalyptic talk from conservative commentators preaching revolution and warning of gun-grabbing plans by the Obama administration may set off unstable minds.

Hedgecock, Roger, "Disagree with Obama? Gov't has eyes on you," WorldNetDaily, April 13, 2009, http:// wnd.com/index.php?fa=PAGE.view&page Id=94799.
The conservative columnist who obtained the first leaked copy of the Department of Homeland Security's recent assessment of the far right attacks it as a justification for political surveillance of Obama administration critics.

Jenkins, Philip, "Home-grown terrorism," *Los Angeles Times,* **March 10, 2008, p. A17.**
During the presidential campaign, a prominent Penn State historian of religion forecast a new wave of right-wing extremism — and of repressive Democratic response.

Roddy, Dennis B., "An Accused Cop Killer's Politics," *Slate,* **April 10, 2009, www.slate.com/id/2215826/.**
A reporter who investigated the man charged in the recent Pittsburgh police killings finds his political ideas jumbled.

Serrano, Richard A., " '90s-style extremism withers," *Los Angeles Times,* **March 11, 2008, p. A1.**
Writing before the latest wave of concern about extremism, a veteran correspondent reported that the far right hadn't recovered from the blows it suffered early in the decade.

Shapiro, Walter, "Long Shadow," *The New Republic,* **April 1, 2009, www.tnr.com/politics/story.html? id=9b2152b7-07fc-4503-9f33-4e2d222161d8.**
A veteran political writer sees a likely surge in populist rage with violent undertones.

Reports and Studies

"The Modern Militia Movement," Missouri Information Analysis Center, Feb. 20, 2009, www.scribd.com/ doc/13290698/The-Modern-Militia-Movement Missouri-MIAC-Strategic-Report-20Feb09.
The report, later repudiated by Missouri officials, triggered a nationwide controversy over government intrusion in political debate.

"Rightwing Extremism: Current Economic and Political Climate Fueling Resurgence in Radicalization and Recruitment," Department of Homeland Security, April 7, 2009, www.fas.org/irp/eprint/right-wing.pdf.
The controversial evaluation of the potential for a resurgence of the far right prompted a backlash against governmental monitoring of ideological trends.

"White Supremacist Recruitment of Military Personnel since 9/11," Federal Bureau of Investigation, July 7, 2008, http://wikileaks.org/wiki/FBI:_White_Supremacist_ Recruitment_of_Military_Personnel _2008.
This recent and more focused FBI report on extremists' interest in recruiting veterans received little attention, except among specialists.

For More Information

The American Cause, 501 Church St., Suite 315, Vienna, VA 22180; (703) 255-2632. Educational organization founded in 1993 by conservative commentator Pat Buchanan that supports "conservative principles of national sovereignty, economic patriotism, limited government and individual freedom."

Anti-Defamation League, Law Enforcement Agency Research Network; http://adl.org/learn/default.asp. A monitoring and research program aimed mainly at keeping law enforcement agencies up to date on extremism.

Federal Bureau of Investigation, J. Edgar Hoover Building, 935 Pennsylvania Ave., N.W., Washington, DC 20535; www.fbi.gov/hq/cid/civilrights/hate.htm. Provides statistics, information on the agency's anti-hate crime program and links to other sites.

Political Research Associates, 1310 Broadway, Suite 201, Somerville, MA 02144; (617) 666-5300; www.publiceye .org. A left-oriented think tank that investigates the far right.

Southern Poverty Law Center, 400 Washington Ave., Montgomery, AL 36104; www.splcenter.org/. Specializes in suing extremist organizations; maintains a research arm that monitors the extreme right.

Stormfront, P.O. Box 6637, West Palm Beach, FL 33405; (561) 833-0030; www.stormfront.org/forum. A heavily trafficked far-right site.

White Aryan Resistance, Tom Metzger P.O. Box 401, Warsaw, IN 46581; www.resist.com. A Web site maintained by a longtime extremist leader.

5

Cyberbullying

Are New Laws Needed to Curb Online Aggression?

Thomas J. Billitteri

After cyberbullies drove his son Ryan to suicide, John Halligan created a Web page devoted to the 13-year-old, who had been harassed for months by classmates in Essex Junction, Vt., including instant messages calling him gay. "He just went into a deep spiral in eighth grade," said his father, who advocates a state law forcing schools to develop anti-bullying policies. "He couldn't shake this rumor."

From *CQ Global Researcher*,
May 2008.

The episodes are hurtful, ugly — and sometimes deadly. In Lakeland, Fla., a group of teenagers records the beating of another teen and threatens to show the video on the Internet. The local sheriff says the attack was in retaliation for online trash-talking by the victim.[1]

At a high school near Pittsburgh, an anonymous e-mail list features sexually explicit rankings of 25 female students, names and photos included.[2]

In suburban Dardenne Prairie, Mo., near St. Louis, 13-year-old Megan Meier hangs herself after receiving cruel messages on the social-networking site MySpace. She thinks the messages are from a boy she met online, but the messages are a hoax.[3]

In Essex Junction, Vt., 13-year-old Ryan Patrick Halligan kills himself after months of harassment, including instant messages calling him gay. "He just went into a deep spiral in eighth grade," said his father, who advocates a state law forcing schools to develop anti-bullying policies. "He couldn't shake this rumor."[4]

The cases, albeit extreme, highlight what school officials, child psychologists, legal experts and government researchers argue is a fast-spreading epidemic of "cyberbullying" — the use of the Internet, cell phones and other digital technology to harass, intimidate, threaten, mock and defame.

Experts say cyberbullying has become a scourge of the adolescent world, inflicting painful scars on youngsters and vexing adults unable to stop the abuse. While many instances are relatively harmless, others can have serious, long-lasting effects, ranging from acute emotional distress, academic problems and school

Social Networking Facilitates Cyberbullying

Nearly 40 percent of teens who engage in online social networking report having been cyberbullied at least once, compared to just 23 percent of non-social network users.

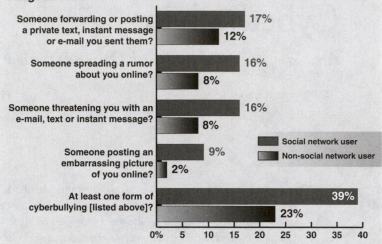

Have you, personally, ever experienced any of the following things online?

Someone forwarding or posting a private text, instant message or e-mail you sent them? — 17% / 12%

Someone spreading a rumor about you online? — 16% / 8%

Someone threatening you with an e-mail, text or instant message? — 16% / 8%

Someone posting an embarrassing picture of you online? — 9% / 2%

At least one form of cyberbullying [listed above]? — 39% / 23%

Social network user / Non-social network user

0% 5 10 15 20 25 30 35 40

Source: Amanda Lenhart and Mary Madden, Pew Internet & American Life Project, Jan. 3, 2007

absenteeism to violence, a desire for revenge and vulnerability to sexual predation.

Studies show cyberbullying affects millions of adolescents and young adults and can be more prevalent among girls than boys, especially in the earlier grades. The Centers for Disease Control and Prevention last year labeled "electronic aggression" — its term for cyberbullying — an "emerging public-health problem."[5] Still, a reliable profile of cyberbullying is difficult to construct. Research is in its infancy, experts who measure online abuse define it in different ways and many incidents are difficult to tally accurately. Studies leave little doubt, however, that cyberbullying is growing, as the following small sampling of recent research makes clear:

- Roughly a third of teens who use the Internet said they'd received threatening messages, had e-mail or text messages forwarded without consent, had an

embarrassing picture posted without consent, had rumors about them spread online, or experienced some other kind of online harassment, according to the Pew Research Center.[6]

- About 9 percent of respondents ages 10 through 17 said they were victims of threats or other offensive behavior, not counting sexual solicitation, that was sent online to them or about them for others to see, according to a 2005 University of New Hampshire survey. That rate was up 50 percent from a similar survey five years earlier.[7]

- More than 70 percent of heavy Internet users ages 12 through 17 — mostly girls — said they had experienced at least one incident of online intimidation via e-mail, cell phones, chat rooms and other electronic media in the previous year, according to a national survey posted on a teen Web site in 2005 by Jaana Juvonen, a psychology professor at the University of California at Los Angeles. A fifth of respondents reported seven or more incidents.[8]

Some cyberbullies are angry loners or misfits, sometimes seeking revenge for having been bullied themselves. But experts say it is common for online abusers to be popular students with plenty of self-esteem who are trying to strengthen their place in the social hierarchy. They do it by intimidating those they perceive to have less status.

"It's not really the schoolyard thug character" in some cases, says Nancy Willard, executive director of the Center for Safe and Responsible Internet Use, a research and professional development organization in Eugene, Ore. "It's the in-crowd kids bullying those who don't rank high enough."

What fuels cyberbullying is "status in schools — popularity, hierarchies, who's cool, who's not," says Danah Boyd, a fellow at the Berkman Center for

Internetand Society at Harvard Law School who studies teens' behavior on MySpace, Facebook and other social-networking sites. Peer pressure for status is further aggravated by adult pressure on teens to succeed, which can breed a cruel game of one-upmanship, Boyd says. "That pressure exerted by parents and reinforced and built out in peer groups is sort of the Petri dish for bullying."

Of course, bullying itself is nothing new. In some respects, cyberbullying is simply a new manifestation of a problem that in earlier days played out chiefly in playground dustups and lunch-money shakedowns.

What's new is the technology. More than 90 percent of teens are online.[9] More than half of online teens have profiles on social-networking sites.[10] And cell phones — many with photo and instant-messaging capabilities — are ubiquitous. The rise of networking sites, personal Web pages and blogs brimming with the minutiae of teen antics and angst has helped to create a rich climate for cyber mayhem: locker-room photos snapped with cell phones and broadcast on the Internet, fake profiles created on social-networking sites, salacious rumors spread in chat rooms, threats zapped across town in instant messages.

Child advocates also tie the increase in cyberbullying to a rise in incivility in the broader culture, from gratuitous insults on popular TV shows like "American Idol" to cynical sniping on the presidential campaign trail.

"I think the culture is angrier," says Mark Weiss, education director of Operation Respect, a nonprofit group in New York City founded by folk singer Peter Yarrow (a member of the legendary trio Peter, Paul and Mary) that promotes safe and compassionate educational climates. While kids have always picked on each other, Weiss says "the virulence is greater" today than in past generations.

"It's more intense, it might be more widespread, and I think you see more of it. The things on TV, the laugh tracks of situation comedies, it's all about making fun of each other and putting each other down, and reality TV is all about humiliation."

Cyberbullying has impelled lawmakers, especially at the state level, to either pass anti-bullying laws that encompass cyberbullying or add cyberbullying to existing statutes. Some laws are propelled by a mix of

Older Girls Typically Create Profiles

Girls ages 15-17 are far more likely to create profiles on social-networking sites than any other age or gender group. Disparities aren't as significant across economic and racial lines.

Percentage of Online Teens Who Create Profiles Online

Sex	
Boys	51%
Girls	58
Age	
12-14	45
15-17	64
Age by Sex	
Boys 12-14	46
Girls 12-14	44
Boys 15-17	57
Girls 15-17	70
Household income	
Under $50,000	55
Over $50,000	56
Race/ethnicity	
White, non-Hispanic	53
Non-white	58

Source: Amanda Lenhart and Mary Madden, Pew Internet & American Life Project, Jan. 3, 2007

concern about electronic bullying and online sexual predators.

But using laws and courts to stop cyberbullying has been tricky and sometimes highly controversial. "There's a big conflict in knowing where to draw the line between things that are rude and things that are illegal," says Parry

Aftab, an Internet privacy and security lawyer who is executive director of wiredsafety.org, an Internet safety group in Irvington-on-Hudson, N.Y., that bills itself as the world's largest.

School officials, for instance, must negotiate the treacherous shoals of cyberbullying content transmitted by a student who is off school grounds. Legal precedents on student expression allow educators to suppress speech that substantially disrupts the educational process or impinges on the rights of others. Some argue that school officials' authority to regulate cyber communication stops at the schoolhouse door, while others say they should regulate it when it affects the school climate. (*See "At Issue," p. 128.*)

"Even when it's off campus, the impact is coming to school in the form of young people who have been so tormented they are incapable of coming to school to study, which leads to dropouts, fights, violent altercations and suicide," says Willard, a former attorney and former teacher of at-risk children. "It has an incredibly long-lasting effect on the school community."

But the law on that question can be confusing, and the U.S. Supreme Court has yet to decide a case involving student Internet speech. Trying to regulate what students do or say on their home computers or in text messages sent from the local mall could wind up trampling students' constitutional rights or the rights of parents to direct their children's upbringing as they see fit, say free-speech advocates.

"There are more questions than answers in this emerging area of law," David L. Hudson Jr., research attorney for the First Amendment Center, a free-speech advocacy group, noted recently.[11]

As cyberbullying grows, here are some of the questions educators and legal experts are asking:

Are new laws needed to curb cyberbullying?

Jane Clare Orie, a state senator in Pennsylvania and majority whip for the Republican Caucus, says criminal laws have failed to keep up with the technological revolution, including the onset of cyberbullying.

A former prosecutor, Orie has introduced a bill that would leave both minors and adults open to potential criminal charges for cyberbullying a student or school employee.[12]

Bullying "has risen to a level so much further than what we grew up with," Orie says. "Anything done in a computer lasts forever."

But civil libertarians and others express concerns about the wave of new cyberbully laws. Some argue that educating students and parents on the harmful consequences of online abuse, instituting school-based prevention programs and promulgating clear school policies on harassment are more effective than passing laws.

Cyberbullying is "a big deal," with serious consequences for victims, says Justin W. Patchin, an assistant professor of criminal justice at the University of Wisconsin-Eau Claire who has done extensive research on the phenomenon. But he adds, "I don't know if it's something that we can legislate away."

Boyd, the Berkman Center fellow at Harvard, says highly publicized cases like the Megan Meier suicide are "absolutely horrible," but rare. Most cyberbullying occurs among peers jockeying for status, and much of the electronic bullying takes the form of taunting and jokes taken too far, she says. Technologies from social-networking sites to cell phones are also used to extend everyday bullying beyond the schoolyard.

Legislators are overreacting, Boyd says. "These laws aren't doing anything. What we desperately need is education and discussion," along with greater attention from parents and other adults to the heavy pressures and expectations weighing on adolescents.

Still, many lawmakers are moving to add provisions to existing anti-bullying laws or writing new codes. Legislatures including Iowa, Maryland, Minnesota, New Jersey and Oregon have passed cyberbullying laws recently, and a number of others are considering such statutes.[13]

"Those who bully and harass stand in the way of learning and threaten the safety of our children," said Matt Blunt, the Republican governor of Missouri, Megan Meier's home state, after the state Senate passed a cyberbullying bill in March.[14]

In Florida, Republican state Sen. Stephen Wise (Jacksonville), chairman of the Education Pre-K-12 Appropriations Committee, relented this year and let the committee consider a bill named after a 15-year-old boy who killed himself after enduring cyberbullying by a classmate. The bill would require all school districts to develop anti-bullying and harassment policies and let school districts punish students who use an electronic device to bully or harass their peers, even if the acts take place off campus and during non-school hours.[15]

Wise said he had opposed the measure because he thought existing law offered protections.[16] But proponents said it sends a message about bullying's gravity and potential harm. The Florida bill "provides a more formalized and transparent process for dealing with bullying situations, for the schools, the parents and for the student," said Republican state Rep. Gary Aubuchon (Cape Coral), a cosponsor. "By making it law rather than school board policy, we are adding an extra layer of emphasis on how important it is to protect our children at all times."[17]

Thomas Hutton, senior staff attorney for the National School Boards Association, says that while it may be acceptable for legislatures to require school districts to formulate cyberbullying policies, laws mandating that school districts deal with cyber abuse in a specific way are "missing the boat."

The desire of school districts to base policy decisions on "local conditions" makes specific directions to school districts a bad idea, Hutton says. Moreover, he says, "a lot of the real action [on cyberbullying] is happening in the courts."

Judicial rulings are evolving quickly, Hutton says, and state laws can create confusion among school districts as to the scope of their power to control online bullying. A new court ruling might limit what a school can do, putting administrators who act more broadly in legal jeopardy, he says. On the other hand, a court might broaden the power of schools to fight cyberbullying beyond what legislators contemplated when they passed a state cyberbullying law.

"Let's say a state attempts to read what the courts have said thus far and boil it down to a statute," Hutton says. "Then we get a ruling saying, 'We're going to allow [school districts] a little more leeway.' Now the statute has locked in place a more restrictive" approach.

Aftab, the Internet privacy and security lawyer, argues that more state laws are unnecessary because states already have cyber stalking and harassment laws on the books. What is needed, she says, is uniformity in those laws "so we know that what's illegal in one state is illegal in the next." Moreover, she says, "prosecutors need to know what laws are on the books."

Child advocates see a link between the increase in cyberbullying and the rise in incivility in the broader culture, such as gratuitous attacks on popular TV shows like "American Idol" and cynical sniping on the presidential campaign trail.

Aftab also argues that schools can fight cyberbullying using a little-known federal anti-stalking provision that President George W. Bush signed into law in 2006 as part of the reauthorization of the Violence Against Women Act. It makes it a crime to anonymously "annoy, abuse, threaten or harass" someone over the Internet.[18] Critics have said the law is vague and subjective.[19]

Aftab says she has a surefire way for school districts to attack cyberbullying, whether it originates at school: write a policy that covers cyberbullying wherever it occurs among students, then ask all students and parents to sign the policy at the beginning of the school year. Once that happens, Aftab argues, the document becomes a binding contract that gives the school legal authority to take action.

Of course, a student or parent could always wind up challenging a school's interpretation of a particular incident or its definition of cyberbullying. Many experts expect the same thing to occur with the raft of state laws hitting the books. So far, case law provides uneven guidance on what constitutes electronic harassment.

"The rub in almost all these statutes is that when you try to regulate speech, [the challenge is] writing a statute that singles out bullying and distinguishes it from legitimate expression," says Dale Herbeck, who teaches communications and cyber law at Boston College. "The way to solve it is to write a statute that is very, very, very specific. The problem is that a lot of the behavior you think is bullying doesn't qualify as bullying. I'm aware that a lot of states have kind of stepped up on this," he says. "But I'm not aware of these laws being challenged."

Do cyberbully laws violate constitutional rights?

In 2003, New Jersey eighth-grader Ryan Dwyer created and briefly maintained a Web site from home that included criticism of his school and postings by others in a "guest book." Some visitors ignored his plea that they not use profanity or threats in their postings. The principal "is a fat piece of crap," one declared. "He should walk his fat a— into oncoming traffic."[20]

School officials punished Dwyer, but the American Civil Liberties Union (ACLU) helped him and his parents sue, claiming violation of his constitutional rights. In a settlement, the district apologized and agreed to pay $117,500 in damages and attorney fees.[21]

"I'm hopeful this will help ensure that free-speech rights of students aren't trampled on again," Dwyer said.[22]

The case points to the difficult legal terrain surrounding abusive cyber expression, especially when it originates away from school. "Schools have a growing concern about the problem, and their concern is whether they can discipline students and how far the bullying has to go before they can get involved," said Kim Croyle, a lawyer in Morgantown, W.Va., who represents several school boards and lectures on cyberbullying.[23]

Under a legal standard set by the Supreme Court in 1969 in *Tinker v. Des Moines Independent Community School District*, educators can prohibit student speech if it causes substantial interference with school discipline or the rights of others.[24] *Tinker* remains the chief yardstick in cyberbullying cases, but it can be tricky to apply.

If, for example, a student is afraid to go to school because of a cyberbullying incident, a school might be hard-pressed to justify harsh action under the *Tinker* ruling. What constitutes substantial interference can be in the eye of the beholder.

The fact that *Tinker* isn't the sole yardstick for deciding students' First Amendment rights further complicates matters. For example, the Supreme Court has said that "true threats" are not protected by the First Amendment.[25] And it has allowed educators to crack down on vulgar student speech at school and to exert control over school-sponsored expression such as school newspapers.[26]

Perhaps the most nettlesome circumstance is cyberbullying that is transmitted at home or the local mall or skating rink, but that nonetheless causes disruption at school.

"There's always the legal discussion of 'if it doesn't happen at school, can a district take action?' " said Joe Wehrli, policy-services director for the Oregon School Boards Association. "If a student is harassed for three hours at night on the Web and they come to school and have to sit in the same classroom with the student that's the bully, there is an effect on education, and in that way, there is a direct link to schools."[27]

But free-speech advocates say educators sometimes punish students whose speech is protected by the First Amendment.

"Off-campus behavior that is not connected to the school in any way — no use of school computers, no transmission of messages in school — is not within the purview of school officials," contends Joan Bertin, executive director of the National Coalition Against Censorship, an advocacy group in New York. "It may have some play-out within school, but the actual speech took place in a protected zone. The school can't go after the speech, but it can go after the behavior that occurs on campus" as a result of the speech.

An exception would be speech that constitutes a true threat, Bertin says, but true threats must meet a high standard, she says. "A kid e-mailing another kid saying, 'I'm going to knock your brains out' or 'I wish this teacher were dead' — these are not, in my opinion, true threats."

Still, most courts would say the school could address any "speech that constitutes the equivalent of stalking or harassment, which would potentially fall under the criminal code," she continues, especially if it is directed at fellow students, teachers or the administration.

Bertin acknowledges that cyberbullying can be a "terrible problem" and understands why teachers and parents are concerned about childhood cruelty. But on the other hand, "There are limits about what schools can and should do," she argues. "Punitive, censorious response tends to be the first line of attack" by state lawmakers. "If people sat down in a more thoughtful, dispassionate way and thought about what they're trying to achieve, they might well reconsider that response."

Some argue, though, that the ability of cyber communication to quickly spread far and wide demands that school officials step in even when the bullying is generated off school grounds. Rumors spread by cell phone or embarrassing photos posted online can often create a disruptive buzz at school and sometimes lead to other problems, including absenteeism or violence.

In Bethesda, Md., at Walt Whitman High School, known for its high academic achievement, students got into fist fights twice in April to settle disputes that arose on Facebook. The incidents prompted Principal Alan Goodwin to ask parents to monitor their children's postings on the site. "I am becoming increasingly frustrated by negative incidents at school that arise from students harassing other students on Facebook," he wrote. Goodwin told *The Washington Post* that the students involved "had not been involved in such things before, and we could have prevented [the fights], I think, if we had known."[28]

In Washington, D.C., last month, Francis Junior High School Principal Stephannie Crutchfield spent two class periods counseling a group of seventh-grade students who began arguing at school as a result of a conflict over "boyfriend-type stuff" that started on MySpace over the weekend. The parents of one girl had called Crutchfield, concerned that her child had been threatened. When the spat turned ugly in the school hallways, Crutchfield didn't hesitate to move in.

"I cannot discipline what a child has written off campus, but if the end result is a behavior infraction inside the school, then that's what I have to deal with," Crutchfield says. "Disorderly conduct or whatever behavior in my building is what I address."

The University of Wisconsin's Patchin argues that "just about everything kids do on or off campus ultimately will come back to the school," and therefore "school officials absolutely must do something." But

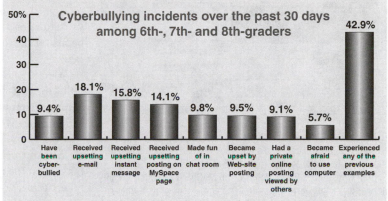

Many Middle-Schoolers Report Cyberbullying

Over 40 percent of middle-school students are cyberbullied in one way or another in the course of a typical month. Only 9 percent, however, report being cyberbullied when asked specifically. The most common forms of abuse involve negative e-mails, instant messages or postings on social-networking sites such as MySpace.

Cyberbullying incidents over the past 30 days among 6th-, 7th- and 8th-graders

Category	Percent
Have been cyberbullied	9.4%
Received upsetting e-mail	18.1%
Received upsetting instant message	15.8%
Received upsetting posting on MySpace page	14.1%
Made fun of in chat room	9.8%
Became upset by Web-site posting	9.5%
Had a private online posting viewed by others	9.1%
Became afraid to use computer	5.7%
Experienced any of the previous examples	42.9%

Source: Sameer Hinduja and Justin W. Patchin, www.cyberbullying.us

that doesn't necessarily mean having to take punitive measures, he says. Schools should be proactive in teaching students about cyberbullying and its consequences and in promoting safe school climates, Patchin says. "We advocate doing the brunt of the work ahead of time."

Sometimes it is not civil libertarians but school officials themselves who argue that off-campus cyber expression is outside their purview. They might be concerned, for example, that if they begin to regulate speech that occurs off school grounds, their liability grows if they fail to catch a specific off-campus incident ahead of time and violence ensues.

But schools shouldn't back away from confronting cyberbullying that impinges on school order and safety, some experts contend.

"Schools want to say cyberspace is beyond our control, but you can't be in denial," says Juvonen, the UCLA researcher. "You can't be saying this is not our business. It is the schools' responsibility to address it when it is so closely connected to what goes on at school."

Willard, at the Center for Safe and Responsible Internet Use, strongly advises educators to step in even

CQ Press/Screenshot

Cyberbullying is fueled by "status in school — popularity, hierarchies, who's cool, who's not," says Danah Boyd, a fellow at the Berkman Center for Internet and Society at Harvard Law School who studies teens' behavior on MySpace and other social-networking sites. Early this year, in an agreement with attorneys general from 49 states and the District of Columbia, MySpace said it would develop technology and work with law-enforcement officials to improve children's protection.

when cyberbullying occurs away from school if the clear potential exists that it would affect students and the educational climate. Even so, she says the manner in which administrators act is important.

"They may impose discipline if . . . they're protecting the school's ability to deliver instruction, the security of students coming to school and [to avert] violence," she says.

But she also says that excessive discipline frequently exaggerates a problem. It can undermine feelings of remorse among bullies and also lead to vicious online retaliation by victims. "I strongly encourage an approach that helps bring the students to a greater level of understanding of the true harm caused by these online activities," she says.

Some administrators err by coming down hard on a student not because the speech endangers school order or safety but simply because it angers or upsets the school officials, Willard says.

"I would remind school administrators that the founders of our country called King George a tyrant."

Should parents be held liable for cyberbullying offenses?

When juveniles do commit serious online abuses, the question often arises: Where were the parents?

Shouldn't they be held accountable, or at least share the blame?

"The question isn't 'should,' the question is 'can,' and the answer is 'yes,' " says Willard. Under parental-liability statutes or parental-negligence standards, parents may be held liable for the harm caused by their children, she says.

Willard says she hopes cases don't reach that point. Still, "the fact that there is the potential for liability can help get parents motivated" to monitor their children's actions, she says.

In the civil-litigation system, "financial consequences for cyberbullying are now serious enough to make even the most lenient parent of a bully sit up and take notice," Millie Anne Cavanaugh, a family-law attorney in Los Angeles, wrote recently on the Web site of a group that provides programs for troubled adolescents. "In addition to liability against the cyberbully himself on theories such as defamation, invasion of privacy, disclosure of private information and intentional infliction of emotional distress, parents could now [be] held accountable for their child's cyberbullying if they failed to properly supervise the child's online activity."[29]

The University of Wisconsin's Patchin sees the issue in a similar light as vandalism cases. "If a parent knows it's going on or creates the opportunity where they're unwilling to supervise the behavior of their kids, certainly we should consider holding them responsible as well," he says.

But Patchin is cautious on the subject. "If you've got a 16- or 17-year-old kid who's logging on at a friend's house" and the parent is unaware of what's going on, "then I don't know. A lot of parents simply don't know much about computers and may be unwilling to educate themselves. Is that deliberate indifference? I don't know."

Experts say parents are often clueless about their children's online activity and that adolescents tormented by cyberbullies often hide their victimization from parents for fear of losing their computer and cell phone privileges.

Researchers say both situations — victims' silence and parents' obliviousness — help cyberbullying to grow.

Aftab, of wiredsafety.org, who speaks regularly to middle- and high-school students, says 45,000 students — 85 percent to 97 percent of her audiences — reported having been victims of cyberbullying last year. Yet, "only 5 percent will tell a trusted parent or adult," she says.

"We've found that over 90 percent of kids did not tell their parents about these incidents," echoes Juvonen, the UCLA researcher. Among 12- to 14-year-old girls, almost half were concerned about their parents restricting their Internet access if they revealed they were victimized, she says. Half of the adolescents Juvonen surveyed wanted to deal with incidents of cyberbullying by themselves rather than seeking help from adults.

"We're very concerned about this belief and the fear of parental restrictions," Juvonen says. "It's what is making cyberbullying so very dangerous."

Susan Limber, a Clemson University psychologist who studies bullying, says many adolescents in focus groups say parents and teachers don't seem to talk enough with them about online behavior. "Kids on the one hand say parents should be a little more involved," Limber says. "But as one kid said, they want supervision, not 'snoopervision.' "

In other words, Limber says, "They want appropriate rules, but they don't want parents poking into every last e-mail or text message. But that's a fine line."

Parents can have an especially difficult time keeping track of what adolescents are posting on social-networking sites. Some child advocates say parents should create their own accounts so they can monitor what their children are doing on the sites.

The sites allow people to post online pages featuring personal facts, photos, gossip and other information for others to read. Social scientists say such sites can serve a useful, and even vital, purpose by helping adolescents build friendships, learn tolerance for others' views and form a sense of self-identity. But critics say the sites have the potential to be incubators for cyber abuse, magnets for sexual predators and embarrassing archives of a student's immature behavior that college admissions officials or employers may wind up seeing.

"Putting something on the Internet is a whole lot different than whispering it on the playground," says Witold "Vic" Walczak, legal director of the ACLU in Pennsylvania.

Many parents and other responsible adults often neglect to impart that message to youngsters.

Weiss, of Operation Respect, says engaging adolescents in "conversation around moral issues" like cyberbullying "is really important for kids" but that many adults — teachers among them — don't know how to do so.

"We're not having this conversation enough," he says. "If we did, it would be the strongest thing we could do."

BACKGROUND

Students' Rights

Inflammatory speech by young people is nothing new, and neither is adults' desire to suppress it. In 1908, the Wisconsin Supreme Court ruled that school officials could suspend two students who ridiculed their teachers in a poem in a local newspaper.[30] Seven years later, a California appellate court said a student could be suspended for criticizing school officials in an assembly.[31]

Courts gradually broadened students' rights, but those liberties remain limited.

In 1969, the Supreme Court said in the watershed *Tinker* case that school officials had no right to suspend students for wearing black armbands to protest the Vietnam War. "It can hardly be argued that either students or teachers shed their constitutional rights to freedom of speech or expression at the schoolhouse gate," Justice Abe Fortas wrote.

Yet, students do shed some rights. Under the *Tinker* standard, school officials can discipline students whose speech disrupts school activities or interferes with the rights of others. Other rulings allow schools to suppress students' lewd speech and punish those who make credible threats.[32]

Cases involving cyberbullying can be especially difficult for school officials and judges to weigh, however. Distinguishing true threats and defamation from harmless adolescent high jinks can be a matter of debate.

In a decision last year, a federal judge ruled that a Pennsylvania school district violated a student's First Amendment rights when it punished him for creating on his grandmother's computer a parody profile on MySpace that crudely made fun of his principal.[33] Still, the judge called the decision, which is being appealed, a "close call."

The school district had based its defense partly on an earlier Pennsylvania case in which the state Supreme Court upheld the expulsion of an eighth-grader — whose initials were J.S. — who created a "Teacher Sux" Web site containing derogatory material aimed at an algebra teacher and the principal. The court said the site created a substantial disruption of school activities.[34]

"[T]he advent of the Internet has complicated analysis of restrictions on speech," Justice Ralph J. Cappy wrote in the J.S. case. "Indeed, *Tinker's* simple armband, worn silently and brought into a Des Moines, Iowa, classroom, has been replaced by J.S.'s complex multimedia Web site, accessible to fellow students, teachers and the world."

Growing Phenomenon

Judges aren't the only ones who struggle to distinguish juvenile antics from truly troublesome behavior.

"I have been teaching in public schools for 13 years. I am not sure what bullying is," a reader responded to a newspaper blog on anti-bullying legislation in Georgia last year. "Is it when a child calls another child's mama ugly or fat? Is it breaking in line after recess? . . . Children are cruel to each other, and they always have been. If a child does smell to high heaven, kids are going to talk about it. When did all this become 'bullying'? I am just asking."[35]

Some experts say that in many ways, face-to-face bullying remains more problematic than online abuse, but that teachers and parents often perceive cyberbullying as more of a threat because it is delivered through new and perhaps bewildering technology. Still, researchers say cyberbullying affects so many youngsters that it cannot be taken lightly.

An anonymous survey of nearly 4,000 middle-school students by Limber and fellow Clemson University psychologist Robin Kowalski found that 18 percent reported being bullied at least once in the previous two months through e-mail, instant messaging, chat rooms, Web sites and cell-phone text messaging. Girls were roughly twice as likely as boys to be victims. Eleven percent of the students — slightly more girls than boys — admitted bullying someone else.[36]

The University of Wisconsin's Patchin says in a random-sample study of about 2,000 middle-school students in 30 schools in a major school district, he and his colleagues found that less than 10 percent of youngsters said they had been victims of cyberbullying — defined as repeated abuse — in the previous 30 days. But when asked about specific types of online harassment and aggression, nearly 43 percent said they had experienced at least one incident in the previous 30 days, such as receiving an e-mail or instant message that made them upset, having something upsetting to them posted on their MySpace site or being made fun of in a chat room.

Because cyberbullying does not require physical confrontation and is often anonymous, it can appeal more to girls than boys, researchers say. "Girls have really taken on a bullying role that has changed in the last couple of years with the electronic age," said Kristy Hagar, a neuropsychologist at Children's Medical Center in Dallas.[37]

Aftab of wiredsafety.org says she has noticed that online bullying is growing, especially among second- and third-graders, and that "by the fourth grade it is institutionalized."

"Fourth-graders use extortion as a form of cyberbullying: 'If you don't do this, I will tell,' " Aftab says. "Sometimes they think it's funny and say they don't mean it." By middle school, she says, cyberbullying can get "more malicious." In high school, many students will claim cyberbullying doesn't exist — not because that's true, Aftab says, but because high-school students don't want to admit that someone else may have power over them and can hurt their feelings.

"Bullying is for babies — that's just stuff that happens," Aftab says she hears high-school students say.

Aftab says cyberbullying is most prevalent among 13- and 14-year-olds. A Harris Poll found that the incidence is highest among 15- and 16-year-olds, particularly girls.[38]

Impact of Technology

The pell-mell expansion in the use of technology has fueled cyberbullying's growth. Nearly half of online youths ages 12-17 have uploaded photos where others can see them (though many restrict access to the pictures), and 14 percent have posted videos online, according to the Pew Research Center.[39]

Technology can make cyber abuse an especially potent form of bullying. For one thing, transmission is instantaneous to a potentially limitless audience — including recipients in the next state or even overseas. "It's not like being called 'four eyes,' " Herbeck of Boston College says. "It's being blasted across cyberspace."

C H R O N O L O G Y

1960s-1970s *Supreme Court upholds students' rights to free speech and due process; computers take root in American society.*

1969 Supreme Court rules in *Tinker v. Des Moines Independent Community School District* that school officials violated students' First Amendment rights by suspending them for wearing armbands to protest the Vietnam War.

1975 Supreme Court rules in *Goss v. Lopez* that suspended students are entitled to a hearing.

1976 Apple computer is founded.

1980s *Supreme Court limits students' rights in speech and discipline cases; computers continue to gain a foothold in society.*

1981 IBM introduces its personal computer.

1985 Supreme Court rules in *New Jersey v. T.L.O.* that school officials do not need to get a search warrant or show probable cause before they search students at school.

1986 Supreme Court rules in *Bethel School District No. 403 v. Fraser* that school officials did not violate the First Amendment rights of a student suspended for delivering a vulgar speech to a school assembly.

1988 Supreme Court rules in *Hazelwood School District v. Kuhlmeier* that school officials can limit school-sponsored student expression if they have a legitimate educational reason.

1990s *Internet becomes big part of American life, spurring Congress to protect juveniles and others from online abuses.*

1997 Supreme Court rules in *Reno v. ACLU* that Internet speech merits First Amendment protection.

1998 Congress passes Child Online Protection Act in bid to limit access by minors to adult-oriented Web sites, but the law runs into court challenges.

2000-Present *Growth of technology and advent of social-networking sites present school and law-enforcement officials with new challenges in fighting adolescent bullying.*

2000 Children's Online Privacy Protection Act takes effect, giving parents the power to decide whether and what information can be collected online from children under 13.

2002 U.S. Secret Service says bullying played a significant role in some school shootings.

2002 Friendster, a global social-networking site, is launched, followed by MySpace (2003) and Facebook (2004).

2003 Ryan Halligan, a Vermont 13-year-old, commits suicide after online harassment.

2006 Suicide of Missouri teenager Megan Meier prompts calls for tougher laws on Internet harassment.

2007 Supreme Court rules in *Morse v. Frederick* that school officials can punish student speech that can be interpreted as advocating illegal drug use; the case involved a student who held up a "Bong Hits 4 Jesus" banner outside school grounds. . . . House passes bill to provide grants to fight online crime, including cyberbullying; Senate proposes separate measure. . . . Centers for Disease Control and Prevention calls "electronic aggression" among adolescents an "emerging public-health problem." . . . MySpace agrees to give states information on convicted sex offenders with accounts on the site.

2008 In an agreement with attorneys general from 49 states, MySpace says it will take additional steps to protect children from online abuses. . . . Eight Florida teens are charged as adults with battery and kidnapping in an attack on another teen that was videoed and posted on the Internet. . . . Consumer officials in New Jersey announce investigation of college-gossip Web site Juicy Campus. . . . AOL enters into agreement to acquire global social-networking site Bebo. . . . Florida Senate on April 30 is scheduled to consider an anti-cyberbullying measure, the Jeffrey Johnston Stand Up for All Students Act, named after a Cape Coral, Fla., teenager who killed himself in 2005 after enduring two years of cyberbullying by a classmate.

Suicide Uncovers Adult Role in Internet Shaming

Controversial practices include attacks on sex offenders.

Cyberbullying isn't just a problem among adolescents. Adults engage in it, too. From online vigilantism and angry blogs to e-stalking and anonymous ranting on newspaper Web sites, grownups can be as abusive as the meanest schoolhouse tyrant.

The suicide of 13-year-old Megan Meier in 2006 thrust adult cyberbullying into the open. The Dardenne Prairie, Mo., girl killed herself after receiving cruel messages on MySpace from imposters posing as a 16-year-old boy named "Josh Evans."

Lori Drew, the mother of one of Megan's friends, was accused of participating in the hoax along with her teenage daughter and a former teenage employee. Drew has denied sending messages to Megan.[1] While questions remain about Drew's role, the case has left no doubt that the Internet is rife with adult cyber passion.

After the suicide came to light, an outraged mother several states away ferreted out Drew's identity and posted it on a blog.[2]

Soon, "an army of Internet avengers . . . set out to destroy Lori Drew and her family," forcing them from their home and "vowing them no peace, ever," newspaper columnist Barbara Shelly wrote. "Who are these people who have made it their business to destroy her? They are a jury with laptops, their verdict rendered without insight into the dynamics of two families or the state of mind of a fragile 13-year-old girl or even a complete explanation of what actually occurred."[3]

Internet shaming is a growing cultural phenomenon, but Daniel Solove, a professor of law at George Washington University and author of the 2007 book *The Future of Reputation: Gossip, Rumor and Privacy on the Internet*, says it can backfire.

"Internet shaming is done by people who want actually to enforce norms and to make people and society more orderly," he said. But instead, "Internet shaming actually destroys social control and makes things more anarchic, and it becomes very hard to regulate and stop it."[4]

Among its many controversial uses, online technology is employed by some citizens to track or expose sex offenders — including those who themselves use the Internet to exploit others.

Perverted-justice.com is famous for its efforts, sometimes in combination with televised sting operations, to expose online predators. In 2006, a former Texas district attorney committed suicide when police tried to arrest him on a warrant linked to a child-predator sting that was a joint operation between Perverted Justice and NBC's "Dateline."[5]

While some criticize such stings as a form of vigilantism, others worry about those who use state online sex-offender registries to pursue their own brand of justice.

In a report last year of U.S. sex-offender policies, Human Rights Watch, an advocacy group in New York, concluded that unfettered public access to online sex-offender registries left former offenders open "to the risk that individuals will act on this information in irresponsible and even unlawful ways. There is little evidence that this form of community notification prevents sexual violence."[6]

In a section of the report on "vigilante violence," Human Rights Watch wrote: "A number of convicted sex offenders have been targets of violence from strangers who take it

And cyberbullies can avoid witnessing the damage they inflict. Researchers say adolescents often don't grasp that a vulnerable human being is on the receiving end of hateful words and images. "A lot of kids who engage [in cyberbullying], when confronted, say, 'I didn't mean it' or 'I didn't know the outcome,' " Wisconsin's Patchin says. "If I am bullying in real life, I can see the effect immediately."

Moreover, bullies tend to think their messages can't be traced back to them — often a faulty assumption. "They may think they have achieved anonymity," says Willard of the Center for Safe and Responsible Internet Use, "but they're really bad at hiding their identity."

Cyberbullying also has staying power. Words and images in the virtual world can exist in perpetuity in cyberspace. That means victims may review tormenting

upon themselves to 'eliminate' sex offenders from communities. In April 2003, Lawrence Trant stabbed one New Hampshire registrant and lit fires at two buildings where registrants lived. When he was arrested, police found a printout of New Hampshire's sex-offender Internet registry, with checkmarks next to the names of those already targeted."

Cyber vigilantism also can occur in the realm of global terrorism. Some experts say that private citizens who seek to monitor and close down terror-linked Web sites are hurting the government's own investigations.[7]

"It is very unlikely they will find something of significance on the Internet that the government doesn't already know," said Michael Radu — a senior fellow at the Foreign Policy Research Institute, a think tank in Philadelphia — who studies revolutionary and terrorist groups. "They are redundant at best."[8]

Sometimes it's an adult's private blog, podcast or video that gets others the most upset. In April, Tricia Walsh Smith, being divorced by Philip Smith — president of the Shubert Organization, Broadway's biggest theater chain — put a video on YouTube containing derogatory information about their sex life.[9]

Yet, just as adolescents may learn to ignore the online gossip and cyber belittling that course through their cell phones and MySpace pages, adults may tire of what some call "net-venting."

Getty Images/Bruce Glikas/FilmMagic

Actress Tricia Walsh Smith, who is being divorced by Philip Smith, president of the biggest theater chain on Broadway, posted a video on YouTube containing derogatory information about their sex life.

"Most people who confront Web sites devoted to 'getting back' at other people for social sins may find them entertaining at first, but will tire of the novelty of electronic trash talk," David A. Furlow, a Houston attorney, wrote in a recent commentary. "Folk wisdom suggests that one should not wrestle with a pig, both because the wrestler gets dirty and the pig likes the challenge. The best response to the venom and vitriol of spite speech is to ignore it."[10]

[1] Kim Zetter, "Cyberbullying Suicide Stokes the Internet Fury Machine," *Wired*, Nov. 21, 2007.

[2] Rebecca Cathcart, "MySpace Is Said to Draw Subpoena in Hoax Case," *The New York Times*, Jan. 10, 2008, p. A19.

[3] Barbara Shelly, "Online avengers perpetuate the problem," *Kansas City Star*, Dec. 7, 2007, p. 9B.

[4] Quoted in Zetter, *op. cit.*

[5] Richard Abshire, Marissa Alanis and Jennifer Emily, "Sex sting leads to suicide for former Kaufman D.A.," *Dallas Morning News*, Nov. 6, 2006.

[6] "U.S.: Sex Offender Laws May Do More Harm Than Good," Human Rights Watch, Sept. 12, 2007. The report, "No Easy Answers: Sex Offender Laws in the United States," http://hrw.org/reports/2007/us0907/.

[7] See, for example, Carmen Gentile, "Cyber Vigilantes Track Extremist Web Sites, Intelligence Experts Balk at Effort," Fox News, March 22, 2008, www.foxnews.com.

[8] Quoted in *ibid.*

[9] Leslie Kaufman, "When the Ex Blogs, the Dirtiest Laundry Is Aired," *The New York Times*, April 18, 2008, p. A1.

[10] David A. Furlow, "Net-Venting: Should a Server or a Speaker Face Civil Liability for Spite Speech on the World Wide Web?," *Privacy Litigation Reporter*, September 2007, www.tklaw.com/resources/documents/PRV0501_FurlowComm.pdf.

words and images again and again. In fact, in charting cyberbullying incidents, some researchers wrestle with whether to count only the initial transmission or the number of times a victim views it.

Effect on Students

While experts contend that cyberbullying is a large and growing social problem, it is too new for definitive data on its effects to have been collected. Nonetheless, Clemson University's Limber says some clues can be drawn from past studies on traditional bullying.

In the short term, children who are victims of traditional, face-to-face bullying are more likely than their peers to have lower self-esteem and higher rates of anxiety, she says: "One can hypothesize that there may be similar short-term effects of cyberbullying," she adds, but "there

Iowa high-school students Mary Beth and John Tinker, shown in 1968, were suspended along with three other students for wearing black armbands to oppose the Vietnam War. In 1969, the Supreme Court said in the watershed *Tinker v. Des Moines School District* case that school officials had no right to suspend the students. "It can hardly be argued that either students or teachers shed their constitutional rights to freedom of speech or expression at the schoolhouse gate," Justice Abe Fortas wrote. However, under *Tinker* school officials can discipline students whose speech disrupts school activities or interferes with the rights of others.

experienced name-calling, pushing, hitting, teasing or other abuses during their school years, 67 percent said yes. Among the effects the respondents reported: depression, unexpressed rage and absenteeism from school.[41]

"You're really talking about post-traumatic stress and school phobia," Peterson says.

Gifted students may not be used to aggression, Peterson adds. When a bully strikes, they can feel betrayed, especially if the bully is part of their close social network, she says. "It's about what is real versus what is unreal. You can think something is real, like a friendship, and all of a sudden it's not." One casualty can be a student's self-identity, particularly if a rumor spreads about the victim's sexuality, she says.

While Peterson's research focuses on regular bullying, she says cyberbullying "kind of hits you without warning and [thus] might even have more impact."

One reason for cyberbullying's growth, experts say, is adults' unfamiliarity with the alien landscape of chat rooms and social networking, allowing online abuse to slip by unnoticed.

"Parents are kept in the dark intentionally by the kids," says Aftab of wiredsafety.org. "Even the victims hide from parents. The only time they tell is if they're under 10."

Patchin of the University of Wisconsin says teens often refrain from reporting cyberbullying because they don't think adults can or will do anything about it. School administrators frequently say they can't address off-campus behavior, Patchin points out, and police and prosecutors typically go after only the most egregious or threatening kinds of cyber harassment. In deciding not to tell adults, Patchin says, many young victims conclude: "What's really going to change?"

Sometimes adults respond to cyberbullying in what many experts say is the wrong way: by trying to ban teens' access to technology. For example, the Deleting Online Predators Act, which sailed through the then-Republican-controlled U.S. House of Representatives in 2006, would have required schools and libraries receiving special federal technology funds to block minors from accessing chat rooms and social-networking sites like MySpace. The bill apparently has stalled.

"I'm concerned that this [crackdown] is going to be as simplistic and thoughtless as the drug programs out there, which is 'Just say no,' when that is not a feasible, meaningful way to go about it," says UCLA's Juvonen.

are elements of cyberbullying that may make it even more disturbing for kids. In many cases kids don't know the identity of the individual doing the bullying. That can create higher rates of anxiety."

More than half of adolescent girls responding to a survey by Patchin and two colleagues reported no negative effects from cyberbullying, but others "reported a wide variety of emotional effects . . . including feeling 'sad,' 'angry,' 'upset,' 'depressed,' 'violated,' 'hated,' 'annoyed,' 'helpless,' 'exploited' and 'stupid and put down.' Some girls described how the victimization made them feel unsafe." Many girls responded to the bullying by retaliating or "cyberbullying back," the study found.[40]

Jean Sunde Peterson, an associate professor of educational studies at Purdue University, in West Lafayette, Ind., studies the effects of bullying on gifted students, a group that she says is generally highly sensitive, acutely perceptive and disinclined to seek help. While her work has not focused on cyberbullying per se, she says many of her findings apply to it.

When Peterson and doctoral student Karen E. Ray asked 432 gifted eighth-graders in 11 states if they had

Juvonen says that used properly, technology can help adolescents navigate through periods of angst and insecurity. "Online communication with even an unknown peer can alleviate the temporary stress of feeling rejection," Juvonen says. "The online world enables them to connect even from that lonely bedroom at home. It would be a pity if parents restrict all communication without better understanding how rich this world is. It has its pluses and negatives."

Potential Solutions

Child advocates and researchers continue to look for ways to curb cyber abuse. One approach encourages young people to police themselves. Social-networking sites offer tools to help them do that, including safety tips, settings to block unwanted communications and protect users' privacy and admonitions to report hateful or harassing content.

For example, Bebo, a San Francisco-based social-networking site aimed at users 13 and older, has an online "safety" tab that includes anti-bullying animations, resources for schools and advice for parents.[42]

Schoolwide programs designed to change a school environment to reduce or prevent behavior problems are also being used to fight cyberbullying. The Olweus Bullying Prevention Program, for instance, founded by Dan Olweus, a European researcher who has studied bullying for more than three decades, is being used by about 2,000 elementary and middle schools in the United States, according to Clemson University's Limber, who leads its U.S. implementation.

The approach includes training programs for teachers and administrators, surveys of students, classroom discussions about the effects of traditional and online harassment, efforts to raise community awareness of bullying, and when needed, individualized intervention with victims or perpetrators.

The program's effectiveness at fighting cyberbullying remains unclear, Limber says, because questions to assess cyberbullying were added only in the past year. But schools using the program to fight traditional bullying often see a 20 percent reduction in incidents, she says.

Limber acknowledges that some cases of cyberbullying call for strong action by school authorities and that online abuse that occurs off-site can create havoc at school.

Still, she says, "there is a lot a school and school personnel can do to raise kids' and kids' parents' awareness about cyberbullying even if it does happen off school grounds. It's important to focus on prevention and intervention. I'm more a proponent of the carrot than the stick."

CURRENT SITUATION
Action in Congress

Moves to improve online safety have been building in Congress and the states for years, spurred in part by concerns over the vulnerability of children to online predators and pornography. For example, the Children's Online Privacy Protection Act, which took effect in 2000, gives parents the power to decide whether and what information can be collected online from children under 13 and how the information can be used.

A bill sponsored by Sen. Ted Stevens, R-Alaska, would direct the Federal Trade Commission to carry out a public-awareness campaign focusing on the safe use of the Internet by children.[43] It also would substantially increase fines for Internet service providers, or those who provide computers for Internet access, such as café owners, who fail to report online child pornography.[44] In addition, it would require schools receiving special federal "E-Rate" technology funds to educate students about cyberbullying and "appropriate online behavior," including interaction with others on social-networking sites and in chat rooms.[45]

Congressional efforts to fight Internet crime are not without controversy, though.

In November 2007, for example, the House passed a bill sponsored by Rep. Linda Sanchez, D-Calif., who has proposed several anti-bullying measures in Congress. The bill would authorize grants for educational programs to fight Internet crime, including cyberbullying, sexual exploitation and privacy violations.[46]

Specifically, the measure would authorize the appropriation of $50 million over five years, half to i-SAFE — a nonprofit group in Carlsbad, Calif., that provides Internet safety programs in all 50 states — and half for a competitive grant program under which online-safety groups could vie for funding.

A coalition of online safety groups criticized the bill, saying it was funneling too much money to i-SAFE and would suppress competition and innovation in cyber-protection programs.[47]

Abusive Online Gossip Thrives on College Campuses

Juicycampus.com allows anonymous postings.

Librarian Graham Mallaghan wondered why students at the Kent University library in Canterbury, England, would laugh at him and sometimes take his picture. After a suggestion from a colleague, Mallaghan went to Facebook.com and found out why. On the site he found a page titled "For Those Who Hate the Little Fat Library Man," with hateful comments from many of the students he had disciplined in the library, telling them to stop eating or not to make noise.

After Mallaghan notified school authorities, his bike's brakes were cut and he was threatened with violence while leaving work. When the students responsible for the page had their computer access suspended, they simply passed on the password and user information to other students, who continued the abuse.

Mallaghan says he was so troubled that he sought therapy over the abuse and became underweight. The site eventually was removed.

At George Washington University in Washington, D.C., an argument between two female roommates led one of the young women to post negative comments on Facebook about her roommate, who had accused her of using drugs. The roommate complained about the mean-spirited comments to campus authorities, but the school said it did not have the authority to act. Facebook eventually stepped in, however,

threatening to block the bullying roommate from using the social-networking site if she continued to run the page.

One of the latest and most abusive gossip sites is eight-month-old Juicycampus.com, now being used at some 60 campuses nationwide, including the U.S. Naval Academy and West Point.[1] The site promises posters complete anonymity. Many of the comments posted about sorority girls, football players and professors are sexist, homophobic, racist or anti-Semitic. Juicycampus postings at such schools as Loyola Marymount University in Los Angeles, Colgate University in New York state and the University of North Carolina at Chapel Hill have included students threatening shooting rampages, a fake "sex tape" of murdered UNC student-body President Eve Carson and a crude "photoshopped" picture of a female Vanderbilt University student.

"For students who have been identified by name on Juicy Campus, the results can be devastating," wrote Richard Morgan recently in *The New York Times*. "In a tearful phone conversation, a 21-year-old junior at Baylor who majors in public relations recounted her experience when her name surfaced on the site in a discussion about the "biggest slut" on campus. " 'I'm trying to get a job in business,' she said. 'The last thing I need or want is this kind of maliciousness and lies about me out there on the Internet.' "[2]

The coalition expressed support instead for a Senate measure introduced by Sen. Robert Menendez, D-N.J., that calls for a $50-million competitive grant program for Internet education through 2012.[49]

"There are many good Internet safety organizations working hard in our schools and communities, and we feel that all organizations should have an equal opportunity to receive funding through an open and transparent grant process," said Judi Westberg-Warren, president of Web Wise Kids, an online safety group in Santa Ana, Calif.[49]

Willard, of the Center for Safe and Responsible Internet Use, criticized i-SAFE's approach and called the Sanchez

legislation "a very bad bill that, if passed in its current form, will ensure mediocrity in the delivery of Internet safety education for years."[50]

But Sanchez stood up for her bill. "Authorizing i-SAFE ensures that this program, which has already helped over 3 million children in all 50 states, will be able to continue its work," she said, adding that the group has a "proven track record for teaching kids how to be safe on the Internet."[51]

Likewise, Teri Schroeder, founder and president of i-SAFE, defends her group and its curriculum, which is distributed free to schools. She says the House bill is more comprehensive than the Senate's and would protect the

As of late April, Juicy Campus had not been banned on any campus, but student governments at several schools, including Pepperdine, Columbia and Yale universities, have called for school administrators to block the sites. At the University of California at Berkeley, Panhellenic Council President Christina Starzak urged sorority leaders in an e-mail not to use the site. Students at Pepperdine asked campus administrators to block the site from campus servers, but administrators declined on free-speech grounds. Some administrators, however, say that blocking Juicy Campus will force them to regulate hundreds of other offensive sites. Additionally, administrators and students simply hope the sites will eventually become less popular and fade away.[3]

Attorneys general in New Jersey and Connecticut, meanwhile, have recently subpoenaed the records of Juicycampus.com in hope of shutting down the site using consumer fraud statutes.[4]

"Me, I'm waiting for a horrific tragedy to happen — followed by a huge lawsuit (or 20) that cuts into the profits of Juicycampus.com," wrote columnist Debra J. Saunders in the *San Francisco Chronicle*. "I'll be rooting for the plaintiff's

AP Photo/Damian Dovarganes

Andy Canales, student body president at Pepperdine University in Malibu, Calif., opposes the juicycampus.com gossip site.

attorneys. There have to be some advantages to living in an overly litigious society."[5]

For his part, Facebook victim Mallaghan says his experience with cyberbullying has made one thing clear to him: Children must be taught that things "could get worse by staying quiet about Internet abuse. You need to find someone you trust to take you to the authorities. If nobody knows, nobody can protect you."

— *Kristina Ryan*

[1] Richard Morgan, "A Crash Course in Online Gossip," *The New York Times*, March 6, 2008.

[2] *Ibid.*

[3] Debra J. Saunders, "Tawdry, Not Juicy," SF Gate (the online edition of the *San Francisco Chronicle*), March 25, 2008, www.sfgate.com/cgi-bin/article.cgi?file=/c/a/2008/03/24/EDCPVPK55.DTL.

[4] "California Scrutinizes Juicy Campus Web Site for Potential Legal Violations," California Attorney Lawyers Web site, http://attorney2-california.com/california-scrutinizes-juicy-campus-web-site-for-potential-legal-violations/.

[5] Saunders, *op. cit.*

federal government's investment in i-SAFE, which has totaled $13 million since 2002.

The i-SAFE approach faces several financial pressures, Schroeder says. It has received no federal money for the past year-and-a-half but will nonetheless educate 6 million youths this year in Internet safety, relying on money raised from donors, she says. Moreover, she says, the federal government this year allocated federal funds through a competitive-bid process to other grantees besides i-SAFE to disseminate i-SAFE's program materials, putting an additional financial burden on i-SAFE. If Congress doesn't authorize new money to keep i-SAFE's programs current and available, those programs would be at risk, Schroeder says.

Social-Networking Sites

Cyber safety continues to draw close attention in the states, and no online mechanisms are drawing more scrutiny than social-networking sites.

MySpace agreed last year to hand over to state officials the names, addresses and online profiles of thousands of known convicted sex offenders with accounts on the networking site. It also said it had deleted the online profiles of 7,000 convicted sexual predators.[52]

And early this year, in an agreement with attorneys general from 49 states and the District of Columbia, MySpace said it would develop technology and work with

Should schools be able to regulate off-campus cyberbullying?

YES

Nancy Willard
*Executive Director, Center for
Safe and Responsible Internet Use*

Written for *CQ Researcher*, April 2008

Two high-school students have created a racist profile on a social-networking site, including racist language and cartoons about lynching. Other students are linking to the site and have posted ugly comments. Teachers report that many of the school's minority students are frightened.

At another high school, students created a "We Hate Ashley" profile that includes crude sexual innuendos and cracks about their classmate's weight. Ashley is no longer willing to come to school, and her grades have plummeted. Her parents report she is under psychological care and on suicide watch.

Do school officials have the authority to impose discipline in response to harmful off-campus online speech? Should they? This is a major challenge facing school administrators today.

The problem is grounded in the fact that the most harmful incidents of cyberbullying occur when students post or send material while they are off-campus, because they have more unsupervised time. But the harmful impact is at school, because this is where students are physically together. Cyberbullying incidents lead to school avoidance and failure, youth suicide and school violence.

Studies on cyberbullying reported in the December 2007 *Journal of Adolescent Health* reveal that both perpetrators and targets of cyberbullying report significant psychosocial concerns and increased rates of involvement in off-line physical and relational aggression. Targets of cyberbullying were eight times more likely than other students to report bringing a weapon to school. The concerns for student safety are very real. Students who do not believe school officials can help them may seek their own revenge — or refuse to come to school.

Courts have consistently ruled that school officials can respond to off-campus student speech if that speech has caused — or a reasonable person would anticipate it could cause — a substantial disruption at school or interference with the rights of students to be secure. Situations that have met this standard include violent physical or verbal altercations, a hostile environment interfering with the ability of students to participate in school activities and significant interference with school operations and delivery of instruction.

School officials do not have the authority to respond to off-campus speech simply because they find the speech objectionable or repugnant. Response to such speech is a parent's responsibility. But when off-campus speech raises legitimate concerns about student safety and well-being, school officials must have the authority to respond — because every student faces the potential of harm.

NO

Witold J. Walczak
*Legal Director, American Civil
Liberties Union of Pennsylvania*

Written for *CQ Researcher*, April 2008

If a school principal observed two students bullying another student at the local park or mall, she might speak to the children, alert the parents or, if really serious, call the police. Most likely she would not, however, contemplate using her principal's authority to suspend or otherwise discipline the bullies. Like most people, she would think that's outside of school and beyond her authority. The same standard should apply to cyberbullying.

School officials act *in loco parentis* (in place of a parent) when children are in school or in school-sponsored activities. Teachers are given leeway to instruct, direct and discipline to ensure a safe environment conducive to learning. And while students don't shed all their constitutional rights at the schoolhouse gate, courts have given administrators some leeway to restrict students' free speech, privacy and other rights while in school custody.

Once students leave the school's custody, they not only reacquire their full constitutional rights, but their parents or guardians regain theirs too, including their right to direct and control their children's upbringing. Parents' values and families' dynamics differ. Some parents prefer to turn the other cheek while others promote an eye for an eye. School officials have their own values and ways of addressing problems, and those may differ from the parents'. When it comes to their children's out-of-school behavior, parents have the right to decide if and how to discipline.

Limiting schools' disciplinary authority for out-of-school speech does not preclude school officials from taking steps, short of discipline, to address problems. Parents typically don't know everything their children do, and that's particularly true for Internet activity. Most parents would probably want school officials to alert them to bullying activity but leave disciplinary decisions to them. And for bullying that may cross the line into criminal behavior, contacting the police might be appropriate.

Finally, while school officials need to recognize that legally they have no authority over students' out-of-school speech, students should understand that Internet speech often carries real-world consequences. Unlike intemperate and stupid things uttered at the mall, speech posted on the Internet endures and is more widely accessible. Colleges, universities and prospective employers increasingly tend to uncover those mean and stupid Internet postings.

In sum, school officials have latitude to discipline students for bullying, cyber or otherwise, that occurs in school, but only parents (or police if necessary) have the authority to handle such matters off campus.

law-enforcement officials to improve children's protection. "Our responsibility is to show the way for social-networking sites," said Hemanshu Nigam, MySpace's chief security officer.[53]

The plan includes a police hotline to report suspicious behavior, automatically making the default setting "private" for profiles of 16- and 17-year-olds, allowing parents to submit their children's e-mail addresses to block them from establishing a MySpace profile and creating a separate section of MySpace for users younger than 18.[54]

MySpace also created a task force to explore how children can avoid unwanted contact and content when using it and other online sites. The task force will be run by Harvard's Berkman Center for Internet and Society, but the center's executive director said the group will operate independently. Recommendations by the task force will be non-binding.[55]

Connecticut Attorney General Richard Blumenthal called the agreement with MySpace "a profoundly significant step towards social-networking safety." He wrote that MySpace "commendably agreed to create and lead a task force of social-networking sites, technology companies and others to explore and develop age- and identity-verification technology." But, he warned, "If the task force fails to deliver, or if other social-networking sites decline to join, attorneys general stand ready to take aggressive steps, including litigation or legislative initiatives, if appropriate."[56]

Yet critics say it is easy for children to circumvent MySpace's safeguards by passing themselves off as adults, and for adults to manipulate MySpace by pretending to be adolescents. Texas Attorney General Greg Abbott, the lone holdout in signing the agreement, said he could not support the pact unless MySpace takes action to authenticate users' ages.

"We do not believe that MySpace.com — or any other social-networking site — can adequately protect minors" without an age-verification system, he said. "We are concerned that our signing the joint statement would be misperceived as an endorsement of the inadequate safety measures."[57]

Age-verification systems are difficult to implement and can lead to problems, some experts point out. Aftab, of wiredsafety.org, a task-force member, characterized the agreement as a good first step but said it could have unforeseen consequences.[58] "Age verification requires that you have a database of kids," she said, "and if you do,

that database is available to hackers and anyone who can get into it."[59]

Still, Aftab said the task force will be "looking to see if age-verification or any other technology is out there that we don't know about that will help." The 20-member group includes such companies as Google, Microsoft, Yahoo and Verizon as well as networking sites Facebook, Xanga and Bebo (recently acquired by AOL), she said.

But Keith Durkin, chairman of the Department of Psychology and Sociology at Ohio Northern University, in Ada, said an effective age-verification system is nearly impossible. A predator or child could use a pre-loaded credit card to circumvent a system that uses credit cards to verify age and identity. And, he said, no hardware or software solutions will be effective unless they are expensive, intrusive and violate current privacy laws — something that would turn a law-enforcement problem into a political controversy.[60]

"You can't monitor your kids 24/7," he said. "Parents need to have a conversation with their children at an early age."[61]

Actions in States

Along with efforts to monitor social-networking sites, anti-bullying measures proposed or passed by state lawmakers are also stirring debate.

In Washington state, for example, legislators last year amended the state's anti-bullying statute, calling on school officials to develop policies barring harassment, intimidation or bullying by electronic means but limiting the scope to actions by students "while on school grounds and during the school day."[62]

The Center for Safe and Responsible Internet Use's Willard is critical of the law, saying it prevents school officials from responding to cyberbullying that originates off campus, even if the abuse causes disruption at school or threatens student safety.

In Oregon, Willard's home state, an anti-bullying statue was amended to include cyberbullying. The law defines bullying as any act that "substantially interferes" with a student's education and occurs "on or immediately adjacent to school grounds," at school-sponsored activities, on school-provided transportation or at school bus stops. The law's language creates the potential for incidents arising off campus to be off-limits, Willard says.[63]

Some states have adopted laws with broadened scopes. Arkansas, for example, last year added cyberbullying to its anti-bullying policies and included provisions for schools to act against some off-campus activities. The measure applies to actions originating on or off school grounds "if the electronic act is directed specifically at students or school personnel and is maliciously intended for the purpose of disrupting school, and has a high likelihood of succeeding in that purpose."[64]

In Maryland, lawmakers approved a bill in April that requires public schools to develop a policy barring cyberbullying and other kinds of intimidation.[65] The bill says that even if the bullying occurs off school grounds, administrators can report it if it "substantially disrupts the orderly operation of a school."[66]

But Hudson, the research attorney for the First Amendment Center, said the school's power to reach off campus creates a "bit of tension in the First Amendment arena as to just how far school jurisdiction extends. There's no doubt that [the bill] is well-intentioned, but the question is whether it's going to sweep too much speech within its reach."[67]

In Kentucky, state Rep. Tim Couch, R-Hyden, filed a bill this year that would require anyone who contributes to a Web site to register a real name, address and e-mail address on the site. The name would then be used whenever the person posted a comment. Couch's intent was to call attention to anonymous cyberbullying.[68] "Some nasty things have been said about high-school kids in my district, usually by other kids," he said. "The adults get in on it, too."[69]

But Couch said because the measure is "probably unconstitutional," he isn't pursuing it.[70]

That's a good thing, opined the conservative *Washington Times*, citing what it called the bill's "bald violation of First Amendment rights."

"We're all concerned about cyberbullying," the newspaper said, "but we're more concerned when a lawmaker threatens our civil liberties and wastes public dollars on dim-witted legislation."[71]

OUTLOOK

Guidance Needed

As technology gets faster, cheaper and more far-reaching, cyberbullying is sure to grow, many experts say.

And that growth will demand clearer guidance from courts and policymakers on the responsibilities of schools, law-enforcement officials and online-network providers.

With state lawmakers and lower courts now focusing more on issues of defamation and cyberbullying, it may be only a matter of time before the Supreme Court rules on those issues. Still, it may be a while before the justices render guidance in a case involving adolescent cyberbullying.

"The cyber laws are emerging," says Boston College's Herbeck, noting that the initial cases involved pornography, followed by those on privacy and file-sharing issues.

In Congress, bills such as the Sanchez and Stevens measures "are raising the profile" of the cyberbullying issue, says Kim Mills, a spokeswoman for the American Psychological Association. The association is "pleased to see the recognition of cyberbullying as a serious issue," Mills says. But, she adds, "it's hard to know in this climate what the prospects are" for such legislation. It's an "election season," she notes, "and people's minds are focused on a number of other things, such as the economy and war."

Boyd, at Harvard's Berkman Center, is less than sanguine about the likelihood of finding solutions to cyberbullying through legislation. Lawmakers, she says, continue to "focus on the extreme cases" and "Band-Aid the issue" without addressing the root cause of cyber abuses: social pressures that drive adolescents to compete for status and the lack of adequate attention to those pressures from busy or distracted parents and other adults.

Cyberbullying and other abuse can be expected to get worse among adolescents "because kids are so stressed," Boyd says. The most obvious source of that stress, she says, "is the pressure to get into college." But "anything that increases pressure for status increases bullying."

And that includes a change in the financial standing of a youth's family, Boyd says, noting that the nation's shaky economy could increase the pressure for status and validation among adolescents' peers.

NOTES

1. Billy Townsend, "High Bail Set In Beating Case," *Tampa Tribune*, April 12, 2008.
2. Mary Niederberger and Nikki Schwab, "Explicit ranking of high school girls sparks outrage; Mt. Lebanon's 'Top 25' List Details Students' Looks, Bodies," *Pittsburgh Post-Gazette*, April 26, 2006, p. 1A.

3. Kathleen Haughney, "Cyberbullies could face penalties," *St. Louis Post-Dispatch*, March 24, 2008.

4. Justin Norton, "Some states pushing for laws to curb online bullying," The Associated Press, Feb. 25, 2007, www.pantagraph.com/articles/2007/02/24/news/doc45df611de8ca0765543652.txt.

5. Corinne David-Ferdon and Marci Feldman Hertz, "Electronic Media, Violence, and Adolescents: An Emerging Public Health Problem," *Journal of Adolescent Health* 41, 2007.

6. Amanda Lenhart, "Data Memo: One in three online teens have experienced online harassment," Pew Internet & American Life Project, June 27, 2007, www.pewinternet.org/pdfs/PIP%20Cyberbullying%20Memo.pdf.

7. Janis Wolak, Kimberly Mitchell and David Finkelhor, "Online Victimization of Youth: Five Years Later," National Center for Missing & Exploited Children, 2006, www.missingkids.com/en_US/publications/NC167.pdf.

8. Publication of the study by Juvonen and Elisheva Gross is forthcoming in the *Journal of School Health*. The survey was posted on bolt.com, a popular teen Web site, in fall 2005, and responses were invited. Among the 1,454 respondents, half reported daily e-mail use, and 60 percent reported daily instant-messaging. Also see Marcia Clemmitt, "Cyber Socializing," *CQ Researcher*, July 28, 2006, pp. 625-648.

9. Alexandra Rankin Macgill, "Data Memo: Teens are more likely than their parents to say digital technology makes their lives easier," Pew Internet & American Life Project, Oct. 24, 2007, www.pewinternet.org/pdfs/PIP_Teen_Parents_data_memo_Oct2007.pdf. Also see John Greenya, "Bullying," *CQ Researcher*, Feb. 4, 2005, pp. 101-124.

10. Amanda Lenhart and Mary Madden, "Teens, Privacy & Online Social Networks," Pew Internet & American Life Project, April 18, 2007, www.pewinternet.org/pdfs/PIP_Teens_Privacy_SNS_Report_Final.pdf.

11. David L. Hudson Jr., "Student Online Expression: What Do the Internet and MySpace Mean for Students' First Amendment Rights?" First Amendment Center, posted Dec. 19, 2006, www.firstamendmentcenter.org/PDF/student.internet.speech.pdf.

12. The bill, SB 1329, was introduced on April 8, 2008, and referred to the state Senate Judiciary Committee.

13. See, for example, Abbott Koloff, "States push for cyberbully controls," *USA Today*, Feb. 6, 2008.

14. Ryan Bowling, "Missouri Senate passes new cyberbullying law," *Christian County Headliner News*, March 30, 2008, www.ozarksnewsstand.com.

15. Jason Wermers and Betty Parker, "Bully bill breakthrough: Senate committee chairman relents, lets panel consider measure," *News-Press*, March 11, 2008.

16. *Ibid.*

17. *Ibid.*

18. Richard Willing, "Cyberstalking law opens debate on what's annoying," *USA Today*, Feb. 14, 2006.

19. *Ibid.*

20. *Dwyer v. Oceanport School District, et al.*, U.S. District Court, District of New Jersey, Civ. No. 03-6005 (SRC), March 31, 2005.

21. Press release, "ACLU-NJ Announces Settlement in 8th Grade Webmaster Case," Nov. 6, 2005, www.aclu-nj.org/news/aclunjannouncessettlementi.htm.

22. *Ibid.*

23. Tresa Baldas, "As 'Cyber-Bullying' Grows, So Do Lawsuits," *The National Law Journal*, Dec. 10, 2007.

24. *Tinker v. Des Moines School District* (1969).

25. *Watts v. United States* (1969)

26. *Bethel School District No. 403 v. Fraser* (1986) and *Hazelwood School District v. Kuhlmeier* (1988), respectively.

27. Quoted in Anne Marie Chaker, "Schools Act to Short-Circuit Spread of 'Cyberbullying,' " *The Wall Street Journal Online*, Jan. 24, 2007.

28. Daniel de Vise, "Schoolyard Face-Offs Blamed on Facebook Taunts," *The Washington Post*, April 27, 2008, p. 1C.

29. Millie Anne Cavanaugh, "Cyberbullying Can Have Deadly Consequences," Aspen Education Group, 2007, www.aspeneducation.com/Article-cyberbulling-consequences.html.

30. "Does the First Amendment apply to public schools?" First Amendment Center, www.firstamendmentschools.org. The case is *State ex rel. Dresser v. Dist. Bd. of Sch. Dist. No. 1*, 135 Wis. 619, 116 N.W.

31. *Ibid.* The case is *Wooster v. Sunderland*, 27 Cal. App. 51, 148 P. 959 (Cal. App. 1915).

32. Last year in *Morse v. Frederick*, 439 F. 3d 1114, the Supreme Court upheld a principal's right to punish a student who displayed a "Bong Hits 4 Jesus" banner across the street from school during a parade. The court construed the parade as a school-sanctioned event at which the school district's discipline rules applied.

33. *Layshock v. Hermitage School District, et al.*, U.S. District Court, Western District of Pennsylvania, 2007.

34. *J.S. v. Bethlehem Area School District*, 807 A.2d. 803 (Pa. 2002), summarized at www.firstamendment schools.org/freedoms/case.aspx?id=1687.

35. Bridget Gutierrez, "Get Schooled: Getting Tough on Bullying," *Atlanta Journal-Constitution*, March 7, 2007, www.ajc.com/blogs/content/shared-blogs/ajc/education/entries/2007/03/07/bully_this.html#comments.

36. Robin M. Kowalski and Susan P. Limber, "Electronic Bullying Among Middle School Students," *Journal of Adolescent Health* 41, 2007.

37. Quoted in Katie Menzer, "Boy Scouts preparing for a new threat: bullies handbook addresses how to deal with aggressive teasing — both online and face-to-face," *Dallas Morning News*, Jan. 20, 2008, p. 1B.

38. "Teens and Cyberbullying: Executive Summary of a Report on Research Conducted for National Crime Prevention Council," Harris Interactive, Feb. 28, 2007, http://vocuspr.vocus.com/VocusPR30/Newsroom/ViewAttachment.aspx?SiteName=NCPCNew&Entity=PRAsset&AttachmentType=F&EntityID=99295&AttachmentID=57d58695-7e1d-404c-a0f0-d5f6d0b18996.

39. Amanda Lenhart, Mary Madden, Alexandra Rankin Macgill and Aaron Smith, "Teens and Social Media," Pew Internet & American Life Project, Dec. 19, 2007, www.pewinternet.org/pdfs/PIP_Teens_Social_Media_Final.pdf.

40. Amanda Burgess-Proctor, Justin W. Patchin, and Sameer Hinduja, "Cyberbullying: The Victimization of Adolescent Girls," www.cyberbullying.us/cyberbullying_girls_victimization.pdf.

41. Press release, "Study: Gifted children especially vulnerable to effects of bullying," Purdue University, April 6, 2006.

42. www.bebo.com. See also the "Safety Tips" link on www.myspace.com.

43. The bill is S 1965.

44. Kathryn A. Wolfe, "Bill Outlines Program to Help Children Stay Safe Online," *CQ Today*, Sept. 26, 2007.

45. *Ibid.*

46. The bill is HR 4134.

47. Andy Carvin, "Debating Federal Funding for Online Safety Curricula," PBS Teachers, learning. now weblog, Dec. 7, 2007, www.pbs.org/teachers/learning.now/2007/12/debating_federal_funding_for_o_1.html. Carvin is founding editor of the Digital Divide Network, an online community of Internet activists seeking to bridge the digital divide.

48. The bill is S 2344.

48. Quoted in Andrew Noyes, "Bill's Passage Divides Child-Safety Groups," *National Journal's Technology Daily*, Nov. 16, 2007, http://techdailydose.nationaljournal.com/2007/11/bills_passage_divides_childsaf.php.

50. *Ibid.*

51. *Ibid.*

52. Brad Stone, "MySpace to Share Data With States on Offenders," *The New York Times*, May 22, 2007.

53. Quoted in Eric Benderoff and Kristen Kridel, "MySpace steps up security," *Chicago Tribune*, Jan. 15, 2008, p. 1C.

54. *Ibid.*

55. "MySpace picks Harvard to study Internet safety," *Chicago Tribune*, Feb. 29, 2008, p. 10.

56. Richard Blumenthal, "Our agreement is a big step," *USA Today*, Jan. 23, 2008, p. 12A.

57. Quoted in Clare Trapasso, The Associated Press, "MySpace agrees to new safety measures," *USA Today*, Jan. 14, 2008.

58. The Associated Press, "MySpace promises safeguards for youths," *Newsday*, Jan. 15, 2008, p. 8A.

59. *Ibid.*

60. Roy Bragg, "Texas AG's refusal to sign deal with MySpace called right move," *San Antonio Express-News*, Jan. 16, 2008, p. 1A.

61. Quoted in *ibid.*

62. The bill is SB 5288.

63. "State action on cyber-bullying," *USA Today*, Feb. 6, 2008.

64. *Ibid.*

65. The bill is HB 199.

66. Kathleen Fitzgerald, "Md. legislators approve bill aimed at curbing cyberbullying," Student Press Law Center, April 9, 2008, www.splc.org/newsflash .asp?id=1734&year.

67. *Ibid.*

68. John Cheves, "Anonymous Web postings targeted," *Lexington Herald Leader*, www.kentucky.com/454/ v-print/story/338489.html.

69. Quoted in *ibid.*

70. Joanne Kaufman, "If You Don't Have Anything Nice to Post . . . ," *The New York Times*, March 17, 2008, p. 4C.

71. "Kentucky Roadkill," *The Washington Times*, March 20, 2008, p. A18.

BIBLIOGRAPHY

Books

Kowalski, Robin M., Susan P. Limber and Patricia W. Agatston, *Cyber Bullying: Bullying in the Digital Age,* **Blackwell Publishing, 2008.**

Two Clemson University psychology professors and a professional counselor provide an up-to-date overview of electronic abuse. "As bullying over the Internet becomes more commonplace," they write, "educators must become equally prepared to address this new form of bullying."

Solove, Daniel J., *The Future of Reputation: Gossip, Rumor, and Privacy on the Internet,* **Yale University Press, 2007.**

A law professor at George Washington University writes that "as social reputation-shaping practices such as gossip and shaming migrate to the Internet, they are being transformed in significant ways."

Willard, Nancy E., *Cyberbullying and Cyberthreats: Responding to the Challenge of Online Social Aggression, Threats, and Distress,* **Research Press, 2007.**

A lawyer and expert on technology in schools explores the legal, social and technical aspects of electronic aggression and offers a useful compendium of cyberbullying definitions.

Articles

Areheart, Bradley A., "Regulating Cyberbullies Through Notice-Based Liability," *Yale Law Journal Pocket Part 41*, **2007, http://thepocketpart .org/2007/09/08/areheart.html.**

An attorney argues that the government should provide recourse for cyberbully victims by curbing the nearly absolute immunity Internet service providers enjoy and implementing a "notice and take-down scheme" in certain cases of wrongdoing.

Barry, Dan, "A Boy the Bullies Love to Beat Up, Repeatedly," *The New York Times,* **March 24, 2008, p. A1, www.nytimes.com/2008/03/24/us/24land.htm l?scp=2&sq=dan+barry+and+bullies&st=nyt.**

A newspaper columnist profiles Billy Wolfe, a high-school sophomore in Fayetteville, Ark., who has been the target of bullies since age 12.

Collins, Lauren, "Friend Game: Behind the online hoax that led to a girl's suicide," *The New Yorker*, **Jan. 21, 2008, www.newyorker.com/reporting/2008/ 01/21/080121fa_fact_collins.**

A journalist provides a revealing look at the suicide of Megan Meier and offers a close-up look at the personalities and neighborhood atmosphere behind a notorious cyberbullying case.

David-Ferdon, Corinne, and Marci Feldman Hertz, "Electronic Media, Violence, and Adolescents: An Emerging Public Health Problem," *Journal of Adolescent Health 41*, **2007, pp. S1-S5.**

Two experts from the Centers for Disease Control and Prevention provide an overview of a series of articles that examine the benefits and risks of adolescents' access to new communications technology. The articles can be accessed at www.jahonline.org/issues/contents?issue_ key=S1054-139X%2807%29X0249-0.

Reports and Studies

Englander, Elizabeth, and Am M. Muldowney, "Just Turn the Darn Thing Off: Understanding

Cyberbullying," Proceedings of Persistently Safe Schools: The 2007 National Conference on Safe Schools and Communities, Hamilton Fish Institute, The George Washington University, http://webhost.bridgew.edu/marc/marc%20research/hamfish%20paper.pdf.
Two researchers from the Massachusetts Aggression Reduction Center provide a useful overview of the available research on cyberbullying and help to shed light on the characteristics of its perpetrators.

Hudson, David L., Jr., "Student Online Expression: What Do the Internet and MySpace Mean for Students' First Amendment Rights?" First Amendment Center, Dec. 19, 2006, www.firstamendmentcenter.org/PDF/student.internet.speech.pdf.
A First Amendment scholar explores the legal terrain of student electronic expression and recommends that educators adopt clear policies, open lines of communication with parents and students and teach students that their postings can return to haunt them. But he recommends against punishing online expression simply because school officials don't like it.

Lenhart, Amanda, *et al.*, "Teens and Social Media," Pew Internet & American Life Project, Dec. 19, 2007, www.pewinternet.org/pdfs/PIP_Teens_Social_Media_Final.pdf.
One of a series of studies on teens and digital technology, this survey-based study found that more than 90 percent of teens use the Internet, "and more of them than ever are treating it as . . . a place where they can share creations, tell stories and interact with others."

Thierer, Adam, "Social Networking and Age Verification: Many Hard Questions; No Easy Solutions," The Progress & Freedom Foundation, March 2007, www.pff.org/issues-pubs/pops/pop14.5ageverification.pdf.
The director of the market-oriented think tank's Center for Digital Media Freedom argues that proposals to impose age-verification rules on social-networking sites "raise many sensitive questions with potentially profound implications for individual privacy and online freedom of speech and expression."

For More Information

Center for Safe and Responsible Internet Use, 474 W. 29th Ave., Eugene, OR 97405; (541) 344-9125; www.cyberbully.org. Provides guidelines, research and other resources for educators, parents and children to encourage safe use of the Internet, including avoiding cyber threats.

i-SAFE Inc., 5900 Pasteur Ct., Suite 100, Carlsbad, CA 92008; (760) 603-7911; www.isafe.org. A nonprofit foundation dedicated to educating students on how to avoid inappropriate and unlawful online content; various services include the i-Learn Online program and the i-Mentor network to provide an "On Demand" learning experience.

Internet Crime Complaint Center; www.ic3.gov. Enables victims of Internet-related crimes to file complaints, which are then referred to law-enforcement and regulatory agencies.

National Crime Prevention Council, 2345 Crystal Dr., Suite 500, Arlington, VA 22202; (202) 466-6272; www.ncpc.org/newsroom/current-campaigns/cyberbullying. Educates the public about cyberbullying and strategies for protection against Internet harassment. The NCPC's Web site links to publications and other organizations for research on cyberbullying.

NetSmartz Workshop, 699 Prince St., Alexandria, VA 22314; (703) 274-3900; www.netsmartz.org. Created by the National Center for Missing and Exploited Children and the Boys and Girls Clubs of America, the interactive workshop offers a wide variety of resources warning parents, teens, educators and law-enforcement officials about the dangers that exist on the Internet. The site links to videos, Cyber-Tiplines and personal accounts of Internet exploitation.

Take a Stand. Lend a Hand. Stop Bullying Now!, 5600 Fishers Lane, Rockville, MD 20857; 1 (888) 275-4772; http://stopbullyingnow.hrsa.gov. The Health Resources and Services Administration campaign educates children and adults about cyberbullying and improving community prevention efforts.

WiredSafety, 1 Bridge St., Suite 56, Irvington-on-Hudson, NY 10533; (201) 463-8663; www.wiredsafety.org. The online safety group offers educational and help services to victims of cybercrimes like cyberbullying, hacking, identity theft and child pornography. In conjunction with WiredKids.org and WiredTeens.org, the group promotes safe and responsible technology use.

Prostitution Debate

Should the United States Legalize Sex Work?

Marcia Clemmitt

6

So-called D.C. Madam Deborah Jeane Palfrey was convicted on prostitution-related racketeering and financial charges on April 15, 2008. Facing a likely four-to-six-year prison term, Palfrey hung herself. High-profile johns — such as Sen. David Vitter, R-La. — a Palfrey client who has campaigned on the need to protect the sanctity of marriage — often escape the toughest censure and keep their careers.

From *CQ Global Researcher*, May 2008.

O n April 10, Navy Lt. Cmdr. Rebecca Dickinson, a 38-year-old divorced mother of three, testified in a federal courthouse in Washington, D.C., about the interview process she went through to get a second — civilian — job.

In need of money a few years ago, Dickinson answered an Internet ad for an escort service and scheduled a tryout appointment with a customer in a Maryland suburb. "We had small talk for a little bit, and then we began to have sexual relations," she said. "He tried to remove the condom. I was fighting to keep it on."

Later, when Dickinson told her prospective boss — so-called D.C. Madam Deborah Jeane Palfrey — that she was upset that the man tried to force unprotected sex, Palfrey warned her: "Don't talk about such things on this phone."[1]

Dickinson told her story after the prosecution called her to testify under a grant of immunity at Palfrey's trial on prostitution-related racketeering and financial charges. On April 15, a jury convicted Palfrey, who faced a likely four-to-six-year prison term. Palfrey hung herself a few days later, leaving behind a note that said she could not face prison again.[2]

Dickinson hasn't been charged but has already suffered her punishment. Forced to publicly admit providing sexual services for pay, she has been stripped of her Navy job and may be forced to leave her 19-year military career without retirement benefits.[3]

Dickinson's story typifies many of the tough truths about the "high-end" prostitution that makes front-page news when powerful clients are involved, say sex-industry analysts.[4] Overwhelmed by economic or other personal pressures, many like Dickinson turn

Prostitution Is Legal in Many Countries

Out of 51 countries surveyed, prostitution is legal in 28 — mostly in Western Europe and Latin America — but brothel ownership is legal in only 11 of those countries. In the United States, prostitution is legal only in 11 rural counties in Nevada.

Policies Governing Prostitution and Brothel-Keeping
(in 51 selected countries)

Countries with Legalized Prostitution

Argentina	England	Iceland	New Zealand
Austria	Estonia	Israel	Norway
Belgium	Ethiopia	Italy	Peru
Brazil	France	Kyrgyzstan	Senegal
Canada	Germany	Latvia	Singapore
Costa Rica	Greece	Mexico	Switzerland
Denmark	Guatemala	Netherlands	Turkey

Countries Where Prostitution Is Illegal

Angola	Japan	Saudi Arabia	Uganda
China	Kenya	South Africa	United Arab Emirates
Cuba	Liberia	South Korea	United States*
Egypt	Philippines	Sweden	
India	Romania	Taiwan	
Iran	Rwanda	Thailand	

Countries Where Prostitution Has Limited Legality

Australia	Spain

Countries With Legal Brothel-Keeping

Belgium	Greece	New Zealand	Switzerland
Costa Rica	Guatemala	Peru	Turkey
Germany	Netherlands	Singapore	

Countries Where Brothel-Keeping Is Illegal

Angola	Estonia	Kyrgyzstan	South Africa
Argentina	Ethiopia	Latvia	South Korea
Austria	France	Liberia	Sweden
Brazil	Iceland	Mexico	Taiwan
Canada	India	Norway	Thailand
China	Iran	Philippines	Uganda
Cuba	Israel	Romania	United Arab Emirates
Denmark	Italy	Rwanda	United States*
Egypt	Japan	Saudi Arabia	
England	Kenya	Senegal	

Countries Where Brothel-Keeping Has Limited Legality

Australia	Spain

* Except in 11 counties in Nevada, where it is legal

Source: "Prostitution Policies Around the World," www.procon.org

to escort work and end up losing their reputations and, often, their jobs and homes when their sex-work pasts are discovered. Meanwhile, high-profile johns — such as Sen. David Vitter, R-La. — a Palfrey client who has campaigned on the need to protect the sanctity of marriage — often escape the toughest censure and keep their careers.[5]

The sex industry operates in the shadows, making it virtually impossible to gather reliable data about prostitution. Estimates of the proportion of women who've worked as prostitutes vary wildly, ranging from less than a quarter of 1 percent to about 1 percent in the United States and up to 7 percent in some other countries.

What is known is that around 90,000 prostitution arrests occur in the United States annually, with sex workers, not their customers, making up the overwhelming majority of those arrested. Most return to prostitution after their arrests, including many who would like to leave the work, in part because virtually no comprehensive social services exist for prostitutes. That's especially troubling, given that many prostitutes enter the industry as homeless teenagers, who've run away or been evicted from dysfunctional families. As prostitutes, they are at high risk for violence, including rape and murder.

Even though some countries are seeking new ways to limit the harm caused by prostitution, it continues to be illegal in the United States except in 11 Nevada counties, and debate on alternatives — such as decriminalization — is less robust than in other countries. That's partly because denial and ambivalence characterize most American attitudes on the sex trade.

Other recent high-profile revelations demonstrate that ambivalence, says Martha Shockey-Eckles, an assistant professor of sociology at Saint Louis University. Earlier this year, for instance, Democratic New York Gov. Eliot Spitzer, a fierce foe of prostitution and sex trafficking in his previous post as state attorney general, was named as a client of an escort service that charged customers up to $5,000 a night. Spitzer resigned his job but blamed his longtime use of prostitutes on "a sex addiction," she says. Most johns "think themselves to be morally upright individuals," she says. (Spitzer has not yet been indicted but could eventually face money-laundering or other charges.)[6]

If johns' attitudes seem inconsistent, so do U.S. laws relating to prostitution.[7] For example, in New York state, because the age of consent for sex is 18, a 17-year-old girl who has consensual sex is considered a victim of statutory rape, and her partner is considered a criminal. But if she's a prostituted girl under 18, she is arrested as a criminal and her john usually escapes punishment, says Taina Bien-Aimé, executive director of the international women's advocacy organization Equality Now.

Prostitutes — many of whom got into the business as abused or homeless teenagers who left or were cast out of dysfunctional families — also face a high risk of rape and murder, including as victims of serial killers. "We're so often in this society pointing the finger of blame that we forget that a lot of women are in danger," says Shockey-Eckles. "And they have little means of protecting themselves, because law enforcement is not their friend."

Bringing the ordinary lives of prostitutes into the open could help remove some stigma, she suggests. "If I try to discuss it, I hear about a woman having no values, that the woman is slimy," she says. "But they do have

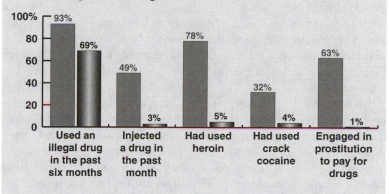

Drug Use Highest Among Street Prostitutes

More than 90 percent of street-walking prostitutes in Great Britain used illegal drugs compared to 69 percent of higher-end, indoor workers, known as "call girls." Disparities in usage of the more destructive drugs — such as heroin and crack — are even more significant. Nearly two-thirds of street sex workers say they engage in paid sex in order to fund their drug habit, compared to just 1 percent of indoor workers.

Drug Use Among Street and Indoor Prostitutes

	Used an illegal drug in the past six months	Injected a drug in the past month	Had used heroin	Had used crack cocaine	Engaged in prostitution to pay for drugs
Street workers	93%	49%	78%	32%	63%
Indoor workers (call girls)	69%	3%	5%	4%	1%

Source: Timothy Brain, et al., "Policing Prostitution: ACPO's Policy, Strategy and Operational Guidelines for Dealing with Exploitation and Abuse Through Prostitution," Association of Chief Police Officers, Oct. 1, 2004

values, and very often they are the same values as ["Leave It to Beaver" mom] June Cleaver. I've asked many prostitutes, 'What's the most important thing in your life?' And over and over the answer is, 'My son.' "

"You always hear, 'I'd do anything before I'd be a prostitute,' " says Shockey-Eckles. "But what if you couldn't feed your child?"

While little policy debate is occurring in the United States, numerous other countries are trying to deal with the issue in new ways. New Zealand has decriminalized prostitution and categorizes sex work as a form of labor in an effort to end the stigmatization. Several Australian states — including, most recently, Western Australia, in April — have legalized prostitution and some brothel-keeping in an attempt to improve prostitutes' lives through regulation. In Greece, where both selling sex and brothel-keeping are legal and regulated, prostitutes are required to have biweekly health checks.[8] Sweden has taken a different approach, decriminalizing the selling of sex while toughening penalties for johns.

Ronald Weitzer, a sociology professor at George Washington University, agrees there is room for a public discussion of such measures in the United States, but he acknowledges that most U.S. politicians "are very wary to touch it." Nevertheless, he points out, polls show that — depending on wording — 25 to 47 percent of Americans favor some kind of legalization, especially if it would help curb the spread of sexually transmitted diseases (STDs).[9]

Although prostitution is largely ignored by legislators and the public, activists hotly debate issues relating to prostitution, such as whether it could be legalized and regulated or whether law enforcement should crack down on johns.

"When are we as a society going to grow up and face the fact that, although sex can be spiritual and emotional, it can also be a commodity?" asked sexologist Susan Block, author of *Advertising for Love.* "What about all the single johns? They aren't even cheating" on anyone. Besides, she continues, "many perfectly legal sex acts are business transactions, from . . . guys who sleep with women to stay rent-free in their apartments to gold-diggers who simply marry for money."[10]

But Bien-Aimé insists that "prostitution isn't sex, it's sexual exploitation . . . and we have to make the distinction between those two."

Clinical psychologist Melissa Farley, director of the San Francisco-based anti-prostitution group Prostitution Research & Education, agrees. "I don't think it's OK that, because some of us don't have to prostitute to pay the rent, we set aside a given class of women and say, 'OK, have at them!' " she says.

As sex-worker-rights advocates and anti-prostitution activists mull how to move prostitution from titillating front-page news into serious public-policy debate, here are some questions being asked:

Should the United States legalize or decriminalize prostitution?

Ceasing the arrest and prosecution of people for selling sex — either through legalization or decriminalization — makes it easier for prostitutes to leave the life if they choose and saves taxpayers money, since most prostitutes return to work after being arrested.

"Decriminalization" merely removes the sale of sex from the realm of law enforcement. "Legalization" establishes rules under which sex work could proceed, such as size and location of brothels and requirements for disease testing. Under legalized systems, prostitutes operating outside the regulated industry face prosecution.

But legalization gets mixed reviews.

Shockey-Eckles at Saint Louis University observes that legalization means health standards could be monitored, and the now underground earnings could be taxed. It would also bring the sex trade "out into the open," so some of the problems associated with the industry could potentially be corrected, she says, adding, "Whatever we're doing now certainly isn't working."

Legalization also would provide some protection for sex workers. "In the counties in Nevada that have legal brothels, clients can walk in and have a business exchange, and there are mandatory condom laws," says Kathryn Hausbeck, an associate professor of sociology at the University of Nevada, Las Vegas. The condom law gives the women "leverage to demand that clients practice safe sex." The women also do not fear being arrested "and feel safe from the extreme violence" that most prostitutes risk, she adds.

But former prostitute Jill Brenneman, executive director of the Sex Workers Outreach Project (SWOP) East, in Chapel Hill, N.C., says legalization gives too much power to the government and brothel owners, while offering sex workers few rights. Women working in Nevada's brothels, she says, must pay brothel owners for food and other items and must pay additional fees to the county. And brothel rules strictly limit the comings and goings of sex workers during their time off, she says.

Moreover, she says, if a prostitute is raped in a brothel, the incidents are often covered up in order to preserve the brothels' and the counties' financial interests.

Nevada's system works in the small counties where prostitution is legal "mostly because it's always been there," but it's not easily replicable elsewhere, Hausbeck says. If the United States is going to adopt an alternative prostitution policy other than criminalization, it should not copy the Nevada plan, she says.

Decriminalization seems to be a more popular proposal. Under decriminalization, "hopefully over time the stigma drops," Brenneman says, so that prostitutes can come out of the shadows and report crimes against them, receive assistance if they want to leave the life and report their health-care problems honestly. But decriminalization would be just the beginning of "a long-term project to change social values," she says, adding that women in general would benefit if society stopped taking the view "that a woman who comes out of a bar in miniskirt and heels" is wearing a deserved-to-be-raped tag, she says.

Since most prostitutes return to sex work soon after being arrested and released, "arrest just cycles people through and doesn't solve anything," says Juline Koken, project director of the Center for HIV Education Studies and Training (CHEST) at Hunter College in New York City. In fact, "the legal persecution makes things worse" because arrest records make it even harder for sex workers or former sex workers to find jobs and homes, she says.

"The more you involve police in the lives of sex workers, the more it gets driven underground and the more opportunity there is for corruption and harassment by the police," says Juhu Thukral, director of the Sex Workers' Project at the Urban Justice Center in New York City.

Decriminalization would allow police resources to be spent on problems that accompany prostitution, such as assaults against sex workers and nighttime noise and disorderly behavior in nearby neighborhoods, says Barbara G. Brents, an associate professor of sociology at the University of Nevada, Las Vegas. And if prostitution were decriminalized, authorities who find underage prostitutes "can take care of them rather than arrest them," she adds.

Many of those who oppose legalization and decriminalization also oppose arresting prostitutes but favor arresting customers, pimps and madams. "When a government says, in effect, 'This is a [legitimate] job for women,' it's like putting out a legal welcome mat for johns and pimps," says psychologist Farley. Research shows that in cities where prostitution is legalized, illegal activities crop up and expand even faster than the newly legal prostitution industry, she says.

Legalizing prostitution doesn't dignify prostitutes so much as it offers an open field to those who exploit sex workers for personal gain, said Janice G. Raymond, a professor emerita of women's studies at the University of Massachusetts-Amherst and co-executive director of

Deputy Secretary of State Randall Tobias resigned in 2007 after he was named as a client in a prostitution sting. He had been the chief U.S. government spokesperson for banning HIV/AIDS funding to groups that aid or advocate on behalf of sex workers.

Getty Images/Chip Somodevilla

the international advocacy group Coalition Against Trafficking in Women (CATW). Most people believe legalization means "dignifying and professionalizing the women in prostitution," she says, but instead, "it simply dignifies the sex industry [by] legalizing pimps as legitimate sex entrepreneurs, [and] men who buy women for sexual activity are . . . accepted as legitimate consumers."[11]

"No woman should be punished for her own exploitation," she continued. "But states should never decriminalize pimps, buyers, procurers, brothels or other sex establishments."

In addition, points out the San Francisco-based advocacy group Standing Against Global Exploitation (SAGE), "Because the sex industries are more legitimized under legalization, there is no basic presumption that buying or selling someone else's body is a crime," making it harder for prostitutes to prove that they were forced or trafficked into their situations.[12]

Furthermore, normalizing prostitution leads to a lack of support services, which "are often curtailed by brothel owners" who fear the services will enable sex workers to leave the industry, wrote British freelance journalist and activist Julie Bindel and Liz Kelly, director of the Child and Woman Abuse Studies Unit at London Metropolitan University.[13]

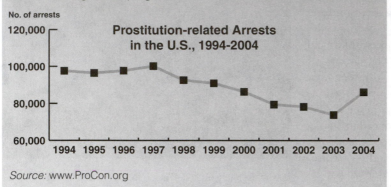

Prostitution Arrests on the Rise Again

Arrests for prostitution-related offenses in the United States reached a peak of more than 100,000 in 1997 and then declined for six years before starting back up again in 2004.

Prostitution-related Arrests in the U.S., 1994-2004

Source: www.ProCon.org

Should law enforcement focus on johns rather than prostitutes?

Although most anti-prostitution laws call for penalizing customers as well as prostitutes, in reality prostitutes bear most of the brunt of enforcement. In fact, only 10 percent of those arrested in connection with prostitution are johns.

To overcome that problem, the Swedish government in 1999 decriminalized the selling of sex but criminalized the buying of sex. Swedish lawmakers concluded that prostitutes "were in it for survival, and it was men who knew that vulnerability and were exploiting it," says Rachel Durchslag, director of the Chicago Alliance Against Sexual Exploitation. "So they shifted the paradigm."

Most analysts of all stripes agree it's unfair to target sex sellers while ignoring buyers, but some advocates of sex-worker rights say the Swedish approach may actually harm prostitutes.

"In New York, the ratio is six to one" — women to men — "who get arrested and charged" in prostitution busts, says Bien-Aimé of Equality Now. "And the women get time while the men get a slap on the wrist."

Durchslag says johns — not prostitutes — create the sex market. "Were there no demand there would be no prostitutes and no trafficking," she says.

For a variety of reasons, however, no U.S. cities have considered criminalizing demand. Law enforcement for vice crimes is "woefully under-resourced," Durchslag says, and it's difficult to establish probable cause unless the officer actually sees money changing hands. Police also may shy away from targeting johns because they're afraid they'll snag powerful citizens in the net, she says.

Contrary to myth, targeting johns doesn't penalize lonely, possibly disabled, men whose "unmet needs" compel them to buy sex, said Gunilla Ekberg, an adviser to the Swedish government on trafficking and prostitution. One of every eight Swedish men over 18 has paid for sex with a prostitute, and the majority of them have wives, live-in girlfriends or other non-paid partners, she said. "Men who have or have had many sexual partners are the most common buyers . . . effectively dispelling the myth that the buyer is a lonely, sexually unattractive man with no other option for his sexual outlet."[14]

Saint Louis University's Shockey-Eckles says law enforcement currently taps into traditional views that women are the root of the world's evils — myths dating to the dawn of history. "She's the . . . dastardly temptress who drags the innocent man off into her lair. It comes from deep-seated ways of dealing with gender," says Shockey-Eckles.

Advocates of Sweden's criminalization of buying sex say it's helping to quell both prostitution and international trafficking of people into the sex trade. "Sweden has provided us with a very effective model" that gives women an exit strategy by offering social services, such as therapy, job training and educational opportunities, says Norma Ramos, co-executive director of the Coalition Against Trafficking in Women.

Demand can be significantly quelled if customers are jailed or punished rather than being subjected only to "shame-based" treatment, such as having their names publicized, and being allowed to walk way without being locked up, says Ramos.

Trafficking of women from elsewhere to work as prostitutes under coercion in Sweden has dropped off drastically after 1999, according to Ekberg. The European Law Enforcement Organisation and national police forces in several European countries have indicated that Sweden "no longer is an attractive market for traffickers," she said.[15]

And while helping prostitutes find jobs and start new lives is "not a quick fix and it's not cheap," says psychologist Farley, it may be cheaper over the long term, according to some studies.

But others argue that prosecuting customers doesn't help prostitutes much. "I have no sympathy for the clients, couldn't care less about them," says Brenneman of the Sex Workers Outreach Project. However, the Swedish approach siphons off scarce resources from helping sex workers and from arresting and prosecuting what Brenneman calls the real criminals — the rapists, those who hire underage girls and traffickers who coerce women and teenagers into prostitution. "If Joe Client pays and doesn't force the sex worker to do what she doesn't want to do," then the transaction amounts to "consensual adult activity, so what's the problem?"

Swedish sex-worker-rights advocates also complain that arresting johns only drives prostitution underground, further endangering the women.

"The negotiations must happen a lot faster than before since the police may be around the corner," said Isabella Lund of Sweden's Sex Workers and Allies Network. "It is therefore hard to do a correct risk assessment" of whether the john is likely to be dangerous, she said. In addition, the risk of spreading sexually transmitted diseases has risen, because men who've been customers of an infected prostitute are afraid to contact authorities, said Lund.[16]

Younger Prostitutes Have Rougher Upbringings

Teenagers who become prostitutes before age 16 are more likely to have had sex and used drugs at an early age — and to have an unhappy homelife and divorced parents — than those who become prostitutes when they are older. By contrast, those who began between ages 16 and 18 were more likely to have been raped or arrested.

Comparisons Among Prostitutes by Beginning Age

Experiential Variable	Began Under 16	Began 16-18	Began 19+
Unhappy homelife	14.30%	3.00%	10.30%
Parents divorced/separated	57.00	44.00	21.80
Distant father	00.00	17.60	15.00
Distant mother	43.00	26.00	11.50
Sexual assaults by "uncles" etc.	14.30	17.60	15.00
Sexual assault by close relative	14.30	20.60	10.30
Coitus by 16	100.00	70.60	33.30
Initial coitus as rape or incest	14.30	20.60	6.90
First male lover 5 years older	28.50	23.50	27.60
Juvenile arrest	28.50	59.00	23.00
Raped outside work	28.50	50.00	39.00
First drug used by 16	57.00	44.00	24.00
Narcotic use past and present	85.70	53.00	36.80
Pills, LSD, "speed" use past and present	100.00	61.80	39.00
Street working experiences	42.80	32.30	12.60
Brothel experiences	85.70	88.20	57.50
Escort experiences	57.00	47.00	30.00
Bondage experiences	14.30	3.00	4.60
Private experiences	43.00	26.50	18.40
Other prostitutions in past	0.00	8.80	1.20
No previous experiences	0.00	6.00	28.70

Source: "Australian studies in law, crime and justice," Australian Institute of Criminology, 2008

Should society concentrate on ending forced prostitution rather than ending all prostitution?

Some feminists insist that prostitution by definition is a form of gender oppression and slavery and must

More Females Are Arrested Than Males

Seven in 10 prostitution-related arrests during the 1980s were of female prostitutes, more than three times the rate of arrest among their male counterparts. Only 10 percent of arrests involved customers.

Prostitution Arrests in the United States, 1980-1989

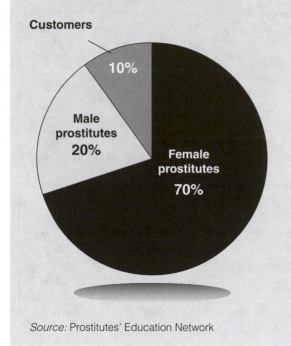

Customers 10%

Male prostitutes 20%

Female prostitutes 70%

Source: Prostitutes' Education Network

Most prostitutes work for madams or pimps, who are often involved with organized crime, and "take 50 percent off the top" of prostitutes' earnings, says Farley. "I don't care if she's paid $10 or $1,000 for a blow job. That's a human-rights violation."

"I think people don't want to look up close at prostitution because when you do, it is about as brutal an act of one person against another as you can get," Farley says. "Johns sexually humiliate women every day. They refuse to use condoms. Then there are the physical things that happen — the coming on people's faces, ass-to-mouth" acts. "The only reason to do any of that is to humiliate and endanger a woman."

Focusing laws only on cases in which demonstrable force or coercion is used to recruit and hold a prostitute misses subtler but no less compelling forms of coercion, Farley says. Ashley Dupre, the purported Emperors' Club VIP escort involved in the Spitzer case, "may not have had a gun to her head, but she had no job or home," which compromised her freedom of choice, she points out.

"The consent of the victim should be irrelevant" in trafficking and prostitution law because even prostitution that looks voluntary is likely the product of poverty or past abuse, said Raymond of the University of Massachusetts-Amherst.[17]

Others say treating all prostitution as criminal behavior demeans women who say their participation in sex work is consensual and diverts resources from helping those who have been forcibly trafficked or prostituted.

"Nobody wants to see someone forced, and the truth is, if you really believe that every single sex worker is forced into it, of course you want to help," says Thukral of New York's Sex Workers' Project, which provides legal representation for prostitutes. However, "we have had clients pulled out" of sex-work venues and identified as victims in police anti-trafficking raids "when they weren't trafficked or forced," and those women shouldn't be categorized as trafficking victims, she says.

Brenneman at the Sex Workers Outreach Project, who was trafficked as a teenager and held captive in her pimp's home and entered the escort business voluntarily

therefore be stamped out in all forms before women and men can attain equality. Others argue that, in at least some cases, prostitution is a form of adult consensual sex, so law enforcement should focus its resources on eliminating cases where a third party has pressured a woman or young person into selling sex.

as an adult, says the two experiences are very different. "I hate to see them pushed together," she says.

"You do have the 14-year-olds who are forced" into prostitution, and they need help, including strong prosecution of their traffickers or captors, but Brenneman insists some women do enter prostitution by choice. Deeming every act of paid sex an instance of rape denies women the right "to make choices in their lives, even the wrong choices," she says.

"Sex work can, in many circumstances, be a relatively lucrative and attractive alternative to repetitive and demoralizing factory work or the ill-paid harum scarum of the fast-food empires," wrote two British academics, Peter Davies, a professor of the sociology of health at the University of Portsmouth, and Rayah Feldman, a lecturer in health at South Bank University.[18]

"People are concerned about the risk in selling sex when they believe that sex is different from every other human experience, or that it is sacred and belongs in the same room with love and should never be tainted by money" or that "women are sexually vulnerable by definition, always in danger of being violated," said independent researcher Laura M. Agustin, author of the 2007 book *Sex at the Margins: Migration, Labor Markets and the Rescue Industry.*[19]

"But not everyone feels that way," she said. "Some migrants who sell sex do hate what they are doing but stay on because the money is better and faster than in any other job they can get. Some don't mind selling sex because they learn how to 'act' in it, and keep it separate from the rest of their lives. Some like doing it. Everyone does not feel the same way about sex."[20]

To reduce prostitution's harms, says independent cultural anthropologist Jennifer James, "do everything possible to stop the second-party trafficking of women and men in any form, but leave the individual entrepreneurs alone; that is a lost cause.

"Most of the prostitutes I met were women and men with lives that had been distorted in childhood — battered, sexually abused, abandoned — all the things that destroy a sense of self and possibility," she says. "I met very few thoughtful, fully conscious women who had made an economic choice based on their talents and options. But

I did meet a few, and they seemed to have good lives and good clients."

BACKGROUND
Moral Panic

A public movement to ban or strictly limit prostitution didn't get off the ground in the United States until the waning decades of the 19th century, when feminists joined both political progressives and church-based activists to protest the widespread acceptance of red-light districts. By 1915, however, all states had enacted anti-prostitution laws.[21]

"In the first half of the 19th century, because the law treated women and children as the property of men, it offered them little protection from men," leaving prostitution to flourish unchecked by concern for prostitutes' health and safety or wives' qualms, wrote John Lowman, a professor of criminology at Canada's Simon Fraser University in Burnaby, British Columbia.[22]

"Most U.S. cities had [clearly identified] brothels and red-light districts," often operating under the eye of cities' political machines — the powerful, unofficial organizations that controlled city governments by dispensing favors to constituents in return for votes — says Brown University Professor of Political Science James A. Morone. These "red-light districts were pretty safe, and at the time the big debate was whether the United States should follow the French example and medically regulate" prostitution.

Many believed that "even good women don't want to put up with their husband's depravity, making a red-light district a good alternative," especially if it's regulated to prevent the spread of sexually transmitted diseases, Morone says. By the turn of the 20th century, however, opposition to prostitution had grown, ultimately mushrooming into a nationwide "moral panic" about what was dubbed the "white slave trade," Morone says.

Feminist groups condemned prostitution as a sign of society's double standard, which decreed that men could buy sexual services and married men have extramarital, paid sex, while wives were required to remain "pure" or become prostitutes condemned as "fallen" women. Religious groups and some political progressives began to view the ubiquitous red-light districts as evidence of a troubling moral laxity. Meanwhile, progressives in the so-called Social Gospel movement deemed prostitution one of many social ills that had arisen from unrestrained capitalism.

Anti-prostitution sentiment finally coalesced into a national movement after *McClure's* magazine published a fabricated 1909 story about Jewish immigrants in the Northeastern United States who lured white American farm girls into brothels with the covert cooperation of city political machines. Author George Kibbe Turner's primary goal had been to arouse national ire against the corruption of city-machine politicians, says Morone. But in an era of rapid urbanization, immigration and a burgeoning car culture that allowed young people to get away from the homestead, the stories tapped into widespread anxieties over sexuality and the loosened morals of modern life, obliterating the message about corrupt politics, he says.

Outcry arose about the white slave trade that supposedly led to the deaths of more than 50,000 women a year, says Morone. Girls were advised to avoid "Italian fruit stands" and "German skating rinks" where traders might lurk, and President William Howard Taft quickly earmarked $50,000 in federal funds — $20 million today — to fight white slavery.[23]

The Mann Act

Although the white slavery scare stories were largely untrue, "there was lots of forced prostitution in that era," says Morone. But it mostly involved Asian women, some of whom were sold into sexual slavery by their families. Nevertheless, "Northeastern girls did come to the city and do things that they wouldn't have done in the country," which helped keep anxiety alive, he says.

In 1910, the Mann Act made it a felony to transport or assist in the transport of a woman across state or national boundaries "for the purpose of prostitution or debauchery, or for any other immoral purpose, or with the intent and purpose to induce, entice or compel such woman or girl" into such actions. Although legislators were reluctant to bring federal law enforcement into an area traditionally the province of states and localities, "a

good old-fashioned panic makes it very simple to get a bill through Congress," says Morone.

The new law and a dedicated force of federal agents recruited to enforce it sent red-light districts and brothels underground. Most likely, it also put some brothel-keepers out of business and cleaned up the look of cities.

The Mann Act was not, however, an unalloyed victory for pro-woman forces, says Morone. "Not to romanticize [the days of ubiquitous red-light districts], but almost everybody who has studied it says things became much worse for prostitutes after they shut the brothels," he says. "It made it a more difficult trade that became dominated by pimps. Closing the brothels may have served everybody's need except the women's."

Law enforcement soon seized upon the very general wording of the Mann Act — banning the transportation of females for "prostitution or debauchery, or for any other immoral purpose" — to prosecute some non-commercial sex, such as adulterers or eloping underage couples.

In 1911, the Supreme Court ruled that the 1907 Immigration Act's similarly worded ban on importation of alien women for prostitution justified prosecution of John Bitty, a cigarette-factory owner who had brought an English mistress into the country.[24] "The words, 'or for any other immoral purpose' . . . show beyond question that Congress had in view the protection of society against another class of alien women" than prostitutes, wrote Justice John Harlan. "In construing an act of Congress . . . regard must be had to the views commonly entertained among the people of the United States . . . and concubinage is generally regarded in this country as immoral."[25]

In 1917, in *Caminetti v. United States*, the Supreme Court cited the *Bitty* precedent in ruling that two men who bought railroad tickets for their mistresses were liable for prosecution under the Mann Act. Writing for the court majority, Justice William R. Day said denying the law's relevance to the case "would shock the common understanding of what constitutes an immoral purpose."[26]

Critics of the act's general wording argue that it has allowed selective prosecution of politically unpopular people. For example, racial resentment apparently spurred the 1913 Mann Act conviction of Jack Johnson, boxing's first black heavyweight world champion. Johnson was sentenced to a year in prison after being convicted of sending a railroad ticket to a white girlfriend.

CHRONOLOGY

1900s-1950s *Reformers spur national outrage over brothels operating openly in many U.S. cities.*

1907 Congress investigates trafficking of women into the U.S. for prostitution.

1909 Iowa becomes first state to allow court injunctions to close a brothel.

1910 Mann Act makes it a federal felony to transport women or girls across state lines for prostitution.

1917 Draft Act of 1917 outlaws prostitution near military bases, spurring closure of red-light districts.

1944 British actor Charlie Chaplin is acquitted of politically motivated Mann Act charges related to his affair with actress Joan Barry.

1945 As World War II ends, prostitution flourishes near military bases.

1960s-1980s *U.S. troops in Vietnam contract sexually transmitted diseases from prostitutes; sex workers begin organizing to seek labor rights; feminists define pornography and prostitution as violence toward women. The HIV/AIDS epidemic fuels fears about prostitution.*

1961 American Law Institute proposes specific punishments for buyers of sex.

1969 Brig. Gen. David Thomas, the Army's top medical officer in Vietnam, recommends that the military run brothels. No action is taken.

1971 Brothels are legalized in rural Nevada. . . . California legislature rejects a bill allowing legalized prostitution in counties.

1973 San Francisco prostitute Margo St. James forms Call Off Your Old Tired Ethics (COYOTE), a sex-workers' rights group calling for decriminalization. National Organization for Women supports decriminalization.

1975 American Civil Liberties Union calls for decriminalization of prostitution.

1976 Rep. Joseph D. Waggonner, D-La., is re-elected after being arrested in a prostitution sting.

1980 Rep. Robert E. Bauman, R-Md., loses his bid for re-election after being arrested for patronizing an underage male prostitute.

1988 Nevada legislature requires condom use in brothels.

1990s-2000s *Global concerns about human trafficking heat up the debate over banning all prostitution.*

1990 The Hollywood film "Pretty Woman," with Julia Roberts and Richard Gere, presents a glamorized vision of prostitution.

1992 Switzerland legalizes ownership of brothels.

1996 Advocacy group Equality Now calls for prosecution of the sex-tour company Big Apple Oriental Tours.

1999 Sweden decriminalizes selling sex and threatens prostitutes' customers with up to four years in prison.

2000 President Bill Clinton signs the Trafficking Victims Protection Act.

2003 New Zealand decriminalizes prostitution.

2007 Deputy Secretary of State Randall Tobias, chief government spokesperson for banning HIV/AIDS funding to groups that aid or advocate for sex workers, resigns after he's named as a client in a prostitution sting. . . . Congress hears testimony about the suffering of "comfort women" kidnapped and trafficked by the Japanese government to work as sex slaves for the military during World War II. . . . House passes the William Wilberforce Trafficking Victims Protection Act Reauthorization, to expand federal powers to prosecute U.S.-based prostitution as sex trafficking.

2008 Gov. Eliot Spitzer, D-N.Y., resigns after federal investigators name him as a client of a prostitution ring. . . . So-called D.C. Madam Deborah Jeane Palfrey commits suicide after being convicted of racketeering charges connected to her Washington escort business.

Prostitutes' Stories Reflect Larger Society

Sex workers are remarkably like everybody else.

Jill Brenneman was a "throwaway" 14-year-old — out of money and 1,000 miles from home — when a good-looking man approached her in a shopping mall.

"He looked like [Fleetwood Mac singer] Lindsay Buckingham" and said he ran a modeling agency, says Brenneman, a former prostitute who is executive director of the Chapel Hill, N.C.-based Sex Workers Outreach Project (SWOP) East. She agreed to go with the man. "I knew it was wrong, but I was hungry, eating out of Taco Bell dumpsters, sleeping in graveyards."

Hung by the wrists in the stranger's basement until she agreed to work as a submissive in a sex "dungeon," Brenneman says she became a captive for several years until the pimp's arrest freed her, with permanent injuries to her wrists from bondage scenarios and to her throat from a beating after she tried to escape.

Brenneman's story of her path into teenage prostitution may be typical, but there are other — quite different — paths as well. The reality is that prostitutes and their customers are everywhere, though largely hidden from view by centuries-old stigma, say prostitution researchers.

"A lot of people know a sex worker and don't realize it, and a lot of people have a relative who's been a sex worker and don't realize it," says Tracy Quan, author of *Diary of a Manhattan Call Girl* who worked as a call girl for 15 years beginning in her teens. "It's like gay issues in the '60s."

A few women enter escort work out of curiosity or sexual adventurousness, at least in part, says Juline Koken, project director of the Center for HIV Education Studies and Training (CHEST) at Hunter College in New York City. One woman she interviewed "was into sexual experimentation in her early 20s and started meeting people on Craigslist for sex but not for money," says Koken. "Then one offered to pay her, and she took the money," eventually becoming a $1,000-an-hour escort. The woman told Koken that escorting allowed her to be sexual without getting emotionally involved, something she felt she needed at the time.

Many sex workers are the working poor, says Juhu Thukral, director of the Sex Workers' Project at the New York City nonprofit Urban Justice Center. "They are a part of the fabric of the community, but we get so caught up in seeing them as victims or criminals that we don't notice that."

"Some people say they'd rather work flexible hours to take care of their kids or work their way through school," says Thukral. "A common thread is that 'I'm looking around at the options, and I could work at a minimum-wage job somewhere, or do this.'"

Among escorts she interviewed, most had goals, many were in school and nearly half had a bachelor's degree or more, says Koken. Many had other jobs that they loved, like teaching yoga or running a dance studio. But escort work "is how they made their money," since even educated women can "often can make much more money there than in other jobs," she says.

"Some women had the goal of staying in the business because they really enjoyed it," says Koken. They "saw it as a calling and often were radiant," when they described their work, she says.

But many women did want to transition out of sex work, Koken says. Such plans met with varying success, however, with some successfully working toward real-estate

---

As social norms changed in the second half of the 20th century, Congress faced pressure to amend the Mann Act to eliminate prosecution of acts no longer widely accepted as crimes, such as unmarried people living together.

In 1978, the phrase "immoral purpose" was replaced with "prohibited sexual contact," which limited the law's application to actions criminalized by states. In response to growing worries about teenage male prostitution, boys were included in the underage prostitution provisions. In 1986, the entire law was made gender neutral.

Feminist Split

In the 1980s, a new generation of feminists began focusing on the sex industry — including pornography, prostitution and sex-trade businesses like strip clubs — as a primary purveyor of the double standard that kept women subjugated to men. At the same time, a new openness

licenses but others finding it extremely difficult to leave because of lack of work skills or "calamitous life experiences," like divorce, she says.

While economics is one reason women enter sex work, many prostitutes have a troubled past, says Martha Shockey-Eckles, assistant professor of sociology at Saint Louis University, who studied street and indoor prostitutes in the Quad City area of Bettendorf and Davenport, Iowa, and Moline and Rock Island, Ill. In her study, "almost all of the women had a history of abuse — physical, emotional or sexual," she says.

Researchers disagree about how many prostitutes are alcohol or drug addicted.

"Typically, what I found was, regardless of the level a woman started in, and regardless of whether she came in drug addicted, most became involved in drugs" before they were through, says Shockey-Eckles. "It's the drug addiction that keeps them in."

But many escorts Koken interviewed said drug addiction is rampant only among street-based prostitutes. "They were emphatic that it was not them," she says.

High-priced call girls tend to be "hedonistic" women who like to party. "You're selling pleasure, after all," says Quan. Nevertheless, "as far as drugs and alcohol go, sex

Former prostitute Tracy Quan, author of *Diary of a Manhattan Call Girl*, says, "What we are is people who work for a living and happen to work with our bodies."

Circe Hamilton

workers are remarkably like everybody else. I've been among guys from every industry, and there's lots of drug and alcohol use."

Social stigma and having nowhere to turn for help when they encounter trouble are constant, painful features of prostitutes' lives, regardless of where they are on the economic spectrum, most analysts agree. "Imagine what it would be like if you couldn't tell anybody what you did for a living," says Koken. "For many who want to leave the business, that's the top reason" they give for not getting out — having nothing to put on a résumé.

"I was terrified of police officers," says Brenneman. "Some of my clients were police officers, and they were often the roughest ones."

In many ways, the sex industry reflects the society at large. For example, class and racial stratification are alive and well in prostitution.

"If you're a white women and you either are or can pass yourself off as someone at the upper-middle-class level" in looks and speech, "then you can charge the higher rates," says Koken. Among the $150- to $1,000-per-hour escorts she studied, "women of color, even highly educated women, were getting $100 less" per hour than comparable white women.

In this way, as in so many others, "the sex industry is nothing more than a microcosm of the culture. It reflects us in every way," Koken says.

toward sex encouraged some prostitutes to speak openly about their work as legitimate labor that they should be able to pursue without fear of arrest and with legal protection against discrimination and violence.

In recent decades debate between opponents and proponents of legalization or decriminalization has grown increasingly heated. At the same time, globalization has increased awareness of laborers being forcibly trafficked around the world for the sex trade and other industries.[27]

Feminists opposed to prostitution argue that to effectively tackle sex trafficking and violence against women, lawmakers must eliminate all forms of prostitution.

"We categorically reject any approach that normalizes" prostitution of any kind, such as treating prostitutes' problems as labor issues, says Ramos of the Coalition Against Trafficking of Women. Quoting a prostituted woman who calls prostitution "prepaid rape," she says that it results entirely from the "negative social condition"

Internet Lures More Men Into Sex Trade

But in gay culture prostitution involves less stigma.

The Internet is driving an explosion of male sex work, says David Bimbi, a project director of the Center for HIV Education Studies and Training (CHEST) at Hunter College in New York City.

Gay men have tended to gravitate toward homosexual chat sites because it's "private and anonymous," according to Bimbi. Many homosexuals tell Bimbi: "I never thought about prostitution until somebody offered me money."

But the Internet can also make sex work safer on many levels, he says, such as allowing someone to state up front what their limits are. On the street, "if you get in a car and they drive you away, you feel pressure to do whatever is asked," he says.

While many vulnerable teenagers, such as transgender teens or effeminate boys rejected by their families, still take up prostitution for survival, Internet-based escort work is attracting a larger demographic, with more men — from teens to 40-somethings — looking for supplemental income, Bimbi says. In particular, college students and men in relatively low-paying service-sector jobs like nursing, teaching and social work are among today's escort ranks.

Unlike with female prostitutes, most men work independently rather than through pimps, says Bimbi. As a result, male sex work is the only field in which men's hourly rates are less than women's — about half as much, between $100 and $500 in the escort field (non-street prostitutes), compared to the approximately $200 to $1,000 per hour pay range among female escorts, he says.

"The more classically attractive and the better built, the higher the rates," Bimbi explains. "If a male sex worker has done a porn movie, he can raise his rates, because he's a star."

Despite the emphasis on looks, it's not all about the physical, however. Many customers want conversation and emotional connection from escorts, male or female, says Juline Koken, another CHEST project director. For example, a male escort may be "the only male-to-male intimate contact" in a married client's life, she says. Many "take a lot of pride" in providing that intimacy, even comparing their work to therapy.

"The sex can be the least part of it" in escort work, says Bimbi. "The sex takes five minutes."

of gender inequality and not from women's free choice. "Many people don't understand that — like some professors at elite institutions" who buy into the idea that some women may participate in the trade willingly.

Others argue that prostitution has always existed — and always will — because of "men's needs," but that view is too dismissive of what humans are capable of, says Bien-Aimé of Equality Now. "We are supposed to have evolved. Why are we thinking that men are so animalistic that they can't control their urges? We shouldn't be in a society where people are for sale."

Prostitutes active in the sex-worker-rights movement and academics sympathetic to them are, in fact, acting as unwitting mouthpieces of the "pimp lobby," the big-money sex industry, which has the most to gain from making prostitution a legally protected enterprise, says psychologist Farley. Three forces — "sexism, race and poverty" — sustain all prostitution, since the people most

vulnerable to being coerced into the business are the poor and ethnic minorities, she says.

Sex-worker-rights advocates, many of whom self-identify as feminists, generally agree that many women are forced into prostitution as underage girls or trafficked immigrants or accept the work because they can't find other jobs that pay a living wage. However, they argue that it's a matter of respect and human dignity to trust the word of adults who say they've chosen sex work freely and that further stigmatizing sex work by calling for its total elimination will do nothing to protect sex workers.

Sex work is not selling oneself but selling services, says former prostitute Tracy Quan, author of *Diary of a Manhattan Call Girl*. "What we are is people who work for a living and happen to work with our bodies," she says.

Sex-worker-rights groups reject the perspective that there is something inherently degrading about exchanging money for sexual services. "We choose to trust our clients

Gay sex workers also may suffer less from the social stigma that isolates female sex workers, says Bimbi. In gay culture, people are more likely to say, "Wow, you're hot enough to be a sex worker," he says.

Many gay prostitutes are like young female prostitutes — homeless teenagers, drug addicts and people from abusive and difficult backgrounds. "Many effeminate young men are tossed out of their homes and can only get money this way," and some straight drug addicts end up performing sex acts on gay males to pay for their drug habits, says Bimbi.

However, sex work is looked down upon less in the gay community, and "there are also men who are very well adjusted and enjoy what they do," he says. "They say, 'I like to have sex, and the average man has sex two times a week, but I have it five times.' " In male prostitution "the higher up the echelon you go [in price], the gayer the men get," and "the higher-end men will see it as a career," he says.

Nevertheless, as in female prostitution, some male-to-male encounters are emotionally violent, says Melissa Farley, an anti-prostitution activist and a clinical psychologist who is director of the San Francisco-based nonprofit Prostitution Research & Education. One ex-prostitute told her that his worst john was a regular who paid top dollar but verbally abused him, calling the prostitute names in a "sexist, homophobic rant." The prostitute found this "worse than being beaten or raped," says Farley.

"There are people with identity issues who come in and want to be punished for what they are, called a faggot," says Bimbi. That's emblematic "of how people internalize oppression" in our society, he observes.

In addition, police treat male prostitutes and female prostitutes differently, says Martha Shockey-Eckles, assistant professor of sociology at Saint Louis University. "Cops will take the women and book them," but they're more likely "to humiliate and harass a gay male prostitute," she says. "This whole notion of gay male prostitutes often strikes a homophobic nerve" among cops.

Police sting operations are rare, partly because "the police don't want to find out who their customers are," says Bimbi. Individual men "do get harassed" on Craigslist, however, "but the men feel, when it does happen, it's not a police department directive but comes from an individual cop."

Transgender women prostitutes have few options besides the street, largely because of the stigma they face in society, says Bimbi. "More than any other group, they are doing sex work for survival. They have absolutely no other choices," he says.

"Of 20 women we interviewed, two-thirds were forced out of their family homes, and half were forced out before age 18," he says. As adults, "the more passable and pretty ones go stealth" and find work in the mainstream economy, "but the minute they're out [as transgender people] in the work force, they're in trouble," he says.

when they tell us they don't feel degraded," says Thukral of the Urban Justice Center. "Part of looking at human rights means respecting what people are saying about their own lives."

"Even though I was abused and harmed in the sex industry, I advocate for sex-workers' rights" because to do otherwise deprives people of the dignity of taking responsibility for their own decisions, says Brenneman of SWOP East.

Furthermore, treating sex work as unlike other business puts sex workers — many of whom have painful histories of poverty and abuse — in a position no one else in society is in, says David Bimbi, a project director at Hunter College's Center for HIV Education Studies and Training. Keeping prostitution illegal makes prostitutes fear asking for help from authorities, even in dire circumstances, he says. "If a client is high on drugs and potentially dangerous or in a medical emergency, why shouldn't

a sex worker be able to call someone for help without getting into trouble?"

Former prostitute Quan disputes the idea that no man has a need to buy sex. "That's obviously wrong and very dogmatic. It's a very narrow way of looking at somebody else's sexual needs," she says "Everyone should ask themselves, 'Is there something that I need that others would be surprised about and say is not really a need?' " Most people would find that there is, and for some men, for a variety of reasons, that's purchased sex, she says.

Regardless of the law, some women "will exchange sex for money, so if you allow them a safer way to do it," such as by legalizing brothels, "you do empower them," insists Hausbeck of the University of Nevada.

AIDS and Trafficking

The debate over what to do about prostitution has played out in the national and international policy arena over the

Who Buys Sex?

The typical client is married with children.

Perhaps the biggest mystery in the largely hidden world of sex work is who buys sex from prostitutes and why. Little research exists on sex-work customers, but what is known is that they are pretty much like everyone else, says Martha Shockey-Eckles, assistant professor of sociology at Saint Louis University. "People are shocked" to hear that "the typical client is 40ish and up, middle to upper class, and married with children," she says. "The average citizen thinks that if somebody's buying a hooker, they're dirty, unkempt and down on their luck," and are surprised to learn that a man may still buy sex elsewhere even "if he can get it at home," she says.

About 18 percent of men consistently tell national surveys that they have paid or been paid for sex during their lifetimes, says Ronald Weitzer, a professor of sociology at George Washington University. "So if that's the percentage that admit to it, I would say that the actual number may be about a quarter of men" who have engaged in paid sex, he says.

Their motivations may be as various as the people themselves — from satisfying a particular fetish to emotional closeness to the power fantasies of a serial killer, many of whom have preyed exclusively on prostitutes.

Men from every income level seek paid sex, including some lower-income men, says Tracy Quan, a former prostitute and author of *Diary of a Manhattan Call Girl.* Partly for economic reasons, the range of sex services sought is also wide, she says. For example, "there's a huge market for manual release" — men paying women or men to masturbate them, she says. "That's affordable."

In the few existing studies of customers, "some will say they want a certain kind of sex or want a friend because they're lonely," says Weitzer. One study focused on whether the men held aggressive views of women — which might indicate a potential for violence — but only a few did, he says.

Some customers take a paternal interest in prostitutes they come to know, but in many cases "the john is in it to humiliate the woman," says Shockey-Eckles.

That makes distinguishing the safe client from the unsafe client a key skill needed by sex workers, says Quan. She entered sex work as a teenager and says she was initially "clueless" about judging customers and relied on accumulated experience along with feedback from others she worked with, including a madam, to hone her judgment. "It took me five years" to become good at screening clients, she says.

For many prostitutes, especially those who work "indoors," sex work is as much a matter of the mind as of the body. "Women provide services both sexual and emotional," says Juline Koken, project director of The Center for HIV Education Studies and Training (CHEST) at Hunter College in New York City. They "want to get the men off and make them feel cared for and loved."

The "energy is put toward giving him that, and the focus is on the client," says Koken. That's how sex work differs from a relationship and why some can consider it to be a selling of services rather than a selling of self, she says. "When a person is with a partner, it's reciprocal — I let you come into my life," she says. "But in a professional-client relationship," the sex worker "only lets a client see one side of herself."

Reportedly, "sex tourism" is a growing phenomenon — paying local men for sex and "romance" when visiting resort areas. "I buy him a nice shirt and we go out for dinner," said a 56-year-old Englishwoman of her month-long hookup in a Kenyan beach town with a 22-year-old local man. "For as long as he stays with me he doesn't pay anything."[1]

Julia Davidson, a senior lecturer in criminology at England's Nottingham University, equates such sex tourism to a "return to the colonial past, where white women are served, serviced and pampered by black minions."[2]

---

[1] Quoted in Jeremy Clarke, "Older White Women Join Kenya's Sex Tourists," Reuters, Nov. 26, 2007, www.reuters.com.

[2] *Ibid.*

Should Congress make the anti-trafficking law more applicable to the domestic sex industry?

YES

Robert Brannon
Co-Founder, National Organization for Men Against Sexism

From the NOMAS Web site, Jan. 24, 2008, www.nomas.org/node/142

On Dec. 4, the House . . . overwhelmingly passed H.R. 3887, which not only extends the Trafficking Victims Protection Act of 2007 (TVPA) — which is about to expire and must be reauthorized by Congress — but greatly improves it. The trafficking issue now moves to the Senate Judiciary Committee. NOMAS is joining many feminist and other groups in strongly urging the Senate to pass this bill.

African-Americans and Latinos are the persons most victimized by domestic traffickers, who exploit and harm [the] most vulnerable: "young people of color, often immigrants, often children, almost always women, almost always poor."

The 2000 bill was valuable and important, but it was the result of a compromise and had major flaws. "Sex trafficking" was defined as "the recruitment, harboring, transportation, provision, or obtaining of a person for the purpose of a commercial sex act." But a second category, termed "Severe Sex Trafficking," was narrowly limited to the few acts that could actually be proved in court to have been performed by "force, fraud, or coercion," or to have involved a minor. And all legal penalties were limited to the "severe" category. This has meant that very few trafficking prosecutions have been possible.

Proving "force, fraud, or coercion" in a court setting is practically impossible, even when it has certainly occurred, as the trafficking victims are often terrified, vulnerable, in poverty and far from home. Few if any victims can take the stand and testify at length about their sexual abuse, try to "prove" what was said or done to them and undergo a brutal, humiliating cross-examination. And this coercion focus totally ignores all the complexities of poverty, economic desperation and "consent."

The new bill will treat proof of force, fraud or coercion, or the use of minors as grounds for enhanced punishment, but not as the sole basis for convictions. It will ensure that all persons convicted of sex trafficking will receive significant sentences. Incorporating and updating the earlier Mann Act, originally called the White Slave Traffic Act, the new bill will make it a felony to engage in trafficking or other unlawful commercial sex activities while "being in or affecting" interstate or foreign commerce.

In other significant provisions, the bill will treat international and domestic trafficking as interconnected, recognizing that we cannot reduce international trafficking if we fail to combat our own trafficking slavery, expand penalties and support the prosecution of "sex tourism" providers.

NO

Brian W. Walsh
Senior Research Fellow
Andrew M. Grossman
Senior Policy Analyst
Center for Legal and Judicial Studies, Heritage Foundation

Written for *CQ Global Researcher*, April 2008

H.R. 3887 trivializes the seriousness of human trafficking by equating it with run-of-the-mill sex crimes — such as pimping, pandering and prostitution — that are neither international nor interstate in nature.

The net effect of this unconstitutional federalization of local crime [is] to blur the lines of federal and state authority and assert federal supremacy without providing sufficient federal resources.

Most dramatically, the William Wilberforce Trafficking Victims Protection Reauthorization Act of 2007 [TVPRA] would create a new federal offense, "sex trafficking," encompassing common prostitution-related offenses. Any person who "persuades, induces or entices any individual to engage in prostitution" . . . would face large fines and imprisonment for up to 10 years. [T]he bill's provisions would transform all pandering, pimping and hiring of a prostitute into federal crimes.

Congress must not sweep aside the long-standing authority of state and local governments to define what immoral conduct should be criminalized and punished.

Further, the TVPRA's overbroad criminal provisions would criminalize "knowingly" making travel arrangements for those intending to engage in "any commercial sex act." This may sound good, but once again the language suffers from a lack of precision that would cause federal law enforcement to be diverted from the worst trafficking crimes. The Department of Justice currently focuses its efforts against "sex tourism" on overseas sex crimes that involve children. These cases are, unsurprisingly, highly resource-intensive. The TVPRA's new definition of sex tourism encompasses adult travel to engage in adult prostitution where such prostitution is legal, thus diverting scarce federal resources from efforts against trafficking and sex tourism that involves children.

Prostitution is a problem common to many states, so federal involvement may seem like a good idea. To warrant federal involvement, however, an activity must fall within Congress' constitutionally granted powers. The bill's drafters have attempted to cure the serious problem of its constitutionality by limiting [it] to infractions that occur "in or affecting interstate or foreign commerce." However, the Supreme Court [has] ruled that this sort of language is not alone sufficient to bring an act within the scope of Congress' commerce power. It must be truly interstate in nature and "substantially affect" interstate commerce. For this reason, Congress does not have the constitutional authority to federalize most street crimes.

past decade or so. During the 1990s the Clinton administration and international bodies like the United Nations took a harm-reduction approach to the sex industry, in line with the philosophy of sex-worker-rights groups.

For example, the 1995 United Nation's Fourth World Conference on Women, held in Beijing, adopted language stating that "all forced prostitution and pornography" are "incompatible with the dignity and worth of the human person and must be eliminated" — language preferred by sex-worker-rights advocates — rather than calling for elimination of "all prostitution and pornography" as anti-prostitution advocates recommended.[28]

By the late 1990s, however, many feared that slavery, including sex slavery, was growing at unheard of rates because of the new ease of global travel. Prostitution prohibitionists in the United States and elsewhere took up sex trafficking as their foremost cause, espousing the view that international sex trafficking and domestic prostitution are essentially the same enterprises and that elimination of one requires elimination of the other.

In response to these concerns, President Bill Clinton signed into law the Trafficking Victims Protection Act (TVPA) on Oct. 28, 2000, which was designed to crack down on international sex trafficking.

However, the bill did not go nearly as far as anti-prostitution advocates would have liked because it continued to distinguish between forced and voluntary prostitution and dubbed as "severe" sex trafficking only prostitution involving minors or using "force, fraud, or deception" to coerce adults into the sex industry.

Anti-prostitution forces gained a stronger White House ally in 2001, when President George W. Bush took office. The Bush administration stepped up enforcement efforts under the TVPA and increased funding to groups pursuing traffickers. It also offered services to women and children who'd been trafficked.[29] Between 2001 and 2006 the government provided about $375 million in anti-trafficking funds to foreign governments and nongovernmental organizations.[30]

In 2003, Congress reauthorized the law, making it easier to target the domestic sex industry. The revised law raised from 15 to 18 the minimum age at which victims must cooperate in the prosecution of their traffickers; authorized victims to file civil damage suits against traffickers and classified U.S.-citizen sex workers who've never crossed a border as potential victims of sex trafficking.[31]

The Bush administration's international HIV/AIDS funding plan — the President's Emergency Plan for AIDS Relief (PEPFAR) — also includes anti-prostitution language. The 2003 law includes the controversial "anti-prostitution pledge," which requires governments or other organizations that receive PEPFAR funds to have explicit policies opposing prostitution and to certify that they in no way support the "legalization or practice" of prostitution, such as providing counseling or even condoms to help protect the prostitutes from AIDS.[32]

But some public-health officials argue that walling off sex workers from anti-HIV/AIDS funding is short-sighted. "Sex workers are part of implementing our AIDS policy and deciding how to promote it," said Pedro Chequer, former director of Brazil's anti-sexually transmitted diseases program. "They are our partners. How could we ask prostitutes to take a position against themselves?"[33]

CURRENT SITUATION
Moving Online

Prostitution made news the old-fashioned way — a married high-profile official linked to high-priced hookers — when Gov. Spitzer got caught early this year. But changes in the industry brought about by new technology and contemporary economic realities may be the more important story.

"Globalization has hit every economic sector, and it's becoming hard to think of the sex industry as operating within any borders," says Hausbeck of the University of Nevada. Globalization has not only complicated efforts to research and regulate prostitution but may actually be expanding it, she added.

"Some sex workers are trafficked, and some prostitutes of their own volition cross national boundaries and serve clients all over the world," she explains. The increasing ease of travel and communication — via Internet and cell phone — also means that "you don't just go to a certain part of town to find the sex industry any longer. It's everywhere, 365 days a year."

Furthermore, "our economy is changing to service jobs, and service work doesn't pay" enough to support families, potentially driving more women into sex work, says the University of Nevada's Brents.

Rising prices and a materialistic culture may already have broadened the demographics of sex sellers in the gay community, says Bimbi of the Center for HIV Education Studies and Training at Hunter College. Traditionally, poverty and homelessness drove young men into performing "survival sex" for money, but today some teenagers and college students are also looking for things to acquire, he says, such as the iPod — which made the wish list of one young male escort offering his services on the Craigslist classified ad Web site. "When you're in Manhattan and an average one-bedroom apartment costs $1,800 a month, and you're also trying to pay off student loans," it's not surprising young people seek supplemental income, Bimbi says.

Koken of the HIV education center calls the move to offering services online a "really radical shift" for the industry. Relying on the Internet and cell phones to conduct transactions rather than storefronts and the street is "good in a lot of ways because when people come indoors they encounter less violence and they're less visible for arrest," says Thukral at the Sex Workers' Project in New York.

The Internet also helps bring escorts together, reducing their social isolation — a big problem for sex workers — says Koken.

"But the downside [to the online shift] is that people think they're not going to be arrested, when, in fact, the police are interested" and now regularly scan Craigslist and other sites, Thukral says. "It's also harder for outreach programs to reach people indoors" with offers of assistance, she says.

Koken contends that the Internet is also allowing more female sex workers to operate independently. "The online venue has made it easier for women to work independently" from escort services and pimps — something many male prostitutes have done all along, she says. Escort agencies are getting fewer calls while more women are posting their own online ads, making "the third party" — the one who takes the money — obsolete, she says.

"I'm surprised we're not hearing as much about it in the media, but it doesn't fit the 'victim' frame" that governs most reporting about sex work, Koken says. One escort Web site that she's monitored since 1997 is "five times as big today," and the ad section for independents has grown the most, she says.

Some analysts disagree that the online shift means more prostitutes work independently. "A lot of people want to work alone, be their own boss," says Shockey-Eckles of Saint Louis University. "But at most levels you will still see a women under management of some kind. Independents are very rare." Many "women have a hard time admitting that they aren't independent business people, so they call their manager their boyfriend."

And psychologist Farley of Prostitution Research & Education says a massive, highly profitable sex industry continues to control prostitution. It's "misinformation" to say the online world is fostering more independent operators. "That's just wild speculation, and there's no research evidence behind it at all," she says. "Pimps are still out there in major numbers."

Government Action

Governments around the world are re-examining prostitution laws in light of today's realities and changing social norms. Several nations have legalized prostitution and related acts like brothel-keeping, and more are mulling such moves.

New Zealand decriminalized prostitution and registered brothels in 2003. Four of Australia's eight states also recently legalized the running of regulated brothels. Denmark decriminalized prostitution in 1999, though brothel ownership is still illegal.

Reviews of these efforts are mixed. Although lawmakers in the Australian state of Victoria believed legalization would enable the sex industry to be controlled, "the illegal industry there is now out of control," said Richard Poulin, a professor of sociology at Canada's University of Ottawa, and sex trafficking of women and children from abroad has "increased significantly."[34]

But in the Netherlands, which legalized brothels in 2000, a government report claims regulation has curbed "criminal excesses" in legalized brothels, making it unlikely the number of trafficking victims is rising. "Before the lifting of the general ban on brothels," trafficking was "taking place in all sectors of prostitution."[35]

The United Kingdom is considering Sweden's model — decriminalizing the selling of sex but making the buying of sex illegal, says Farley.

But Sweden's approach also draws mixed reviews. Between 1999 and 2004, the number of women involved in street prostitution in Sweden dropped from 650 to 500, and "there is no evidence that the sale of women has moved from the streets to the Internet," said government adviser Ekberg. She said Sweden's experience shows that attacking demand limits the size of the sex industry.[36]

But others say the law has left prostitutes worse off. The johns who remain "are the ones with a twisted mindset, and street prostitutes today are more exposed to robbery, assault and rape than before," said Lund of Sweden's sex workers' advocacy group. And the government has not provided enough resources to help sex workers leave prostitution, she says.[37]

In the United States, where prostitution law is mostly a local and state matter, most of the prostitution debate has occurred at the national level and focused on trafficking. An exception occurred in 2004, when voters in Berkeley, Calif., debated and eventually rejected a ballot measure to decriminalize prostitution.[38]

Also, mimicking somewhat Sweden's approach, some cities have tried focusing more negative pressure on johns. But unlike in Sweden, American johns seldom face jail time. Instead, cities rely on shame-based approaches.

In 2006, Atlanta Mayor Shirley Franklin launched a "Dear John" public-awareness campaign aimed at shaming men who buy sex from underage people. "When you buy sex from our kids, you hurt them, you hurt our families and you hurt our city. It's over, John. No more — not in my city," reads one Atlanta public-service announcement.[39]

In San Francisco, men picked up as first-time-offending johns can have the misdemeanor charge dropped if they pay a $1,000 fee and spend a Saturday afternoon in "john school," listening to ex-prostitutes and others give presentations on STDs and trafficking. Attendees are 30 percent less likely to be rearrested for buying sex than non-attendees, according to Michael Shively — a criminologist at the Massachusetts-based research company Abt Associates, who studies such programs for the Justice Department.[40]

This spring both houses of Congress passed versions of a bill to reauthorize PEPFAR HIV/AIDS funding to governments and groups that oppose prostitution.

Sex-worker-rights advocates are disappointed. "We had very realistic hopes that PEPFAR's anti-prostitution clause would go," says Thukral at the Sex Workers' Project, because "good data show sex workers are leaders in sexual health" when they're officially included in anti-disease efforts.

Federal anti-trafficking programs also are up for reauthorization. In December, the House overwhelmingly passed the William Wilberforce Trafficking Victims Protection Act of 2007, which broadens the programs' scope. Named after the 19th-century British abolitionist, the House bill would make it easier to include as trafficking victims U.S. citizens who have not crossed national borders, partly by easing a requirement for prosecutors to demonstrate that a person was brought into the sex industry through "force, fraud or coercion." (*See "At Issue," p. 151.*) The Senate has not yet acted on the matter.

Current U.S. trafficking law is "really outdated," in the same way that "the old rape laws were outdated, because they told women, 'We want to see the bruises on you' " before claims of rape were believed, says Farley of Prostitution Research & Education.

But Thukral says the government's attention is diverted from egregious cases of internationally trafficked women and young people when the law targets prostitution generally.

OUTLOOK
Common Ground?

While the prostitution debate remains bitter, advocates on both sides say enough common ground exists for progress to be made against the harms of prostitution if government and the public have the will.

"We all agree that we should fight child prostitution," first and foremost, despite disagreement about whether adult prostitution should be targeted, says Hausbeck of the University of Nevada.

And virtually everyone involved in the issue argues that prostitutes themselves should be offered social services rather than being arrested. Arrest actually lessens a person's chances of leaving prostitution, says Thukral, of the Sex Workers' Project in New York City, because a police record can prevent women from getting a new job or housing and increase their risk of deportation if they are immigrants.

Proponents and opponents also widely agree that many more social services are needed, such as drop-in centers for underage sex workers and gay and transgender teens, who are at high risk for ending up in prostitution. "You'd think this would be an area people could agree on quite a bit, but so far there are virtually no comprehensive services," says Thukral.

"There is such a huge need for some kind of transitional housing" for kids who get kicked out of the house — such as gay and transgender teens and others ejected from dysfunctional families who frequently end up selling sex, says Bimbi of Hunter College.

Also needed are judgment-free medical care and chemical-dependency programs for addicts as well as training in computer skills and résumé writing, says sex-worker-rights advocate Brenneman.

"Everybody on all sides of this issue agrees the number of prostitutes would go down if we offered people jobs and tackled the issue of offering women equal opportunity," says Farley of Prostitution Research & Education in San Francisco.

Teaching effective parenting skills is also important, says Saint Louis University's Shockey-Eckles, so fewer youths wind up getting kicked out of the house and on the streets.

Tackling racial and class inequalities also would help, Farley says, because some women are brought into prostitution because of the color of their skin or because poverty makes them vulnerable, she adds.

Better public understanding of how deeply prostitution is woven into society would help ease the disgrace sex workers face, say many analysts. Today, "people risk stigma by coming out" as sex workers or ex-sex workers, but, "ironically, if everyone told their stories, then things would change," says Koken at Hunter College.

"We have huge knowledge gaps about what really goes on in the industry," which cripples the ability to make sound policy, says the University of Nevada's Hausbeck. "Everybody is afraid to fund good research." She would like to see the National Science Foundation fund research on prostitution, so that it would be as agenda-free as possible.

"I hope we would evolve toward the belief that sex is a healthy human attribute that you don't have to pay for," says Bien-Aimé of Equality Now. "With healthier sexual relationships, I don't think exploitation would be nearly as pervasive or rampant as it is now."

NOTES

1. For background, see Chris Amos, "Academy Officer Led Double Life as Call Girl," *Army Times*, April 15, 2008, www.armytimes.com.

2. Paul Duggan, "Escort Service Boss Found Guilty," *The Washington Post*, April 16, 2008, p. B1. See also Petula Dvorak, "Palfrey Described 'Exit Strategy,' " *The Washington Post*, May 6, 2008, p. B3.

3. Amos, *op. cit.*

4. For background, see Charles S. Clark, "Prostitution," *CQ Researcher*, June 11, 1993, pp. 505-528, and M. Costello, "Legalization of Prostitution," *Editorial Research Reports*, Vol. II, Aug. 25, 1971, available at www.cqpress.com.

5. For background, see "Vitter Statement on Protecting the Sanctity of Marriage," press release, campaign Web site of Sen. David Vitter, www.vitter2004 .com/News/Read.aspx?ID=20.

6. For background, see Joseph Goldstein, "Prosecutor Move Suggests Spitzer May Face Charges," *New York Sun*, April 8, 2008, www2.nysun.com/ article/74326.

7. "1994-2004 U.S. Prostitution-Related Arrests," Prostitution ProCon.org, www.prostitutionprocon .org.

8. Susan Block, "Amsterdamize New York!" *Counterpunch online*, March 17, 2008, www.counter punch.org.

9. For background see Sarah Glazer, "Sexually Transmitted Diseases," *CQ Researcher*, Dec. 3, 2004, pp. 997-1020.

10. For background, see "Prostitution Policies Around the World," Prostitution ProCon.org, www .prostitutionprocon.org/international.htm.

11. Janice G. Raymond, "10 Reasons for Not Legalizing Prostitution," Coalition Against Trafficking in Women International, March 25, 2003, www .prostitutionresearch.com.

12. "Frequently Asked Questions about SAGE and CSE," SAGE, March 9, 2007, Prostitution Pro and Con Web site, www.procon.org/faqs.php.

13. Julie Bindel and Liz Kelly, "A Critical Examination of Responses to Prostitution in Four Countries: Victoria, Australia; Ireland; the Netherlands; and Sweden," Routes Out Partnership Board, 2003, www.nswp.org/pdf/BINDEL-CRITICAL .PDF.

14. Gunilla Ekberg, "The Swedish Law that Prohibits the Purchase of Sexual Services," *Violence Against Women*, October 2004, p. 1194.

15. *Ibid.*, p. 1200.

16. Quoted in "Sweden Has Not Made It Safer for Women," All Women Count Web site, http://all womencount.net.

17. Quoted in Eric Goldscheider, "Prostitutes Work — But Do They Consent," *The Boston Globe*, Jan. 2, 2000, p. C1.

18. Peter Davies and Rayah Feldman, "Selling Sex in Cardiff and London," in Peter Aggleton, ed., *Men Who Sell Sex: International Perspectives on Male Prostitution and AIDS* (1999), p. 1.

19. Quoted in Susie Bright, "The Truth Behind the Sex Trade," Alternet Web site, Oct. 11, 2007, www .alternet.org.

20. *Ibid.*

21. For background, see James A. Morone, *Hellfire Nation: The Politics of Sin in American History* (2003).

22. John Lowman, "Submission to the Subcommittee on Solicitation Laws of the Standing Committee on Justice, Human Rights, Public Safety, and Emergency Preparedness," http://24.85.225.7/lowman_ prostitution/SCJHPE/Submission_to_the%20 Subcommittee_on_Solicitation%20Laws_Brief.pdf.

23. Based on comparative-value calculations from the Measuring Worth Web site, Institute for the Measurement of Worth, www.measuringworth .com/index.html.

24. For background, see Ariela Dubler, "Immoral Purposes: Marriage and the Genus of Illicit Sex," www.law.columbia.edu/null/Dubler?exclusive= filemgr.download&file_id=94747&showthumb=0.

25. *United States v. Bitty*, 208 U.S. 393 (1908).

26. *Caminetti v. United States*, 242 U.S. 470 (1917).

27. For background, see David Masci, "Human Trafficking and Slavery," *CQ Researcher*, March 26, 2004, pp. 273-296.

28. For background, see "Violence Against Women," The European Online Resource Center, www.eurowrc .org/13.institutions/5.un/un-en/04.un_en.htm.

29. For background, see Laudan Y. Aron, Janine M. Zweig and Lisa C. Newmark, "Comprehensive Services for Survivors of Human Trafficking: Findings from Clients in Three Communities," Urban Institute, June 2006, www.urban.org/ UploadedPDF/411507_human_trafficking.pdf.

30. "Human Trafficking: Better Data, Strategy, and Reporting Needed to Enhance U.S. Antitrafficking Efforts Abroad," Government Accountability Office, July 2006, www.gao.gov/new.items/d06825 .pdf.

31. For background, see "Response to Human Trafficking," The Salvation Army, www.salvation-armyusa.org/usn/www_usn.nsf/vw-sublinks/ A19410276D968DBE85256F650071663E?open Document.

32. For background, see Nicole Franck Masenior and Chris Beyrer, "The U.S. Anti-Prostitution Pledge: First Amendment Challenges and Public Health Priorities," *PLoS Medicine*, July 2007, p. 1158, www.plosmedicine.org.

33. Quoted in *ibid.*

34. Quoted in "Does Legal Prostitution Lead to Human Trafficking and Slavery?" Prostitution Pro/Con.org, www.prostitutionprocon.org/questions/trafficking .htm.

35. Anna G. Korvinus, "Trafficking in Human Beings: Third Report of the Dutch National Rapporteur," Bureau NRM, The Hague, 2005, www.prostitution procon.org/pdf/NL-NRMEngels3.pdf.

36. Ekberg, *op. cit.*, p. 1193.

37. "Sweden Has Not Made It Safe for Women," *op. cit.*

38. For background, see Kristin Bender, "Berkeley Battles Over Prostitution Measure," *Oakland Tribune*, Aug. 31, 2004.

39. "Mayor Franklin's Dear John Program," Human Trafficking Atlanta Web site, http://humantrafficking atlanta.wikidot.com.

40. Quoted in Justin Berton, "John School Takes a Bite Out of Prostitution," *San Francisco Chronicle*, April 14, 2008.

BIBLIOGRAPHY

Books

Agustin, Laura Maria, *Sex at the Margins: Migration, Labor Markets and the Rescue Industry*, Zed Books, 2007.
An independent scholar argues against regarding poor working women who emigrate from developing nations to work in the sex industry as simply victims of sex trafficking — a label she regards as demeaning to the variety of motives women have for emigrating.

Albert, Alexa, *Brothel: Mustang Ranch and Its Women*, Ballantine Books, 2002.
A public-health researcher and Harvard Medical School graduate describes the lives of the prostitutes in one of Nevada's legal brothels, among whom she lived for an extended period during a six-year study.

Davies, Peter, and Rayah Feldman, eds., *Men Who Sell Sex: International Perspectives on Male Prostitution and AIDS*, UCL Press, 1999.
Professors of sociology and health in Great Britain assemble research studies by a group of international scholars detailing the experiences of male prostitutes.

Farley, Melissa, *Prostitution, Trafficking, and Traumatic Stress*, Routledge, 2004.
A clinical psychologist and anti-prostitution activist uses prostitutes' own testimony to argue that prostitution is organized violence against women.

Morone, James A., *Hellfire Nation: The Politics of Sin in American History*, Yale University Press, 2004.
A Brown University political science professor chronicles attempts by American reformers of many stripes to turn morality into law, including an account of the Mann Act, an early 20th-century federal anti-prostitution law.

Ringdal, Nils Johan, *Love for Sale: A World History of Prostitution*, Grove Press, 2005.
A Norwegian historian offers an overview of prostitution in many cultures.

Articles

Phillips, Tom, "Weary of War but Ready for Action: American Soldiers Set Their Sights on Delights of Rio," *The Guardian* (UK), Jan. 18, 2007, www.guard ian.co.uk.
Troops on leave from war zones enjoy sex tourism.

Rosen, David, "The Double Life of Prostitution in America," *Counterpunch*, Jan. 27-28, 2007, www.counterpunch.org.
Stigmatization of prostitutes exposes sex workers to mortal dangers.

Studies and Reports

"Behind Closed Doors: An Analysis of Indoor Sex Work in New York City," The Urban Justice Center, 2005, www.sexworkersproject.org/downloads/BehindClosedDoors.pdf.
Based on interviews with 52 indoor sex workers, an organization involved in sex-worker rights describes the lives of brothel workers, escorts, dominatrices and bar workers.

"Human Trafficking: Better Data, Strategy, and Reporting Needed to Enhance U.S. Antitrafficking Efforts," Government Accountability Office, July 2006.
Congress' nonpartisan audit office says the lack of both a coordinated federal anti-trafficking strategy and solid information on how many people are victims of trafficking has seriously hindered implementation of anti-trafficking laws.

"Revolving Door: An Analysis of Street-Based Prostitution in New York City," The Urban Justice Center, 2003, www.sexworkersproject.org/downloads/RevolvingDoor.pdf.
Based on interviews with 30 prostitutes in the New York City area, a sex-worker rights organization describes the lives of street prostitutes and the "revolving-door" of arrests that repeatedly cycles them through the justice system.

"Seminar on the Effects of Legalization of Prostitution Activities — A Critical Analysis," The Government Offices of Sweden, November 2002, www.regeringen.se/content/1/c4/22/84/0647d25a.pdf.
Anti-prostitution feminists and others offer their perspectives on the fallout from legalization of prostitution in several countries.

"Sex Worker Health and Rights: Where is the Funding?" Sexual Health and Rights Project, Open Society Institute, June 2006, www.soros.org/initiatives/health/focus/sharp/articles_publications/publications/where_20060719/where.pdf.
A sex-worker advocacy group argues that anti-prostitution policies by governments and nonprofit groups leave sex workers in many countries exposed to disease, violence and police brutality.

Farley, Melissa, "Bad for the Body, Bad for the Heart: Prostitution Harms Women Even if Legalized or Decriminalized," *Violence Against Women***, October 2004, pp. 1087-1125.**
A clinical psychologist argues that no legal framework can limit prostitution's harms.

Weitzer, Ronald, "The Social Construction of Sex Trafficking: Ideology and Institutionalization of a Moral Crusade," *Politics & Society***, September 2007, pp. 447-475.**
A George Washington University sociology professor argues that equating prostitution with sex trafficking is based on dubious data and is shaping unsound and ineffective U.S. policy.

For More Information

COYOTE (Call Off Your Tired Old Ethics) L.A., www.coyotela.org. Prostitutes' rights organization assists sex workers and advocates for decriminalization.

Equality Now, P.O. Box 20646, Columbus Circle Station. New York, NY 10023; (212) 586-1611; www.equalitynow.org. A women's-rights group that opposes sex trafficking and prostitution.

Girls Educational and Mentoring Services (GEMS), www.gems-girls.org. Nonprofit group that provides information about and assistance to girls and young women who have been prostituted or experienced sexual violence.

Official Website of Father Depaul Genska, Catholic Theological Union, 5401 South Cornell Ave., Chicago, IL 60615; (773) 753-5315; www.depaulgenska.com/ministering.html. Provides contact information for groups that minister to heterosexual prostitutes and their customers or work to eliminate sex trafficking.

Prostitution ProCon.org, www.prostitutionprocon.org. An educational Web site providing information and commentary on the sex industry, including updated summaries of prostitution laws worldwide and a list of experts.

Prostitution Research & Education, Box 16254, San Francisco CA 94116; (415) 922-4555; www.prostitutionresearch.com. A feminist anti-prostitution group providing information and advocacy about the harms of the sex industry and sex trafficking.

Prostitution Resources, http://arapaho.nsuok.edu/~dreveskr/prolinks.html-ssi. A Web site run by a criminal justice professor at Oklahoma's Northeastern State University; contains links to research and commentary on the sex industry.

Sex Workers Outreach Project — East, P.O. Box 2881, Chapel Hill, NC 27515-2881; (202) 470-0534; www.swopeast.org. Provides information on the sex industry from a sex-worker rights perspective.

Sex Workers Outreach Project — USA, www.swopusa.org. Provides information and services to sex workers and advocates for decriminalization of prostitution and for labor rights in the sex industry.

Sex Workers' Project, Urban Justice Center, 123 William St., 16th Floor, New York, NY 10038; (646) 602-5617; www.sexworkersproject.org. Provides information, legal services and advocacy on behalf of sex workers who choose or are forced to work in the sex industry.

Whore College, P.O. Box 210256, San Francisco, CA 94121; (415) 751-1659; www.whorecollege.org. Presents information and commentary on prostitution-related news and legislation from a sex-worker rights perspective.

Child Welfare Reform

Will Recent Changes Make At-Risk Children Safer?

Tom Price

Sally Ann Schofield was sentenced in Augusta, Maine, to 20 years in prison for killing her 5-year-old foster child in 2002. Logan Marr suffocated after being bound to a highchair with 42 feet of duct tape. More than 900,000 children were abused or neglected in the United States in 2003 and 1,390 died. Today about a half-million children live in foster homes under the jurisdiction of state child welfare agencies.

AP Photo/Joel Page

From *CQ Researcher*,
April 22, 2005.

D aisy Perales, a 5-year-old San Antonio girl, died on Dec. 1, 2004, a week after she was found unconscious and bleeding, with head trauma, bruises, a fractured rib and a lacerated spleen. She weighed just 20 pounds.

Texas Child Protective Services had investigated her family seven times. Daisy was one of more than 500 Texas children to die of abuse or neglect from 2002 to mid-2004. The agency had looked into at least 137 of the cases.[1]

At the beginning of 2003, in Newark, N.J., police entered a locked basement to find Raheem Williams, 7, and Tyrone Hill, 4. Both were starving and covered with burns and excrement. The next day, police found the body of Raheem's twin, who had been dead for more than 30 days. The state Department of Youth and Family Services had received repeated warnings that the children were being abused.[2]

"Our system is broken, and we need to make monumental changes," New Jersey Human Services Commissioner James Davy declared a year later, after more scandals surfaced.[3]

A decade earlier, police in Chicago had discovered 19 children, ages 1 to 14, living in a filthy two-bedroom apartment with a half-dozen adults. Police described a horrific scene of dirty diapers, spoiled food, roaches and dog and rat droppings. One child had cigarette burns, cuts and bruises. The Illinois Department of Children and Family Services had been in contact with six of the children.[4] Following the discovery, the department placed the children with various caregivers, later admitting it had lost track of them. The department eventually confessed it had a backlog of

159

U.S. Probe Faults State Programs

No state child welfare programs fully comply with federal child safety standards, according to a three-year investigation by the Bush administration. Sixteen states did not meet any of the seven federal standards (below) used to assess children's programs, and no state met more than two of the standards.

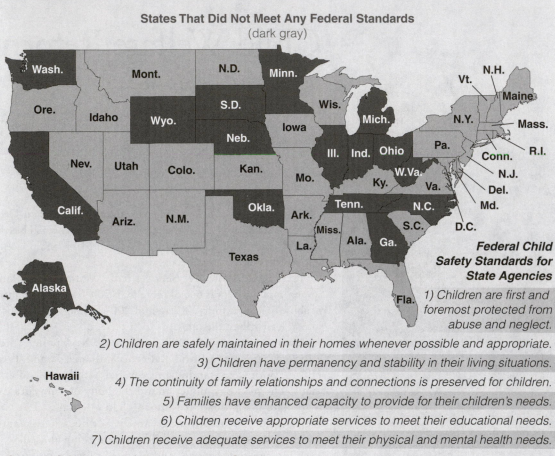

States That Did Not Meet Any Federal Standards
(dark gray)

Federal Child Safety Standards for State Agencies

1) *Children are first and foremost protected from abuse and neglect.*

2) *Children are safely maintained in their homes whenever possible and appropriate.*

3) *Children have permanency and stability in their living situations.*

4) *The continuity of family relationships and connections is preserved for children.*

5) *Families have enhanced capacity to provide for their children's needs.*

6) *Children receive appropriate services to meet their educational needs.*

7) *Children receive adequate services to meet their physical and mental health needs.*

Source: U.S. Department of Health and Human Services

4,320 uninvestigated complaints of abused or neglected children.

But then consider these hopeful signs of reform:

- Legislation being considered in Texas this year would increase spending on child welfare programs, improve training for caseworkers and encourage the administration to reduce caseloads. Republican Gov. Rick Perry calls reform an "emergency issue."[5]
- New Jersey is planning to hire hundreds of new child welfare workers, speed investigations and reduce

caseloads to no more than 25 children or 15 families per worker — down from the current maximum of more than 40 children and 20 families. Children who have lived in institutions for 18 months or more will be moved into "familylike" settings. An independent committee of child welfare experts, appointed in a lawsuit settlement, has approved the plan.[6]
- And Illinois has been transformed into "sort of the gold standard" for child welfare, in the words of Sue Badeau, deputy director of the Pew Commission on Children in Foster Care, a bipartisan group of political

leaders and child welfare experts that promotes child welfare reform. After the state's child welfare scandal in the mid-1990s, new leadership and a new philosophy have turned the Illinois system around, says Mark Testa, co-director of the University of Illinois' Children and Family Research Center and former research director of the state children's services department.

The department reduced caseloads and focused on keeping families together or quickly placing children in alternative permanent-living situations. It obtained federal waivers from regulations preventing subsidies for placements with relatives, such as grandparents or aunts and uncles. As a result, Illinois has reduced the number of children in foster care from 52,000 in 1997 to fewer than 17,000 today, according to Testa.

So it goes in the American child welfare system: Scandal triggers public outrage which spurs reform, leaving children's advocates and child welfare workers constantly ricocheting between hope and despair. Meanwhile, more than 900,000 American children age 17 and younger were abused or neglected in 2003.[7]

"Reading the newspapers of late has been more like reading a horror novel, with case after case of abuse and neglect," said Texas state Sen. Jane Nelson, reflecting the nationwide despair generated by the unending reports of children who were mistreated while supposedly being protected by state agencies charged with doing so.[8] But, as the Republican author of reform legislation, Nelson also represents the potential for improvement that gives advocates hope.

Not a single state received a passing grade last year when the U.S. Health and Human Services Department (HHS) completed its review of state and local child welfare systems, and 16 states did not meet *any* of the seven federal child-care standards used to evaluate the programs. But the first eight states given follow-up reviews met all their initial targets for improvement,

Nearly 1 Million Children Are Maltreated

More than 900,000 children in the United States were victims of abuse or neglect in 2003, about a 5 percent increase over the 1990 total. Most of the cases involved neglect, but 19 percent involved physical abuse and 10 percent sexual abuse.

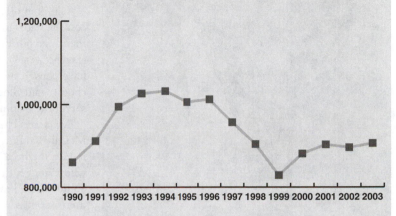

Abused or Neglected American Children, 1990-2003*

*2003 is the most recent year for which data are available

Source: Child Trends Data Bank, based on Department of Health and Human Services Reports, 1990-2003

says Wade F. Horn, the department's assistant secretary for children and families.[*9]

State and local officials throughout the country agree on the need for substantial improvements in their child welfare systems, and even critics acknowledge that significant improvements are under way. Private organizations are adding to the ferment, from public-interest law firms demanding reforms in court to foundations that are supporting innovation. The Bush administration has offered up its plan for restructuring federal funding of child welfare, and both Republicans and Democrats in Congress agree not only on the need for reform but also on how that reform should be carried out.

"The consensus is: Where we can, we should protect the family," says Fred H. Wulczyn, an assistant professor at the Columbia University School of Social Work and a research fellow at the University of Chicago's Chapin Hall Center for Children. "Where we need to place kids in

* The states are: Arizona, Delaware, Indiana, Kansas, Massachusetts, Minnesota, Oregon and Vermont.

Getty Images/Melanie Stetson Freeman

Foster child Daphane Irvin, a senior at Chicago's South Shore High School, hopes to become an actress. Only 2 percent (1,900) of all foster care adoptions in 2002 were older teens, ages 16 to 18. Another 19,500 teens "aged out" of foster care without being adopted and must face the transition to adulthood alone.

foster care, we should proceed to permanent placement — such as with adoptive parents — as soon as possible."

Child welfare workers, government officials and children's advocates agree that it's best for children to live with their parents in healthy families, and that agencies should help families stay together. When children must be removed from their parents because of abuse or neglect, it's best to quickly return the children home safely or to place them permanently with adoptive parents or relatives.

Failure to do so can have disastrous consequences, as Maryland residents learned in early April.

Maryland houses 2,700 children in 330 privately operated group homes that are not adequately supervised by state agencies, according to an investigation by *The Baltimore Sun.*[10] In some of those homes, children have been denied needed medical treatment, served inadequate food, assaulted by employees and even supplied by employees with illegal drugs. At least 15 group home residents have died since 1998.

Children often are placed in group homes — which cost the state far more than foster family homes — when there is no other place for them. "There were some providers who were good, but there were others who we would have chosen not to be bothered with, but we had no choice," said Gloria Slade, former child placement supervisor for the Baltimore Social Services Department.

Maryland Human Resources Secretary Christopher J. McCabe said the state will recruit more foster parents to reduce the need for group homes. But Charlie Cooper, who manages the Maryland Citizens' Review Board for Children, said the state must offer a wider range of children's services.[11]

"You have a lot of things going on at the same time" to improve services to children, says Susan Notkin, director of the Center for Community Partnerships in Child Welfare, a nonprofit organization that funds and consults with agencies implementing innovative programs. "A lot of innovation is being tested. There's a lot of interest in looking at the financing."

Madelyn Freundlich, policy director for Children's Rights, a New York-based advocacy organization, agrees. "There is a lot of energy in the field right now," she says. "There has been a joining together of public agencies and the private sector to really look at foster care, and there is a growing awareness among the general public about foster care and the support needed to provide the right services for kids and families."

But the challenge is complex. And the road from good intentions to effective accomplishments is neither short nor straight. There are stark disagreements about how much spending should be increased (or whether it should be increased at all), how much federal control should be exercised over federally funded state and local programs, and which reform proposals are most likely to be effective.

Widespread agreement on the need for reform represents just "superficial consensus," says Douglas J.

Besharov, director of the American Enterprise Institute's (AEI) Social and Individual Responsibility Project and a former director of the U.S. Center on Child Abuse and Neglect.

"The Democrats who say they want to give states more flexibility want to make it open-ended [entitlement] spending," Besharov, a University of Maryland public affairs professor, says. "This is just an excuse to put in more money, while Republicans say they're looking for ways to cap expenditures. It's just like we're all in favor of long life and fighting cancer, but getting from here to there requires a lot more agreement than what I see."

As the nation struggles to help children from troubled families, here are some of the questions child welfare experts are trying to answer:

Do state and local governments do enough to keep families together?

Most headline-grabbing child welfare horror stories spring from parents mistreating children whom the system has failed to protect. But many child welfare experts believe the more common problem stems from agencies removing children from parents too frequently. It's not that the children didn't need protection but that agencies failed to provide early services that could have kept the kids safe and at home.

In fact, concern about taking children from their parents is so prevalent that a common measure of agency success is reducing the number of youngsters removed from their homes. Several private organizations are promoting reforms designed to improve services to troubled families before the children have to be removed. But there's still a long way to go.

Illinois' newfound reputation for quality stems in part from cutting its foster care population by two-thirds since the mid-1990s and removing fewer than half as many children from their parents each year, Testa says. Improvement in New York City's system is marked by a foster care caseload that dropped from just under 50,000 in the mid-1990s to just below 20,000 today, according to Columbia University's Wulczyn.

Nationwide, the foster care caseload also is declining, but it did not peak as early and is not falling as rapidly as in Illinois and New York. In 1999, nearly 570,000 American children lived in foster homes — an historic high. That number dropped to just above 520,000 in

2003, the most recent figure available. But the dip wasn't because fewer children were removed from their homes; it was because states did a better job of returning foster children to their parents or placing them in other permanent homes.[12]

Because child welfare systems differ from state to state, Wulczyn says, "it's hard to come up with one overarching statement about where the system is, except to say that it's not as good as it should be, but it's better than it was."

Illinois succeeds, Testa says, because it is "doing a better job making family assessments, working with families who can take care of their kids in the home and not putting those children unnecessarily into foster care." Child welfare experts would like to see that approach expanded throughout the country.

"Most places do not have the services and support that families need, so they would never get put into the child welfare system in the first place," says Judy Meltzer, deputy director of the Center for the Study of Social Policy, who serves on panels monitoring court-ordered reforms in New Jersey and Washington, D.C. "The infrastructure does a really bad job of being able to reach out and work with families before they get to the point where crises occur and kids have to be removed from their homes."

Meltzer and others say that even the best child welfare agencies can't provide those services by themselves. "If we think child welfare agencies alone will do it, we will always be stuck," says Wanda Mial, senior associate for child welfare at the Annie E. Casey Foundation, a leading operator and funder of programs for disadvantaged children.

"Government can't do it alone," either, says Notkin, whose Center for Community Partnerships promotes cooperation among many public and private organizations.

Parental substance abuse causes or exacerbates 70 percent of child neglect or abuse incidents, says Kathryn Brohl, author of the 2004 book *The New Miracle Workers: Overcoming Contemporary Challenges in Child Welfare Work*.[13] Abuse also stems from poverty, poor housing, ill health, lack of child care, parental incompetence, domestic violence, arrest and imprisonment, Brohl adds. Some children enter the child welfare system because they run afoul of authorities by committing a crime or frequently skipping school, says Mial, a former child welfare worker in Philadelphia.

Judges' Hearings Help Kids Feel Loved

"So, I [see] you want to be a cosmetologist," Judge Patricia Martin Bishop said to the teenager sitting before her. "What's that?" the girl asked.

"Someone who fixes your hair, does your nails — things like that," Bishop replied.

"I can't even do my own hair," the girl exclaimed. "I want to be a lawyer."

Bishop, the presiding judge in the Child Protection Division of Cook County Circuit Court in Chicago, looked at the girl's caseworker, who explained why she had changed the girl's answer on a questionnaire about her future. "I changed it to cosmetologist because she's reading at such a low level she'll never be a lawyer."

But Bishop quickly set the caseworker straight: "I'm not convinced she can't become a lawyer until we help her get through high school and give her the support she needs to get into college and get her through college and get her through law school. Until we've made some concerted effort to help her achieve her dreams, I'm not prepared to channel her to our dreams for her."

That moment, Bishop says, demonstrated exactly why she created "benchmark hearings" for teenagers.

Since 1997, Illinois has reduced its foster care rolls from 52,000 to fewer than 17,000, thus reducing demands on the court. Bishop was able to relieve Judge Patricia Brown Holmes of her regular caseload, and now they both conduct special hearings for unadopted teens about to leave foster care for independence.

The benchmark hearings are held when the child is 14, 16 and $17^1/_2$. The children, as well as their caseworkers, teachers, doctors, coaches and other adults with whom they have important relationships, attend the meetings, which can last up to two hours. "I require the psychiatrist to face me and tell my why this kid's on meds," the judge explains. "I make the basketball coach come in and tell me how basketball helps or hurts this kid."

Every Illinois foster child attends a juvenile court hearing every six months, but they can be brief, Bishop says. The benchmark meetings tend to be longer because the judges want to get a clear picture of the child's capabilities and needs.

"The idea is to look at kids more holistically," Bishop explains, "to coordinate with the agencies, to help [the teens] for the present and for their dreams for the future. If there are unresolved issues after a benchmark hearing,

---

To avoid removing children from their parents in these circumstances, Brohl and other experts say, child welfare workers must be able to call on other agencies to address such problems as soon as they are discovered — or even before.

According to social psychologist Kristin Anderson Moore, who heads the Child Trends research organization, the most effective ways to deter child abuse and neglect include "helping people establish healthy marriages before they have children, helping teenagers delay child-bearing and helping parents delay having second births."

Some "very rigorous studies" have shown that starting home-visitation programs shortly after birth can reduce abuse and neglect by 50 percent, says Shay Bilchik, president of the Child Welfare League of America. A visiting nurse trains new parents, monitors the well being of the child and arranges for additional services needed by the family. "If you track those babies

15 years down the road," Bilchik says, "home visitation has been shown to reduce those babies' entering into the criminal world."

Rep. Wally Herger, R-Calif., chairman of the House Ways and Means subcommittee that oversees child welfare, noted that the federal government spends 10 times as much on state and local foster care and adoption services as it does on programs designed to hold families together.

"As a result," he said, "rather than focusing on the prevention of abuse and neglect, today's funding structure encourages the removal of children and breakup of families. That is unacceptable."[14]

There are deep disagreements about how that problem should be fixed, however.

"I don't have any doubt Wally cares about kids," says Rep. Jim McDermott of Washington, the ranking Democrat on Herger's subcommittee. "It's a question of how you do it."

I keep it on my benchmark calendar and have follow-up hearings."

The needs for follow-up can vary widely. "A girl came to one of my benchmarks wearing sandals and a short skirt in dead of winter," the judge says. "She had moved from one group home to another, and her allowance hadn't kept up with her so she couldn't buy the things she needed. I kept the case on my benchmark hearing calendar until we were able to resolve the allowance problem."

At another hearing, Bishop discovered that a boy had maintained a relationship with his mother, whose parental rights had been terminated years before — a not uncommon occurrence. "His mother had continued drugging," Bishop says. "My position was, if he's maintained this relationship it's incumbent upon us to make it work as best we can. We put the mother back into [drug-treatment] services. She got clean. We sent this kid back home before he turned 18."

Presiding Judge Patricia Martin Bishop of Chicago created "benchmark" hearings to protect teens' rights — and their dreams.

Cook County Courthouse

Adolescents need relationships that will help them make the transition to adulthood when they leave foster care, Bishop explains. Sometimes the relationship can be as unlikely as with a drug-addicted mother who had lost her parental rights. Sometimes it can continue to be the child welfare system.

Bishop is authorized to keep a foster child within the jurisdiction of the Department of Children and Family Services until age 21. And, using private donations, the department can even provide higher-education assistance until age 23.

Bishop doesn't have empirical data to establish the value of benchmark hearings, but she has heard encouraging anecdotes. "Lawyers who didn't want to do this now are requesting that I extend this down to age 12," she says. "Kids come and say, 'I want Judge Holmes to have my case, or Judge Bishop to have my case.'

"The state is such a poor parent. We [judges] can look a child in the eye and talk about what he or she hopes to do in the future. They feel as if they're heard. They feel as if they've gotten attention. They feel loved."

Does the federal government give state and local child welfare agencies enough financial support and flexibility?

As they lobbied on Capitol Hill last month, volunteers from the Child Welfare League of America boldly proclaimed their top legislative priority on oversized campaign buttons pinned to their lapels: "No caps on kids!"

The slogan is shorthand for their opposition to President Bush's proposal to convert the main source of federal child welfare funding — the foster care entitlement — into a flexible, capped block grant, or a single grant that the states can spend in various innovative ways with less federal control.

Under current law, states are entitled to federal reimbursement for every foster child whose parents would have qualified for welfare under the old Aid to Families with Dependent Children program in 1996. Overall, the federal government pays about half the nation's $22

billion child welfare bill, according to an Urban Institute study, while the rest comes from state and local governments.[15]

The welfare league argues that not only should the existing entitlement regime be preserved but also that the federal government should increase spending on various child welfare programs.

However, HHS Assistant Secretary Horn says groups like the Child Welfare League "live in a dream world where money grows on trees," adding that he himself prefers to live "in the world of the achievable."

Both sides agree that child welfare agencies should be able to spend more federal money on helping families stay together and on alternatives to traditional foster care, which receives the bulk of federal aid today. The administration contends this can be accomplished by letting states spend their existing federal foster care allotment for other activities, such as helping troubled families or supporting guardians. But many child welfare

Number of Foster Kids Has Declined

The number of foster children began declining after peaking in 1999, due largely to a rise in adoptions. Even so, more than a half-million American children were in foster care in 2003, a 31 percent increase over 1990.

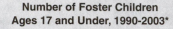

Number of Foster Children Ages 17 and Under, 1990-2003*

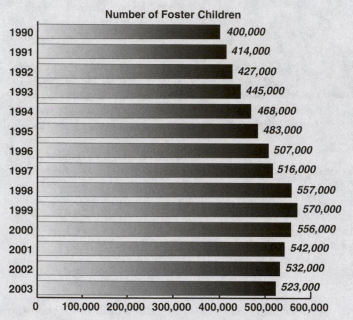

Number of Foster Children

Year	Number
1990	400,000
1991	414,000
1992	427,000
1993	445,000
1994	468,000
1995	483,000
1996	507,000
1997	516,000
1998	557,000
1999	570,000
2000	556,000
2001	542,000
2002	532,000
2003	523,000

* 2003 is the most recent year for which data are available

Source: Child Trends Data Bank, based on Department of Health and Human Services Reports, 1990-2003

advocates argue that the agencies need more money and warn that eliminating the entitlement could leave them with less in the long run.

The administration proposes giving states the option of accepting a block grant that could be spent on foster care and other services. Unlike the entitlement, the grant would not rise and fall with changes in the foster care caseload. For the first five years, each state would receive the same amount it would have received under the entitlement program based on the caseload change during the previous five years. That means states that had declining caseloads would receive less federal money. After five years, Congress would decide how to continue to fund the program.

Some states have implemented well-regarded innovations by obtaining waivers from federal regulations, leading administration officials to contend that allowing flexibility works. Pointing to the drop in welfare rolls that followed similar welfare reforms in the mid-1990s, the administration also argues that flexibility allows the states to be more effective while cutting costs.[16]

"We think if states are better able to focus money on prevention — which is cheaper than intervention — there would be less need for expensive out-of-home-care, in the same way that when states focused on work instead of simply cash, welfare caseloads declined," Horn says.

States would be hard pressed to shift money from foster care to other services, however, because child welfare systems already are underfunded, contends Liz Meitner, vice president for government affairs at the Child Welfare League. "We think a better strategy is to increase investments for prevention that will ultimately reduce the number of kids in foster care," Meitner says.

The Pew Commission on Children in Foster Care proposed maintaining the entitlement and beefing up federal aid while increasing flexibility.[17]

The commission calculated it would cost $1.6 billion annually just to extend federal aid to all foster children. Acknowledging the pressure to contain federal spending, the commission proposed extending aid to all but cutting the amount given for each child, so total federal aid would not rise. The commission suggested hiking other, more flexible, federal grants by $200 million the first year and by 2 percent above inflation in later years.

"Every child who experiences abuse or neglect deserves the protection of both the federal and state governments," said commission Chairman Bill Frenzel, former Republican representative from Minnesota, making a key argument against ending the entitlement.[18]

"Child welfare has traditionally been the safety net for vulnerable children and families," Freundlich of Children's Rights says. "It does not have waiting lists. It's had to be there for the children."

Block grant opponents point to the crack cocaine epidemic that devastated many families and caused child welfare caseloads to soar in the 1980s and '90s. Without the entitlement, states would have had to spend much more of their own money or agencies could not have cared for all the children coming through their doors. Many warn methamphetamine abuse could become the next crack. They also note that, over time, block grant programs haven't kept pace with inflation, and funding for some has declined.

The Social Services Block Grant, for example, dropped from $3 billion in 1981 to $1.7 billion in 2003, according to the Child Welfare League. Had it tracked inflation, she says, it now would total more than $6 billion.

But Assistant HHS Secretary Horn replies that if states reduce foster rolls they would receive more money through a block grant program than through an entitlement program. That's because the entitlement, which is based on the number of children served, would drop if the rolls dropped, while the block grant would not. If caseloads rise significantly, he adds, the administration plan includes an emergency fund that states could tap.

The federal government can't afford to give states both flexibility and an entitlement, the American Enterprise Institute's Besharov argues. "The only way to give states flexibility in a federal grant program is to cap it. Otherwise, they will steal you blind."

Besharov suggests extending the waiver option, which gives the states supervised flexibility, and "tying it to rigorous evaluations" to document what works best.

Testa, of the Children and Family Research Center, also supports more waivers, although he doesn't share Besharov's fear of entitlements. "We have to invest a lot more in demonstrations that will prove what works," he says. "We should be giving states permission to innovate but requiring them to demonstrate that what they're doing is working."

Because states have to match the federal funds under current law, he adds, they will not be motivated to spend more than they need.

Does the child welfare system prepare foster adolescents for adulthood?

Mary Lee's foster care judicial reviews always seemed the same. She'd wait for hours in the courthouse, then have what felt like a one-minute session during which the judge would "pat me on the back and say everything's great."

Then, when she was 16, a judge actually asked: "Mary, what do you want for your life?" And she told him.

"I said I want a family," she recalls. "I want to be adopted. I want to know that when I go to college I'm going to have a family to come home to, that I'm going to have a dad to walk me down the aisle and grandparents for my children. And if I stay in foster care, when I leave I'm not going to have anything. I'm going to be totally on my own."

A week before her 18th birthday, after five years in foster care, Mary was adopted by Scott Lee, her caseworker, and his wife in Montgomery County, Tenn. Now 23, Mary has graduated from Vanderbilt University and plans to attend law school. She traces her good life and bright future to that moment the judge asked her about her dreams.

"Adoption is not about your childhood," she explains. "It's about the rest of your life. You always need a mom and a dad. You always need your grandparents. You always need the family support."

Mary's happy-ending story is, unfortunately, rare. According to the latest available statistics, 92,000 teens ages 16 to 18 lived in foster homes in 2002 — 17 percent of the total foster population. Just 1,300 of them were adopted that year — 2 percent of all foster care adoptions. That same year, 19,500 teens "aged out" of foster care, usually by turning 18, and many of them faced the transition to adulthood the way Mary Lee feared she would face it — alone.[19]

Four years after leaving foster care, nearly half of these older teens had not graduated from high school, a quarter had been homeless, 40 percent had become parents and fewer than a fifth were self-supporting, according to the Jim Casey Youth Opportunities Initiative, which works with those young people.[20]

"Effective middle-class families parent their kids into their 20s, and these kids are cut off at 18," Moore of Child Trends notes. "From age 18 to 24 is a time kids need contact and care and monitoring from adults."

CHRONOLOGY

1800-1900 *Charitable organizations open "orphan asylums." Courts allow child protection societies to remove children from homes. Later, child-protection organizations pay families to take in homeless children.*

1853 Children's Aid Society of New York is founded and begins sending homeless children to Western families on "orphan" or "baby" trains in 1854.

1872 New York Foundling Asylum begins putting unwanted infants and toddlers on westbound "baby trains."

1900-1930s *First juvenile courts created. Child welfare agencies increase supervision of foster homes.*

1912 U.S. Children's Bureau established.

1935 Social Security Act provides federal funds for rural children's services, social-worker training.

1960-1970s *Federal role expands, focus intensifies on preserving families and alternatives to adoption.*

1961 Federal aid extended to poor foster children; more children's services are offered in urban and rural areas.

1962-69 Child-care professionals are required to report suspected abuse.

1974 Child Abuse Prevention and Treatment Act provides federal funds for protecting endangered children.

1976-79 Child welfare agencies try to reduce need for foster care. California, New York and Illinois subsidize adoptions.

1977 Foster care caseloads total about 550,000.

1980s-2000 *Single-parent households, unmarried births, child abuse and neglect reports all soar. Demands for reform increase. Lawsuits force improvements in state and local child welfare systems.*

1980 Congress creates federal adoption-assistance program. Social Security Act becomes main source of federal child welfare support.

1986 Foster caseload drops below 300,000; crack cocaine epidemic soon causes foster care rolls to soar.

1993 Federal government grants waivers for states to test innovative child welfare services.

1993-94 Discovery of 19 children living in squalor, death of another, spur shakeup of Illinois child welfare system.

1995 Foster caseloads hit nearly 500,000.

1997 Adoption and Safe Families Act increases federal support for adoption, family preservation.

1999 Foster caseloads peak at 570,000. Federal government increases aid for youths aging out of foster care.

2000s *Courts get federal money to reduce abuse and neglect backlogs, improve information technology.*

2001 Federal government offers new education assistance for aging-out youths.

2002 Authorities report 900,000 confirmed cases of child abuse or neglect nationwide, including 1,390 deaths.

2003 Foster rolls decline to 525,000. General Accounting Office says high caseloads and low salaries inhibit recruitment and retention of effective child welfare workers.

2004 Concern arises that a methamphetamine epidemic could raise foster care rolls. Pew Commission on Children in Foster Care argues that states need more child welfare money and flexibility. About 20 states receive waivers to offer support services not normally funded by federal programs.

2005 President Bush asks that federal foster care funding be converted to block grants. Illinois, now representing child welfare's "gold standard," cuts foster care population by two-thirds since mid-1990s and reduces average caseload from more than 50 to fewer than 20.

After Chris Brooks left foster care in Nevada at age 19, he slept in a car and on friends' couches. At age 18, Terry Harrak figured out how to sleep and scrounge food amid the bustle of a busy hospital in Northern Virginia.

But both Chris' and Terry's stories have happy endings, thanks to serendipitous relationships with caring adults. A professor studying homeless youth "took me under his wing" and "became kind of like an uncle," Chris says. Now 23, he attends college in Las Vegas and mentors homeless youth. While living in a shelter, Terry met a Child Welfare League staff member who was looking for homeless young people to testify before Congress. Now 25, she attends college and works as the league's youth leadership coordinator, staffing an advisory council on which Chris and Mary serve.

Chris and Terry both say they were ill-prepared for independent living. And both cite the need for ongoing relationships and training in such basic skills as balancing a checkbook, filling out a tax form and applying for college aid.

"Historically, in child welfare we never thought about the permanent lifetime relationships that these kids need," says Gary Stangler, head of the Casey program for older teens and former director of the Missouri Social Services Department. "If we got them to age 18 alive, we did our job.

"Adoption, especially the older you get, is difficult and uncommon. So the solution was training for independent living, which is the opposite of permanent lifetime relationships."

Stangler has observed "an awakening to the fact that we were doing a very poor job for kids once they left the foster care system without the support we take for granted for our own kids." Slowly, he says, things are getting better.

Legislation passed in 1999 provides federal aid for housing and education for former foster youths, but many young people do not know how to apply for it. States are allowed to keep them on Medicaid beyond age 18, but most don't. Private organizations and some states are helping older teens build the adult relationships they need. And a few courts are institutionalizing the kind of court procedure that turned Mary Lee's life around.

In Chicago, the Cook County Circuit Court's Child Protection Division conducts "benchmark hearings" when foster children turn 14 and 16 and six months before they age out. (*See story, p. 164.*) The hearings can last up to two hours. Participants include the most important individuals in the children's lives, such as caseworkers, teachers, doctors and adults with whom the children have or might build long-lasting relationships.

"All of us were grappling with how could we, the court, get a handle on this road to being independent," says Patricia Martin Bishop, the division's presiding judge, who established the hearings. "The thought was, if we had more time to concentrate on each of these kids, we'd get a better handle on what needs they have that aren't met."

Among the questions Bishop requires the children to answer during the hearings: "What do you want to do when you get out of school? What do you intend to do with your life?"

BACKGROUND

Orphan Trains

In the beginning, America's child welfare system provided a kind of residential vocational education: Families took in needy children, then fed, clothed and trained them in a trade. Such apprenticeships were common, even for youngsters who were not parentless or poor. But it was considered an especially attractive way to place orphans and other children whose parents couldn't care for them. The child got a home and learned a trade; the host family benefited from the child's work.[21]

In the early 19th century, religious and charitable organizations began opening orphan asylums, which became the most common means of caring for children without parents between 1830 and 1860.

Also in mid-century, Charles Lorring Brace organized the Children's Aid Society of New York, which created the "orphan train" or "baby train" movement. Urban centers like New York attracted hordes of immigrants who took difficult, dangerous and sometimes deadly jobs. Diseases like typhoid, diphtheria and cholera also hit the poor especially hard. Deceased adults left orphans or

How Illinois Reformed a Broken System

Clearer information is needed

Three times, the Illinois Children and Family Services Department took Joseph Wallace away from his mentally ill mother, and three times the youngster was returned to her. There was no fourth time, because on April 19, 1993, she tied an extension cord around the 3-year-old's neck and hanged him from a transom in their Chicago apartment.[1]

Early the next year, Chicago police discovered 19 children living in a squalid, two-bedroom apartment with a half-dozen adults. Again, the department knew about six of the children but had left them with their mothers.[2]

Although the tragedies were only tiny tips of an enormous iceberg of bureaucratic failure, they shined a media spotlight on the Illinois child welfare system and outraged the public. In the end, they spurred dramatic reforms in the system, making it a font of successful innovation.

"They've addressed preventing kids from coming into foster care in the first place, as well as strengthening reunification for children who return home safely and strengthening alternative forms of permanency through subsidized guardianship and adoption," says Sue Badeau, deputy director of the Pew Commission on Foster Care, who says the system is now the "gold standard" of child care.

The Illinois system was "sort of average" in the 1980s, became "a mess" by the mid-'90s and now is one of the best, says Jill Duerr Berrick, associate dean of the School of Social Welfare at the University of California, Berkeley. "We've seen tremendous innovation coming out of Illinois."

Illinois probably ran America's worst child welfare system in the mid-1990s, says Mark Testa, co-director of the University of Illinois' Children and Family Research Center. It had the nation's highest prevalence of children in foster care — 17.1 per 1,000 — where they remained in care longer than children in other states. The total foster care rolls soared from 20,000 in the late-'80s to 52,000 in 1997. But when horror stories repeatedly hit the media, public outrage triggered changes.

Feeling intense pressure from the public, the state legislature and a lawsuit by the American Civil Liberties Union, Republican Gov. Jim Edgar appointed a new department director, Jess McDonald. He launched a comprehensive overhaul of the system and hired Testa as in-house research director.

"Lawsuits are critical to reform," says Marcia Robinson Lowry, executive director of Children's Rights, a New York organization that sues local and state governments to get them to improve child welfare systems. "There is sustained pressure for reform because of a court order."

McDonald and Testa discovered a system engaged in self-destruction. It was taking custody of thousands of children who didn't need to be removed from their homes, which limited caseworkers' ability to take care of children who really were in danger.

"The state was stepping in and taking these kids into protective custody because they were living with someone other than their parents — grandmother, aunt, uncle —

single parents who couldn't support their children. And as immigrants or the offspring of immigrants, many of the children had no extended families they could turn to for support.

Besides worrying about the children's well being, Brace warned they might grow up to be violent criminals, referring to them as the "dangerous classes." He convinced businessmen to support shipping the children west, where they presumably would live healthy and wholesome lives on farms.

The first orphan train carried children to Dowagiac, Mich., in 1854. Over the next 80 years, some 150,000 to 200,000 children were shipped to states in the West.

In 1872, the New York Foundling Asylum, which took in unwanted babies, began putting infants and toddlers on the trains, a practice that lasted into the 20th century. As in colonial days, the farmers benefited from the labor of the children they took in.

In the 1870s growing public concern about child abuse and neglect spurred the founding of societies for the prevention of cruelty to children, and courts began to empower them to remove children from neglectful homes.

What we now know as foster care took root in the last two decades of the 19th century, when some child protection organizations began to pay families to take in homeless children so the children would not have to work.

even though they were living safely," Testa explains. "Children were building up in long-term foster care because there were no pathways for moving kids into more permanent homes, and folks weren't asking the relatives if they were willing to adopt. There was this myopia of only recognizing nuclear families, and if you're not in a nuclear family you're taken into the child welfare system."

The new managers forced the department to stop taking children who were living safely with relatives and start offering those families services available to nuclear families. "That reduced the number of kids coming into foster care right off the bat," Testa says. "But large numbers were still remaining in long-term foster care, so moving kids out needed attention."

The Illinois child welfare system delivers most foster care services through private contractors rather than local government agencies. "The financial incentives were all geared toward keeping kids in foster care," Testa explains, because they were paid only for foster children. "There was no reward for moving kids into permanent homes."

The state began paying incentives for adoption and reunification with parents, and the foster rolls dropped again.

The state also sought a waiver from federal rules in order to use some of its federal foster care funds to subsidize guardianships. Guardianship does not require termination of parental rights as adoption does, but it creates a permanent relationship between the child and the guardian and removes state supervision. Many relatives willing to care for children do not want to adopt, Testa says, because that would require termination of the biological parents' rights.

Since obtaining the waiver in 1997, Illinois has moved more than 8,000 children from foster care to guardianship, Testa says, reducing state costs and freeing caseworkers to concentrate on families that really are in trouble. During the decade of reform, the average worker's caseload has dropped from more than 50 cases to fewer than 20, Testa says.

"Illinois takes far fewer kids into foster care than many other states," he explains, "because we're doing a better job making family assessments and working with families who can take care of their kids with some help."

Now the department's biggest challenge is helping older adolescents who remain in foster care and are less likely to be adopted. "The solution is to attach every child as early as possible to a permanent family, a mentor, someone who's going to care about them," Testa says.

One hurdle to adoption is that older adolescents lose foster services that help in the transition to adulthood. The department has obtained a new federal waiver to extend those services after adoption or while the child is in guardianship. The department also is working with universities to support former foster children while they're in school. And it's developed a program to recruit families to host college students during vacations and to maintain connections with them during the school year.

"The Illinois system has not achieved perfection," Berrick says, "but it's certainly made a remarkable turnaround."

---

[1] Phillip J. O'Connor and Zay N. Smith, "Woman Charged In Son's Hanging," *Chicago Sun-Times*, April 20, 1993, p. 3.

[2] Phillip J. O'Connor and Ray Long, "Police Rescue 19 Kids In Filthy Apartment," *Chicago Sun-Times*, Feb. 2, 1994, p. 1; Colin McMahon and Susan Kuczka, "19 Kids Found In Filth," *Chicago Tribune*, Feb. 2, 1994, p. 1.

As the century neared its end, states began to organize charity boards that tended to favor home placements over institutional care.

The modern child welfare system began taking shape in the early 20th century. In 1912, the federal government created the U.S. Children's Bureau, now part of the Health and Human Services Department, to conduct research and distribute information to state children's agencies. States began to create separate juvenile court systems, which ordered more children into government care. In the 1920s, child welfare agencies began to exercise greater supervision of foster homes. And the New Deal brought federal money into the picture.

The Social Security Act of 1935 made the Children's Bureau responsible for administering the new Aid to Dependent Children program, later known as Aid to Families with Dependent Children, or AFDC. Congress intended the program to preserve poor families that otherwise might not be able to afford to keep their children at home. Aimed primarily at widowed mothers, it supported state aid programs for children living with a parent or other relative. States also received federal assistance to establish or strengthen children's services in rural areas and to train child welfare workers.

The federal government didn't extend aid to foster children and to urban services until 1961. To receive that

Linda and Mike Hurley and adopted daughter Courtney pose for their first family photo after signing adoption documents in Tampa on June 4, 2004. Child welfare agencies around the nation are seeking adoptive parents or guardians to help older foster children make the transition to adulthood.

aid, the foster child had to come from a family with income low enough to qualify for AFDC. Assistance also was offered for a broader range of child services, including family preservation.

Child Abuse and Crack

Also during the early 1960s, Denver physician Henry Kempe called public attention to the "battered child syndrome," revealing that many hospitalized youngsters whose injuries had been attributed to accidents actually had been abused by a parent or other caregiver. Before the decade ended, all 50 states passed laws requiring doctors, teachers and other child-care professionals to report suspected abuse. Congress followed suit in 1974 with the Child Abuse Prevention and Treatment Act (CAPTA), which provided federal funds for child protection services, including procedures for reporting and investigating abuse and protecting endangered children.

During the late-'70s, child welfare agencies began focusing on moving children from foster care into permanent homes and on helping families avoid the need for out-of-home placements in the first place. Advocates of the shift in focus said it was better for children and would cost less than foster care.

Congress established a national adoption-information exchange program in 1978. California, New York and Illinois became the first states to subsidize adoptions in order to counteract the financial penalty suffered by foster parents who lose their foster payments when they finally adopt their foster children.

In 1980, Congress created a federal adoption-assistance program and merged it with the old AFDC foster care funds. Known as Title IV-E of the Social Security Act, it is now the main source of federal support for child welfare. The law required states to make "reasonable efforts" to keep children with their parents or return them as soon as possible. When families couldn't be reunited, the law declared placement with relatives or adoption to be superior to long-term foster care.

These efforts collided with the crack cocaine epidemic and other social pathologies from the mid-1980s through early-'90s.

From 1980 to 1994, single-parent households increased from 22 percent to 31 percent of all families. Births to unmarried teens soared from 27.6 per 1,000 females in 1980 to 44.6 in 1992. In 1993, 2.9 million child abuse and neglect reports were filed, up from 1.7 million in 1984.[22]

Foster caseloads — which dropped from a little more than 500,000 in 1977 to fewer than 300,000 in 1986 — soared back to nearly 500,000 by 1995.[23]

Federal and state governments, with support and prodding from private organizations, continued to press for family preservation and adoption as better alternatives to foster care.

In 1993, Congress authorized $1 billion over five years to help states strengthen troubled families. More federal money was distributed to help courts improve their handling of foster care and adoption cases. Congress gave the Health and Human Services secretary authority to grant waivers so states could use federal child welfare grants to finance innovative programs.

President Clinton declared adoption to be a national priority in 1996, saying "no child should be uncertain about what 'family' or 'parent' or 'home' means." The 1997 Adoption and Safe Families Act provided more incentives for adoption and family preservation. The Foster Care Independence Act of 1999 increased federal funding for counseling and other services for youths making the transition from foster care to adulthood. The money could be used for housing and other living expenses, and states could extend Medicaid coverage beyond the youths' 18th birthday.

In 2000 Congress authorized federal aid to help courts reduce backlogs of abuse and neglect cases and improve information technology systems. New federal educational assistance for so-called aging-out youths — those leaving the system — was authorized in 2001.

CURRENT SITUATION

Rigid Rules and Budgets

When Katie Sutton's grandchildren wanted to sleep over at a friend's house, Philadelphia child welfare caseworkers had to investigate the friend's family first. If she wanted to take a child to the doctor, she had to get a caseworker's instructions. When she wanted to take them across the nearby border into New Jersey, she had to get a caseworker's permission.

To Sutton, who had custody of five grandchildren as a foster parent, this was more than a nuisance.

Investigating a friend's family felt like "a way of invading their privacy and just automatically assuming that they have a bad background," she explained. For the grandchildren, the frequent involvement of caseworkers sent the message that "we're foster care kids, we don't belong anywhere, we have a label and we're different from everyone else."[24]

The children don't feel different anymore, because Sutton has become their permanent legal guardian, and they have left government supervision behind them. She hadn't wanted to adopt because she didn't want to terminate her son's parental rights. He's not a bad father, she said, just immature and emotionally and financially unable to care for his offspring. She couldn't afford to keep them outside the foster care system until Pennsylvania offered to subsidize her guardianship.

Her story encapsulates the state of the U.S. child welfare system today. Rigid rules and tight budgets make it difficult for agencies to tailor services to the specific needs of individual children and families.

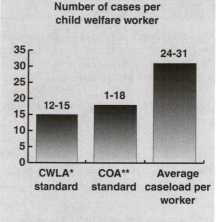

Caseloads Are Double Recommended Levels

The average American child welfare caseworker oversees two-dozen or more children — twice as many as child advocate and accreditation organizations recommend. Some caseworkers manage as many as 110 cases.

Number of cases per child welfare worker

Category	Number of cases
CWLA* standard	12-15
COA** standard	1-18
Average caseload per worker	24-31

* Child Welfare League of America

** Council on Accreditation for Children and Family Services

Source: "HHS Could Play a Greater Role in Helping Child Welfare Agencies Recruit and Retain Staff," U.S. General Accounting Office, March 2003

But federal, state and local governments — often in cooperation with private organizations — are moving toward more flexible policies that emphasize holding families together and placing children in alternative permanent homes when that's not possible.

It's common for relatives not to want to adopt, even when they're willing to make permanent homes for grandchildren, nieces or nephews, Testa at the University of Illinois says. "They don't want to get embroiled in an adversarial battle with a daughter or sister," he explains. "Many of them feel it's odd that they'd have to adopt someone to whom they were already related."

Stephen McCall of Brooklyn, N.Y., has been a foster parent for five years for, from left, Marshawn, Maleek, Brandon and Marcus. New York's child welfare agency is encouraging more potential foster parents to take adolescent and special-needs children.

In Sutton's case, Pennsylvania uses state funds to help her give the grandchildren a stable home. Sixteen other states do the same, while nine redirect surpluses from their share of the federal welfare program. Another nine have negotiated waivers with the HHS to spend some of their federal foster-care funds on subsidies for guardians.[25]

Waivers have become an important vehicle for reform of the child welfare system, just as they were for welfare reform in the mid-1990s. About 20 states have used them in varied ways, including for guardian assistance, drug-abuse treatment for parents, training of staff in private and public child services agencies, adoption promotion and other services to children and families not covered by federal foster care assistance.[26]

Whole Child Approach

Some state and local agencies have teamed up with private organizations and volunteers to improve the way they do business.

Some 70,000 volunteer court-appointed special advocates — or CASAs — represent the interests of children under court supervision throughout the country, for instance. Started in Seattle in 1976, the CASA movement has grown to 930 local programs that are united in the National Court Appointed Special Advocate Association.[27] The volunteer builds a relationship with a child and tells the court whether the child is receiving the care and services the judge has ordered.

Child welfare workers often don't have enough time to keep close watch on the children in their charge, says Kenneth J. Sherk, who helps lead an organization that supports CASAs and children in the Phoenix-area child welfare system. "They're overworked and underpaid and all bogged down in red tape, and often as not things just don't get done for these kids," Sherk explains. "The CASAs tell the court and the Foster Care Review Board here when a child needs counseling, dental work, new clothes, school books — the basic needs."

In 2002 child welfare agencies in St. Louis, Louisville, Cedar Rapids, Iowa, and Jacksonville, Fla., agreed to work with the Center for Community Partnerships in Child Welfare. The center funds and advises efforts to bring a broad array of public and private organizations and individuals together to help troubled families. It's now working in 80 communities, Director Notkin says.

"The problems of families at risk of child abuse and neglect are complex," Notkin explains. "Therefore, it's necessary to develop a neighborhood network of services and support that involves public agencies, private agencies, nonprofits, the business community, the faith community, neighbors and relatives."

The center also stresses creation of a unique plan for each family, Notkin says. "If substance abuse is a problem, make sure someone from substance-abuse treatment is at the table," she explains. "If job training is needed, the job-training folks need to be there."

A key component is the participation of neighborhood volunteers who may tutor the parents in the skills of parenting, help to care for the children and help integrate the family into the community. "Our fundamental principle is that in order to have safe children we need strong families, and strong families need healthy communities that they're connected to," Notkin says.

Comprehensive approaches must be advocated, says Rosemary Chalk, director of the National Academy of Sciences Board on Children, Youth and Families, because "there's no sense of overall accountability for the whole child within the child welfare system."

"We know these kids are in bad shape and in many cases may have serious health problems or serious educational deficits," she explains. "But no one is stepping up and saying we're prepared to deal with the whole child."

Such services work, child welfare experts say, but the demand exceeds the supply. In a study of mothers who

Should states be allowed to convert federal foster care funds into capped block grants?

YES
Wade F. Horn, Ph.D.
Assistant Secretary for Children and Families,
U.S. Department of Health and
Human Services

Written for *CQ Researcher,* April 2005

States should be allowed to convert the Title IV-E foster care entitlement program into a flexible, alternative-financing structure. President Bush's proposed Child Welfare Program Option would allow them to do that. But the president's proposal is not a block grant. Its very name, Child Welfare Program Option, says it all: It is an option. If a state does not believe it is in its best interest to participate in this alternative, it may continue to participate in the current title IV-E entitlement program.

The states for many years have criticized the Title IV-E program as too restrictive. For instance, it only provides funds for the maintenance of foster children who have been removed from a home that would have been eligible for assistance under the old welfare program and for child welfare training. Under current law, Title IV-E funds cannot be used for services that might prevent a child from being placed in foster care in the first place, that might facilitate a child's returning home or that might help move the child to another permanent placement.

Under the proposed Program Option, states could choose to administer their program more flexibly, with a fixed allocation of funds over a five-year period. States would be able to use funds for foster care payments, prevention activities, permanency efforts, case management, administrative activities and training of child welfare staff. They would be able to develop innovative systems for preventing child abuse and neglect, keeping families and children safely together and quickly moving children toward adoption and permanency. They also would be freed from burdensome income-eligibility provisions that continue to be linked to the old welfare program.

Although states would have greater flexibility in how they use funds, they would still be held accountable for positive results. They would continue to be required to participate in Child and Family Services Reviews and to maintain the child safety protections, such as conducting criminal-background checks and licensing foster care providers, obtaining judicial oversight for removal and permanency decisions, developing case plans for all foster children and prohibiting race-based discrimination in placements. States also would be required to maintain their existing level of investment in the program.

Thus, the proposal allows — but does not force — states to enhance their child welfare services while relieving them of unnecessary administrative burdens. This option for flexible funding represents good public policy.

NO
Shay Bilchik
President and CEO,
Child Welfare League of America

Written for *CQ Researcher,* April 2005

It is too common an occurrence to read a newspaper or listen to the news and learn about yet another seriously abused or neglected child or a child welfare system struggling to protect the children in its care. Recently, every state, the District of Columbia and Puerto Rico had the performance of their child welfare system measured as a part of a federal review. States fell short in a variety of areas, including having excessive caseloads, inadequate supervision, inadequate training and lack of treatment services.

Each of these shortcomings relates to a failure to provide resources that would support high-quality performance — resources that should be provided through investments made by the federal, state and local governments responsible for protecting abused and neglected children.

Yearly, states confirm nearly 900,000 reports of abuse and neglect. There are more than 550,000 children in the nation's foster care system. Too many of these children stay in foster care far longer than necessary because of the lack of appropriate support services. In fact, nearly 40 percent of abused and neglected children don't receive treatment to address the emotional trauma they have experienced. In addition, much of this abuse could have been avoided through prevention services.

There is indeed a need for greater flexibility in the use of federal funds to help address these service gaps. Proposals that condition flexibility on capping federal funding, however, are shortsighted and reflect a lack of responsiveness to the results of the federal review. While it may seem difficult to argue against an option being presented to the states that trades funding level for flexibility, it actually is quite easy when it is being presented as the federal government's solution to the problems facing our nation's child welfare system. Such a proposal is tantamount to a freeze on the federal commitment to protecting children and contradicts the vital role that the federal government plays in keeping children safe.

Flexibility is needed, but new federal investments are also needed so that fewer children are hurt and more parents can safely care for their children. The federal review clearly tells us that this is the case. It seems a fair demand, therefore, that our federal leaders bring forward a reform proposal that presents serious solutions to the trauma and horror that confront our abused and neglected children — and no less.

AP Photo/Elise Amendola

A mourner leaves the funeral service of Dontel Jeffers, 4, in Boston's Dorchester section on March 16, 2005, wearing a photo of the abused child on his shirt. Dontel died in a foster home where he had been placed by the Department of Social Services. The boy's relatives claim his foster mother beat him.

received drug abuse treatment, for example, slightly more than half had custody of their children before entering treatment while three-quarters had custody six months after completing treatment, the Child Welfare League reported. Three-quarters of parents with children in the child welfare system need treatment, the league said, but only a little more than 30 percent receive it.[28]

In 2003 authorities received about 2 million child abuse or neglect reports involving more than 3 million children. Agencies found that more than 900,000 of the children had been neglected or abused and that 1,390 had died. Most of the confirmed cases involved neglect, but 19 percent involved physical abuse and 10 percent sexual abuse.[29]

Although most agencies prefer to keep children with their parents, about 525,000 lived in foster homes in 2003, a number that has steadily declined since peaking at 570,000 in 1999. The Congressional Budget Office estimates that the number of federally supported foster care children will drop from 229,000 this year to 225,000 next year and 162,000 by 2015. Because federal aid goes only to children from families with very low income, only about half of the foster caseload receives a federal subsidy.[30]

Many child welfare workers complain that this caseload exceeds the capabilities of the work force, and the Government Accountability Office (GAO) has endorsed that view. "A stable and highly skilled child welfare work force is necessary to effectively provide child welfare services," Congress' nonpartisan investigating arm said in a 2003 report.[31] However, workers' salaries tend to be too low to attract and maintain a well-qualified staff, and caseloads tend to be higher than those recommended by widely recognized standards, the agency found. (*See graph, p. 173.*)

"Large caseloads and worker turnover delay the timeliness of investigations and limit the frequency of worker visits with children," the GAO said.[32] In reviewing the performance of state child welfare agencies, HHS attributed many deficiencies to high caseloads and inadequate training.[33]

The Child Welfare League suggests a caseload of 12 to 15 children per worker, and the Council on Accreditation for Children and Family Services recommends no more than 18, GAO said.[34] Actual caseloads last year ranged from nine to 80, with medians ranging from 18 to 38 depending on the type of cases a worker was handling, according to a survey by the American Public Human Services Association.[35]

Beginning caseworkers earned a median salary of about $28,500 in 2002, and the most experienced workers about $47,000, the Child Welfare League reported.[36] Child welfare administrators complain about losing workers to jobs in schools, where the workers can continue to work with children while earning more in a safer environment.[37] Child welfare staff turnover ranges from 30 to 40 percent annually.

To induce workers to stay in their jobs, Rep. Stephanie Tubbs, D-Ohio, has introduced legislation to forgive their college loans. Ohio Republican Rep. Mike DeWine introduced a similar bill in the previous Congress but had not done so again this year.

OUTLOOK

Hope and Fear

Children's advocates view the future of child welfare with optimism and concern. Their hope springs from the reform movements spurring changes in many state and local programs, the trends in child welfare policies that seem to be moving in effective directions and the agreement among liberals and conservatives that more attention must be focused on early services to troubled families and speedy placement of foster children into permanent homes.

They worry that the federal financial squeeze might strangle child welfare funding and that a threatened increase in methamphetamine addiction could imitate the devastating crack cocaine epidemic of the 1980s and '90s and cause caseloads to soar once more.

"You have a lot of things going on, a lot of innovation being tested, a lot of interest in looking at the financing," says Notkin, of the Center for Community Partnerships in Child Welfare. "You also have, in the last few years, some really horrific stories coming to the attention of the public that dramatize the crisis in child welfare.

"The question is whether there will be enough political will to honestly confront the problems of the child welfare system, which are reflective of and connected to other problems in our society."

The Child Welfare League's Bilchik foresees "a three- to five-year window where we're going to see tremendous change in practice and a continuing push for reduction of federal support. Either states are going to ratchet up their support in tough economic times or we're going to see a reduction in the level and quality of care.

"I think we're going to go through another cycle where they push for less investment, which will result in more harm for children and that will lead to recognition that more resources are needed," he says. "At the same time, good practices will be adopted as we get better at keeping kids closer to home, reducing the number of times they move and placing them more often with kin."

Columbia University's Wulczyn predicts foster care rolls will shrink because "we're doing a better job of providing appropriate services," but he adds a caveat: "as long as we don't experience an unexpected social upheaval that mimics the crack cocaine epidemic."

The Casey Foundation's Stangler expects agencies to do "a much better job of promoting permanency arrangements for older youth. And I expect states to get better at connecting the dots between emancipating youth, education and the work force."

He looks to expansion of current programs through which families volunteer to provide home-like relationships to former foster children, offering them a place to come home to during college vacations, for instance, and adults to whom they can turn for parent-like guidance year-round.

An important challenge, says Meltzer, of the Center for the Study of Social Policy, is getting other parts of society to solve problems that shouldn't have been left to child welfare agencies to fix. "Ultimately, the child welfare systems have become services of last resort for a lot of problems related to poverty, mental health and substance abuse," she explains. "Figuring out how you build up resources so fewer kids and families need child welfare intervention is where you want to go."

HHS Assistant Secretary Horn is confident that the government and child welfare community know more today than 15 years ago about how to prevent child abuse and neglect. "I'm very encouraged by the renewed focus on helping families form and sustain healthy marriages," he adds, "because two parents in a healthy marriage don't come home one day and decide to abuse and neglect their children. Parents in unhealthy, dysfunctional and violent households do."

Rep. McDermott concedes the possibility of "some improvements here or there. But, if you're digging the kind of debt hole we've created, the first ones who are sacrificed into the hole are the kids."

"Republicans and Democrats do care a lot about kids," says Mial of the Casey Foundation. "What it comes down to is how well connected are they to what's happening."

Research and education are needed, for child welfare workers as well as for politicians, she adds.

And despite Horn's optimism about knowledge gained in the last 15 years, she says, "We know how to send kids to adoption. We don't necessarily know how to keep kids in a family or how to reunite them with their family."

NOTES

1. Lomi Kriel, "Bill to Overhaul Kid Agency Is Filed," *San Antonio Express-News*, Feb. 4, 2005, p. A8. And

Robert T. Garrett, "New bill on child abuse proposed; Police would become involved in most reports of juvenile injuries," *The Dallas Morning News*, Dec. 2, 2004, p. A4.

2. Suzanne Smalley and Brian Braiker, "Suffer the Children," *Newsweek*, Jan. 20, 2003, p. 32.

3. Leslie Kaufman, "State Agency For Children Fails Its Tests, U.S. Says," *The New York Times*, May 22, 2004, p B5.

4. Phillip J. O'Connor and Ray Long, "Police Rescue 19 Kids In Filthy Apartment," *Chicago Sun-Times*, Feb. 2, 1994, p. 1; Colin McMahon and Susan Kuczka, "19 Kids Found In Filth," *Chicago Tribune*, Feb. 2, 1994, p. 1.

5. Michelle M. Martinez, "Senators Giving CPS Reform Bill a Thumbs up," *Austin American-Statesman*, March 3, 2005, p. B1; "Senators Approve Protective Services Bill," *Austin American-Statesman*, March 4, 2005, p. B6.

6. Richard Lezin Jones, "Child Welfare Plan Approved," *The New York Times*, June 13, 2004, Section 14NJ, p. 6; Jones, "Monitor Approves Child Welfare Plan," *The New York Times*, June 10, 2004, p. B4; Jones, "New Jersey Plans to Lighten Load for Child Welfare Workers," *The New York Times*, June 9, 2004, p. B5; Jones, "Plan for New Jersey Foster Care Removes Many From Institutions," *The New York Times*, Feb. 16, 2004, p. B1.

7. "The Number and Rate of Foster Children Ages 17 and Under, 1990-2003," Child Trends Data Bank, available at www.childtrendsdatabank.org.

8. Robert T. Garrett, "Changes Urged for Care Agencies," *The Dallas Morning News*, Dec. 8, 2004, p. 4A.

9. "Trends in Foster Care and Adoption," U.S. Department of Health and Human Services, Administration for Children and Families, August 2004, available at www.acf.dhhs.gov/programs/cb/dis/afcars/publications/afcars.htm.

10. Jonathan D. Rockoff and John B. O'Donnell, "State's Lax Oversight Puts Fragile Children at Risk," *The Baltimore Sun*, April 10, 2005, p. 1A. Additional stories in the series, "A Failure To Protect Maryland's Troubled Group Homes," published April 11-13.

11. Rockoff and O'Donnell, "Leaders Vow To Fix Group Homes," April 14, 2005, p. 1A.

12. Child Welfare League of America press release, 2004.

13. House Ways and Means Committee, Human Resources Subcommittee, "Hearing to Examine Child Welfare Reform Proposals," July 13, 2004, transcript and documents available at http://waysandmeans.house.gov/hearings.asp?formmode=detail&hearing=161&comm=2.

14. Roseana Bess and Cynthia Andrews Scarcella, "Child Welfare Spending During a Time of Fiscal Stress," Urban Institute, Dec. 31, 2004, available at www.urban.org/url.cfm?ID=411124.

15. "Budget in Brief, Fiscal Year 2006," U.S. Department of Health and Human Services, pp. 6 and 98, available at http://hhs.gov/budget/06budget/FY2006BudgetinBrief.pdf.

16. For background, see Sarah Glazer, "Welfare Reform," *The CQ Researcher*, Aug. 3, 2001, pp. 601-632.

17. "Fostering the future: Safety, Permanence and Well-Being for Children in Foster Care," Pew Commission on Children in Foster Care, May 18, 2004, available at http://pewfostercare.org/research/docs/Final Report.pdf.

18. House Ways and Means subcommittee hearing, *op. cit.*

19. "The AFCARS Report" (Adoption and Foster Care Analysis and Reporting System), U.S. Department of Health and Human Services, August 2004, available at www.acf.dhhs.gov/programs/cb/publications/afcars/report9.pdf.

20. www.jimcaseyyouth.org/about.htm.

21. Except where noted, information for this section is drawn from these sources: Rachel S. Cox, "Foster Care Reform," *The CQ Researcher*, Jan. 9, 1998. Kasia O'Neill Murray and Sarah Gesiriech, "A Brief Legislative History of the Child Welfare System," Pew Commission on Children in Foster Care, available at http://pewfostercare.org/research/docs/Legislative.pdf; Mary-Liz Shaw, "Artist Recalls the Rough Rumbling of the Orphan Trains," *Milwaukee Journal Sentinel*, Feb. 2, p. E1; Mary Ellen Johnson, "Orphan Train Movement: A history of the Orphan Trains Era in American History," Orphan Train Heritage Society

of America, available at www.orphantrainriders.com/otm11.html.

22. "National Study of Protective, Preventive and Reunification Services Delivered to Children and Their Families," U.S. Department of Health and Human Services, 1994, available at www.acf.hhs.gov/programs/cb/publications/97natstudy/introduc.htm#CW.

23. Margaret LaRaviere, "A Brief History of Federal Child Welfare Legislation and Policy (1935-2000)," the Center for Community Partnerships in Child Welfare, Nov. 18, 2002, available at www.cssp.org/uploadFiles/paper1.doc.

24. Press conference, Washington, D.C., Oct. 13, 2004, transcript, pp. 7-9, available at www.fosteringresults.org/results/press/pewpress_10-13-04_fednewsbureau.pdf.

25. *Ibid.*, p.12, for updated waiver figure. Also: Mark Testa, Nancy Sidote Salyers and Mike Shaver, "Family Ties: Supporting Permanence for Children in Safe and Stable Foster Care With Relatives and Other Caregivers," Children and Family Research Center, School of Social Work, University of Illinois at Urbana-Champaign, Oct. 2004, p. 5, available at www.fosteringresults.org/results/reports/pewreports_10-13-04_alreadyhome.pdf.

26. "Summary of Title IV-E Child Welfare Waiver Demonstration Projects," U.S. Health and Human Services Department, May 2004, available at www.acf.hhs.gov/programs/cb/initiatives/cwwaiver/summary.htm.

27. "History of CASA." Available at www. casanet.org/download/ncasa_publications/history-casa.pdf.

28. "The Nation's Children 2005," the Child Welfare League of America, pp. 2-3.

29. *Ibid.*, p. 1. Also: "Child Maltreatment 2002," Health and Human Services Department, available at www.acf.hhs.gov/programs/cb/publications/cm02/summary.htm.

30. Child Trends Data Bank, *op. cit.* Also: "CBO Baseline for Foster Care and Adoption Assistance," Congressional Budget Office, March 2005, available at www.cbo.gov/factsheets/2005/FosterCare.PDF.

31. "HHS Could Play a Greater Role in Helping Child Welfare Agencies Recruit and Retain Staff," General Accounting Office, (now called the Government Accountability Office) March 2003, available at www.gao.gov/new.items/d03357.pdf.

32. *Ibid*, pp. 3-4.

33. *Ibid*, p. 21.

34. *Ibid*, p. 14.

35. "Report From the 2004 Child Welfare Workforce Survey: State Agency Findings," American Public Human Services Association, February 2005, p. 22, available at www.aphsa.org/ Home/Doc/Workforce%20Report%202005.pdf.

36. Child Welfare League of America National Data Analysis System, available at www.ndas.cwla.org/data_stats/access/predefined/Report.asp?ReportID=86.

37. General Accounting Office, *op. cit.*, pp. 3, 11.

BIBLIOGRAPHY

Books

Brohl, Kathryn, *The New Miracle Workers: Overcoming Contemporary Challenges in Child Welfare Work,* **CLWA Press, 2004.**
A veteran child welfare worker and family therapist explains new challenges facing workers and administrators, including meeting legislature-imposed timelines for case management, working collaboratively with clients, understanding diverse cultures and nontraditional families, keeping up with research, improving pay and training and overcoming worker burnout.

Geen, Rob, editor, *Kinship Care: Making the Most of a Valuable Resource,* **Urban Institute Press, 2003.**
A collection of essays edited by an Urban Institute researcher examines how child welfare agencies are using relatives as foster parents, how this differs from traditional foster care, and how the caregivers describe their experiences.

Shirk, Martha, and Gary Stangler, *On Their Own: What Happens to Kids When They Age Out of the Foster Care System,* **Westview Press, 2004.**
A journalist (Shirk) and the former director of the Missouri Social Services Department (Stangler) who now runs a program for older foster children offer alternately inspiring and heartrending stories of 10 young

people who must leave foster care and learn to live on their own without the family and community relationships that most young people lean on as they make the transition from teen to adult.

Articles

Campbell, Joel, "Encourage Access to Juvenile Courts: The Time Is Right for Lifting Juvenile Court and Child Welfare System Secrecy," *The Quill*, Aug. 1, 2004, p. 36.

A leader of the Society of Professional Journalists' Freedom of Information Committee argues that one way to improve the child welfare system is to let the news media into juvenile courts.

Colloff, Pamela, "Life and Meth," *Texas Monthly*, June 2004, p. 120.

Methamphetamine is destroying families in East Texas — an epidemic child welfare authorities worry could spike foster care rolls nationwide.

Humes, Edward, "The Unwanted," *Los Angeles Magazine*, Jan. 1, 2003, p. 64.

The reporter exposes a dysfunctional Los Angeles children's home.

Rockoff, Jonathan D., and John B. O'Donnell, "A Failure to Protect Maryland's Troubled Group Homes," *The Baltimore Sun*, April 10-13, 2005.

In a four-part exposé, the authors reveal child abuse, neglect and even death within Maryland's state-supervised group homes for children.

Reports and Studies

"Fostering the Future: Safety, Permanence and Well-Being for Children in Foster Care," *the Pew Commission on Children in Foster Care*, May 18, 2004, available at http://pewfostercare.org/research/docs/FinalReport.pdf.

This influential report by a blue-ribbon panel headed by two former U.S. representatives — Republican Bill Frenzel of Minnesota and Democrat William H. Gray III of Pennsylvania — explores the need to improve the child welfare system. The commission argues for more flexibility and more federal funds while acknowledging need to moderate federal spending.

"HHS Could Play a Greater Role in Helping Child Welfare Agencies Recruit and Retain Staff," *General Accounting Office* (now the Government Accountability Office), March 2003, available at www.gao.gov/new .items/d03357.pdf.

A report by Congress' nonpartisan investigating arm presents evidence that child welfare agencies' effectiveness suffers because caseworkers are underpaid and given too many cases to manage.

Testa, Mark F., "Encouraging Child Welfare Innovation through IV-E Waivers," *Children and Family Research Center, School of Social Work, University of Illinois at Urbana-Champaign*, January 2005; http://cfrcwww.social.uiuc.edu/briefpdfs/cfrc.

An academic study by the former research director of the Illinois Department of Children and Family Services examines how states have used waivers of federal regulations to spend federal funds on innovative programs and suggests how to use waivers more effectively. Testa is co-director of the University of Illinois' Children and Family Research Center.

Vandivere, Sharon, Rosemary Chalk and Kristin Anderson Moore, "Children in Foster Homes: How Are They Faring?" *Child Trends Research Brief*, December 2003; www.childtrends.org/files/FosterHomesRB.pdf.

An analysis of surveys of children and families concludes that foster children are less healthy than other children, have more developmental and behavioral problems and often have problems in school.

For More Information

Annie E. Casey Foundation, 701 St. Paul St., Baltimore, MD 21202; (410) 547-6600; www.aecf.org. Advocates, conducts research and supports programs to benefit disadvantaged children and families; known for its Kids Count Data Book, an annual compilation of state-by-state statistics.

Child Trends, 4301 Connecticut Ave., N.W., Suite 100, Washington, DC 20008; (202) 572-6000; www.childtrends .org. Conducts research about children and publishes reports and statistics on its Child Trends Data Bank.

Child Welfare League of America, 440 First St., N.W., Washington, DC 20001; (202) 638-2952; www.cwla.org. America's oldest and largest child welfare organization advocates, suggests standards and educates welfare workers.

Children and Family Research Center, University of Illinois, 1203 W. Oregon St., Urbana, IL 61801; (217) 333-5837; http://cfrcwww.social.uiuc.edu. Leading university-based institution for studying children, families and child welfare services.

Children's Bureau, 370 L'Enfant Promenade, S.W., Washington, DC 20447; (202) 205-8618; www.acf.hhs .gov/programs/cb. Agency of the U.S. Health and Human Services Department that supports states' delivery of child welfare services, publishes reports and data on its Web site, maintains hotlines for reporting child and domestic abuse and runaway, missing or exploited children (1-800-4ACHILD).

National Court Appointed Special Advocate (CASA) Association, 100 W. Harrison, North Tower, Suite 500, Seattle WA 98119; (800) 628-3233; www.nationalcasa.org. Provides leadership, consultation and resources for more than 900 CASA programs across the country whose nearly 70,000 volunteers serve as advocates for 280,000 abused or neglected children.

Pew Commission on Foster Care, 2233 Wisconsin Ave., N.W., Washington, DC 20007; (202) 687-0948; www .pewfostercare.org. Blue-ribbon, bipartisan panel that proposed more federal funding and more flexibility for states to spend it.

Supporting researchers for more than 40 years

Research methods have always been at the core of SAGE's publishing program. Founder Sara Miller McCune published SAGE's first methods book, *Public Policy Evaluation*, in 1970. Soon after, she launched the *Quantitative Applications in the Social Sciences* series—affectionately known as the "little green books."

Always at the forefront of developing and supporting new approaches in methods, SAGE published early groundbreaking texts and journals in the fields of qualitative methods and evaluation.

Today, more than 40 years and two million little green books later, SAGE continues to push the boundaries with a growing list of more than 1,200 research methods books, journals, and reference works across the social, behavioral, and health sciences. Its imprints—Pine Forge Press, home of innovative textbooks in sociology, and Corwin, publisher of PreK–12 resources for teachers and administrators—broaden SAGE's range of offerings in methods. SAGE further extended its impact in 2008 when it acquired CQ Press and its best-selling and highly respected political science research methods list.

From qualitative, quantitative, and mixed methods to evaluation, SAGE is the essential resource for academics and practitioners looking for the latest methods by leading scholars.

For more information, visit **www.sagepub.com**.